The Mount

Home of Edith Wharton

A HISTORIC STRUCTURE REPORT

The Mount
Home of Edith Wharton

A HISTORIC STRUCTURE REPORT

History of The Mount
and Report Preparation

SCOTT MARSHALL

Existing Conditions,
Problems of Repair,
and Recommendations

JOHN G. WAITE ASSOCIATES,
ARCHITECTS

EDITH WHARTON RESTORATION, INC.

LENOX, MASSACHUSETTS

The publication of *The Mount, Home of Edith Wharton: A Historic Structure Report* has been made possible by a generous grant from the Florence Gould Foundation. In addition, this report has been funded in part by grants from the National Trust for Historic Preservation and its Johanna Favrot Fund for Historic Preservation.

ISBN 0-9665004-0-7

Edith Wharton Restoration, Inc.
The Mount
Box 974
Lenox, Massachusetts 01240
Telephone 413-637-1899
Fax 413-637-0619

This book was published with the assistance of
Mount Ida Press
152 Washington Ave.
Albany, New York 12210
Telephone 518-426-5935

Graphic Design:
The Market Street Group

FRONT COVER: *Tinted postcard of The Mount, viewed across the east garden during Edith Wharton's occupancy. (Lenox Library Association)*

BACK COVER: *The Mount reflected in Laurel Pond, 1986. (Photograph by James Gambaro)*

Edith Wharton Restoration, Inc.

The Mount
Lenox, Massachusetts 01240

Edith Wharton Restoration, Inc., was founded in 1980 to preserve and restore Edith Wharton's home, The Mount, in Lenox, Massachusetts, and to establish it as a cultural and educational center dedicated to the study and promotion of Edith Wharton, literature, and the design arts.

The Mount, Home of Edith Wharton: A Historic Structure Report was initiated in 1986 by Edith Wharton Restoration's House Structure Restoration Committee: Arthur C. Townsend, Chairman; Jonas Dovydenas, Arthur Dutil, Terry Hallock, Tiziana Hardy, Thomas Hayes, Charles Schulze; Scott Marshall, Architectural Historian.

John G. Waite Associates, Architects, PLLC

388 Broadway
Albany, New York 12207

Staff for 1986-87 Report

PARTNER IN CHARGE
John G. Waite, FAIA

ARCHITECTURAL STAFF
Douglas G. Bucher
Charles B. Tonetti
A. Patricia Hughes
Chelle M. Jenkins
Charles E. Barthe, Jr.

This report was prepared initially by Mendel Mesick Cohen Waite Architects in 1986-87. The firm evolved into Mendel Mesick Cohen Waite Hall Architects and then Mesick Cohen Waite Architects. In 1995 Mesick Cohen Waite Architects was dissolved, and John G. Waite Associates, Architects, PLLC, was established. The report was revised in 1995-96 by John G. Waite, Douglas G. Bucher, Michael Curcio, and Chelle M. Jenkins.

Contents

INTRODUCTION 9

PART ONE

History of The Mount   SCOTT MARSHALL

PREFACE   A Passion for Houses 14

CHAPTER 1   Edith Wharton *Designing A Life* 16

CHAPTER 2   Edith Wharton and Design *A Study of Her Earliest Homes and Influences* 21

CHAPTER 3   A House of Her Own Making *The Design of The Mount* 35

CHAPTER 4   Construction of The Mount 46

CHAPTER 5   Life at The Mount, 1902-11 52

CHAPTER 6   History of the Exterior and Interior of The Mount 60

         Forecourt 60

         Terrace 64

         Ground Floor 70

         First Floor (Main Floor) 74

         Second Floor (Bedroom Floor) 94

         Service Areas 104

CHAPTER 7   Proposed Alterations in 1907 118

CHAPTER 8   History of The Mount, 1911 and After 123

         The Whartons Sell The Mount, 1911-12 123

         Mary and Albert R. Shattuck, Owners, 1912-38 125

         Louise and Carr V. Van Anda, Owners, 1938-42 128

         The Foxhollow School, Owner, 1942-76 131

         The Center Incorporated, Owner, 1977-80 137

         Shakespeare & Company at The Mount, 1978-Present 138

         Edith Wharton Restoration, Inc., Owner, 1980-Present 140

CHAPTER 9 Outbuildings. 145

ABOUT THE AUTHOR 153

ACKNOWLEDGMENTS 154

NOTES 156

SELECTED BIBLIOGRAPHY 182

PART TWO

Existing Conditions, Problems of Repair, and Recommendations JOHN G. WAITE ASSOCIATES, ARCHITECTS

EXISTING CONDITIONS, PROBLEMS OF REPAIR, AND RECOMMENDATIONS. 188

  EXTERIOR PROBLEMS OF REPAIR 188

  INTERIOR EXISTING CONDITIONS AND PROBLEMS OF REPAIR 193

      Ground Floor 194

      First Floor (Main Floor). 208

      Second Floor (Bedroom Floor). 228

      Attic. 246

RECOMMENDATIONS 249

JOHN G. WAITE ASSOCIATES, ARCHITECTS, PLLC. 253

KEY TO ILLUSTRATION SOURCES. 255

Introduction

The Mount was the beloved summer estate of Edith Wharton, the noted American author of 21 novels, 11 collections of short stories, nine works of non-fiction, and numerous articles and reviews. The house was constructed in 1901-02 to the design of Francis L. V. Hoppin, of Hoppin & Koen Architects in New York City. It embodies the ideals of a classical house that expressed "human dignity and greatness" as described in the popular book *The Decoration of Houses*, co-authored by Mrs. Wharton in 1897 with architect Ogden Codman, Jr.

Edith Wharton retained ownership of The Mount until late 1911. It continued in use as a private residence until 1942, when it was acquired by the Foxhollow School for Girls. The estate was used as part of the school until 1976; 49 acres of the original property were purchased by Edith Wharton Restoration, Inc., in 1980. Since then the house, outbuildings, and grounds have been the subjects of planning studies and restoration efforts.

This historic structure report is the first step in the preparation and implementation of a comprehensive program for the long-term preservation of the mansion. The building is now in need of extensive stabilization and restoration because of years of hard use and little substantive maintenance.

Today, in preparing a historic structure report, restoration architects follow a disciplined approach in which investigative techniques are applied to the preservation of historic buildings. Too often in the past, preservation and restoration projects have been shaped by romantic notions of history or expedient compromises in repair work. Such unfortunate practices have destroyed the historic integrity of countless structures. For The Mount, a team of architects, architectural historians, and restoration-technology specialists assembled all known documentary materials relating to the mansion, conducted a comprehensive survey of the existing facility, and analyzed the particular problems of the structure. The accomplishment of these tasks enabled plans for the restoration to be formulated without whim or uncertainty and in a logical and sequential manner. This approach will help to ensure that the integrity of The Mount will survive the extensive preservation efforts that are now required to save the building.

JOHN G. WAITE, FAIA
John G. Waite Associates, Architects

On a slope overlooking the dark waters and densely wooded shores of Laurel Lake we built a spacious and dignified house, to which we gave the name of my great-grandfather's place, the Mount. There was a big kitchen-garden with a grape pergola, a little farm, and a flower-garden outspread below the wide terrace overlooking the lake. There for over ten years I lived and gardened and wrote contentedly, and should doubtless have ended my days there had not a grave change in my husband's health made the burden of the property too heavy. But meanwhile the Mount was to give me country cares and joys, long happy rides and drives through the wooded lanes of that loveliest region, the companionship of a few dear friends, and the freedom from trivial obligations which was necessary if I was to go on with my writing. The Mount was my first real home, and though it is nearly twenty years since I last saw it (for I was too happy there ever to want to revisit it as a stranger) its blessed influence still lives in me.

EDITH WHARTON
A Backward Glance, 1934

No one fully knows our Edith who hasn't seen her in the act of creating a habitation for herself.

HENRY JAMES
Portrait of Edith Wharton
by Percy Lubbock, 1947

PART ONE

History of The Mount

SCOTT MARSHALL

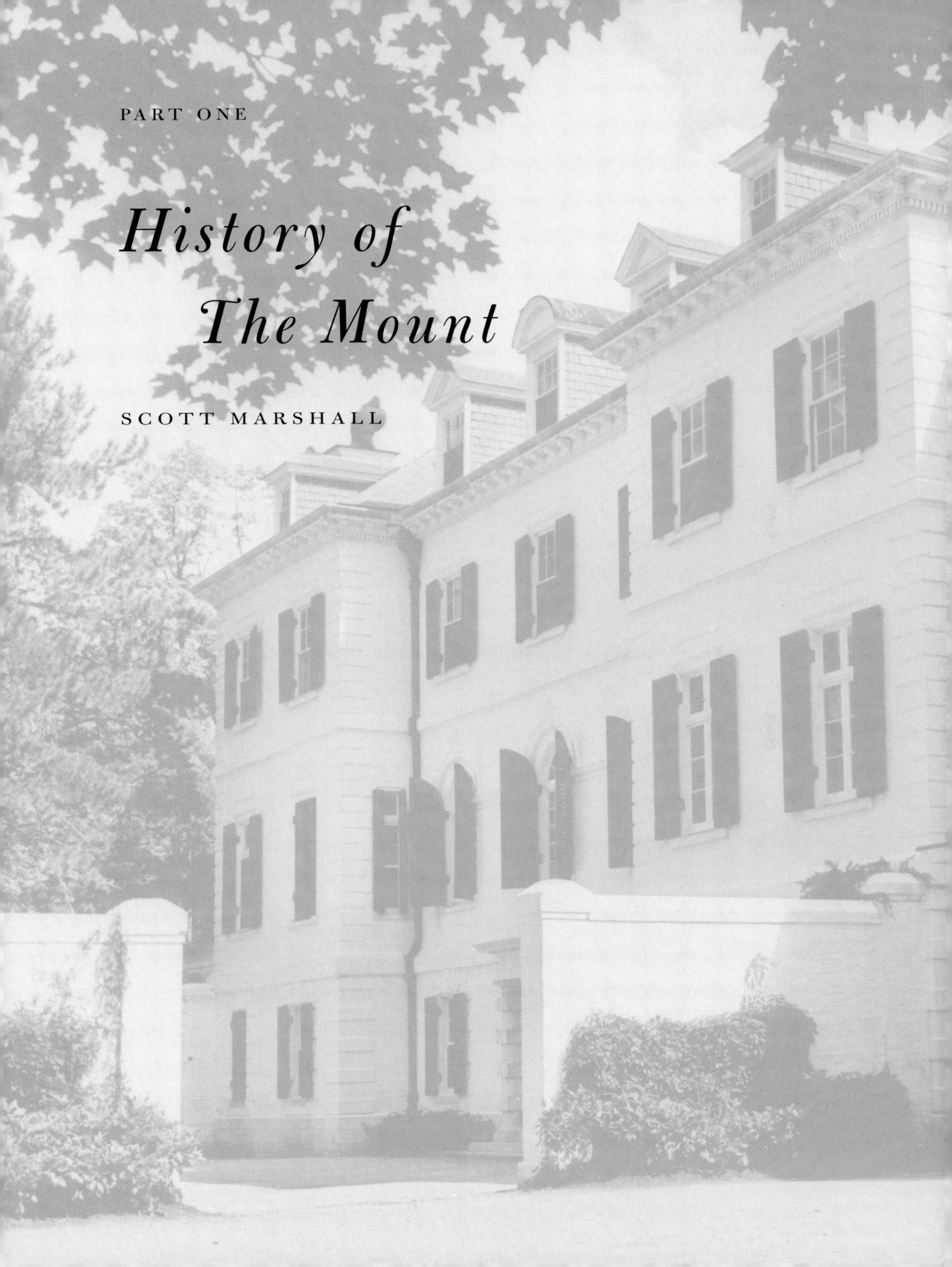

A Passion for Houses

I have sometimes thought that a woman's nature is like a great house full of rooms: there is the hall, through which everyone passes in going in and out; the drawing room, where one receives formal visits; the sitting room, where the members of the family come and go as they list; but beyond that, far beyond, are other rooms, the handles of whose doors perhaps are never turned; no one knows the way to them, no one knows whither they lead; and in the innermost room, the holy of holies, the soul sits alone and waits for a footstep that never comes.

EDITH WHARTON
"The Fullness of Life," 1893

Edith Wharton had lifelong love affairs with her homes. In letters to friends and in her autobiography she often described these houses in passionate and rapturous terms.

Her first love was her family's Victorian country home, Pencraig, in Newport, Rhode Island. She remembered fondly the many happy childhood hours that took place under its "friendly gables."[1]

Her mother's residences in New York City were never finished, as Edith explained in a late memoir, but they lacked something more fundamental: a sense of home. She fled from these cold habitations by marrying Teddy Wharton in 1885.

Their first home together, Pencraig Cottage, was too close to her mother to be a true place of refuge. In the early 1890s, Edith purchased Land's End in Newport, a house with which she had a temperate love affair. Although finding its exterior "intolerably ugly," she confided, "I loved Land's End, with its windows framing the endlessly changing moods of the misty Atlantic, and the night-long sound of the surges against the cliffs."[2]

Her efforts to remake this early object of her affection resulted in her first book, *The Decoration of Houses*, co-authored with Ogden Codman, Jr., which remains in print a century later as an influential touchstone in the field of design. On every home she owned, she lavished her attentions on both the house and its gardens with, as she described it, "such a frenzy of affection and zeal for improvement."[3]

In her later years Edith had two French homes: the Pavillon Colombe in St. Brice-sous-Forêt, outside of Paris, and Ste. Claire du Vieux Château in Hyères, on the Riviera. Her passions for these final abodes were those of an independent woman. Encountering Pavillon Colombe for the first time in 1918, Edith wrote: "I saw the house and fell in love with it... [it] has never failed me since."[4] A few years later, moving into the Château Ste. Claire, she revealed in a letter to a friend: "I am thrilled to the spine... I feel as if I were going to get married — to the right man at last!"[5]

Edith's own words suggest that for her these homes came to assume positions of surrogate husbands. Each house gave her what Teddy Wharton and her lover, Morton Fullerton, could not: order, tranquility, stability, and the freedom from trivial obligations, which she deemed necessary if she was to continue her writing.

At the turn-of-the-century, following her years at Land's End but prior to her permanent move to France, Edith fell in love with a new locale: the Berkshires of western Massachusetts. She wrote to Codman: "The truth is, that I am in love with the place — climate, scenery, life & all."[6] Removing herself from Newport, she created her ideal world: a house and gardens of her own designs. The Mount was to be the scene of many of her greatest triumphs and of some of her deepest sorrows. In this world of her making she wrote her first bestseller, *The House of Mirth*, and entertained illustrious friends such as Henry James. It was at The Mount that Edith Wharton came into her own as one of America's greatest writers.

But it was also at The Mount that she agonized through many of the highs and lows of her love affair with Fullerton. The final chapter of her unhappy marriage was played out there, and the estate, whose management provided Teddy with a principal occupation, was a contributing factor in the dissolution of their marriage tie. Like that earlier commitment, she entered into her relationship with The Mount with permanence in mind, writing years later that she had intended to end her days there, but a grave change in her husband's health had "made the burden of the property too heavy."[7] Although she ultimately divorced Teddy after moving to France, Edith never fully separated herself from The Mount. In her twilight years she admitted poignantly: "The Mount was my first real home... and its blessed influence still lives in me."[8]

The subsequent owners of the property also loved The Mount; they preserved and cared for its basic virtues, allowing it to remain remarkably intact. Thanks to them, The Mount survives today as Edith Wharton's autobiographical house, definitively embodying its creator's spirit and ideas, as well as her distinctive passion for houses. The Mount's restoration is a tribute to the enduring strength of Edith Wharton's many achievements and to the legacy that she has left us.

CHAPTER 1

Edith Wharton
Designing a Life

Edith Newbold Jones was born on January 24, 1862, into the fashionable, tightknit world of old New York society. She was the third and last child of middle-aged George Frederic Jones, an educated and kindly "gentleman of leisure," and his wife, Lucretia Rhinelander Jones, who instilled her passions for high fashion, proper etiquette, and personal discipline into the consciousness of her only daughter.

Despite what she later considered the dull pleasantries and formal constraints of life in a narrow and well-to-do milieu unconcerned with — in fact, vaguely frightened by — matters of intellectual import, Edith developed a prodigious curiosity and imaginative intelligence. These attributes were greatly stimulated between 1866 and 1872 (when she was four through ten years old) as the Jones family travelled in Europe in order to reduce the expenses of maintaining their New York and Newport properties. During this formative period, as her family journeyed to Italy, France, Spain, and Germany, Edith absorbed European culture and languages and began to develop a lifelong passion for travel.

Upon their return to America in 1872, the Joneses routinely divided their time between their brownstone residence at 14 West 23rd Street and their summer home, Pencraig, a rambling Queen Anne-style structure, in then-rural Newport, Rhode Island. Edith's girlhood was calm, lonely, and quite sheltered, hardly remarkable for an upper-class daughter except for her passion to make up stories and write them down on pieces of discarded wrapping paper. Although her father encouraged Edith by allowing her to spend endless treasured hours reading books in his library, Lucretia was distinctly unsupportive, preferring instead to lecture her daughter on proper manners and decorum.

During these early years, a kindly German governess, Anna Bahlmann, guided Edith through her only formal education. All else was self-taught, leading the mature Wharton to refer to herself as a "self-made man." Her lonely life was peopled mainly by the characters and stories that were constantly forming in her imagination.

By 1877, when Edith was fifteen, she had secretly written a melodramatic novella of thirty thousand words, *Fast and Loose*. Though she would parody its title in a later short story, this work (finally published in 1977) marked the beginning of Edith's literary career and revealed that her gifts for style, irony, and character delineation were already well developed.

The following year her mother uncharacteristically encouraged Edith's poetic gifts by underwriting the publication of *Verses*, a slender volume of 29 poems. The eminent author and editor William Dean Howells reprinted one of the poems in the *Atlantic Monthly* in 1880, Edith's first professional appearance in wide-ranging print. Her New York society debut, made in 1879, marked the beginning of the identification enigma with which Wharton would be presented so often during her life: how could she be both a creature of high society (as, by birth, she was) and a serious writer?

Although her debut had been an unhappy experience for a girl who was often intensely shy and withdrawn, Edith soon joined the other members of her set for the youthful activities of the time: evenings at the opera or the theater, midnight suppers and dances, winter skating and sleigh rides, and frequent carriage rides and social calls. Her father's declining health led the family to return to Europe in 1880. Edith greatly welcomed the opportunity to renew the European interests of her youth. Her father's death in 1882 was a key event in her life. It meant the end of her European sojourn, but more importantly it marked the end of a close and affectionate relationship with the only member of her family who had encouraged her interest in reading and her talents for writing.

Alone with her stern and unsympathetic mother, Edith — as a young woman at the age of courtship and marriage — began to develop friendships with eligible young men. A formal engagement to Harry Stevens, a gentle and amiable suitor, was averted only at the last moment, apparently a casualty of social niceties between his mother and hers. At approximately the same time, Edith formed a friendship that would last throughout her lifetime with Walter Berry, an aspiring young lawyer whom she met on holiday in Bar Harbor, Maine. A mutual friend once called Berry the "dominant seventh-chord" in Edith's life. He proved to be her most beloved friend, and his support during both personal and authorial crises was unwavering and influential.

In 1883 Edith was courted by Edward (Teddy) Robbins Wharton, of Boston, a good friend of her brother Henry. Thirteen years older than Edith, Teddy, at thirty-three, seemed an unlikely candidate for marriage to Edith, as he was not at all interested in intellectual matters, preferring outdoor activities such as hunting and fishing. However, his kindly demeanor and even temper, as well as his love of animals and travel, appealed to Edith, and the two were married on April 29, 1885, at Trinity Chapel in New York City.

The young couple established a routine in the early years of their marriage that was not dissimilar to that of Edith's parents in their youth: they spent June through January in Newport at Pencraig Cottage, a small house near her mother's, and February through May traveling through Europe, often in Italy. In 1888 they took a large financial gamble with their limited incomes by chartering a yacht with a friend and spending three months cruising the Aegean and visiting little known Greek islands. Upon returning to New York, Edith discovered that she was now independently wealthy, having inherited a large sum of money from a distant relative.

Her European travels had stimulated Edith to begin writing poetry again. In 1889 she submitted three poems to three New York magazines, all of which were accepted. Edward Burlingame, an editor of *Scribner's Magazine*, published "The Last of the Giustiniani." He evinced a particular interest in Edith's work and also published her first short story, "Mrs. Manstey's View," in July 1891. This flush of success encouraged Edith to write more often and to concentrate on poetry and short stories.

Meanwhile, the Whartons sought to put down roots; they purchased a small brownstone house at 884 Park Avenue in New York in 1891 and a summer home, Land's End, in Newport, in 1893. The remodeling and decorating of these two new homes brought Edith into contact with Ogden Codman, Jr., a Boston architect, who had recently started his own firm and was pleased to add the Whartons as clients. Edith

FIG. 1 *Edith Wharton, c. 1885-86.* (LL)

FIG. 2 *Edith Wharton,*
c. 1902. Although this image
of the author is regularly
dated 1907, it was published
in March 1903 in Women
Authors of Our Day in Their
Homes. (LL)

and Codman found that they shared many of the same ideas on design and similar philosophies of interior decoration. The time they spent together on these projects became an important influence in Edith's development.

In the mid-1890s, Edith suffered from several years of exhaustion and endured undiagnosed and recurring nauseas, which culminated in a series of nervous breakdowns. Biographers surmise that this was an identity crisis concerning her roles of wife and writer, exacerbated by the failure of her marriage to Teddy.[1] Nevertheless, at this time Edith also collaborated with Codman on her first book, *The Decoration of Houses,* which was published in 1897. It was a financial and critical success, and its innovative design precepts have exerted considerable influence on architects and designers. She would almost always publish one book, and sometimes two, each year for the rest of her life.

As her literary life began to flourish, so too did her social life, but Edith was most interested in developing friendships with highly educated, artistic, and culturally refined people. Beginning in the 1890s, she initiated important friendships with Egerton Winthrop, Paul and Minnie Bourget, Vernon Lee, George Cabot Lodge, Howard Sturgis, and ultimately, Henry James. Her first collection of short stories, *The Greater Inclination*, published in 1899 by Scribner's, was followed by a novella, *The Touchstone* (1900), and a second volume of short stories, *Crucial Instances* (1901).

Since the mid-1890s, Edith and Teddy had come to the Berkshire Hills in western Massachusetts for occasional visits to Pine Acre, his mother's home in Lenox. Edith fell in love with the beauties of the countryside and resolved to build a house there. She purchased land in 1901 and hired Codman as the architect. However, disagreements with the Whartons eventually led to Codman's withdrawal. The Whartons hired Francis L. V. Hoppin in his place, but Codman later returned to the project to design the interiors of the principal rooms. Construction of The Mount began in July 1901 and lasted into the fall of 1902. Despite her preoccupations with the design and construction of what she called her "first real home," Edith was also able to oversee the publication of her first novel, *The Valley of Decision* (1902), and to translate Hermann Sudermann's *Es Lebe das Leben* into a Broadway play for the actress Mrs. Patrick Campbell.

The Whartons moved into The Mount in late September 1902, and Edith at last was in a world totally of her own creation. She continued to develop the property, adding a flower garden, an Italian walled garden, and a rock garden; she landscaped parterres that linked the formal garden areas, cleared views, and created striking vistas of the Berkshire countryside. Her niece, Beatrix Jones (later Farrand), designed a kitchen garden, as well as the drive and approach to the mansion. The property also included a well-equipped stable, a superintendent's house near the main gate, a greenhouse, and a collection of farm buildings on a rise overlooking a lake. It was Teddy's responsibility to oversee the day-to-day operations of The Mount, an arrangement that allowed Edith to spend her mornings writing in her room and the rest of her day entertaining a steady stream of guests.

The years that the Whartons owned The Mount — 1902 until 1911 — were productive ones for Edith. Her first great work (and a major bestseller), *The House of Mirth* (1905), was written there, even though much of the story — a skillful dissection of contemporary society — was set in New York City. Her other novels from this period include *The Fruit of the Tree* (1907), which has a Berkshire setting in its mill-town scenes, and large portions of what became *The Custom of the Country* (1913). She also published three novellas: *Sanctuary* (1903), *Madame de Treymes* (1907), and perhaps her most famous work, *Ethan Frome* (1911), which was inspired by a real-life local sledding accident in the Berkshires and by the poverty that she saw surrounding the estates during her frequent drives through the countryside.

Edith also wrote a great many short stories during her years at The Mount, published as collections entitled *The Descent of Man and Other Stories* (1904), *The Hermit and the Wild Woman* (1908), and her first collection of ghost stories, *Tales of Men and Ghosts* (1910). She also wrote essays about her impressions of places that she had visited on her European travels. Usually first appearing as magazine articles, these essays were collected into two volumes of travel sketches: *Italian Backgrounds* (1905) and *A Motor-Flight Through France* (1908).

Edith's great passion for gardens, landscaping, and garden history led her to undertake a series of scholarly articles published as *Italian Villas and Their Gardens* (1904). This topic was hardly a surprising choice, given her prodigious research for her first novel, *The Valley of Decision* (1902), which was set in seventeenth-century Italy, and her learned writing and astute observations first revealed in *The Decoration of Houses* in 1897. She also wrote more poetry for magazines; a volume of some of her best poems, *Artemis to Acteon*, appeared in 1909.

The Mount was the scene of some of Edith's happiest moments, as well as the site of her deepest sorrow. Henry James visited on three occasions — in 1904, 1905, and 1911. He was the brightest luminary of Edith's inner circle of friends that she began to draw around herself as darker events unfolded. Teddy, previously so robust and uncomplicated, soon showed disturbing signs of mental problems, which eventually affected his physical well-being. In 1907 Edith first met Morton Fullerton, a friend of Henry James. By the following year Edith and Fullerton were secret lovers, and she then experienced firsthand some of the pains and pleasures that she had previously ascribed only to her fictional characters.

Edith and Teddy had continued to travel to Europe each year, but in 1909 and 1910 she did not return to America. Instead, she remained primarily in Paris, where she could be near Fullerton and pursue her interest in Parisian society, resulting in a novella set in that milieu, *Madame de Treymes* (1907). Her affair with Fullerton also contributed to her renewed efforts at poetry, including several unpublished erotic poems, most notably "Terminus" (1909), which celebrated their night of passionate love-making at a railroad station hotel.

The Whartons' growing estrangement, initially complicated by the lack of any sexual relationship and their fundamentally different personalities and interests, was exacerbated by Teddy's constant mental and physical problems and by Edith's affair with Fullerton. Possibly because he was suspicious of his wife's infidelity, Teddy embezzled a large sum from Edith's trust fund, which he managed, in 1909 and spent most of it on a house in Boston for a mistress.

Edith could no longer trust Teddy with her money or property. She removed him as a manager of her trust and of The Mount, a thoroughly wounding experience that made Teddy feel even more useless. Both Edith and Teddy attempted sporadically to repair their marriage and tried to continue living together (or at least to give the semblance of it). However, Edith's lack of trust, her exhaustion, and her deep personal unhappiness finally led her to sell The Mount late in 1911 and to obtain a French divorce in 1913.

Edith moved to France permanently in 1911. Her ten years at The Mount — years in which she attained her first great success, wrote prodigiously, formed influential friendships with intellectuals, experienced her only love affair, and witnessed the beginnings of an independent existence—are clearly central to understanding her life and career.

Around the time of her relocation to France, Edith published two novels, *The Reef* (1912) and *The Custom of the Country* (1913). With the outbreak of World War I, she revealed a selfless and heroic side by organizing the American Hostels for Refugees and the Children of Flanders committee to aid Belgian orphans, as well as by doing extensive work on behalf of tubercular soldiers. She visited the front lines and recorded her impressions in *Fighting France* (1915). She also compiled *The Book of the Homeless* (1916), in order to raise funds for these French charities. For her war work, Edith was made a Chevalier of the Legion of Honor by the French government in 1916 and was later awarded the Order of Leopold by the Belgian government. During the war years she published a novel with a Berkshire setting, *Summer* (1917); a collection of short stories, *Xingu and Other Stories* (1916); a novella with a wartime theme, *The Marne* (1918); and a book of essays on French culture, *French Ways and Their Meaning* (1919).

After the war, Edith found a house near Paris, the Pavillon Colombe in St. Brice-sous-Forêt, which she remodeled, landscaped, and made into her first real home since she had left America. Within two years she had also established a winter residence on the French Riviera, Ste. Claire du Vieux Château in Hyères, a former convent. For the final 17 years of her life, she divided her time between these two estates, making only occasional trips abroad. A 1917 trip resulted in another volume of travel essays, *In Morocco* (1920). In 1926 she chartered a yacht and retraced the route of her Aegean cruise of 1888.

Although the war years also brought the deaths of friends, notably Henry James and Ronald Simmons, Edith was already developing, or would soon develop, key friendships with Bernard Berenson, Percy Lubbock, Gaillard Lapsley, John Hugh Smith, Robert Norton, Geoffrey Scott, Logan Pearsall Smith, Kenneth Clark, Nicky Mariano, and Elisina Tyler, her husband, Royall, and their son, William. Edith's friendship with Walter Berry deepened, as did her relationship with her sister-in-law, Mary (Minnie) Cadwalader Jones, the divorced wife of her brother Frederic. Among the literary friendships that she continued or developed were those with Robert Grant, André Gide, William Gerhardi, Aldous Huxley, Vivienne de Watteville, and Sinclair Lewis.

In 1920 Edith published one of her most celebrated novels, *The Age of Innocence,* an evocative return to the New York of her youth. For it she became the first woman to receive the Pulitzer Prize for Fiction, awarded in 1921. Other significant awards included an honorary Doctorate of Letters from Yale University in 1923 (the first woman so honored) and election to the American Academy of Arts and Letters in 1930 (only the second woman to be so recognized).

Perhaps what is most outstanding about Edith Wharton's final years was her deep commitment to her art: she never stopped writing. Her later output included a work analyzing her own metier, *The Writing of Fiction* (1925); an autobiography, *A Backward Glance* (1934); another volume of poetry, *Twelve Poems* (1926); several collections of short stories — *Here and Beyond* (1926), *Certain People* (1930), *Human Nature* (1933), and *The World Over* (1936); and a quartet of novels collectively titled *Old New York* (1924) — *False Dawn, The Old Maid, The Spark,* and *New Year's Day.* Her major efforts, nevertheless, were directed towards a series of novels — *The Glimpses of the Moon* (1922), *A Son at the Front* (1923), *The Mother's Recompense* (1925), *Twilight Sleep* (1927), *The Children* (1928), *Hudson River Bracketed* (1929), and *The Gods Arrive* (1932).

In June 1937, while visiting Ogden Codman, Jr., at his château in Grégy, Edith suffered a devastating stroke, from which she never recovered. She was transported back to the Pavillon Colombe, where she lingered near death until August 11. She was buried in the Cimetière des Gonards in the town of Versailles, close to her companion, Walter Berry. *Ghosts* (1937) and her incomplete final novel, *The Buccaneers* (1938), were published posthumously.

FIG. 3 *Edith Wharton in 1923, when she became the first woman to receive an honorary degree from Yale University.* (AP)

CHAPTER 2

Edith Wharton and Design
A Study of Her Earliest Homes and Influences

Even as a child, Edith Jones was extremely sensitive to her physical surroundings. Her "first conscious recollection" was of being kissed on Fifth Avenue at the age of three by a young cousin as she walked with her father.[1] She noted years later in her autobiography that she and her father "walked up Fifth Avenue: the old Fifth Avenue with its double line of low brown-stone houses, of a desperate uniformity of style."[2] This memory remained a vivid one throughout her life; old Fifth Avenue (and by extension, old New York) would appear again and again in so much of her greatest work.

Her discerning eye and keen mind developed surprisingly early, before she was four years old, according to Wharton. She once recalled that "my visual sensibility seems to me ... to have been as intense then as it is now."[3] She explained that it "must always have been too keen for middling pleasures; my photographic memory of rooms and houses — even those seen but briefly, or at long intervals — was from my earliest years a source of inarticulate misery, for I was always vaguely frightened by ugliness."[4]

Her other early memory was an "ugly" one, but it reveals how the novelist developed from such a sensitive child. Edith spent one summer (probably her third) with her father's sister, Elizabeth Jones, at her country house on the Hudson River. Edith did not like her aunt, whom she remembered as "a ramrod-backed old lady compounded of steel and granite,"[5] or her home called Rhinecliff, which she remembered for "its intolerable ugliness."[6] Then, as in her future work, Edith saw distinct connections between buildings and the people who inhabited them:

I can still remember hating everything at Rhinecliff, which, as I saw, on rediscovering it some years later, was an expensive but dour specimen of Hudson River Gothic; and from the first I was obscurely conscious of a queer resemblance between the granitic exterior of Aunt Elizabeth and her grimly comfortable home, between her battlemented caps and the turrets of Rhinecliff.[7]

The Jones family soon left New York and moved to Europe, where it was less expensive to live. From 1866 to 1872 Edith absorbed the European scene — its customs, culture, and languages. She preferred Europe over New York: "The chief difference was that things about me were now not ugly but incredibly beautiful."[8] The family divided its time between Italy, Spain, France, and Germany.

Edith's susceptibility to the beauty of her surroundings was intense, and her memories were often of great architectural treasures. In Rome she spent hours playing in the gardens of the famous villas and gathering bits of marble among the ruins of the Forum and on the slopes of the Palatine. In Spain she remembered "a fantastic vision of the columns of Cordova, the tower of the Giralda, the pools and fountains of the Alhambra, the orange groves of Seville, the awful icy penumbra of the Escorial, and everywhere shadowy aisles undulating with incense and processions."[9]

FIG. 4 *Edith Jones at age five, decorating with a vase of flowers, oil painting by Edward Harrison May, c. 1867.* (NPG)

With so much to feed the eye and the imagination, it is not surprising that Edith found "the necessary formula" for making up her stories, something she believed had been part of her life from her "first conscious moments."[10] Not yet able to read, she would walk up and down a room holding a richly bound copy of Washington Irving's *The Alhambra*, believing its exquisite binding to be a source of inspiration.

Wharton's later writings repeatedly link her love for beautiful objects and sights with her developing mind and her need to read and to write as a "means of escape"[11] from her lonely childhood. One means of escape was provided by her "love of pretty things — pretty clothes, pretty pictures, pretty sights" and the other by "learning to read."[12] The intensity of her reactions is significant; she later wrote that "I never felt anything *calmly* — & I never have to this day!"[13]

Edith and her family returned to America when she was ten. She experienced a deep depression at leaving the beauties of Europe for New York:

Out of doors, in the mean monotonous streets, without any visible memorials of an historic past, what could New York offer to a child whose eyes had been filled with the shapes of immortal beauty and immemorial significance? One of the most depressing impressions of my childhood is my recollection of the intolerable ugliness of New York, of its untended streets and the narrow houses so lacking in external dignity, so crammed with smug and suffocating upholstery. How could I understand that people who had seen Rome and Seville, Paris and London, could come back to live contentedly between Washington Square and the Central Park? ... this little low-studded rectangular New York, cursed with its universal chocolate-coloured coating of the most hideous stone ever quarried, this cramped horizontal gridiron of a town without towers, porticoes, fountains or perspectives, hide-bound in its deadly uniformity of mean ugliness.[14]

Wharton never changed her feelings about America; she always felt like an exile in her native country.

14 West 23rd Street, New York City

Returning from Europe, the Joneses quickly repaired to their summer home, Pencraig, in Newport in 1872; Edith's happiest childhood memories seem to be connected with that house. However, it was her birthplace at 14 West 23rd Street that would be most influential in her early years. There she would spend most of her life from 1872-82.

The dwelling was a four-and-one-half story brownstone, built in the late 1850s in the then-fashionable Italianate style,[15] on the south side of the street between Fifth and Sixth avenues. It stood opposite the massive Fifth Avenue Hotel,[16] which fronted on Madison Square Park where Fifth Avenue and Broadway converge. Four steps led to double doors framed by an arched surround of rusticated quoins and crowned by a massive pediment.[17] A typical brownstone of this period, Wharton later wrote, had a vestibule "painted in Pompeian red, and frescoed with a frieze of stencilled lotus-leaves, taken from Owen Jones' *Grammar of Ornament*."[18] Although she never stated that this precisely described the decoration in the Jones house, it seems reasonable to assume that it did.[19]

Beyond was what she called "a small room on the ground floor," which measured 16 feet square and served as her father's study.[20] It was dominated by a huge oak mantlepiece supported by knights in visors; similar knights stood at the four corners of a large writing table. A "Turkey rug"[21] covered the floor. Beneath green damask wallpaper were low, glass-fronted bookcases with seven hundred volumes of a "gentleman's library."[22] It was in this peaceful setting, which her mother apparently rarely entered, that Edith was able to read for hours on end. She referred to it wistfully as "the kingdom of my father's library,"[23] and its influence on her life and career cannot be overestimated.

Two other mainstays of the Victorian era — the billiard room and the conservatory — were probably located on the ground floor of the

Jones house.[24] Edith recalled that the billiard room opened onto an unfinished yet "stately conservatory... an empty waste, unheated and flowerless, because the money gave out with the furnishing of the billiard-room."[25]

Upstairs were the principal rooms: the drawing room and the dining room. Although Edith once described her home as "a comfortable town-house, luxuriously mounted,"[26] she recalled the drawing room as "a full-blown specimen of Second Empire decoration, the creation of the fashionable French upholsterer, Marcotte."[27] The floor-length arched windows were "hung with three layers of curtains: sash-curtains through which no eye from the street could possibly penetrate, and next to these draperies of lace or embroidered tulle, richly beruffled, and looped back under the velvet or damask hangings which were drawn in the evening."[28]

The furnishings in the drawing room, like those in other well-to-do homes of the period, included "monumental pieces of modern Dutch marquetry,"[29] as well as a cabinet with glazed doors holding Lucretia Jones's collection of old lace and fans. A table of "Louis Philippe *buhl*, with ornate brass heads at the angles" held a Mary Magdalen "minutely reproduced on copper."[30] Travelers often brought such items as the Mary Magdalen, Venetian furniture, and European paintings copied from accepted old masters to decorate their New York homes; for the most part, Wharton recalled them all as ugly, gloomy, and depressing. "One of these 'awful warnings,' a Domenichino, I think, darkened the walls of

FIG. 5 *Lucretia Jones's drawing room at 28 West 25th Street, c. 1880s. On the back of the photograph Edith Wharton wrote: "The house (my mother's) at W 25th St. New York, from which I was married April 19, 1885." Edith and her mother moved to this house from 14 West 23rd Street following the death of George Frederic Jones in 1882.* (BL)

our dining room,"[31] she wrote many years later.

The upper stories of the house contained bedrooms for her parents, her two brothers (Frederic and Henry), a bedroom and probably a nursery for Edith, and rooms for the servants. In the privacy of her room, away from the constricting eye of her mother, Edith kept a stack of wrapping paper retrieved from packages to be reused for writing. Spreading the sheets out on the floor, she happily scribbled poetry and little stories for hours on end.

Pencraig, Newport

Edith described Pencraig, on Harrison Avenue, as "a charming country-place on the Narragansett Bay, in the outskirts of Newport, where I found everything to delight the heart of a happy, healthy child — cows, a kitchen-garden full of pears & quinces & strawberries, a beautiful rose-garden, a stable full of horses (with a dear little poney [sic] of my own), a boat, a bath-house, a beautiful sheltered cove to swim in, & best of all, two glorious little boys to

swim with! I wonder now that I did not forget all about Europe."[32] After years of traveling, Pencraig represented stability to the young girl.

Unlike her New York home, Pencraig had "friendly gables"[33] and was "roomy and pleasant."[34] A rambling wooden Queen Anne-style structure with dark half-timbering, the three-story house was very much the model of a proper but picturesque mid-century Victorian country home.[35] Half-smothered in ivy, clematis, and honeysuckle, it sported numerous gables topped with finials, striped awnings, window boxes, myriad chimneys, and a spacious veranda. The front lawn sloped towards a meadow of wildflowers; below was a beach and a private boat landing.

Furniture in the style of modern Dutch marquetry that Edith remembered "gracing" New York townhouses was placed prominently in the stair hall. Tables and desk tops were covered with photographs, urns, and objets d'art. A large cupboard held a collection of her mother, Lucretia's, china. Large potted ferns were evident, along with two paintings of Edith by Edward May, one executed when she was five and the other when she was nineteen. The overall feeling, though more relaxed than the New York townhouse, was heavy and dark.

Interestingly, Edith later recalled that her mother had tempered some of her decorating zeal by using Colonial pieces at Pencraig. Because both parents had inherited fine Colonial silver, Edith surmised that her mother had purchased Colonial furniture "that could then be had almost for the asking in New England. At all events, our house in Newport was provided, chiefly through old Mr. Vernon, the Newport antiquarian, with a fine lot of highboys and lowboys, and with sets of the graceful Colonial Hepplewhite chairs."[36] Wharton lamented that her mother had not pursued this line of interior decoration.

Lucretia Jones also had an extensive collection of Italian faience china ("Urbino, Gubbio, and various Italian luster wares"[37]), which was then deemed "more suitable than pictures"[38] in drawing rooms. She had been particularly proud of this collection until an Italian collector praised the pieces too enthusiastically and made her realize that the collection was without true merit. Edith noticed that her mother subsequently restricted her collecting to lace, fans, and old silver.

Apparently, there was no library at Pencraig, for Edith remembered that "in the country we had few books."[39] Indeed, summers at Newport were given over chiefly to outdoor pleasures; her "chief distractions were the simple ones of swimming and riding."[40] At Newport she awoke to the beauty of the outdoors, complimenting her early remarkable feelings about interiors and rooms:

Yet what I recall of those rambles is not so much the comradeship of the other children, or the wise and friendly talk of our guide, as my secret sensitiveness to the landscape — something in me quite incommunicable to others, that was trembling and inarticulately awake to every detail of wind-warped fern and wide-eyed briar rose, yet more profoundly alive to a unifying magic beneath the diversities of the visible scene — a power with which I was in deep and solitary communion whenever I was alone with nature.[41]

In the summers after her debut in 1879, Edith recalled Pencraig was "full of merry young people . . . Every room in our house was always full."[42] The days were filled with riding, drives, fishing, boat races, archery tournaments, yachting parties, and many other pleasurable pursuits. One of the regular annual visitors to Pencraig was Edward (Teddy) Robbins Wharton, who had been an intimate friend of Edith's brother Henry. Familiarity and friendship led Edith and Teddy to marry in 1885. They set up housekeeping at Pencraig Cottage on the grounds of her mother's home.

FIG. 7 *The hall and stairs of Pencraig, c. 1880s. Two portraits of Edith are visible on the left: at age five (see Fig. 4) and in 1881, both by Edward Harrison May.* (BL)

Pencraig Cottage, Newport

In her autobiography, Edith did not discuss her marriage but she made immediate mention of her early decorating efforts: "My first care was to create a home of my own; and for a few months after our marriage my husband and I moved into a little cottage in [sic] the grounds of Pencraig, and rearranged it in accordance with our tastes."[43] Although they were unable to afford a property of their own, the couple established a regular routine: June through February at Pencraig Cottage and February to June traveling in Europe, with intervals in New York City.

Edith had always written happily, almost rapturously, about Newport, but after her marriage she began to complain. She disliked the climate, hated its "watering place mundanities and always longed for the real country."[44] Her life there as a young married woman was more constricting than the carefree, happy days of her childhood. Edith's and Teddy's basic differences in temperaments and interests were also creating strains.

Apparently they did enjoy making their home both comfortable and tasteful. For Edith, interior decoration was a chance to please her husband and an attempt to define herself: "I always saw the visible world as a series of pictures, more or less harmoniously composed, & the wish to make the picture prettier was, as nearly as I can define it, the form my feminine instinct of pleasing took."[45]

Decorating and redecorating their homes were engaging pastimes and creative outlets for society women in Edith Wharton's time. Edith stands out for her simplicity, the result of limited funds and her already highly developed sensibilities.

Pencraig Cottage was a modest two-and-one-half story frame house in the Italianate style.[46] The center section was three bays wide; on either side were irregularly shaped wings. The most dominate exterior feature was a later addition, an airy veranda in a rather ornate style.

The interior was notable for its simplicity and for the personal touches that would always mark Edith's homes. Despite the floral wallpaper, which was typical of the period (and which Edith would describe as distasteful in *The Decoration of Houses*), the rooms conveyed comfort and practicality. The furniture was not heavy or overstuffed nor were the floors overwhelmed with thick carpets. The walls were not excessively decorated with pictures. Personal touches included bookcases filled with books (not for mere decoration), carefully selected objets d'art, and a table heaped with more books and magazines. There were numerous floral arrangements that Edith had probably picked, arranged, and placed. Photographs of family and friends abounded on the mantel, bookcase, and on tables. Furnishings and objects were arranged for the comfort and intellectual fulfillment of the inhabitants, rather than to impress outsiders.

Edith continued to read and to travel as much as possible; she had a passionate interest in Italy, particularly in the Italian Renaissance. In addi-

FIG. 8 *Pencraig Cottage, near Pencraig, date unknown. This was the Whartons' first home after their marriage in 1885.* (LL)

tion, she developed her already strong interest in architecture with the help of a scholarly treatise:

Another book...figured among my more recent Awakeners; and that was James Fergusson's "History of Architecture," at that time one of the most stimulating books that could fall into a young student's hands. A generation nourished on learned monographs, monumental histories, and works of reference covering every period of art from Babylonian prehistory to the present day, would find it hard to believe how few books of the sort, especially on architecture and sculpture, were available in my youth. Fergusson's "History of Architecture" was an amazing innovation in its day. It shed on my misty haunting sense of the beauty of old buildings the light of historical and technical precision, and cleared and extended my horizon...[47]

Another key influence during this time was Edith's newly developed friendship with Egerton Winthrop, a family friend who was almost as old as her father. It was Winthrop who, as Wharton later explained, guided "the cool solitude of my studies...into the warm glow of a cultivated intelligence."[48] He introduced her to important literary and scientific writings and encouraged her fascination with the world of eighteenth-century Italy.

Winthrop also encouraged Edith to fulfill her proper role in society: "he was always pleading with me to fill the part he thought I ought to play in New York,"[49] she remembered. A cosmopolitan man, Winthrop thrived in New York society, and his home on East 33rd Street was acknowledged to be one of its most important. Designed in the French Second Empire style by prominent architect Richard Morris Hunt in 1878-79, the tasteful Louis XVI-style interiors stood in marked contrast to the stuffiness of Victorian New York.[50]

As Edith noted in *A Backward Glance*, Winthrop "had built himself a charming house. Besides being an ardent bibliophile he was a discriminating collector of works of art, especially of the eighteenth century, and his house was the first in New York in which an educated taste had replaced stuffy upholstery and rubbishy 'ornaments' with objects of real beauty in a simply designed setting."[51] She resolved to do the same.

FIG. 9 *The drawing room of Pencraig Cottage, one of Edith Wharton's first efforts at interior decoration.* (BL)

Edith's early design efforts at Pencraig Cottage included a small garden and improvements to the landscaping. Although she and her husband soon moved to a larger home in Newport, she remained interested in both Pencraig and Pencraig Cottage. Gaillard Lapsley wrote of how she would question him after she had moved to France:

Her interest naturally centred on the visit I generally make at Newport where I happen to know the present occupants both of her parents' house and of the cottage opposite its gate where she and Teddy began their married life. I think the little garden with which she surrounded it must have been the first that she actually planned and it was done with amazing skill to conceal the irregular shape of the scrap of land and the roads that held it in on three sides. Its full success depended on the maturity of the numerous trees and tall hedges and that of course she had never seen and was the more delighted therefore to hear about. When I first went to Pencraig (her parents' house) the present occupant her cousin Mrs. Webster begged me to tell her particularly that the washstand china in what had been her bedroom was unchanged and complete, because Edith had been specially attached to it. That touched her sensibly and she asked me more questions about the present arrangements in what I had seen of the house than I could answer, though I had foreseen and had tried to prepare myself for a pretty close examination.[52]

Land's End, Newport

At his death in 1888, Joshua Jones, a wealthy cousin on her father's side, whom she had never met, made a bequest to Edith that gave her financial independence for the rest of her life. A few years later, in March 1893, she purchased a house in Newport known as Land's End.[53] Located on Ledge Road, the property "was at the furthest possible distance from her mother's Pencraig, lying, as its name may suggest, at the far opposite end of the island, at the foot of the cliff walk, its windows looking directly across the Atlantic toward Ireland."[54] The estate included a main house, a stable, and another frame building, as well as gardens on the ocean side.

The house, with its wood clapboards painted white and a bulky mansard roof, had been constructed in 1864 for Samuel G. Ward by architect John Hubbard Sturgis.[55] Although Edith described the outside of Land's End as "incurably ugly,"[56] she and Teddy felt that "within doors there were interesting possibilities."[57]

They discussed the house with "a clever young Boston architect,"[58] Ogden Codman, Jr.,

a nephew of Sturgis. The Whartons had known Codman in Newport, and Edith may have consulted him concerning the decoration of Pencraig Cottage.[59] In 1893, the Whartons hired Codman to alter and decorate Land's End, which Edith noted later was "a somewhat new departure, since the architects of that day looked down on house decoration as a branch of dress-making, and left the field to the upholsterers, who crammed every room with curtains, lambrequins, jardinières of artificial plants, wobbly velvet-covered tables littered with silver gew-gaws, and festoons of lace on mantlepieces and dressing tables."[60]

The transformation began with the exterior; excess details were removed, and a circular courtyard was added. It consisted of high hedges and trelliswork niches that "helped it to a certain dignity"[61] and created areas for Edith to landscape and plant. Inside, Edith and Codman strove for "simple and architectural" decoration.[62]

The main floor of the house contained an entrance hall and stairs, a drawing room, a dining room, a library, and a glass veranda, an informal room that had been an open porch before it was enclosed by Codman and the Whartons. Architectural historian Richard Guy Wilson notes that the rooms were conceived by Edith and Codman to be showpieces "in the manner of the much-admired rooms of Egerton Winthrop," Edith's cultivated friend whose interiors had strongly influenced her.[63] The decoration of Land's End was a tremendous step from the far more simple work at Pencraig Cottage and represented a major step toward the philosophies exhibited ten years later at The Mount.[64]

Surviving period photographs of the interiors of Land's End illustrate the basic concepts that Edith and Codman would draw upon at The Mount. Perhaps the least successful room at Land's End was the drawing room; its low ceiling diminished a spaciousness inherent in Codman's design. Though the French armchairs, bookcases filled with books, and statues (including a table-top Venus de Milo) seem typical of Edith's later inclinations, the heavy draperies at the windows and doors and the busy damask wallcovering sandwiched between the wainscoting and cornice are indicative of Edith's developing tastes. Several framed portraits seem to be lost in the patterns of the wall fabric. French wall sconces holding candles were identical to

those in the dining room and to those later used in the dining room at The Mount.

The dining room seems a more appealing space, perhaps because it was smaller and its low ceiling did not seem so oppressive. There was also damask fabric on the walls, although the design was lighter and more attractive. The white-painted chairs, cabinet, and side tables were later transferred to The Mount, and the dining room carpet was later used in Edith's library there. The ceiling design in the Land's End dining room employed some of the same plaster Rococo scrollwork that abounded in the drawing room, but because it was limited to the corners and ceiling margins, it appeared much less ostentatious.

The stair hall and the library came closest to the ideals that Edith and Codman were to achieve at The Mount. The furnishings of the latter room — most of which were later moved to Edith's library at The Mount — consisted of comfortable armchairs and a sofa grouped around a marble fireplace. To the left of the

FIG. 11 *Boudoir, Land's End, 1890s. The furniture from this room was transferred to Edith Wharton's boudoir at The Mount (see Fig. 69). (SPNEA)*

FIG. 12 *Library, Land's End, 1890s. Codman's design of the medallion of the Roman emperor over the mantel mirror was repeated in Teddy Wharton's den at The Mount (see Figs. 52, 127, and 129). Most of the furniture was transferred to The Mount's library. The eagle andirons may have been the ones that Edith inherited from her great-grandfather, Gen. Ebenezer Stevens. All of her libraries featured a dog bed near the fireplace. (MMA, gift of the estate of Ogden Codman, Jr., 1951)*

fireplace was a round dog bed; on either side were wooden bookcases. Other tables held piles of books and magazines. The plain plaster walls were delineated by strong architectural moldings and hung with engravings of European places and monuments.

The eagle andirons visible in a photograph of the Land's End library may be the ones that Edith inherited from her illustrious great-grandfather, Ebenezer Stevens. In *A Backward Glance*, she wrote that "in his Bonapartist days General Stevens must have imported a good deal of Empire furniture from Paris, and one relic, a pair of fine gilt andirons crowned with Napoleonic eagles, has descended to his distant great-grand-daughter."[65]

Codman designed a medallion of a Roman emperor surrounded by garlands, which was executed in plaster and placed above the tall, inset mirror over the mantel. This design must have appealed to the Whartons, for they had it reproduced almost exactly ten years later in Teddy's den at The Mount.

The stair hall at Land's End featured a French-inspired staircase with wooden balusters framing wrought-iron railings. A dark stair carpet — perhaps a rich red — was held in place by carpet rods. Strong architectural moldings gave a sense of order and proportion to the space. The furnishings included a sofa and a French wall clock (both later transferred to the drawing room at The Mount) and an oriental carpet at the foot of the stairs.

The glass veranda seems to have had no precedent in Edith's former homes nor would it reappear at The Mount. In describing this unusual Wharton interior, Richard Guy Wilson writes: "With its plain floor covering and elegant wooden furniture, this sitting room was the most relaxed and inviting space in the house... When Edith was unable to purchase a suitable ceiling in Italy, Codman designed, probably in 1897, an Adamesque or Pompeiian 'tent' ceiling for the glass verandah. With its patterns of ropes and colored sky and clouds, the space would have become even more intentionally an ambiguously indoors-outdoors room; but it was never installed."[66]

The glass veranda, which overlooked the garden hedges, flowers, statues, trellage, paths, and clipped lawn, seems to have served many functions that later took place on the wide, sunny terrace at The Mount. Despite Edith's comment that the exterior of Land's End was "incurably ugly," some of her feelings about the house were strongly affectionate. She wrote, for instance, that "I loved Land's End with its windows framing the endlessly changing moods of the misty Atlantic, and the night-long sound of the surges against the cliffs."[67] With its windows that "looked straight across to the west coast of Ireland,"[68] the glass veranda must have been a special room for her.

The Whartons sold Land's End to move to the Berkshires. *Berkshire Resort Topics* noted on June 13, 1903, that "Mr. Edward R. Wharton was in Newport on Thursday, arranging for the transfer of 'Landsend' [sic] to Mr. and Mrs. R. Livingston Beekman, to whom Mr. and Mrs. Wharton recently sold the estate."[69]

884 Park Avenue, New York City

In November 1891, Edith and Teddy purchased a brownstone at 884 Park Avenue. The house proved so small (approximately 16 feet wide) that the Whartons decided to rent it for income at $1,300 a year.[70]

Edith joked that she and Teddy "used to say it was the smallest [house] in New York."[71] A few years later, she bought an identical house next door. Teddy, who loved society and disliked the cold, would not live in the country during the winter, so a New York home was a

visible, along with a decorative rounded Italian table-top cabinet) seems stiff and less plush than the furniture at Land's End. The striped wallpaper, an unusual feature in a Wharton home, appears similar to a scheme that Codman had proposed, but not used, for the library at Land's End in 1893.[75]

The use of a wallpaper depicting birds, palms, ferns, and flowering shrubs in the dining room at 884 also seems atypical of Wharton interiors from this period. There was a mirror with an elaborate frame of ribbons and garlands and a gently curving top set above a marble fireplace. Other furnishings included simple, painted chairs with caned seats and dark wooden cabinets that held candles, silverware, china, and glassware flanking the fireplace. While elegant, this interior seems more colorful than the usual Wharton-Codman room, mainly due to the flowing lines of the wallpaper and the prominence of the large mirror.

FIG. 14 *882-884 Park Avenue, the Whartons' New York City home in the 1890s.* (EWR)

FIG. 15 *Parlor, 884 Park Avenue.* (MMA, *gift of the estate of Ogden Codman, Jr., 1951*)

necessity. The Whartons (with their staff living in 882) would spend parts of the next ten or so years at 884.

Edith remembered that "I had the amusement of adorning our sixteen-foot-wide house in New York with the modest spoils of our Italian travels."[72] Once again she called in Codman; he brought his usual flair for perfection, and together they created some charming interiors. Henry James, who stayed at 884 Park Avenue (he once referred to it as "suite 884"[73]), wrote to Howard Sturgis in 1905 that he found himself in "elegant though very gentle bondage" and called the house "a bonbonnière of the last daintiness naturally."[74]

Photographs reveal tastefully furnished but rather formal rooms. The parlor featured books displayed prominently in a bookcase and on a nearby cabinet, hallmarks of a Wharton interior. Yet the furniture (three armchairs and a sofa are

In her autobiography, *After All*, Elsie de Wolfe, the "lady decorator," related a story that may well be apocryphal. Having called upon Edith:

I noticed but eight chairs in her dining room. I remarked about this to her, as it was then the custom to give large and formal dinners. "Yes, Miss de Wolfe," she replied, "there are but eight people in the whole of New York whom I care to have dine with me."[76]

There are few firsthand accounts of 884 Park Avenue, but two people who knew Edith over the course of many years testified to her love for interior decoration and the thought and care that she brought to it. Daniel Berkeley Updike, founder of the Merrymount Press, commented on the small scale of the house. Since he was then designing a number of Edith's first books, he was probably a frequent visitor to 884 Park Avenue:

This house was scarcely sixteen feet wide, but Edith managed to collect furniture and pictures all on a small scale and as she and Teddy were both small in stature and the plan was ingeniously and consistently carried out, the effect of the interior was spacious — unless a very big man or woman entered, when the house seemed to be of normal size and the visitor a giant![77]

In *Portrait of Edith Wharton* (1947), British writer Percy Lubbock quoted the memories of "a young Englishwoman, newly married and established in New York."[78] This unidentified person, actually Sybil Cutting, who later married Lubbock, gives a glimpse into Edith's working relationship with Codman. The account began with a description of the house and drawing room:

At first sight the house was reassuring. It was small, plain and unpretentious, and might have stood unnoticed in a quiet corner of Brompton. Once inside I was not so sure. It was English certainly, but with a minute and studied perfection quite unknown to me in English houses of its kind. The drawing-room too, where I had vaguely hoped to find Mrs. Wharton seated at her literary labours, was as barren of any sign of habitual occupation as all the other New York drawing-rooms in which I had waited.[79]

FIG. 16 *Dining room, 884 Park Avenue.* (MMA, *gift of the estate of Ogden Codman, Jr., 1951)*

During their conversation, the two women were unable to find much mutually comfortable ground, as Edith mentioned names or topics unfamiliar to the younger Englishwoman.

At this moment to my relief a man entered the room. "Oh Edith," he said, "I think I've worked out quite a good plan for those rooms." "Mr. Codman" — she turned to me half in explanation, half in introduction — "is kindly helping me with some plans." But I was already on my feet, glad of the excuse. Mr. Codman politely accompanied me to the front-door, and while I was struggling with my unfamiliar over-shoes, for there was snow on the ground, Mrs. Wharton leant over the banisters, thinking I had already gone, and called to him in a warm, kind, eager voice that I had not yet heard: "What do you think, Ogden — could one in a little house like this allow a Chippendale clock in the hall?" I liked that voice... As I walked home up Park Avenue I reflected that though I had called on another New York lady I had not yet met Edith Wharton.[80]

The Decoration of Houses

In *A Backward Glance*, Edith recalled almost forty years later how she and Ogden Codman came to co-author *The Decoration of Houses*: "Codman shared my dislike of these sumptuary excesses, and thought as I did that interior decoration should be simple and architectural; and finding that we had the same views we drifted, I hardly know how, toward putting them into a book."[81]

R. W. B. Lewis, author of *Edith Wharton: A Biography*, points out that between 1894 and 1896 Edith suffered from a "severe identity crisis."[82] Overwhelmed with what he called "paralyzing melancholy, extreme exhaustion, constant fits of nausea, and no capacity whatever to make choices or decisions,"[83] her life — including sporadic attempts to write poetry and short stories — came to a standstill. This crisis was apparently caused by the recent rejection of some of her writings by Scribner's, her unhappy and unfulfilling marriage, and her confusion with reconciling her conflicting roles of wife, hostess, intellectual, and author.

Yet by the end of 1896, Edith had recovered her health sufficiently to begin work on what would become her first widely-published book. The young woman who, in her own words, had once "trembled with a sensuous ecstasy at the sight of beautiful objects, or the sound of noble verse"[84] had matured into a writer able to analyze her love of beautiful things in discerning and more dispassionate prose. Although some writers have been surprised that Wharton's first book would be a learned treatise on the subject of house decoration, William A. Coles, in "The Genesis of a Classic," believes that it "brought to a happy resolution her experiences of the last decade in travel, studying and buying furniture, and interior decoration."[85]

Edith and Codman wrote much of the book in early 1897. After seeing an incomplete manuscript during the summer, Scribner's agreed to publish it by the end of the year. During late July and August, Edith rewrote extensive sections under the careful guidance of Walter Berry, who was staying at Land's End. Edith credited Berry with shaping not only the newly emerging book but also her development as a writer:

Codman and I were struggling with our book. Walter Berry was born with an exceptionally sensitive literary instinct, but also with a critical sense so far outweighing his creative gift that he had early renounced the idea of writing... I remember shyly asking him to look at my lumpy pages; and I remember his first shout of laughter (for he never flattered or pretended), and then his saying good naturedly: "Come, let's see what can be done," and settling down beside me to try to model the lump into a book.

In a few weeks the modeling was done, and in those weeks, as I afterward discovered, I had been taught whatever I know about the writing of clear concise English.[86]

It can never be determined what each author brought to their collaboration; over the years each would remember differently what the other had done. Pauline C. Metcalf, editor of *Ogden Codman and The Decoration of Houses*, concludes that "Edith's crisp prose gave the book its style, while Ogden contributed both

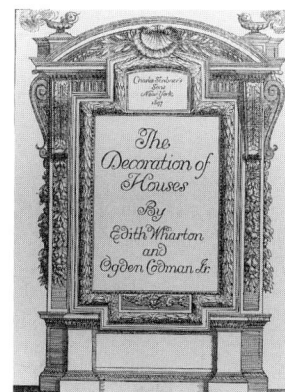

FIG. 17   *Title page of the first edition of* The Decoration of Houses, *1897.* (EWR)

FIG. 18 *Illustration (Plate XVIII) from* The Decoration of Houses, *1897, entitled "Carved Door, Palace of Versailles. Louis XV Period (showing painted over-door)."* (EWR)

a practical understanding of the principles of interior design and many of the illustrations of splendid rooms in the great palaces and country houses of Europe."[87]

The theme of *The Decoration of Houses*, according to Edith, was that "the interior of a house is as much a part of its organic structure as the outside, and that its treatment ought, in the same measure, to be based on right proportion, balance of door and window spacing, and simple unconfused lines. We developed this argument logically, and I think forcibly."[88] Edith and Codman were rebelling against the excessive Victorian interiors and poorly planned designs of their childhoods that they, like everyone else, were expected to live in without regard to common sense. The authors were well aware that their precepts would appear to be quite radical to most readers.

The book was divided into 16 chapters on components (walls, doors, windows, fireplaces, ceilings, and floors) and rooms (entrance and vestibule, hall and stairs, drawing room, boudoir, morning room, ballroom, salon, music room, gallery, library, smoking room, "den," dining room, bedrooms, school room, and nurseries). Introductory chapters discussed historical traditions and general precepts. There were 56 plates, a bibliography, and an index (unfortunately the publishers did not include house plans as Edith had hoped). Daniel Berkeley Updike, a friend of both Edith and Codman and founder of the Merrymount Press in

Boston, designed an appropriately classical title page for the handsome, oversized volume.

The book's popularity surprised both the authors and the publisher. Edith proudly recorded in *A Backward Glance* that the first printing sold out quickly and that "people of taste were only too eager to follow any guidance that would not only free them from the suffocating upholsterer, but tell them how to replace him. It became the fashion to use our volume as a touchstone of taste."[89] Nearly a century later the book's precepts remain as timeless and valuable as when they were first written.

Throughout their exceptional careers, both Edith and Codman took pride in their collaboration and enjoyed the occasional royalty check that it provided. When Edith wrote to Codman early in 1937 about publishing a second edition,[90] he replied with satisfaction that although there had been great progress since the 1890s, "it still seems to me a book that most architects, and *all their clients* should buy: — '*To read, mark, learn, inwardly digest and profit thereby.*' Nothing any thing like as good has appeared since to my knowledge," he continued, "and I have tried to add all books of consequence about Architectural decoration to my library."[91]

Codman proposed that they add a brief preface and photographs of rooms whose designs were based on the philosophies of the book, including his two French châteaux and several of his New York City townhouses, in order for "readers to grasp what we were trying to inculcate."[92]

Edith agreed and stopped to discuss the book at Codman's home in Grégy a few months before her death. Although Edith and Codman would not live to see a reworking of *The Decoration of Houses* as they had envisioned it, there seems an appropriate symmetry in that some of her final literary activities were directed towards a new edition of this first enduring success.

CHAPTER 3

A House of Her Own Making
The Design of The Mount

The design of The Mount involved a combination of Edith Wharton's philosophies and astute knowledge of design and architecture, the initial planning by Ogden Codman, Jr., and the work of the firm of Hoppin & Koen. It is difficult to assign specific design elements to individuals with absolute certainty, due to a lack of documentation.

The idea of locating the house on a rock outcropping to take in the view of Laurel Pond and Laurel Lake was most likely a decision made by Edith and Teddy Wharton in response to the site. The inventive idea of placing the house half-on and half-off the hillside was probably made by Edith with Codman. Codman clearly developed it in his first rough sketches for the Whartons in 1901. This scheme is one of The Mount's most distinctive features, as on the north it allowed for the *piano nobile*, or main floor, of the house to open directly onto the hillside. In some areas the house is three-and-one-half stories, in others it is only two-and-one-half.

Edith and Codman also decided on an H-shaped plan, which was retained in the final design. While Codman did not execute any elevations of The Mount, the H-shaped plan of his rough sketches suggests that The Mount was based on English country houses of the seventeenth century, specifically Belton House in Lincolnshire. It seems likely that Codman may have introduced the Whartons to Belton when they made a trip to Europe in the spring of 1900. Upon their return to Lenox, where they were renting a cottage, Edith wrote to Codman in July:

I must begin by thanking you for your thoughtfulness in writing me so often during my European tour, and more especially for sending me the list of English country houses that you promised me before we left. Your list added very much to our enjoyment of England...[1]

When it came to the realities of planning her own country house, Edith obviously remembered the footnote that she and Codman had added to Chapter 1 of *The Decoration of Houses* in 1897. In it they expressed their preferences for the Italian villa over French and English country houses. However:

Charming as the Italian villa is, it can hardly be used in our Northern States without certain modifications, unless it is merely occupied for a few weeks in mid-summer; whereas the average French or English country house built after 1600 is perfectly suited to our climate and habits. The chief features of the Italian villa are the open central *cortile* and the large saloon two stories high. An adaptation of these better suited to a cold climate is to be found in the English country houses built in the Palladian manner after its introduction by Inigo Jones. See Campbell's *Vitruvius Britannicus* for numerous examples.[2]

In Colin Campbell's *Vitruvius Britannicus, or The British Architect* (1715-25), there is an illustration of Belton House, the seat of Lord Brownlow in Lincolnshire. In addition, Belton House had been featured in 1898 issues of

FIG. 19 *Belton House, the seat of Lord Brownlow, in Lincolnshire, England, constructed in 1684, as illustrated in a plate by Colin Campbell from* Vitruvius Britannicus *(1715-25).* (EWR)

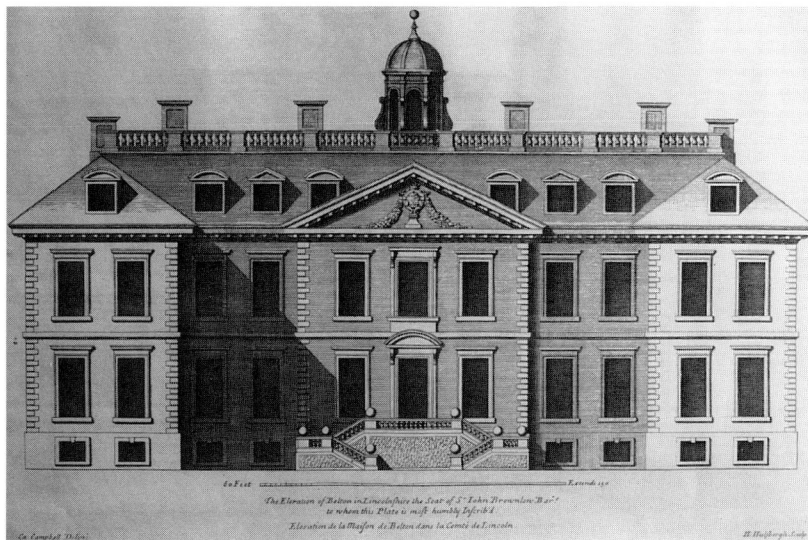

35

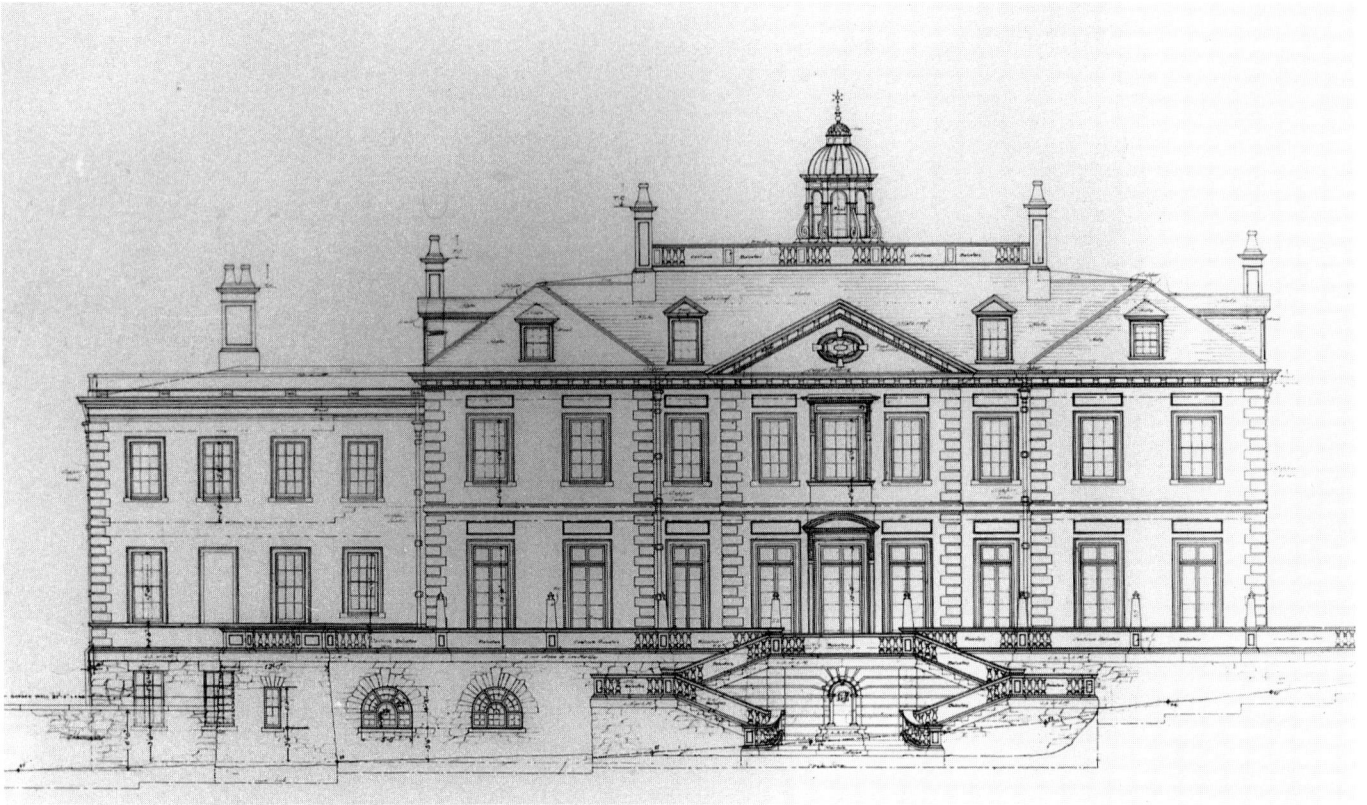

FIG. 20 *East elevation of The Mount, Hoppin & Koen, 1901. This aspect of the house was inspired by the elevation of Belton House in Lincolnshire, England, published in* Vitruvius Britannicus *(see Fig. 19; also compare to Fig. 90).* (AAFAL)

Country Life,[3] probably increasing Edith's familiarity with it. Belton probably represented one of most perfect images of the proper English estate of the period. Built during 1684-86, it was attributed at the turn-of-the-century to architect Sir Christopher Wren,[4] with interior ornamental carvings by Grinling Gibbons.

The east facade of The Mount was most closely inspired by Belton House, but it is not an exact copy. The Mount is smaller than the English house. Instead of being built of gray stone, The Mount's appearance is affected by the use of stucco painted white (with the green shutters, the effect is that of a proper New England house). And instead of Belton's flat site, The Mount's unusual hillside perch and the large terrace anchoring it to the landscape are distinctive features. John Summerson's *Architecture in Britain 1530 to 1830* shows no other English house with a terrace even remotely resembling that of The Mount. The Mount's Palladian staircase, which leads from the terrace to the formal gardens below, was

most likely taken almost exactly from the Belton plate in *Vitruvius Britannicus* by Francis Hoppin at Edith's direction.[5]

The Belton House prototype was used several times by Codman previous to the design of The Mount: for example, the Coats House (c. 1884) in Newport, Rhode Island, and the Lloyd Stephens Bryce House (c. 1901) in Roslyn, New York. According to Pauline C. Metcalf, "The plan and form of all his country houses was based on a classical prototype."[6] This form consisted of "a central block with projecting 'H' wings [which] provided the ideal solution for an enfilade arrangement of rooms."[7] Hoppin & Koen had also used the Belton House prototype, including three houses designed by the firm in Aiken, South Carolina (all c. 1902), and to some extent Armsea Hall (1900-04) in Newport, Rhode Island, and Blithewood (1900-01) in Barrytown, New York.

The service wing at The Mount was designed by Hoppin & Koen. Although Belton House had various additions to the main

FIG. 21 *West elevation of The Mount, Hoppin & Koen, 1901. The five arched windows of the gallery were modified to three windows, and the entrance portal from the courtyard was simplified substantially (compare to Figs. 37 and 89).* (AAFAL)

house, none resembled this wing. The original rough sketches by Codman presented a completely symmetrical structure with the service functions incorporated within. A specialty of Hoppin & Koen was to design homes that could be added to if future needs or desires permitted, and this would eventually be so at The Mount, although the 1907 project to extend the service wing was never realized.

The west facade of The Mount departed significantly from the model of Belton House. The unusual entrance sequence of arriving in the forecourt, entering a vestibule, turning to the right and climbing a flight of stairs to the *piano nobile*, had no relation to any seventeenth-century English country house. Richard Guy Wilson postulates that the origin of this sequence "was undoubtedly French, possibly the Petit Trianon at Versailles (1762-68) by Ange-Jacques Gabriel, where the same spatial sequence takes place with entry from forecourt into a three-story block."[8] Landscape architect David H. Bennett argues that Edith and

Codman envisioned the house as a "gateway to the garden"[9] and that the real inspiration for the floor plans and design of The Mount was that of the Villa Pratolino, near Florence, Italy. The Whartons were visiting Italian villas and gardens around the time that plans for The Mount were in formation. Regardless of whether the design was more French or more Italian, the point is that it was inspired by European antecedents and adapted for an American setting. Much of the genius of Edith's design of The Mount is in the skillful blending of the best of French, English, and Italian classical design elements to create a new American vocabulary.

The original Hoppin & Koen drawings for both the east and west facades of The Mount reveal that Edith made some significant changes. For example, on the east there would be only three French doors in the drawing room, although the illusion of five was maintained on the exterior with two blind windows. The five windows proposed for the gallery on the west were also changed to three and the rather elaborate scheme of narrow loggia, balustrades, and other exterior decorative elements was likewise dropped. The more decorative scheme around the main entrance from the forecourt was also simplified.

The idea of a forecourt on the west elevation is attributable to Edith and Codman. The forecourt was crucial to the way the house sits on the hillside, because it obscures that natural feature from the entrance approach while serving the practical purpose of a retaining wall. The forecourt also clearly separates the owners' entrance from the service yard. The actual design incorporates elements of a "split-level house, [which] is decidedly modern."[10] Edith and Codman had previously created a forecourt at Land's End using hedges and trelliswork. The final design of The Mount's forecourt, as executed by Hoppin & Koen, was roundly ridiculed by Codman, although the real problem may have been the Whartons' tight budget, since various more elaborate Hoppin & Koen schemes were rejected by the Whartons.

Edith Wharton's ideas concerning the design of her home made The Mount unique. A detailed examination of the design of each room, including Codman's initial sketches and the Hoppin & Koen floor plans, may be found in Chapter 6.

Ogden Codman, Jr., Preliminary Architect of The Mount

Ogden Codman, Jr., (1863-1951) was the architect to whom Edith first turned in 1901 to realize her ideas for The Mount. More than just a friend and social acquaintance, he had collaborated with her in 1897 on her first published book, *The Decoration of Houses*, an influential treatise advocating a common-sense approach to house decoration using classical eighteenth-century French, English, and Italian designs.

Born in Boston in 1863 (one year after Edith Jones), Codman came from a distinguished old New England family, whose home, The Grange in Lincoln, Massachusetts, would serve as inspiration and a design laboratory for the future architect. Like the Jones family, which had gone to Europe in 1866 when Edith was four, the Codmans moved to France in 1872 due to financial constraints. Codman spent the formative ages of nine to twenty-one mostly in Dinard, developing an acute appreciation for French life, manners, and architecture. In particular he was drawn to French architecture and decorative arts of the eighteenth century, a period that approximated the Colonial era in America, to which he was also attracted. His deft mixing of these classic styles became the trademark of his future work.

FIG. 22 *Ogden Codman, Jr., at nineteen in Dinard, France, 1882.* (SPNEA)

Codman's early training in the mid-1880s included learning from his uncle, the architect John Hubbard Sturgis (a partner in the Boston firm of Sturgis & Brigham), two years in the office of an unidentified architect in Lowell, Massachusetts, then work for the firm of Andrews & Jacques in Boston in 1889.[11] As early as 1884 he carried out his first commission, a parlor redesign for a cousin in Newport. By 1891 he had resolved to start his own firm; two years later he had opened offices in Newport and New York City.

One of his first clients was Edith Wharton, who possibly sought his services for work on Pencraig Cottage in Newport circa 1891.[12] In 1893, when the Whartons purchased the large Victorian cottage, Land's End, Edith called on Codman to transform the house, which she considered "incurably ugly."[13] Codman's solutions addressed the entire house. The exterior treatments, consisting of garden areas, trellis-work, and hedges, formed a forecourt, and the removal of excess detailing helped "to lend" the house "a certain dignity,"[14] as Edith later explained. Most successful and influential were the interiors, in which Codman and Wharton exercised their strong predilections for eighteenth-century French design, decoration, and furnishings.

A growing friendship between Codman and Edith, who found that they shared many of the same ideas on design, decoration, and architecture, also resulted in Codman's doing work on the Whartons' New York City townhouse on Park Avenue. Of great interest to Codman was Edith's influence among the social set in New York and Newport, where he wished to find commissions; soon "her friendship and patronage were of invaluable assistance to him in obtaining some of his most important clients."[15]

In December 1893, Codman found that Edith was responsible for his selection to decorate the two upper bedroom floors of The Breakers, the enormous Newport cottage of Cornelius Vanderbilt.[16] Architect Richard Morris Hunt and the prestigious French firm of

J. Allard et Fils decorated the other principal rooms. As Codman wrote ecstatically to his mother: "Just think what a client! The nicest and richest of them all..."[17] Herein were the seeds of some of the subsequent financial disagreements that eventually caused a falling-out between Codman and Edith and Teddy Wharton; Codman received highly lucrative fees from clients like the Vanderbilts, which the Whartons were simply unable to match.

Codman designed his first entire house for Mrs. Charles Coolidge Pomeroy in 1895-96 in Newport. The structure was "not much more than an interrupted cube with a classical pediment, corbels, and arched windows on the first floor."[18] Although the house was named "Seabeach," it soon became known to the locals as "the mud palace,"[19] perhaps due to the use of stucco for its exterior. Edith, in an 1896 short story, "The Valley of Childish Things, and other Emblems," clearly satirized this first effort by referring to the work of an architect in the story as "a mud hut,"[20] an allusion that must have infuriated Codman.

At this time Codman did a second house, Landfall, for Mr. and Mrs. Alfred M. Coats. Constructed c. 1895-96, this house was a key one in Codman's early work; it was based on "late seventeenth-century English models [and] contained many elements that would recur in his country houses — a hip roof, dormers, and the massing of a central block with projecting wings."[21] In these aspects, Landfall may be seen as a clear precedent to The Mount as Codman would initially conceive it in 1901.

In 1897 *The Decoration of Houses*, co-authored by Edith and Codman, appeared. As Pauline C. Metcalf notes, this marked

an important watershed in Codman's career. Not only was his reputation considerably enhanced by his association with the book, but his work after 1897 shifted also from the purely decorative approach toward an architectural one. He later wrote that in the process of analyzing the advice that he and Wharton had laid down, he had been able to "inwardly digest" the guidelines and apply them to his own work. Such phrases as "if proportion is the good breeding of architecture, symmetry...may be defined as the sanity of decoration" and "structure conditions ornament, not ornament structure" were hence forth consistently adhered to by Codman... Codman's style had matured by the turn of the century. There would be no further significant changes in his approach to design, although he gradually rid his decorative schemes of the charming but excessive details so characteristic of the Edwardian era.[22]

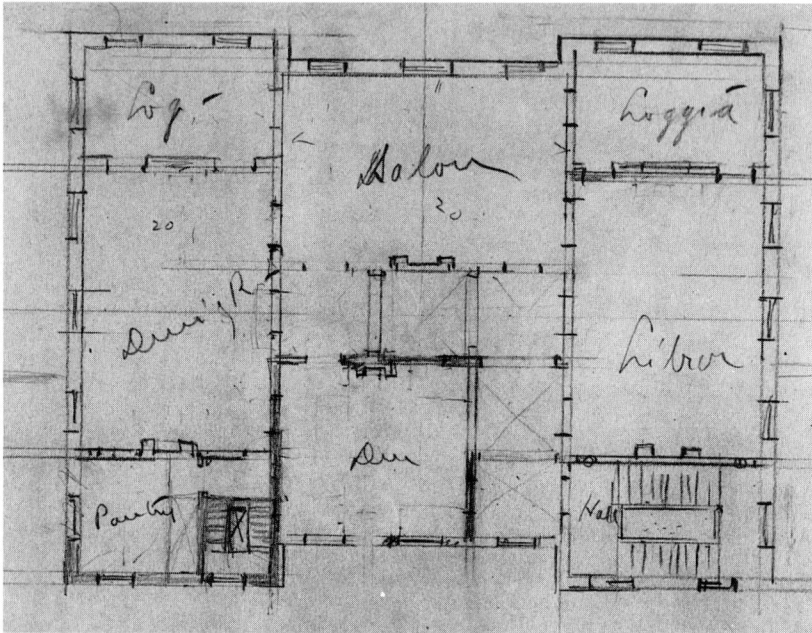

FIG. 23 *First-floor plan for The Mount, Ogden Codman, Jr., c. 1901 (not realized). The center salon was flanked by the dining room and library; the latter two rooms opened onto separate loggias. The den, opposite the salon, would have been connected to the dining room. The only service room was a pantry adjoining the dining room.*

(AAFAL)

Around the turn-of-the-century, Codman agreed to design a country home in Lenox for Edith and Teddy Wharton. This was finally accomplished during February 1901, and Edith wrote to Codman that they hoped to begin construction almost immediately, "in the spring,"[23] as Codman wrote to his mother on February 7, 1901. He began work on some preliminary sketches, but the Whartons' budget for construction and architect's fees proved to be a problem for him; as he wrote to his mother in mid-February 1901, "I have already made some plans they like but I don't know what they mean to spend."[24]

A week later, on February 25, he again wrote to his mother, but in a more threatening tone concerning the Whartons: "They have been fussing about their house so I almost wish I was not going to build it. They do not seem to realize that I am very different from when I did their other house [Land's End]. But they *will* learn."[25] He went on to add with irritation:

"There are times when I fully realize what an idiot Teddy is."[26] Teddy had apparently tried to get Codman to lower his fees, but, as the architect continued, "I won't have any nonsense...he failed and was upset. I guess he won't try that again."[27]

Despite his upbeat ending to the February 25th letter ("it will all come out right in the end"[28]), things soon went from bad to worse. On March 9 Codman explained to his mother: "I think the final break with the Whartons is now on hand as they are very much offended because I do not care to do their Lenox house. Teddy has been so foolish."[29] Two days later, the decision made and the obligation ended, he wrote in a happier tone with regard to his summer plans for 1901:

now that I am not doing the Whartons' house I am more free to move about at my own desire. They are nearly enough to drive me crazy when they are clients... Don't be worried about the Whartons as I am not in the least disturbed about them. They would have interfered with all my most important plans and spoiled my *whole* summer, besides keeping me in a constant state of irritation. They are now rather stunned and don't know what to make of it. The idea of my asserting myself and becoming quite independent never seems to have occurred to them as a possibility.[30]

Another letter on March 13 elaborated that he had not wanted to spend the summer in Lenox while other friends (and influential clients) were elsewhere: "The Nat Thayers, the Eugene Thayers, the Coates and I think the Morses and Ameses will be gone themselves, and I think the Frank Harrisons will be in California. This you see is one reason I did not care to do the Whartons' house which would have tied me here."[31]

The break between Codman and the Whartons had to do with money and an inability for friends to work together in an architect-client relationship once the architect felt that he no longer needed their patronage and their advice. Codman was quite pleased to be left to his own devices on the Lloyd Bryce estate in Roslyn, New York (under construction 1900-01). He remarked to his mother in a November 26,

1900, letter: "The Lloyd Bryces keep enlarging the plans for their house which ought to be very handsome. I seem to be pretty well 'lancé' as an architect when you think this is only my second year at building whole houses."[32]

A letter of February 7, 1901, links financial matters to the difficult problems of dealing with each other: "This looks like the best year [1901] I ever had, much better than the Vanderbilt years [1894-95] because I am making double the money because I have so many clients instead of only one good one. The Whartons' house instead of being my first house is my sixth, and the smallest of the four now building [Codman was still the architect of The Mount at this point of writing]. The Morses' [house], Coates' & Thayers' cost more than double what the Whartons expect to spend. I am glad of it because they cannot *train* as they would have if they were the most important clients and wear me to a shadow with their nonsense…"[33]

According to Eleanor Dwight in *Edith Wharton: An Extraordinary Life*, the problem was that "Codman and Teddy disagreed on Codman's commission of 25 percent, and he [Codman] refused to change his terms."[34] Shari Benstock in *No Gifts from Chance: A Biography of Edith Wharton* explains that "the threesome got off to a bad start" because "Edith and Teddy rejected Codman's first rough sketches for the house (probably because the design was too costly) and asked for revised plans. Teddy then suggested that he could purchase fittings (mantels, columns, cornices) direct from Codman's Paris supplier, thus saving the architect's 15 percent commission. Codman coolly responded that this would violate rules of the American Institute of Architects. Teddy flew into a rage, telling Codman he was not 'easy to get on with.' "[35]

On March 25, 1901, Edith wrote to Codman:

I was very glad to get your letter, for it is always a pleasure to know that a friendship on which one has set great store has been worth something to the other "contracting party." In fact, it is of much more importance to me that we should maintain our old relation as

good friends than risk it by entering in the new and precarious one of architect and client. We are in such close sympathy in things architectural that it would have been a pleasure for me to work with you, but perhaps after all we know each other too well, & are disqualified by that very fact for professional collaboration. At any rate having avoided that peril, I feel that our escape ought to unite us more closely, and now that you need not be on your guard against me as a client, perhaps I shall be all the more useful as a friend. I shall certainly try to be, for it has always been a great interest to me to follow your work and try to make people understand what it represents; and I hope you will not be too busy to be interested in *my* undertaking, and to come and talk over our plans some day when you have the time to spare.[36]

Clearly the problems between Codman and the Whartons were those of three strong-willed people, all of whom knew what they wanted and believed that their way was the only way. Codman may well have been irritated that the Whartons seemed to treat him as the inexperienced new architect whose career should be managed to his benefit; meanwhile his confident attitude, willingness to argue and assert himself, *and* his high fees must have wounded old friends who felt that because of all that they had done for him, they were entitled to special consideration.

Despite the earlier unpleasantness, the feud was over once a new architect (Francis L. V. Hoppin) had been hired. "I think myself that Teddy was the whole trouble and not Pussy [Edith]. Meantime Hoppin is *doing the house* which lets me out of a very disagreeable business as Teddy and I would have come to blows over the bills,"[37] Codman explained in a letter. In a letter to his mother on April 7, 1901, Codman confided: "Peace reigns with the Whartons. I lunched there alone with them today and it was very nice."[38] On April 16th he again wrote on this subject: "The Wharton feud is really over & you may feel sure it was entirely due to Teddy who has such a big head & thought he owned the earth. The more unreasonable he became the less he got."[39]

Walter Berry wrote to Edith in spring 1901 that Codman's behavior as architect had been "disgusting... He ought to have made half a dozen plans, free, and begun over again, if necessary. You're dead right in chucking him."[40]

On New Year's Day 1902, Codman had dinner with the Whartons at 884 Park Avenue and, after hearing about their unhappy experience with an unidentified French decorating firm that had done some designs for The Mount, agreed to design the principal rooms for his old friends. This must have seemed the perfect compromise for everyone and gone some way towards erasing the bad feelings from the February and March 1901 disagreements.[41]

Hoppin & Koen, Architects

Francis Laurens Vinton Hoppin (1866-1941), the new architect of The Mount, was born in Providence, Rhode Island.[42] His father, Washington Hoppin, was a physician and a caricaturist. Two of Francis's uncles were also creative men, which probably had a strong effect on his development. Thomas Frederick Hoppin (1816-73) designed the evangelists windows for the chancel of Trinity Church in New York City. Augustus Hoppin was an author and illustrator who did drawings for works by Oliver Wendell Holmes, Harriet Beecher Stowe, and Mark Twain. One of his books, *Auton House* (1882), the story of a mid-nineteenth-century Providence, Rhode Island, family, was actually based on the real-life Hoppin family and their home. It was dedicated to fifteen-year-old Francis and to his brother.[43]

After attending the local high school in Providence, Francis went to the Trinity Military Institute in Tivoli-on-the-Hudson, New York, and later Pomfret Academy in Pomfret, Connecticut. At each school he was preparing for West Point and a future in the military. Although he would eventually have a distinguished career in the army and would reach the rank of colonel,[44] young Hoppin decided to leave Pomfret Academy and to make a radical change. In 1884 he enrolled at the Massachusetts Institute of Technology (M.I.T.), where he began the study of architecture. The program at M.I.T. was closely based on the principles of design being taught at that time in Paris at the Ecole des Beaux-Arts.

In 1886, for unknown reasons, Hoppin withdrew from M.I.T. after two years of study and began an apprenticeship with the architectural firm of McKim, Mead & White, where he developed his extraordinary facility for watercolor and charcoal renderings of buildings and building perspectives. In 1887 Hoppin interrupted his work for the firm with an extended tour of Belgium, Holland, France, and Italy. His impressions of the people that he met and the buildings that he saw were later published in seven issues of *The American Architect and Building News* in 1889 under the title "Architectural Knockabout." During this time, Hoppin took and passed entrance examinations for the Ecole des Beaux-Arts.[45]

Upon his return to America in 1888, Hoppin worked for a brief time for his brother Howard's Providence architectural firm, Hoppin, Read & Hoppin.[46] By late 1890 he had returned to McKim, Mead & White, where he did more sketches and perspectives and was given increasing responsibility to travel and to meet with some of the firm's many clients.

In 1892 Hoppin once again left McKim, Mead & White to travel, this time to Spain, Portugal, and Gibraltar. As before, his travel sketches were published in *The American Architect and Building News* in 1893.

In 1894, with a friend, Terrence A. Koen (1858-1923), Hoppin started an architectural practice—Hoppin & Koen—at 160 Fifth Avenue in New York City. Koen had also worked for McKim, Mead & White for a significant period of time. As *The New York Architect* explained in 1911:

Eleven years ago they left the offices of McKim, Mead & White, and they consider that they were "graduated" from the best "Classic" training school in America. Mr. Hoppin held the position of designer for a number of years... Mr. Koen spent eighteen years in their service in the more practical end of the work, to which, mainly, he now devotes his energies. Mr. Hoppin is engaged chiefly in the art end.[47]

FIG. 24 *Francis L. V. Hoppin, date unknown.* (EWR)

Koen's expertise on building construction clearly was the necessary complement to "Hoppin's strictly artistic orientation to design."[48]

Within only a few years of opening, the firm's specialty was recognized to be the building of gracious residences, primarily large country houses. Working closely with their wealthy clients, Hoppin & Koen "sought to harmonize the client's point of view with that of the architect's and to effect a happy solution of the definite desires of the clients consistent with the opinions of the architects in regard to their execution."[49]

Involving their clients in the design of the home was a particular strength of the firm, and it covered a multitude of concerns:

The placing of the houses, the arrangement of the rooms, the ventilation, the approaches, the planting and all the other details, which are so innumerable in any house, large and small, and which, if worked out in thorough accord with the owners, make the building of homes a very pleasant and delightful proposition for all concerned.[50]

Classical symmetry was an important design feature of the facades and interior planning of homes by Hoppin & Koen. Using the most modern technologies available, the firm gave great thought to "the conveniences of the owners and the conveniences of the servants… to arrange the necessities of domestic life with the least care in maintenance for the mistress and the domestics; to divide properly and practically the living part from the service; to give access to all rooms from hallways without traversing any apartment to enter another…"[51]

Hoppin & Koen, which often designed in the neo-Georgian, Beaux-Arts, Colonial Revival, Louis XVI or other classical styles, also conceived the facades of houses "which can be easily added to, if it should be desired, yet maintain a symmetrical and pleasing appearance to the facade."[52] Realizing that their wealthy clients often wished to "improve" their properties after initial completion, Hoppin & Koen sought to specialize in this area, advertising in 1911 that they could design or implement the

FIG. 25 *Longitudinal section of The Mount, Hoppin & Koen, 1901. This view from the terrace side looking west (compare to Fig. 20) "slices" the building open to reveal the arrangements of its interior. Dominating the center are the five arched windows of the gallery on the main floor (the center opening was a door to an exterior loggia); in the actual construction, the five windows were modified to three, and the loggia was not realized. (AAFAL)*

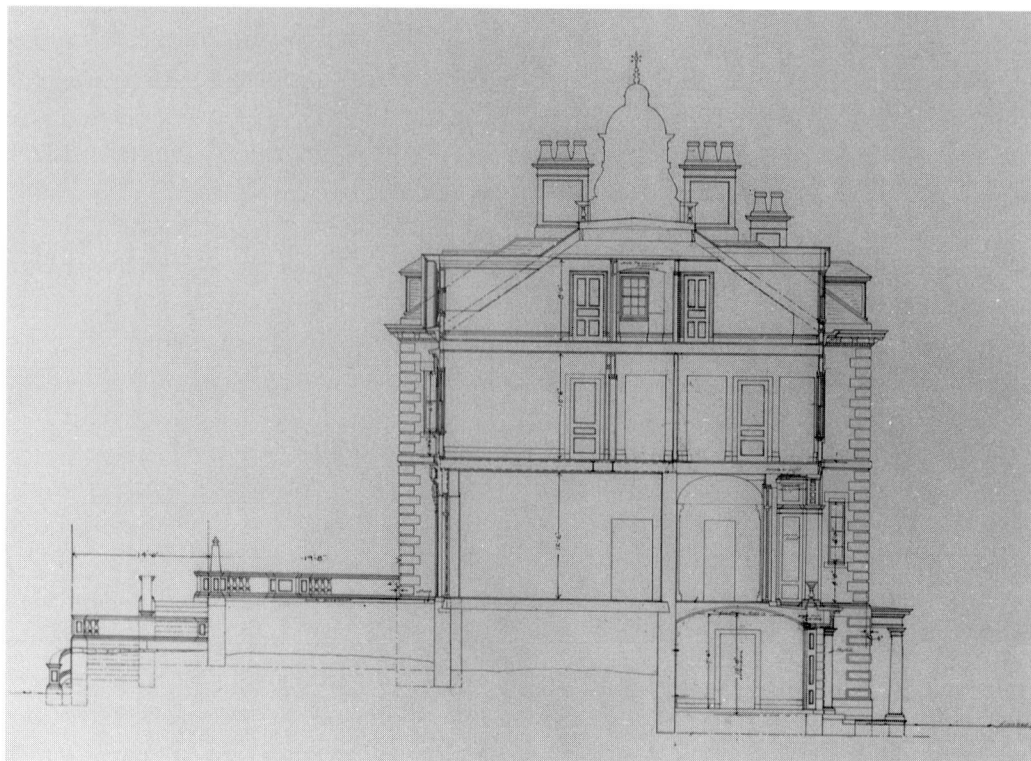

following: "tennis courts, gardens, fountains, summerhouses, studios, and many of the various buildings that an owner might wish for; to provide for the convenience of visitors, or the disposition or parking of carriages or automobiles, always giving special attention to the water supply and drainage systems."[53] After construction of The Mount ended in 1902-03, the Whartons returned twice to the firm for similar assistance: in 1905 for advice (and possible designs) of the Italian walled garden and again in 1907 to design an extension of the service wing, which was not realized.

Edith Wharton was personally acquainted with Francis Hoppin for at least four years prior to hiring him as architect for The Mount. In a letter of June 30, 1897, from Land's End in Newport, Rhode Island, to Ogden Codman, Jr., she concluded: "Who should turn up here yesterday but Hoppin!! However, I'll tell you about it when we meet. Yours in haste E. Wharton."[54] The tone of the letter is ambiguous — it seems to suggest a friendly, but adversarial, relationship between Codman and Hoppin, which would not be surprising. Since

Hoppin had only recently opened his firm in 1894, the two architects would have been competing among the same possible clientele, primarily in New York and Newport.

When Codman and the Whartons parted company in early March 1901, it is understandable that Edith would have turned at once to Hoppin as architect of The Mount. Codman, as his letters to his mother make clear,[55] was irritated at being replaced by Hoppin and belittled the latter's work, insisting that there were numerous problems between the Whartons and their new architect. Although there is little documentation of this aspect of The Mount's history, it would not seem unlikely that Hoppin — despite all the work that his firm had at that time — was eager and grateful for the Wharton commission and the prestige that it conferred, including his replacement of Codman.

Writings by the firm (published in *The New York Architect* in July 1911) and an interview with Hoppin on the house and garden (in *Scientific American Building Monthly* in March 1903) indicate that Hoppin and Edith shared many of the same design philosophies and were able to work together harmoniously. In addition, Hoppin was both able and willing to accommodate the Whartons' tight construction budget. One solution, possibly proposed by Hoppin, was to abandon the more costly brick exterior of the house and to use a wood frame with stucco covering.

Perhaps using Codman's original rough drawings as a beginning point, Edith and Hoppin redesigned the new house in record time, which was necessary to meet the Whartons' demands and construction schedule (work began in July 1901). Though the Hoppin & Koen firm had been in business for only seven years, they already had impressive experience to draw upon: several country houses in Newport; Aiken, South Carolina; Tuxedo Park and Barrytown, New York; seven New York City townhouses; the Church of the Messiah in Rhinebeck, New York; and a New York City fire station.

Although Codman continued to complain in letters to his mother about Hoppin's various failings and the inadequacies of The Mount's design, there is little record that either Edith or Teddy Wharton was dissatisfied with the work of either Hoppin or his firm.[56]

After the completion of The Mount it seems likely that the Whartons and Hoppin and his wife continued to see each other socially. In a postscript to a letter of August 19, 1912, to Gaillard Lapsley, Edith wrote: "I wish I could see Mrs. Hoppin some time when she is in Paris."[57] Edith would also have been aware of Hoppin's subsequent connections to two of her former Newport homes; in 1917 he made alterations (which must have displeased her) to Land's End for Governor R. L. Beeckman, and in 1929 he himself settled into Pencraig Cottage, where she and Teddy had made their first home.

The Hoppin & Koen firm achieved great success in the years immediately following the collaboration with Edith Wharton. A 1903 interview with Hoppin in *Scientific American Building Monthly* by Barr Ferree admiringly began: "Among the younger architects of New York, few have obtained a more rapid success in the building of houses than Mr. F. L. V. Hoppin…"[58] Hoppin held forth on his ideas about house and garden design, discussing his philosophy of the "architectural garden"[59] and that house and garden were "properly parts of a single design."[60] These precepts could have come directly from Edith's essays, which were appearing at that time and which were eventually collected and published as *Italian Villas and Their Gardens* (1904). Hoppin discussed at length the tact necessary to deal with clients and the necessity of retaining "the interest of the client in the operation,"[61] which testifies to his skill in dealing with both Edith and Teddy Wharton during the design and construction of The Mount.

CHAPTER 4

Construction of The Mount

"On a slope overlooking the dark waters and densely wooded shores of Laurel Lake we built a spacious and dignified house, to which we gave the name of my great-grandfather's place, The Mount."[1] Thus did Edith Wharton explain in her autobiography how she and Teddy came to use this name for their Berkshire estate. Although Edith inherited "a pair of fine gilt andirons crowned with Napoleonic eagles" from her great-grandfather Major-General Ebenezer Stevens, it is clear that he left her much more. She admitted a "secret partiality for him," admiring his "stern high-nosed good looks, his gallantry in war, his love of luxury... I like above all the abounding energy, the swift adaptability and the *joie de vivre* which hurried him from one adventure to another."[2]

Throughout January 1901, Edith and Teddy had negotiated vigorously with Georgiana Sargent for 113 acres of her former family farm.[3] Edith arrived at the Curtis Hotel in Lenox in February and apparently by the end

FIG. 27 *Edith and Teddy Wharton, with two of their dogs, standing on "the Mount when we first bought it" in 1901.* (BL)

of her visit had obtained from Miss Sargent a verbal assent to sell. Edith then informed Ogden Codman, Jr., that construction would begin "in the spring."[4]

By mid-February, Codman, in a letter to his mother, mentioned that he had "made some [house] plans they like but I don't know what they mean to spend."[5] This was an ominous note: within three weeks the Whartons and Codman parted company in a battle of egos and finances. Despite this setback, Edith, writing from 884 Park Avenue in New York on March 12, predicted confidently to her friend Sara Norton that "we are going to begin building in April."[6]

The necessity of hiring a new architect, as well as a delay in signing the deed, forced construction to be put off until midsummer. Edith, with her customary thoroughness and concern for even the smallest detail, "spent hours during the spring"[7] with Francis L. V. Hoppin, the new architect, going over the plans

from his firm, Hoppin & Koen. Unfortunately, no correspondence of the working relationship between the Whartons and Hoppin is known to exist, but — from a gossipy distance — Codman reported his own perceptions to his mother by letter: Hoppin was "having an awful time with the house...she telegraphs for him every day or two and fusses terribly over every detail. He has been cut down in every way...and has had to make three sets of plans. It has not been begun yet!! I consider myself well out of it."[8] In addition, he believed that "the more unreasonable she is with Hoppin and the more he complains of it the better will people understand why I did not want to build the house."[9] Codman also revealed that a major new decision had been made by Wharton and her new architect by June 1901: "The house is to be of wood stuccoed not brick,"[10] he wrote.

Although *Lenox Life*, a local society newspaper, announced on May 25, 1901, that "a new cottage for Mrs. Edith Wharton"[11] was underway, the deed for the property was not signed until June 29. She purchased 113 acres of land ("with farm house thereon") from the Sargent family for $40,600.[12] Ensconced at a rental cottage for the summer, Edith had, within several days of signing the deed, gathered together several of the principal participants in the design of the property: Francis Hoppin and her niece Beatrix Jones[13] (the landscape designer, later Beatrix Farrand) were her house guests. Robert W. Curry, the builder, was staying a short distance away at the Curtis Hotel.[14]

The account books for the Hoppin & Koen firm indicate that the contracts to build the mansion and the superintendent's lodge were signed with Curry on July 1 and for the stable on July 24.[15] Construction on all three structures was soon underway. At the end of the month, in a conciliatory letter to Codman, Edith explained that work on The Mount was progressing well and confided that "We are going to ruin ourselves in terraces, but the effect will be jolly."[16]

Edith's mother, Lucretia Jones, died in Paris in late June 1901. A month later, as work was getting underway on the house and she needed funds, Edith found that she had to make a trip to Europe to persuade her two brothers to allow her greater control over her trust fund. Her mission accomplished, she returned to Lenox in September to "the dear dogs and horses and our own woods"[17] and to inspect the progress on the house.

The foundation for the mansion had been completed in mid-August. Grading on the site was done by Barnes and Jenks, of Pittsfield, a firm that was also doing grading nearby at "Blantyre," a Scottish-style castle, for Robert W. Patterson, of New York. Lumber and brick then arrived "for the superstructure" of The Mount. Nelson Martin, of Lee, Massachusetts, contracted to deliver 160,000 bricks to the site.[18]

Codman visited the Whartons in late October and registered his usual disapproval to his mother: "I am not enthusiastic about their new place but the land and the new buildings have many grave defects. I do not care for Lenox or its society which is rather second rate."[19]

In November, as the shells of the three buildings were going up, four local firms signed contracts with Hoppin & Koen for basic interior mechanical systems: Berkshire Electric Company to supply electric-light wiring and bell work; Gillis & Geoghegan to install a hot-water heating apparatus; Wear & Hodgetts to install a hot-air furnace; and John Kirkwood to do all the plumbing and drainage work.[20] Edith and Teddy remained in Lenox until early December to oversee the beginning of this new phase of construction.

Back in New York City at 884 Park Avenue, Edith had a miserable January and February. Preoccupied with the impending publication of her first novel, *The Valley of Decision*, and dissatisfied with the book design and type, she "had a bad attack of grippe."[21] She turned forty on January 24 ("I excessively hate to be forty,"[22] she confided in a letter to Sara Norton), and a more painful blow came with the death of her beloved little dog, Mimi, who had been with Edith for eight years.[23] Despite these difficulties and several weeks of exhaustion, illness, and depression, the new house was much on her mind. On New Year's Day of 1902, Codman dined with the Whartons, and the past difficulties seemed forgotten when he agreed to "decorate the inside of their new house."[24] This must have been a relief to Edith, who apparently had found the work of another interior designer unsatisfactory. Codman's letter noted that the new agreement "is a secret as yet because they have not settled with a Frenchman who made designs which they will have to pay for."[25]

The Valley of Decision was published on February 21 and received a glowing critical reception. Thus cheered, Edith began work on a new novel, *Disintegration*,[26] in mid-spring. Planning for the interior decoration of The Mount went smoothly; Edith and Teddy probably went out of their way to avoid antagonizing the temperamental Codman. A letter to his mother on January 27 found him in a happy mood: "I am glad to be doing the Wharton's house as it is quite fun doing it."[27] By mid-March, Codman reported with satisfaction that Edith and Teddy "have accepted their estimates and their rooms are to be very nice indeed, and more expensive than I supposed they would stand for."[28] What he probably did not know was that the previous February Edith had taken a mortgage of $50,000 on the property from the Berkshire Savings Bank in Lenox.[29] Triumphantly Codman wrote to his mother in March that "The Whartons are now domesticated and eat out of my hand."[30]

A letter from Edith to Codman gives some idea of how the collaboration between the two

FIG. 28 *Edith Wharton in a 1902 publicity photograph, when she was building The Mount and was forty years old.* (BL)

architects and their client worked: "I hope you have sent Hoppin the gallery plan. Please do it today, if you haven't already, for I know that there will be pretexts for delay at that point if we don't give them the alternative promptly."[31] The relationship cannot have been an easy one, given the personalities involved and the fact that both Codman and Hoppin preferred to design and build their houses independently. According to Codman (who was only too delighted to report any perceived weakness or defect), Teddy once went to Hoppin's office "so enraged that he 'foamed at the mouth.'"[32] In March 1902, Codman wrote that both Whartons were "very dissatisfied" with Hoppin's work and concluded that "Their only hope is that I may redeem it."[33]

In April Edith and Teddy learned that Codman planned to sail for Europe and leave the execution of his work to his assistant. Codman explained to his mother that "they do not much like my going although there is nothing more to do on their house and they are always advising me to go abroad and leave other people's houses — I shall be back before it is done… Mr. Wulff [is] quite capable of looking after my work in my absence."[34]

That same month Edith wrote from Lenox to her Berkshire neighbor Richard Watson Gilder, the editor of the *Century* magazine, that "the work [on the house] is now in a peculiarly unbecoming phase. I am going on the 27th & shall be back in four or five days. By that time some of the workmen will have gone, & their scaffoldings with them, & you will be better able to judge of our intentions."[35]

A letter Teddy wrote to Codman on May 11 indicates that interior decoration in the house was already well underway. This correspondence provides a vivid glimpse of Teddy's attitudes and may help explain the behavior that so incensed Codman:

You are at times a demon & have lots of really bad qualities, but I forgave all your baseness of character when I saw the work (woodwork) in Puss's [Edith's] boudoir, which is more than half up. It is perfectly delightful to look at & does your taste credit. I find Wolf [sic] very satisfactory, he gets a move on.[36]

Edith, with her own characteristic impatience, was already planning for guests. In May she wrote to Margaret Terry Chanler indicating that "in the autumn our new house will be ready for visitors" and inviting her and her husband "to come to us for a few days."[37]

In early June the Whartons were back in Lenox, renting the nearby Struthers cottage for the season.[38] Committed to overseeing all aspects of the house, every morning Edith "drove out to The Mount to busy herself with the gardens and orchards, consult with the architect, and keep a sharp eye on the workmen."[39] On June 7, in a letter to Sara Norton, she enthused: "It is great fun out at the place, now too — everything is pushing up new shoots — not only cabbages & strawberries, but electric lights & plumbing. I really think we shall be installed — after a fashion — by Sept 1st."[40]

The exterior of the stable was close to completion by June (interior work would continue through November), while the lodge (except for interior wiring) was also nearly finished, according to the account books.[41] Apparently the mansion was far enough along by early August to begin receiving some furnishings. *Lenox Life* reported on August 9 that "The artistic cottage of Mrs. Edith Wharton on the shores of Laurel lake, which was built from plans inspired by Mrs. Wharton, is almost finished and is now being fitted up with the furnishings which Mr. and Mrs. Wharton picked up abroad, during a trip through France and Italy in company with the famous French

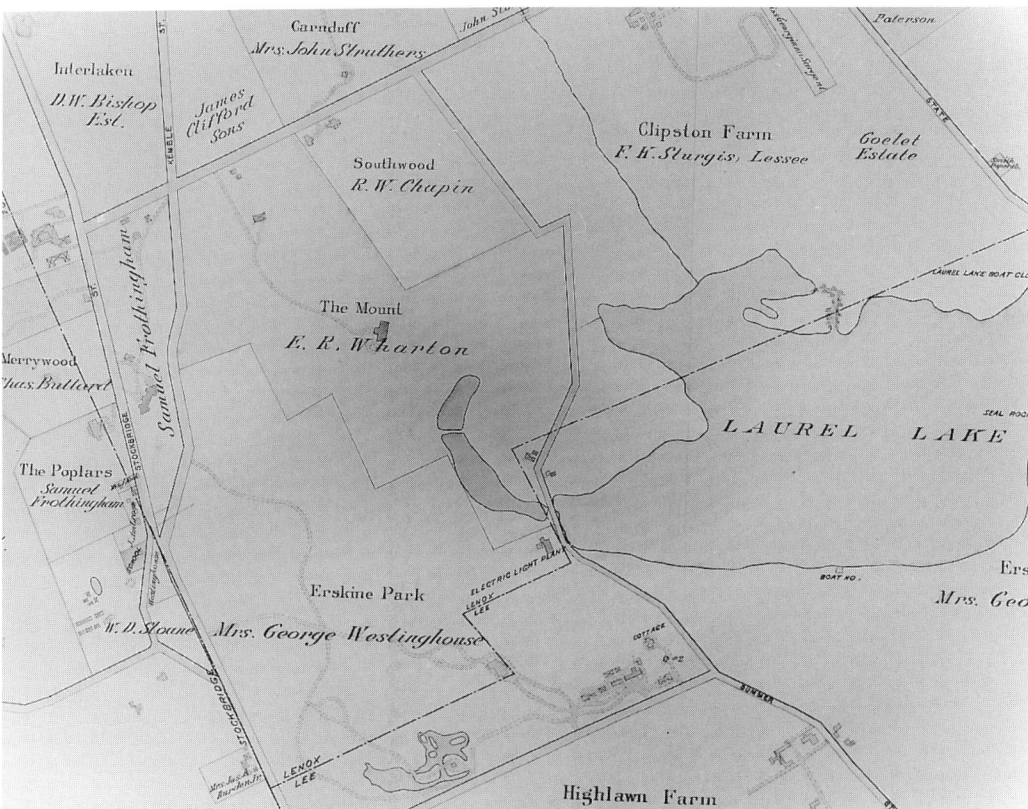

FIG. 29 *"Lenox (south),"* *plate 22,* Atlas of Berkshire County, Massachusetts, *(Pittsfield: Barnes & Farnum, 1904). The Mount (also marked "E. R. Wharton") appears near the center of the map. The superintendent's lodge and the greenhouse are visible on the upper left; further down the drive is the stable, and the mansion is located at the end of the drive directly under "The Mount." The Whartons' working farm is visible between Laurel Lake and Laurel Pond, just over the border in the town of Lee.* (SM)

author, Paul Bourget, and his wife."[42] Already it was clear that The Mount would be different from most other large houses in the area since its owner, the author of *The Decoration of Houses*, had her own very definite ideas. *Lenox Life* carefully explained: "This will be one of the houses whose furnishings reflect the character and taste of its owner, and not that of any upholstering firm, no matter how artistic."[43]

that way). *Zwei Seelen Wohnen, ach, in meine Brust*, & the Compleat Housekeeper has had the upper hand for the last weeks; but I am now beginning to recover my sense of proportion... We have been in the new house ten days, & have enjoyed every minute of it."[45]

Having moved in on a Saturday, Edith and Teddy lost no time in giving a "house warming"[46] party. The following Monday they had

FIG. 30 *Tinted postcard, c. 1902-03, of the east elevation, the earliest known image of The Mount following its completion. Four workmen doing landscaping are visible on the grounds.* (FHS)

Despite Edith's hopes, The Mount was not yet ready for occupancy at the beginning of September, so she and Teddy stayed with his mother at her home, Pine Acre, in Lenox. Edith told her editor at Scribner's, William Crary Brownell, that the final move would take place on September 20. When he sent a check for $2,191.81, she added her thanks "even to the 81 cents, [which] is welcome to an author in the last throes of house-building."[44]

The move occurred on schedule, and by September 30 Edith was writing to Sara Norton to explain why she had not been able to put pen to paper for so long: "*Finalmente!*... The latter weapon [her pen] has rusted in its scabbard since we began to move (the process has been so prolonged that I can only put it in

a small luncheon. Among the guests were Edith's longtime friend and confidante Egerton Winthrop; Mr. and Mrs. William D. Sloane, of nearby "Elm Court"; Col. William Jay and his daughter Eleanor; and Reginald C. Vanderbilt and his fiancé, Kathleen Neilson.[47]

Despite Edith's great pleasure in being "in a home not inherited or rented, not purchased and remodeled, but genuinely of her own making"[48] for the first time in her life, The Mount was still far from finished. One of the earliest visitors was Codman, who arrived in early October to check on his work, which was to his satisfaction. But in a letter to his mother, he found much fault in Hoppin's work regarding the unfinished interiors: "the walls are not properly painted as they were in such a hurry to get in. They were too silly not to wait till the spring before moving in, so as to get the house looking its best before people saw it... The marble floors look and are only half finished... and of course nothing properly arranged as the house was full of gas fitters and other workmen."[49] As the initial euphoria over the move wore off, Teddy suffered from more serious (and undiagnosable) illnesses, while Edith found that "the demands of The Mount, still unfinished inside and out, were in fact getting in the way of new writing."[50] To Sara Norton, Edith confided: "I am bothered about him and tired with the house. There come weary stretches, don't there, now and then?"[51] With the doctor's blessing, the Whartons headed south just before Christmas 1902 to stay at Biltmore, the baronial estate of Mr. and Mrs. George Vanderbilt, postponing the remaining work on The Mount until the following season.

About the same time, Codman wrote to his mother describing Teddy's behavior and the fact that monies were still owed to him for work on The Mount:

Teddy Wharton seems to be losing his mind which makes it very hard for his wife... Well he has been queer for a long time getting slowly worse I noticed it the day he came into my office two years ago [1900]... Part of the time he sat with his arms on the table and held his head in his hands. He looks very old and broken and has lost most of the hair on his head.

He brought up a lot of strange accusations such as that I had written letters no gentleman would write to his wife, etc. I thought there must be no quarrel and no one wants to quarrel with a maniac so I merely remarked that the letters I had written would compare favourably with those I had received from him, after telling me that of course I was losing all my business because he found me so hard to get on with he departed slamming the door.

I was rather prepared for this by what had gone before so was able to keep my cool which was very important: I shall not do anything about it and expect that by end of next week she [Edith] will see that a cheque is sent for my bill... I should think she would send him to Waverly [McLean Hospital] then instead of going abroad as I hear they intend to do.

He has always been very strange about paying his bills, and the contractors have had great trouble getting their money on the house... As I know how Hoppin the other architect talks about the Whartons I feel I have said enough... From something that happened the day I was at Lenox and from what Eliot Gregory and Berkeley Updike have said I am sure Mrs. Wharton is much troubled and worried about him.

I suppose she wants to put off shutting him up as long as she can, as he will probably never get any better...[52]

After a spring spent mostly in Italy where Edith worked on a series of articles commissioned for the *Century* magazine (later collected and published as *Italian Villas and Their Gardens*), the Whartons returned to Lenox in early May 1903. Edith was devastated to find that a two-month drought had destroyed most of her fledgling landscaping; to Sara Norton she wrote: "You may fancy how our poor place looks, still in the rough, with all its bald patches emphasized... I try to console myself by writing about Italian gardens instead of looking at my own."[53] After dismissing a profligate gardener and hiring a new one, Edith began to turn her attention to the final work on the house. Enough had been done since the previous fall to enable her to sigh in a letter to a friend: "It is very pleasant to be taking one's ease in one's own house."[54] Almost all of the accounts for construction were concluded by the end of August 1903.[55] By that time Edith had focused on the landscape and the creation of her gardens, which were to occupy her over the next several years.

The contracts that Edith and R. W. Curry signed in July 1901 estimated the total cost of the mansion to be $41,000, plus $14,000 for the stable and $4,580 for the lodge. The architects' account books indicate that the actual costs were much higher: $57,619.76 for the mansion, $20,354.46 for the stable, and $5,356.63 for the lodge, excluding interior appointments and furnishings.[56] Although work on The Mount continued until late summer of 1903, the majority of construction had taken place from July 1901 through September 1902, a period of approximately 15 months.

CHAPTER 5

Life at The Mount, 1902-11

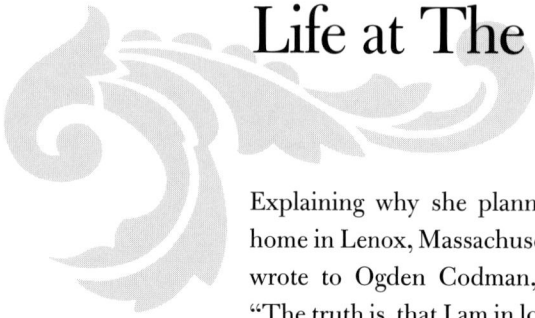

Explaining why she planned to build a new home in Lenox, Massachusetts, Edith Wharton wrote to Ogden Codman, Jr., in the 1890s: "The truth is, that I am in love with the place — climate, scenery, life & all."[1] Edith and Teddy had begun visiting his mother's Lenox home, Pine Acre, in the 1890s and soon were regular visitors to the fashionable Berkshire resort colony.

Although she had spent happy childhood summers by the sea in Newport, Edith began to grow weary of the place as it was transformed by the ostentatious displays of millionaire cottagers, even though many, including the Cornelius Vanderbilts, were her friends. In *A Backward Glance* she explained how much she had "disliked the relaxing and depressing climate, and the vapid watering-place amusements in which the days were wasted"[2] and how in coming to the Berkshires she had finally "escaped from watering-place trivialities to the real country. If I could have made the change sooner," she continued, "I dare say I should never have given a thought to the literary delights of Paris or London; for life in the country is the only state which has always completely satisfied me."[3]

Although Lenox at the turn-of-the-century was known to many as the "inland Newport," the two resorts were very different. Lenox had also begun to change during the 1880s as wealthier people chose to build large mansions, villas, and estates along its hillsides, but it was quieter, less populated, more rural, and more exclusive than Newport. The Newport season consisted of the months of June and July, while the fall (particularly September and October) belonged to Lenox.

During the heyday of each resort, newspapers tried to explain the differences between them to a public that could probably fathom few

distinctions. In 1901, *Lenox Life* printed an editorial extolling the virtues of the Berkshires:

Newport is known as the greatest watering place and "resort" in America; Lenox has never aspired to that position. Newport is filled with magnificent mansions; Lenox has many beautiful country houses comfortable in the extreme, but not "show" places. Newport's life is fast in a way, with countless balls, yachting parties, and a constant round of "bridge," whist and other sources of amusement; Lenox has none of these things, with the possible exception of a little "bridge" now and then…

A visit to Newport, and a visit to Lenox at the height of the season will show more conclusively than anything else why the better classes of New York society, and people of more conservative tastes prefer life in the Berkshires to life at Newport. No one with a healthy mind cares to go out in society all winter in town, and continue the round of gaiety in Newport; but what more delightful life, after a winter in town, than to come to quiet, restful Lenox, to play golf, to ride and drive, to go fishing and boating on Lake Mahkeenac, and to enjoy the dinner parties and the informal dances which are the means of entertaining.

Lenox, in its early days, reminded one of one big happy family, and while its summer colony has grown since then, the same neighborhood spirit and lack of formality still exists, especially among those families who have come here year after year. New ideas and new schemes, not to speak of new people, have appeared recently, but nothing can spoil the spirit of *comraderie* [sic] which is one of the principal charms of Lenox life during the summer.[4]

Another factor contributing to the popularity of Lenox was its proximity to New York City. *Lenox Life* noted in 1900 that "when an enterprising railroad, by special trains places Pittsfield three hours and thirty-seven minutes from New York and other places proportionally, there is no reason why people should not live in the country and do business in town."[5] The summer express trains operated on the Berkshire division of the New York, New Haven, & Hartford Railroad. An afternoon train leaving Grand Central Station in New York at 3:30 p.m. could deliver a cottager to the Lenox station by 7:23 p.m. On Sunday afternoon there was a special train for New York leaving at 6:27 p.m., "much appreciated by the young business men and others who come up to Lenox to spend Sunday."[6]

Country life in the Berkshires centered around outdoor activities, such as golfing, driving, walking, boating, picnics, horse shows, tennis tournaments, gardening, parades, dances, and a constant round of parties, dinners, and other entertainments. Of these, the most important was the house party. *Lenox Life* explained the fine art of the Lenox house party in 1901:

Society people of the present age know how to entertain. They have made it something of a study. They know just how much to do for their guests, and just how little.

The art of entertaining is a difficult one. The generally accepted notion now-a-days is that the ideal host or hostess should let their guests severely alone. By this, it is not meant that they should pay no attention to them. A great many amusements should be provided; they usually are. The host who knows his business will very likely tell his guests what is on the day's schedule, and then his visitors will decide to do just what strikes his or her fancy. This is the English idea of entertaining, and if one wishes to lounge about the house and read a novel instead of playing golf or going driving it is considered perfectly proper and right.

A congenial house party will entertain itself. The great thing, however, is to get together a party of people who are congenial. Here in Lenox few strangers are admitted. Most house parties are usually one big happy family. Everyone knows everyone else. That is why it is so delightful to visit at a country house in Lenox, not to speak of the pleasures of being far away from town and its cares, amid the glories of the beautiful Berkshire Hills in the golden light of brilliant September.[7]

The Country House

The focus of the turn-of-the-century house party was the country estate. As the mode of entertaining was along English lines, so too were the country houses where they took place.[8] Architectural historian Richard Guy Wilson delineates the various types of American country houses, of which the "power house" stands at the top, embodied in America

most obviously by such Vanderbilt palaces as The Breakers in Newport and Biltmore House in Asheville, North Carolina. Below such grandiose structures were the country houses of the less wealthy, "the imitations, the country villas, places, and resort cottages."[9] Wilson also explains how the life within these houses was shaped by the perceptions accorded their size, expense, and degree of ostentation: "the life these houses both contained and helped form resembled in many ways what might be thought of as country life. They gave the appearance of — if not the reality of — wealth, luxury, seclusion, easy communion with the out-of-doors, and amplitude of form in which the house becomes a statement of the stature of the owner."[10]

How then to characterize The Mount? According to Wilson, The Mount "was not a 'power' country house, but a country place. Located on limited acreage with stables, gatehouse, gardens, and sometimes a few acres for farming, the country place became the most popular form of country house into the late 1920s... Growing in many cases out of earlier resorts, the country place was designed for sport and relaxation."[11]

The Mount as a "Country Place"

From its inception, The Mount had been designed as a place for the Whartons to relax and to entertain and for Edith to work. The house was divided into areas for the owners, their guests, and the staff. The main floor, or *piano nobile*, was carefully considered with its arrangements of rooms *enfilade* (linked together), opening both onto the gallery to the west and large terrace to the east. Architecture critic Paul Goldberger observes that The Mount "seems at once to celebrate community and privacy. It is ordered and easy to understand, yet complex. What is most remarkable, perhaps, is the circulation system — it is possible to go from almost any room in the house to almost any other without passing through certain main rooms,"[12] because of the gallery and the terrace. Edith's eye for perfection, along with her desire for privacy and a gracious lifestyle, led her to create a special world for herself and her guests. As British author Percy Lubbock, a friend of Edith's, once explained, "Nobody could deny that to be a guest in a house of Mrs. Wharton's was a deeply, deliciously, delicately luxurious experience."[13]

Biographer R. W. B. Lewis notes that Edith's move into The Mount in September 1902 was a key event in her life. "After forty years, Edith Wharton was in a house not inherited or rented, not purchased and remodeled, but genuinely of her own making. She was in the physical location of her own choosing... The achievement coincided precisely with her recognition as the first woman of American letters."[14]

The Mount would be the scene of some of Edith's developing relationships with major figures, many of whom would become lifelong friends. These included Henry James, Howard Sturgis, and Gaillard Lapsley. Lewis explains:

FIG. 31 *Walter Berry holding a Wharton dog in The Mount's east garden niche, probably photographed by Edith Wharton. The trellis, designed by Ogden Codman, Jr., for the garden at Land's End, had originally sheltered a statue in Newport.* (BL)

She was only just now exercising to the fullest her remarkable capacity for warm and enduring friendship — the quality which, almost without exception, her guests best remembered and valued about her. But at the same time, Edith put them in touch with one another. At The Mount they motored together, they exchanged opinions and swapped jokes, they inquired eagerly about the absent ones and passed on the latest news. Within the larger world, with its array of dissatisfactions, Edith was creating a small human community, a society of friends, and the first of a series of its kind. This too was in response to a deeply felt personal need; for Edith, it was not a matter of keeping busy as a much-admired hostess, but of surrounding herself with genuine and like-minded companions.[15]

In July 1903, the Whartons returned to The Mount and began entertaining a group of close friends, a routine that would continue until 1911. *Berkshire Resort Topics* reported on July 4, 1903: "There is quite a house party at 'The Mount,' Mr. and Mrs. Edward R. Wharton's beautiful new estate in Lenox. Among those now being entertained by Mr. and Mrs. Wharton are Mrs. Winthrop Chanler, Mrs. William Cabot Lodge, Mr. Egerton Winthrop, Mr. George Cabot Lodge and Mr. Walter Berry."[16]

Berkeley Updike, a frequent guest at The Mount, found that both Edith and Teddy knew how to care for their guests. Years later he remembered:

Both she and her husband loved simple yet luxurious living, knew how to effect this intelligently, and were past masters of the art of entertaining, and in this there was between them a complete unanimity of taste. In other words, at that period they were fashionable people... and I do not think that there was any great longing on Edith's part that this should be otherwise... I do not remember any house where the hospitality was greater or more full of charm than at The Mount. As one thinks of it in retrospect, the word 'civilized' comes to one's mind.[17]

Henry James arrived in October 1904 and immediately wrote to Howard Sturgis: "The social life, not unnaturally, is the note of this elegant, this wonderful abode... It is an exquisite and marvelous place, a delicate French chateau mirrored in a Massachusetts pond (repeat not this formula), and a monument to the almost too impeccable taste of its so accomplished mistress."[18]

A most discerning guest, James also wrote to Edith's sister-in-law from The Mount of the "charm of the Wharton hospitality...I need scarcely tell you that I am very happy here, surrounded by every loveliness of nature & every luxury of art & treated with a benevolence that brings tears to my eyes."[19] He enjoyed the "adroit grouping of guests and occasions, the fine opportunities for talk or for silence, as one pleased."[20] Updike, noting that the Whartons loved to entertain amusing guests, remarked that The Mount was a delightful house to stay in, "not a bit sophisticated in its atmosphere — full of gaiety and fun of a very simple sort: we laughed until we cried!"[21] Marion Bell said that Edith "could sit for hours over the fire or out on the terrace and tell or hear stories, funny incidents, anything that struck her sense of humor."[22] Novelist Robert Grant remembered "the sparkling talk we heard there,"[23] while Eunice Maynard spoke of things being "so ordered, so gay, so competent."[24]

The Whartons hosted many intimate lunches and dinners in The Mount's dining room or on the terrace for their guests and for local acquaintances. They rarely — if ever — entertained on a lavish scale, preferring quiet evenings of good conversation among friends, reading aloud in the library, or star-charting on the terrace.

To many, The Mount also told them a great deal about Edith Wharton. Henry James remarked to Percy Lubbock that "No one fully knows our Edith who hasn't seen her in the act of creating a habitation for herself."[25] Mrs. Bell observed: "The Mount was a different sort of revelation of herself. Here was Edith Wharton the artist, content with nothing less than the best in gardening, the cooking, the furnishing

and housekeeping of her place. Everything in it was harmonious, brought to the same degree of perfection by minute care combined with a faultless taste. The hard-working writer, the traveller, the woman of letters, seemed merged into the hostess."[26]

FIG. 32 *On the hillside adjacent to the terrace outside Teddy Wharton's den (from left): Henry James, Edith Wharton, and Howard Sturgis, 1904, probably photographed by Teddy.* (CP)

Perhaps George Cabot Lodge summed up The Mount best when he wrote that it was a "really beautiful" house, "the sort of house one longs to live in because of its exquisite harmony throughout and its real luxury and distinction."[27]

When guests arrived at The Mount, Edith would often meet them at the front door with a dog in her arms[28] (as she later explained in *A Backward Glance*, the term family "in my own house, always included two or three busy and extremely interested dogs"[29]). Gaillard Lapsley remarked that she "observed the merciful custom of offering her guests champagne after a long railway journey."[30]

A typical day at The Mount would begin early for Edith. She would awaken around six a.m. and spend hours in bed writing stories or

novels, as well as answering her correspondence. Berkeley Updike explained that "At Lenox her writing was done early in the day, though very little allusion was made to it, and none at all to the infinite pains that she put into her work or her inexhaustible patience in searching for the material necessary to perfect it."[31] Such days were more rewarding than ever for Edith because, as she wrote in *A Backward Glance*, "the country quiet stimulated my creative zeal,"[32] and a great amount of superb writing was done at The Mount. Percy Lubbock has described how Edith (while writing in bed) would also be planning the day's itinerary: "In those early morning hours of Edith's seclusion over her story... a gay little note, thrown off as it were between chapters, would appear for the guest on his breakfast tray, with a greeting and a plan for the day."[33]

While Edith was still in bed writing, Teddy was attending to day-to-day affairs of the estate. As a friend remembered: "her husband at that period had charge of most of the housekeeping, and used to drive over to Pittsfield to do the household errands."[34]

By eleven o'clock, Edith was "ready for friends and engagements, for walking or gardenwork."[35] Several guests have recalled that she would often visit her gardens to check on the flowers or to direct some planting. She entered several competitions of the Lenox Horticultural Society; in 1904 she received one first prize, five second prizes, and two third prizes,[36] while in 1905 she received seven first prizes.[37]

In keeping with the outdoor nature of turn-of-the-century Lenox life, afternoons at The Mount most likely consisted of walks, horseback riding, carriage rides, or driving in the Whartons' motorcar. In her autobiography Edith spoke glowingly of "long happy rides and drives through the wooded lanes of that loveliest region."[38] R. W. B. Lewis notes that at times Teddy, whose domain was the stable at The Mount, "escorted a guest in his Mineola cart on a tour of the region while Edith guided another through the woodlands on horseback."[39]

These activities really became exciting when the Whartons, who had first experienced an automobile trip in Italy during 1903, bought a "little sputtering shrieking American motor,"[40] as Edith characterized it the following year. They had previously owned a European motor but had not brought it to America because of the heavy import duties. In July 1904, Teddy purchased a "very handsome Pope-Hartford light touring car of ten horse-power, with removable tonneau and brass trimmings"[41] from the agency of Thomas S. Morse in Lenox. Teddy and Morse went to Hartford to pick up the car and drove it back to The Mount.

The new car allowed the Whartons the luxury of traveling farther and yet returning to The Mount that evening. Frequent trips were made to Ashfield to visit Charles Eliot Norton at his summer retreat, and the local newspaper in 1904 recorded that the Whartons ventured further afield to eastern Massachusetts in mid-August, including Worcester, Groton, and Beverly Falls.[42] Other destinations included Maine, New Hampshire, Newport, and the top of Mount Greylock, Massachusetts's highest peak.[43]

Henry James, whose first visit soon followed the purchase of the motorcar, immediately became a frequent passenger and companion on countless excursions. He told a friend, "I greatly enjoyed the whole Lenox countryside, seeing it as I did by the aid of the Whartons' big commodious new motor... A great transformer of life and the future!"[44] Edith later wrote that "This mode of locomotion seemed to him, as it had to me, an immense enlargement of life."[45] She also detailed in her autobiography some of the problems that she encountered with the new car, nicknamed George (for writer George Sand):

those were the days when motor-guides still contained carefully drawn gradient-maps like fever-charts, and even "George" sometimes balked at the state of the country roads about Lenox; I remember in particular one summer night when Henry James, Walter Berry, my husband and I sat by the roadside till near dawn while our chauffeur tried to persuade "George" to carry us back to the Mount... In those epic days roads and motors were an equally unknown quantity, and one set out on a ten-mile run with more apprehension than would now attend a journey across Africa. But the range of country-lovers like myself had hitherto been so limited, and our imagination so tantalized by the mystery beyond the next blue hills, that there was inexhaustible delight in penetrating to the remoter parts of Massachusetts and New Hampshire, discovering derelict villages with Georgian churches and balustraded house-fronts, exploring slumberous mountain valleys,

and coming back, weary but laden with a new harvest of beauty, after sticking fast in ruts, having to push the car up hill, to rout out the village blacksmith for repairs, and suffer the jeers of horse-drawn travellers trotting gaily past us.[46]

The Whartons' chauffeur was Charles Cook, a native of Lee, Massachusetts, who would eventually accompany Edith to France in 1911. Many friends remembered Cook fondly as a superb driver who was never fazed by bad roads, lack of signs, confusing directions by backseat drivers, or other traffic.[47] Hired in 1904, Cook remained Edith's chauffeur until 1923.

An outing in the motor with Edith was "no aimless outing; it was an excursion of shapely design, embracing an interesting object,"[48] according to a friend. Edith often arranged a roadside picnic, one of her favorite pastimes. Gaillard Lapsley has contributed a vivid memory of what took place:

I see her at a picnic, on a Massachusetts hill-side, in the forest near Isle-Adam, on the sandy beach of a cove between Hyères and Toulon, wherever it might be, the meticulous ritual was invariable. She chose the position with the care and deliberation of a Roman general selecting the site of a fortified camp. There must be

FIG. 34 *About to embark on a Berkshire "motor-flight" in the Whartons' 1904 Pope-Hartford motorcar from The Mount's front door (from left): Edith Wharton with a dog on her lap, Henry James, chauffeur Charles Cook, and Teddy Wharton, holding two dogs, October 1904.* (LL)

something for her to lean against, in winter we must all be in the sun except Edith and even when she was scrupulously sheltered her reserves of smoked goggles, veils and white parasol lined with green must be within reach. Then the rubber sheeting must be laid on the ground and covered with travelling rugs, and the baskets unstrapped and set on either side of Edith who unpacked and distributed napkins, plates, knives, forks, glasses, and the hard-boiled eggs, salad, cold chicken and ham, fruit and cheese, passed backward and forward from hand to hand on either side of her. When it was over we were all very conscientious about disposing of the fragments and returning our plates and what not as clean as we could make them for Edith to repack in the elaborately fitted baskets. She insisted on doing it all herself and from the moment the ceremony (it was nothing less for all its jolly informality) began until she returned to the motor Edith was a happy woman.[49]

Although the new motorcar soon made the Whartons' carriages obsolete, Teddy still devoted much time to horses, a particular pleasure for him. At the annual Lenox Horse Shows in 1901 and 1902, he won fourth in several classes.[50] *Berkshire Resort Topics* reported that Edith and Teddy were among the many local cottagers who attended the 1904 Horse Show, although that year there were no entries from the Wharton stable.

The Whartons also enjoyed another sport at The Mount: ping pong. In a letter to Helen Brice in August 1903, Edith complained that August had been as cold as October, and that "fires every evening & violent games of ping pong alone keep us from sinking into an Arctic slumber."[51]

According to Elizabeth Norton, daughter of Charles Eliot Norton and sister of Edith's close friend Sara, Edith "had little in common with the summer colony [in Lenox] and they did not find her very sympathetic; her natural shyness unconsciously impressed her intellectual superiority upon people, and she lived remotely."[52] However, the Whartons visited with a number of distinguished Berkshire residents, including Mary and Daniel Chester French and Caroline and Joseph Hodges Choate in Stockbridge, as well as Mr. and Mrs. Richard Watson Gilder in Tyringham. Berkeley Updike also remembered that Edith was friendly with her Lenox neighbors Charlotte Barnes, of Coldbrooke, and Ethel Cram, of Highwood.[53] The Whartons were occasionally listed in the society pages of *Berkshire Resort Topics* as party guests at various homes, most often at Wyndhurst, the neighboring estate of Mr. and Mrs. John Sloane.

Both Whartons were involved with local organizations. Teddy was appointed to a committee of the Lenox Club for "the purpose of taking steps toward reorganizing the Taxpayers' Association, and pursuing a definite line of work in reducing what is believed to be excessive taxation."[54] He also frequently played golf at the club.[55] Edith helped to reorganize the Lenox Library, and in 1902 she was elected a volunteer assistant (or associate) manager, a position she held until 1911.[56] She also became a director of the Lenox Village Improvement Society in 1902 (Teddy's sister, Nancy Wharton, was then its president), an organization dedicated to the care and appearance of the village proper, roadsides, and outlying areas, and of the Lenox Educational Society in 1903.[57]

FIG. 35 *Edith Wharton smoking in Lenox, 1905, while picnicking with friends beside a lake.* (BL)

FIG. 36 *Looking northwest over the pool and dolphin fountain of The Mount's east garden, designed by Edith Wharton, during the Whartons' occupancy, date unknown. The roof of the now-vanished spring-house is visible to the left of center.* (BL)

In addition, the Whartons were continually improving The Mount, particularly its grounds. For Edith, this meant close attention to her gardens and the creation of a rock garden full of sweet ferns and, in 1905, the walled garden. Teddy found "the opening of vistas and the planting of trees" to be a constant amusement.[58] Novelist friend Robert Grant noted that "My last visit to The Mount [1911] seemed the happiest at the moment, for each of my hosts gave the impression of being in love with what they built, and Edith spoke gleefully of hoping to pay for a new terrace with the profits of her next book."[59]

Edith saw The Mount and the Berkshires as places for personal renewal. In the winter of 1906, she wrote to Sara Norton from the Curtis Hotel: "It is delightful to be here, & see trees against the sky, and *hear only silence*. Thank heaven I can get away from the world in a few hours, when I have the chance. It takes me very little time to shake off the accretions that town forms on one."[60] That same year, reinstalled at The Mount, Edith wrote to a friend that their life at The Mount was really much more dull than anyone would suspect or believe: "here

we are sunk into our usual monotonous country life, which would be such a surprise to our European friends, who see us only flying from place to place in our eagerness to crowd all we can into our holiday. Here I write every morning, & then devote myself to horticulture; while Teddy plays golf & cuts down trees."[61]

By 1911 Edith knew it was primarily The Mount that kept her bound to the country of her birth. As she wrote to Bernard Berenson on August 6, 1911, from Lenox: "Really, the amenities, the sylvan sweetnesses, of the Mount (which you would have to see to believe) reconcile me to America."[62] She signed her letter asking him not to forget "The Hermit of Western Massachusetts, Edith Wharton."[63] One month later, with her American "hermitage" sold without her permission while she was at sea, Edith's final true tie to her native country was broken. As she reflected poignantly in her autobiography, "The Mount was my first real home, and though it is nearly twenty years since I last saw it (for I was too happy there ever to want to revisit it as a stranger) its blessed influence still lives in me."[64]

CHAPTER 6

History of the Exterior and Interior of The Mount

FIG. 37 *The west elevation as seen across the forecourt, c. 1940s. The mirror in the gallery glimpsed through the arched window above the front door gives the impression of a view through to the other side of the house. Photograph by H.S. Babbitt, Jr.* (FHS)

Exterior: Forecourt

In 1893 Edith Wharton and Ogden Codman, Jr., designed an entrance courtyard for the Whartons' home, Land's End, in Newport, Rhode Island. "The outside of the house," she later wrote, "was incurably ugly, but we helped it to a certain dignity by laying out a circular court with high hedges and trellis-work niches."[1] Almost ten years later, Edith again elected to have a circular entrance court, but at The Mount it was to be of a much more permanent construction.[2]

Designed in 1902 by Hoppin & Koen, the walls of the forecourt are constructed of brick and painted white to match the exterior of the house.[3] The design features two gateposts standing 10 feet tall flanked by concave walls, which connect in a straight line with the exterior walls of the house. Each of the concave sections

FIG. 38 *Courtyard and west elevation entitled "The Mount — Mrs. Wharton's home at Lenox, Massachusetts," from* The Book News Monthly, *1907.* (SM)

consists of three sections divided by pilasters; in the center of each section is a shallow, arched doorway capped by a keystone. The northern doorway is open, while the southern one is a false or blind door. The walls extending between this area and the house also consist of three sections.[4] For the most part, the walls stand approximately 8 feet tall, with the pilasters slightly higher; only on the sections where the walls meet the building do their heights rise another foot or so. Each of the 16 posts is surmounted by a simple brick cap.

The forecourt of the Mount was conceived as a "*cour d'honneur*, as was generally found in front of great French town and country houses. As an outdoor room, so-to-speak, it is a preview of the spare elegance of the interior of the house."[5] As an extension of the house into the natural landscape, the forecourt serves as a transition from the drive into the entrance hall, as a way to usher visitors into the house, and as a logical separation of the principal entrance from that of the servants.[6] It also blocks off all views of the formal gardens, grass terraces, pond and lake, and of the distant mountains (in the same manner that the entrance hall shields the main rooms of the house from the glance of a casual visitor). As a retaining wall on the north side, the forecourt achieves one of its best effects. Since the house had been fitted into the hillside, the forecourt reinforces a "powerful tie"[7] to the landscape as it holds back the earth while effectively obscuring the hill. This results in "the first impression of the approach from the drive…of a very large three-and-a-half story house in gleaming white stucco."[8]

Codman was unimpressed after examining the forecourt in October 1902; in a letter to his mother he expressed total disapproval: "The enclosed courtyard is *to my* mind an utter failure — it looks like a clothes yard & is all out

FIG. 39 *A Wharton dog crossing the gravel forecourt, date unknown. This photograph, probably taken by Edith or Teddy Wharton, shows the northwest corner of the courtyard, where "creeping vines struggle towards its top," as described in* Berkshire Resort Topics *in 1904.* (LL)

FIG. 40 *Forecourt statue in its niche, c. 1950s. This is one of two statues, which Edith Wharton moved to The Mount from Land's End and which were sold by the Foxhollow School in the early 1970s.* (FHS)

of proportion. There are regular rules for making courtyards & several of the old books in architecture give these rules & the reasons for them. Mrs. Wharton has at least *one* of these books but evidently neither she or Hoppin can have read them."[9] In assessing these remarks, it is necessary to remember that Codman was bitter over his dismissal as architect. The court-yard at this time would also have been lacking in any form of landscaping or decoration.

A newspaper account from 1904 found the forecourt a more successful space: "The drive-way ends in a circular courtyard, surrounded by a high brick wall, and having at its base a narrow border of velvety turf . . . creeping vines struggle towards its top."[10] A photograph clearly reveals these vines during the Whartons' occu-pancy; around the door in the northwest corner, heavy vines had reached the top of the wall. The rest appeared to be about midway up the wall.

The forecourt was decorated with two statues, which Edith had previously placed in her gar-dens at Land's End in Newport, Rhode Island. *Berkshire Resort Topics* reported in 1904 that "a statue rests in a niche at either side"[11] of the entrance posts. The south wall niche, believed to have been located in the center panel of the wall, was eliminated in the mid-to-late 1960s, when the Foxhollow School opened the court-yard to the adjacent service area to accommodate bus turnarounds. The north wall niche, directly opposite, was apparently removed when the

wall was rebuilt after it collapsed in 1972[12] (see also Chapter 8, The Foxhollow School).

Interestingly, two different early schemes for the forecourt by Hoppin & Koen survive. Although neither was carried out, both shed light on the ideas underlying the final design.

One scheme, labelled "Courtyard on the West Front," consisted of a plan, as well as two elevations. The plan, which illustrated the walls of the forecourt as they were built, indi-cated that Hoppin & Koen suggested that there be a circular grass plot in the center; the "X"

FIG. 41 *Exterior view looking west from "Courtyard on the West Front," Hoppin & Koen, 1901; proposed scheme for The Mount's forecourt walls and gates (not realized).* (EWR)

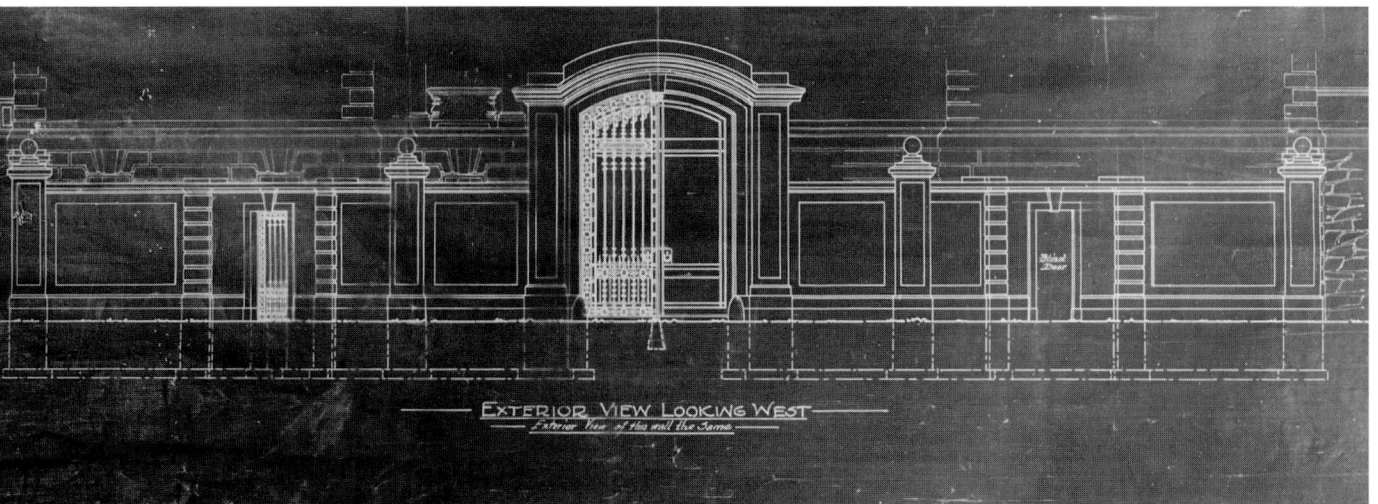

EXTERIOR VIEW LOOKING WEST
Exterior View of this wall the same

FIG. 42 *South elevation, Hoppin & Koen, 1901, illustrating the unrealized south belvedere proposed for the terrace, the unrealized lion's-head fountain in the north wall of the forecourt (left), and a gatepost with an urn finial.* (EWR)

drawn through the design indicates that Edith rejected this idea. The other notable feature of this scheme is Hoppin & Koen's proposal of elaborate iron gates set within an arch. A matching gate was proposed for the arched opening to the garden. The design — never realized — incorporated the opening on the north side and the "blind door" as they were eventually built. Other elaborate features that were not adopted included recessed panels in the walls, quoins on each of the 16 posts, and ball finials atop the posts.

The other scheme is even more intriguing. Labelled "South Elevation," it may have been an earlier design as it incorporated fewer of the final features. Instead of ball finials, elaborate classical urns topped each post. A Romanesque arched door (labelled "Larick arch") opened into the forecourt from the hillside close to the house. The forecourt wall sloped down approximately a foot and then sloped up as it met the building. There was no open doorway leading to the gardens. The most dominant feature was a large, elaborate lion's-head fountain in the center of the forecourt wall. Apparently to have been constructed of terra cotta with a base of limestone or Lee marble, the fountain[13] in many ways mirrored Hoppin & Koen's elevation of the entrance door of The Mount that was scaled down by the Whartons. The two schemes have in common flanking columns supporting a cornice with dentils and a decorative frieze. The walls featured quoining and a large keystone, and the lion's head placed within a recessed arch. The south elevation scheme is reminiscent of the Pitti Palace in Florence, as described by Edith in *Italian Villas and Their Gardens*:

The palace is built against the steep hillside, which is dug out to receive it, a high retaining-wall being built far enough back from the central body of the house to allow the latter to stand free. The ground floor of the palace is so far below ground that its windows look across a paved court at the face of the retaining-wall, which Ammanati decorated with an architectural composition representing a grotto, from which water was meant to gush as though issuing from the hillside.[14]

Certainly the fountain on the Hoppin & Koen elevations would have given much of the same effect to visitors at The Mount. Edith may have proposed the design but later rejected it because of cost or other considerations.[15]

Terrace

DESIGN AND CONSTRUCTION

The wide Italianate terrace at The Mount was built to stretch almost the entire length of the principal, or east, elevation. Although the terrace turns the northeast corner and continues across the north end of the building, it is on the east facade — which overlooks the gardens — where this feature proves most distinctive.

The north facade of Belton House (1685-86) in Lincolnshire, England, served as an inspiration for the design of the east elevation of The Mount. The choice of Belton House for this purpose was probably determined very early in the design process by Edith and Codman. The front facade of Belton House was published in 1771 in *Vitruvius Britannicus* and probably was also the direct source for the Palladian staircase at The Mount,[1] as well as for many design elements on the east elevation. However, Belton House, situated on a flat site, did not have a terrace. Interestingly, Codman's initial pencil drawings did not even suggest a terrace for the main floor of The Mount. Instead, Codman envisioned two separate loggias — one in front of the dining room and the other in front of the library. The salon, which opened onto each loggia from the sides, acted like a wall between them. Neither loggia was very large or wide, and each appears to have been conceived as an enclosed room with windows and a roof.

Codman originally envisioned the Palladian staircase as part of a sequence leading from a grotto-like room at the basement level to the gardens below. Visitors would have entered the vestibule on the west side of the house, proceeded along a narrow passage underneath the main floor, and then passed through the grotto (located under the east end of the salon) and onto the Palladian staircase.[2]

Under Hoppin & Koen, the entrance sequence was reworked radically. The new design did away with the subterranean passage and grotto, elevated the Palladian staircase one story to descend from the *piano nobile*, and added the wide L-shaped terrace on the east and north elevations.[3]

The concept and design of the Italianate terrace most likely was arrived at in discussions between Edith and Francis L. V. Hoppin. A frequent traveler to Italy and a student of Italian architecture and gardens, Edith had observed them firsthand and was determined to adapt them to her own country home. Her knowledge of Italian culture and her love of the outdoors would probably have convinced her to improve Codman's initial plans with the addition of the wide and sunny terrace. In *Italian Villas and Their Gardens*, she commented that the terrace of the Villa Madama by Raphael on the slope of Monte Mario in Rome was "a roofless continuation of that airy hall,"[4] an apt description of the relation between her own Berkshire terrace and adjoining drawing room. Her observation that the Florentine villas from the fifteenth to seventeenth centuries were "strongly planted on their broad terraces"[5] also recalls how The Mount appears to grow from the strong natural rock foundation of its terrace on the east elevation.

It is interesting to note that none of Edith's former homes — Pencraig, Pencraig Cottage, and Land's End — had terraces. She and Codman had virtually nothing to say about terraces in *The Decoration of Houses*, although it is possible that she was planning to cover the subject in a projected book with Codman entitled *Garden Architecture or The Garden in Relation to the House*[6] in 1897. Some credit for the terrace must also be given to the Hoppin & Koen firm, which had previously designed several houses with large terraces overlooking gardens or vistas.[7]

As built, the terrace is 24 feet 4 inches wide at its widest point, opposite the drawing room, and 125 feet long from the southern pier to the northern one. Along the north facade it is 19 feet 8 inches wide and 46 feet 4 inches long.[8] A small arm wraps around the southeast corner, continuing 11 feet in front of the dining room and terminating at the east wall of the service wing. This smallest section is only about 12 feet wide.

The foundation walls of the terrace are composed of large stones or fieldstones and other pebble masonry set in mortar. An unusual feature is the split-level character of the terrace (reflected in the design of the house as well), which ties the house more naturally into the hillside. On its south end, the terrace is a full

The scullery, laundry room, servants' toilet, wine closet, and trunk storage room were located under the south end of the terrace. Beginning at the northeast corner of the projecting wing of the dining room, the area underneath the terrace is unexcavated (or possibly crawlspace).

Hoppin & Koen originally envisioned four sections of grass parterres bordered by white marble panels in the center of the terrace, two on the east (in front of the dining room and library) and two on the north (to the side of the library and in front of the den). A fifth (and larger) section consisting of brick laid within wider marble panels would have been located

story above ground, while at the north end, it becomes progressively lower. The terrace and the hillside meet at a point opposite the French doors of Teddy Wharton's den. The natural stone masonry highlights the tie between house and hillside and helps camouflage the sloping design.

The floor of the terrace is paved in brick laid in sand in a herringbone pattern between marble borders.[9] The lower marble panels of the balustrade are drilled with holes to facilitate water runoff.

directly in front of the drawing room. These parterres, which would have curtailed use of some areas of the terrace and possibly caused major maintenance problems, were never realized.

The balustrades for the terrace are a combination of several materials. The base of the railing and the hand railings are a white marble quarried nearby in Lee, Massachusetts.[10] The balusters, which the 1901 drawings specified as terra cotta, are actually composed of "a concrete-like substance produced by molding stucco and extending it with broken bricks as very large

FIG. 43 *A Wharton dog crossing the terrace outside the library, date unknown. This photograph, also probably taken by Edith or Teddy Wharton, shows the obelisks on the balustrade and (on the far left) some terrace furniture.* (BL)

aggregate"[11] in the center. The piers between balusters are made of brick covered with stucco.[12] Originally the piers had recessed panels on their east and west sides.

The balustrades of the terrace were also decorated with obelisks and two statues. The obelisks, to be made of terra cotta, stood 3 feet 6 inches high and had small knob-like finials. Historic photographs and postcards show only four of these obelisks in place (one on either side of the Palladian staircase and one on either side of the opening on the north end of the "L"); holes in the center of every pier may indicate that all 15 obelisks were anticipated but not installed, as called for on the Hoppin & Koen plan.[13] The two statues were placed on the piers at the top of the Palladian staircase. Presumably executed in marble, these classical-style pieces depicted a man in a casual stance (north statue) and a woman in a short skirt carrying an urn-type object on her shoulder (south statue). It is unknown whether they were original works or reproductions and whether they represented mythological or other subjects. The statues were not indicated on the 1901 plans.

The original Hoppin & Koen plans proposed twin belvederes flanking the north and south ends of the terrace.[14] Designed in an elaborate Beaux-Arts style, the belvederes (each was referred to as a "gazebo" on the plans) would have been supported by the north and south piers. The elevation drawings indicate that the surface ornament (which consisted of quoins, engaged columns, arches, keystones, and recessed panels) was to have been executed in terra cotta and the prominent dome of each pavilion in copper. The belvederes were approximately 10 feet wide on each side and would have towered 13 feet from hand railing to their sloped peak roofs.[15]

THE PALLADIAN STAIRCASE

A gracious Palladian staircase leads from the terrace to a gravel walk below, linking the house and terrace to the lower gardens. The outer walls of the staircase are built of the same masonry as the terrace; panels of white marble separate the fieldstone from the marble steps.

The staircase begins with a landing located one step below the terrace. Seven steps descend on either side to an intermediate landing; seven more steps then lead from the intermediate landing to a lower landing. A lion's-head fountain[16] is placed in a niche on the lower landing. Water issued from the lion's mouth and fell into a small semicircular basin on the landing. The fountain wall was paneled to resemble a rusticated belt-course,[17] similar to the interior plaster paneling of the basement-floor staircase hall. On either side of the fountain, two semi-circular openings in the landing functioned as planters[18] for climbing vines. Period photographs show a profusion of vines growing up the wall and the basin of the fountain. Two broad steps descend to the gravel walk as the balustrade flares out to terminate in piers. The balustrades are identical to those lining the terrace.

USE OF THE TERRACE, 1902-11

The terrace was designed to serve as an important focal point for life at The Mount. The four major rooms on the *piano nobile* open onto it through elegant French doors: the library, drawing room, dining room, and Teddy's den.[19] It was one of the features most often remembered by guests. Berkeley Updike spoke of the "broad terrace overlooking the formal parterres of the garden,"[20] while Marion Bell remembered how Edith "could sit for hours over the fire or out on the terrace and tell or hear stories, funny incidents, anything that struck her sense of humor."[21]

In her autobiography, Edith spoke fondly of "the wide terrace overlooking the lake."[22] Its importance is demonstrated in a letter she wrote to Bernard Berenson on August 6, 1911:

This place of ours is really beautiful; & the stillness, the greenness, the exuberance of my flowers, the perfume of my hemlock woods, & above all the moonlight nights on my big terrace, overlooking the lake, are a very satisfying change from six months of Paris.[23]

A letter from Edith to her friend Daisy Chanler in 1905 gives a glimpse of the terrace as a place to read and rest; Wharton wrote that she had not read Henry Adams's *Mont-Saint-Michel and Chartres* because "it is too obviously meant to be read with recueillement, on our shady terrace, with all the books I want within reach, & great stretches of time in which to turn the matter over as one reads."[24]

Many contented guests held forth on the terrace both day and night under Edith's watchful eye, yet perhaps none so celebrated and appreciated as Henry James. Edith remembered "the shout of laughter with which — on that dear wide sunny terrace of the Mount — his fellow-guests greeted my 'dressing-down.'"[25] She spoke with affection of his "evening talks on the moon-lit terrace"[26] and of how "one summer evening, when we sat late on the terrace at the Mount, with the lake shining palely through dark trees,"[27] James regaled a select group of the inner circle of friends with memories of his Albany, New York, cousins and relatives, the Emmets and the Temples. It was a memorable night; before Edith and her guests he evoked "a series of disconnected ejaculations, epithets, allusions, parenthetical rectifications, and restatements, till not only our brains but the clear night itself seemed filled with a palpable

FIG. 45 *The view from the terrace looking east over Laurel Pond in the foreground to Laurel Lake in the distance. The Mount's farm buildings (see Fig. 88) are silhouetted against the lake.* (BL)

fog; and then, suddenly, by some miracle of shifted lights and accumulated strokes, there they stood before us..."[28]

Teddy Wharton, ever the gracious host but often out of his league with such conversations, was often unable to contribute to the intellectual banter. One visitor remembered "the awkward and slightly tight-lipped silence that would fall upon the company when Teddy smilingly joined them on the terrace."[29]

The terrace was often a gathering place before and after meals. Berkeley Updike remembered: "One day when a party for lunch had gathered on the terrace, Mr. [Joseph Hodges] Choate arrived, accompanied by the Austrian Ambassador. 'Ah, Mrs. Wharton,' he said as he stepped from the house, 'when I look about me I don't know if I am in England or in Italy.'"[30]

An interviewer for *The Book News Monthly* in October 1907 explained that after luncheon,

"We had coffee on the broad terrace overlooking Mr. Wharton's estate, and...we all fell under the spell of meadow-reach and hillside distances..."[31] Another guest recalled that Edith "served high tea on occasion" on her "open plaza."[32]

From the terrace Edith enjoyed her new interest in star-gazing, or "star-charting,"[33] as she called it. It began seriously in the late summer and early fall of 1907. According to R.W.B. Lewis:

She had come upon a little volume called *A Fieldbook of the Stars*, and with its aid, standing on the terrace after dinner, she mapped the heavens, locating among others Capella, "a handsome new luminary" that appeared in the east about nine thirty in the evening. She drew her guests into the game, and, focusing a flashlight on the star chart, she lectured them on her findings.[34]

Lewis explains that although this new activity "was a scientific exercise of sorts...there was also something uncharacteristically romantic about this new nightly ritual."[35] Her interest continued throughout the final summer at The Mount. She wrote to Morton Fullerton in July 1911: "I went out on my terrace last night, and took up my interrupted communion with Vega, Arcturus and Altair..."[36]

TERRACE FURNISHINGS

The most prominent furnishing was "an immense striped awning"[37] that covered the center section approximately the width of the drawing room. Secured by a frame anchored into the facade,[38] the awning stretched from the projecting wing of the dining room to the projecting wing of the library. Quite possibly its broad stripes were green and white to complement the green shutters and white facade.[39] Along the front edge were pendants (the dormers of the servants' rooms had matching striped awnings). The original awning remained in use as late as c. 1942. At the head of the Palladian staircase was a long wooden planter filled with flowering vines, which covered the balustrade and spilled down towards the lion's-head fountain.

Considering the amount of entertaining that went on outside, it seems surprising that so

FIG. 46 *On the terrace, surveying the view (from left): Henry James, Teddy Wharton, and Howard Sturgis, with a Wharton dog, 1904. The photograph was probably taken by Edith Wharton.* (BL)

FIG. 47 *East elevation during the Whartons' occupancy, taken from the lime walk, showing the striped awning over the terrace and the matching awnings on the dormers, date unknown. A Wharton dog on the parterre steps suggests that the photograph was probably taken by Edith or Teddy.* (BL)

little furniture can be discerned in surviving photographs.[40] The author of a letter to the editor of *The Berkshire Eagle* in 1937 asserted: "I think that she [Edith Wharton] was the first to bring iron chairs and tables for her open plaza,"[41] but there is nothing to support this tentative remembrance. The Whartons had Adirondack-style benches along some paths at The Mount. Wharton later used wooden benches and tables and wicker armchairs and chaise lounges, usually with matching (often striped) cushions[42] for the terraces at Pavillon Colombe and at Ste. Claire.

THE TERRACE AFTER 1911

Apparently the terrace remained in reasonably good condition up through the 1940s. Photographs taken during ownership by the Shattucks and the Van Andas reveal that vines and other shrubbery were allowed to grow freely until they eventually covered the foundations. A c. 1942 photograph shows vines completely covering entire balustrades on the

north and east. While this kind of landscaping was probably intended by the Whartons — it certainly gave the desired "aged" look — the overgrowth accelerated deterioration. Lack of maintenance was probably also a factor.[43]

By 1960 problems had become so severe that Foxhollow School headmistress Aileen Farrell spent $35,000 for "shoring up the terrace of The Mount."[44] The brick had worn out over the years, and sections of it were taken up and relaid with dense mortar, which caused moisture to build up.[45] More cracks appeared, along with sink holes where sections of sand had washed away. Water damage caused the foundation walls to bulge and shift.

At some point the recessed panels of the balustrade piers were stuccoed, which robbed the terrace of detail and definition. The obelisks and two statues were also removed; none of these are known to survive.

By the early 1980s the north section of the terrace was threatened with extreme overgrowth from the former rock garden. Most of this over-

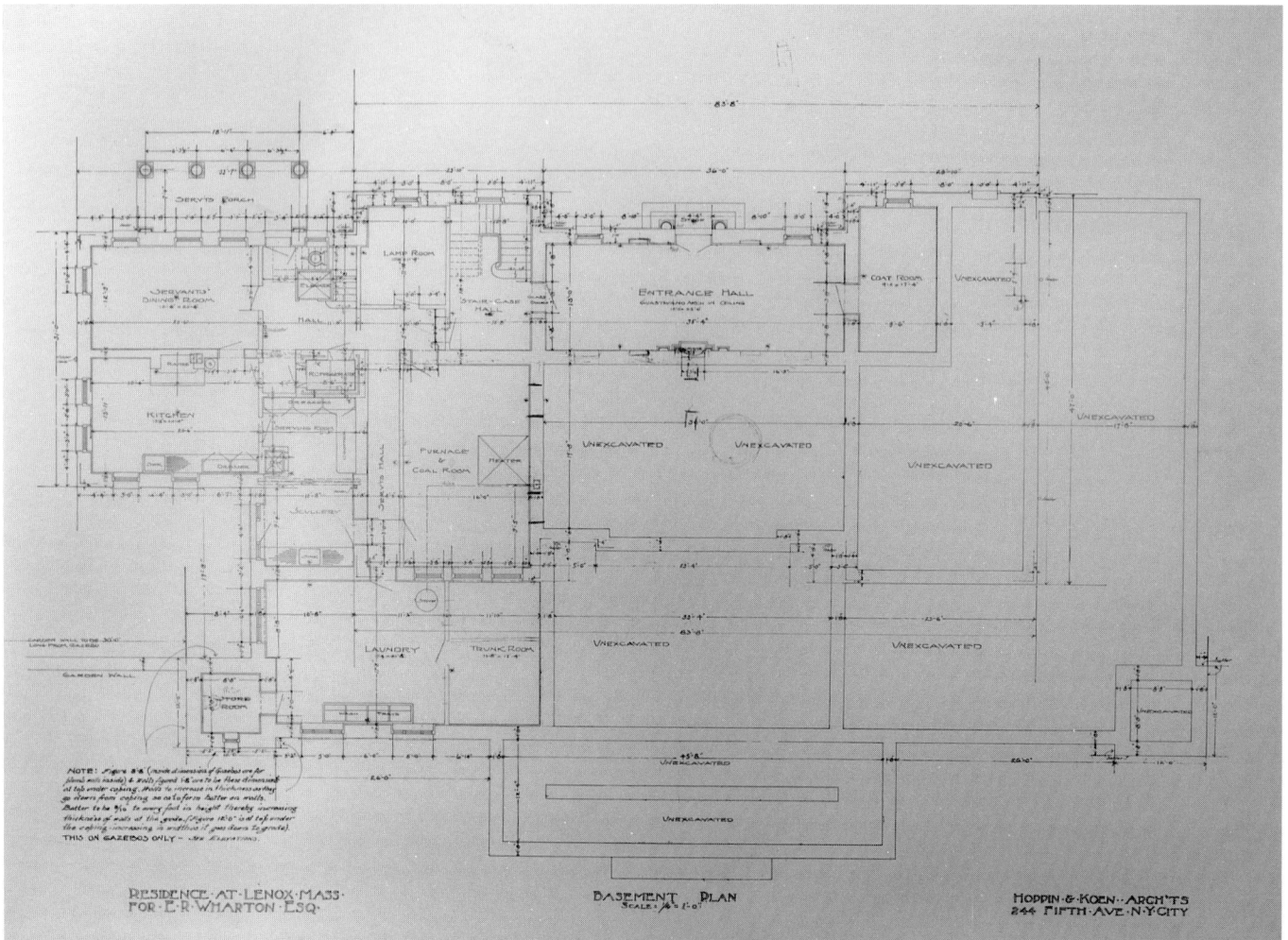

FIG. 48 *Basement plan, Hoppin & Koen, 1901. The area marked "unexcavated" east of the entrance hall became the furnace room.*

(AAFAL)

growth was cut away by 1985 to protect the terrace and to restore the views and vistas that the Whartons had planned.

Although the Foxhollow School used the terrace for occasional dances between the 1940s and the 1960s, its heaviest use has come in the 1980s. EWR and Shakespeare & Company use it for benefits, special events, weddings, rehearsals, and as an outdoor theater.

Interior: Ground Floor

ENTRANCE HALL

A visitor to The Mount during the years of Edith Wharton's occupancy (1902-11) arrived in the entrance courtyard by carriage, horseback, or motorcar. Then, as now, after crossing a threshold of white marble, one enters an entrance hall that is 35 feet by 13 feet in plan and covered by a barrel-vaulted ceiling.[1] The Mount's entrance hall, like those described in *The Decoration of Houses*, forms "a natural and easy transition from the plain architecture of the street to the privacy of the interior."[2] The visitor has clearly entered the building but is not yet admitted into the house or invited to meet its inhabitants.

Edith, who had carefully studied and written about the use of the grotto in Italian villas and gardens, chose a grotto to serve as a model for the entrance hall. Textured stucco wall panels simulate the effect of dripping water, while directly opposite the entrance portal is a fountain set in a shallow niche. The niche is all that remains of Codman's original plan to link the entrance hall to another grotto area on the terrace side of the house. To greet her guests, Edith chose a fountain statue of Pan, sculpted in bronze by Frederick MacMonnies in 1890.[3] As the god of nature, Pan reinforced Wharton's scheme of carefully transitioning the outdoors into the house.

Flanking the niche are window sash with mirrored panes that balance actual windows beside the entrance. The interior windows open into The Mount's furnace room. The mirrored panes thus block off the unsightly views and reflect the outdoors inside the house. The mirrored double doors to the coat room on the north balance the south doors, set with clear glass, leading to the main staircase.[4]

The hall floor is laid with terra-cotta tiles, which are highly durable and were deemed correct by Edith for "so exposed a situation."[5] The baseboard is an elegant black-and-green Italian marble. The painted stucco walls and the tile-and-marble floors are all in complete accord with the recommendation in *The*

Decoration of Houses that for entrances the "decoration should at once produce the impression of being waterproof" and also "be as permanent as possible in character, in order to avoid incessant small repairs."[6]

Edith and Codman cautioned against the use in halls of furniture that could be damaged by weather or need frequent cleaning. Their recommendations for marble or stone benches and tables, statues, and busts were carried out fully at The Mount. According to a 1904 account, the "entrance vestibule and hall have numerous pieces of ancient Italian furniture, including a table of polished Italian marble and marble benches."[7]

The earliest known photograph of the vestibule (c. 1942) shows two rather elaborate light fixtures on pedestals, which may be original, although they do not conform to Edith's stated preference for the lantern as "the traditional form of fixture for lighting vestibules"[8] or her recommendation that such a fixture should

FIG. 49 *The entrance hall, looking north towards the mirrored doors of the coat room, c. 1942, with the original statue of Pan by MacMonnies. The urns on marble pedestals (not extant) may be the original lighting fixtures.* (FHS)

appear to be covered, even when it is electrified. The present silver sconces are not original.

The final drawing of the west elevation by Hoppin & Koen (c. 1901) proposed entrance doors with panes of glass in the upper panels and a porch with an elaborate classical frieze in the entablature. Edith, however, rejected this idea in favor of a more "effectual barrier…to give a sense of security" and "so plain in design as to offer no chance of injury by weather and give no suggestion of interior decoration."[9] The outer doors that were installed are both solid and relatively unadorned, except for their hardware.

The entrance hall has three sets of double doors: the outer doors open in from the court-yard, the second set leads into the staircase hall, and the third set is for the coatroom, an arrangement specified in *The Decoration of Houses*. The outer doors are designed without glass panes; the inner doors, dividing the entrance hall and staircase hall, are constructed with large panes of glass. In *The Decoration of Houses*, Edith explains this design: the outer doors needed to be open during the day while the glass doors inside helped to keep the house warm while "affording a shelter to the servants who, during an entertainment, are usually compelled to wait outside."[10]

For the expected guest, admission through the glass doors and up the stairs was swift. Edith may have met guests at the entrance with a small dog or two in her arms. However, the entrance hall was possibly all the less fortunate visitor saw of The Mount. The glass doors represent well her axiom that "while the main purpose of a door is to admit, its secondary purpose is to exclude."[11]

Although it is known that Codman designed many of the interiors at The Mount, there is no documentation linking him to the entrance hall. However, a comparison of Edith's and Codman's precepts in *The Decoration of Houses* and an examination of Codman's entrance hall at La Leopolda in Villefranche-sur-Mer, overlooking the French Riviera, place the design and deco-ration of the entrance hall at The Mount clearly within Codman's provenance. Although La Leopolda was a late work (1929-31), its vesti-

bule bears many striking resemblances to that at The Mount: a similar ceiling, mirrored windows balancing actual windows, tiled floor, wall panels, and an arched niche for statuary. Existing plans for other country houses by Hoppin & Koen, on the other hand, indicate that the firm most often favored tiny vestibules or none at all. The entrance sequence in the typical Hoppin & Koen country house depended most heavily on a large and imposing hall that opened into the key rooms, an arrange-ment totally unlike The Mount.[12]

STAIRCASE HALL

Edith and Codman thoroughly traced the history and the development of the vestibule, hall, and stairs and the interconnections of these spaces in *The Decoration of Houses*. In planning the hall and stairs at The Mount, they again followed their precepts of 1897.

The placement of the staircase in the hall adjoining the entrance hall was deemed appro-priate when, as at The Mount, all the living quarters were on upper floors. Such an arrangement gave a more reliable "security from intrusion,"[1] while recognizing that the use of the staircase was generally reserved for the inhabitants of a house and their guests.

Therefore, the function of the staircase hall was to link the entrance hall and the outer world to the living areas. In effect it had to serve as both "a public square"[2] and as "a thorough-fare"[3] used by many people, including the household servants.[4]

The dominant feature of this area at The Mount is the French-style staircase, which is as distinctive in its simplicity and modest propor-tions as in its elegance. The wrought-iron railing,[5] a flowing pattern of circles and spirals, perfectly illustrates the idea that a railing should detach "itself from the background in vigorous decisive lines."[6] Edith and Codman argued that the railing be painted black, as was customary in France, to form a "stronger contrast with the staircase walls."[7] In addition, this color is truer to the material of iron, and painting helped prevent rusting.

Although stairs constructed of stone or marble were judged by the two authors as the most distinctive (wooden stairs having been traditionally associated with middle-class medieval homes), Edith chose wood for the stairs and stair molding at The Mount. This choice may have resulted from a somewhat limited budget, but she had also allowed for the use of wood for stairs in *The Decoration of Houses*. The material used for the stairs governed the selection of that for the walls of a staircase hall: "If the stairs are of wood, it is better to treat the walls with wood or plaster paneling."[8] In the decorations for such a passageway, Edith and Codman believed that "only the first impression counts, and forcible simple lines, with a vigorous massing of light and shade are essential. These conditions point to the use of severe strongly-marked paneling."[9] Edith elected to utilize the simple device of a stringcourse, simulating the exterior base of a building and continuing the already established transition of outdoor features along the approach into the house. Both the staircase and the paneling accord strongly with other work done by Codman, to whom the design of these areas at The Mount must be attributed in the absence of other documentation.[10]

It was necessary to paint plaster paneling (as opposed to marble or stone treatments), and the authors of *The Decoration of Houses* advocated either "one uniform tint" or "white for mouldings and buff, gray or pale green for the wall."[11] Recent research has indicated that the staircase hall at The Mount was originally painted a blue green.[12] In order to contrast strongly with the neutral tint of the walls, Edith and Codman felt that the stair carpet should be one solid color and devoid of any pattern. This, no doubt, was the case at The Mount.[13]

Although the green-and-black Italian marble baseboard continues into the staircase hall, the terra-cotta floor tiles of the entrance hall give way to an elaborate parquet design in the staircase hall, consisting of a border of contrasting light, dark, and medium-colored wood, while the center portion is dominated by a pattern of hexagons, each composed of six strips of wood.

In both the heating and lighting of the staircase hall, Edith appears to have deviated from her stated ideals in *The Decoration of Houses*. Instead of having a faience stove, which she admired for its design and color, the hall is heated by hot air from the furnace through a utilitarian heating grate, which may have been hidden from view by a marble bench or console table. Hoppin & Koen's plans indicated wall fixtures for lighting beside the two sets of doors, while in *The Decoration of Houses*, Edith called for a lantern "like that in the vestibule, but more elaborate in design."[14] A fixture now hanging by a chain from the ceiling and enclosed within an opaque glass globe is apparently the original one.

In recognizing that "as the vestibule is the introduction to the hall, so the hall is the introduction to the living rooms of the house,"[15] Edith and Codman recommended that the furnishings be quite formal. To preserve the hall's role as a passageway, the authors eschewed open fireplaces, easy-chairs, books, magazines, or other amenities for lounging.[16] *Berkshire Resort Topics* in 1904 reported that both the entrance hall and staircase hall at The Mount contained marble tables and noted that "a contemporary replica of Mino da Fiesole's bust of the Bishop of Fiesole, with white marble column and base, is one of the most interesting pieces in the hall."[17] The bust probably stood in the space between the stairs and the glass doors.[18]

The upper landing of the staircase hall was built with several modifications to the 1901 Hoppin & Koen floor plan. The stairs were changed so that the treads abut the north, rather than the south, wall. A curve in the wrought-iron railing at the head of the stairs (labeled "balcony," a feature that appears on the stairs of other homes designed by Hoppin & Koen) was rejected by Edith.

The architects also appear to have envisioned glass along the south wall of the upper landing — a single swinging door of glass flanked by an interior window on either side. This feature was amended to become a set of glass double doors centered in the wall and echoing the arch and the doors at the other end of the gallery. A narrow window on the north wall, which would have balanced a similar window in the bathroom off the den in the projecting wing, was omitted in order to hang an oil painting in this area. A blind window was constructed on the exterior. There is no evidence that a service bell, called for on the floor plan, was ever set into the south wall.

Two oil paintings are set into the walls on either side of the staircase hall, one on the north wall and one on the south wall. *Berkshire Resort Topics* noted in 1904 that "the upper landing has two very fine painted panels."[19] Each painting measures 110 inches high by 45 inches wide and consists of stretched canvas held in place by simple wall moldings. Painted by anonymous nineteenth-century artists in an eighteenth-century French style, both paintings feature three elegantly dressed figures in a garden setting. The paintings serve as part of the transitional sequence from the outdoors into the mansion. Before a visitor had actually entered the main body of the house, these figures signaled the motif common to the majority of the interior appointments and furnishings (Louis XV and Louis XVI).

An elaborate overpanel of stylized flaming urns, designed by Codman and executed in plaster, crowns each of the paintings. Each urn is surrounded by leaves, garlands of fruits and flowers, and ribbons. At the base of each urn are a flaming torch and several crossed arrows. The identical overpanels extend from the top of the paintings nearly to the ceiling.

At the top of the stairs, a visitor is met with double doors that open directly into the dining room. An archway to the north opens into the gallery; closed glass double doors to the south open into and partially isolate the main stairs to the bedroom floor.

The floor of the staircase hall's upper landing has the same terrazzo marble found in the adjacent gallery, drawing room, and dining room. The Hoppin & Koen floor plan in 1901 called for a ceiling light fixture; a Wharton-period photograph indicates that it was a chandelier

identical to the beaded crystal ones in the gallery. *Berkshire Resort Topics* identified the furnishings in this area as "two inlaid marble pedestals supporting Italian baroque busts."[20] The busts probably flanked the double doors leading into the dining room.

The hall remains substantially as it was in the Whartons' time. The chandelier, like those in the gallery, was replaced prior to the Foxhollow years with a different style of beaded crystal. The plaster overpanel above the painting on the south wall has suffered severe water damage from the upstairs guest bathroom. In addition, the painting on the north wall — which is most vulnerable because of its proximity to the stairs — has some tears. The area was painted pink in the early 1980s to match the adjacent gallery. In 1990 the original blue green was restored to the walls of the staircase hall, and a deep-plum-colored carpet was laid on the stairs and at the foot of the stairs, covering the parquet floor.

First Floor (Main Floor)

GALLERY

The gallery is of particular interest, having no precedent at Land's End. This magnificent space on the main floor runs along the west from the staircase hall on the south to the den on the north. The room, measuring approximately 44 feet long and 12 feet wide, is dominated by a barrel-arch ceiling and three tall, arched windows facing west, a marble terrazzo floor, and a mirror set in the east wall between the double doors to the drawing room. Symmetry is achieved by eight arches: three arched windows on the west wall face the two arched doorways to the drawing room and the center arched mirror on the east wall, while an arched entryway on the north end faces another on the south end. The walls, ceiling, and trim are a combination of plaster and wood. Double glass doors on the south end match what appears to be a set of double doors leading into the den on the north; one door, however, is false.[1]

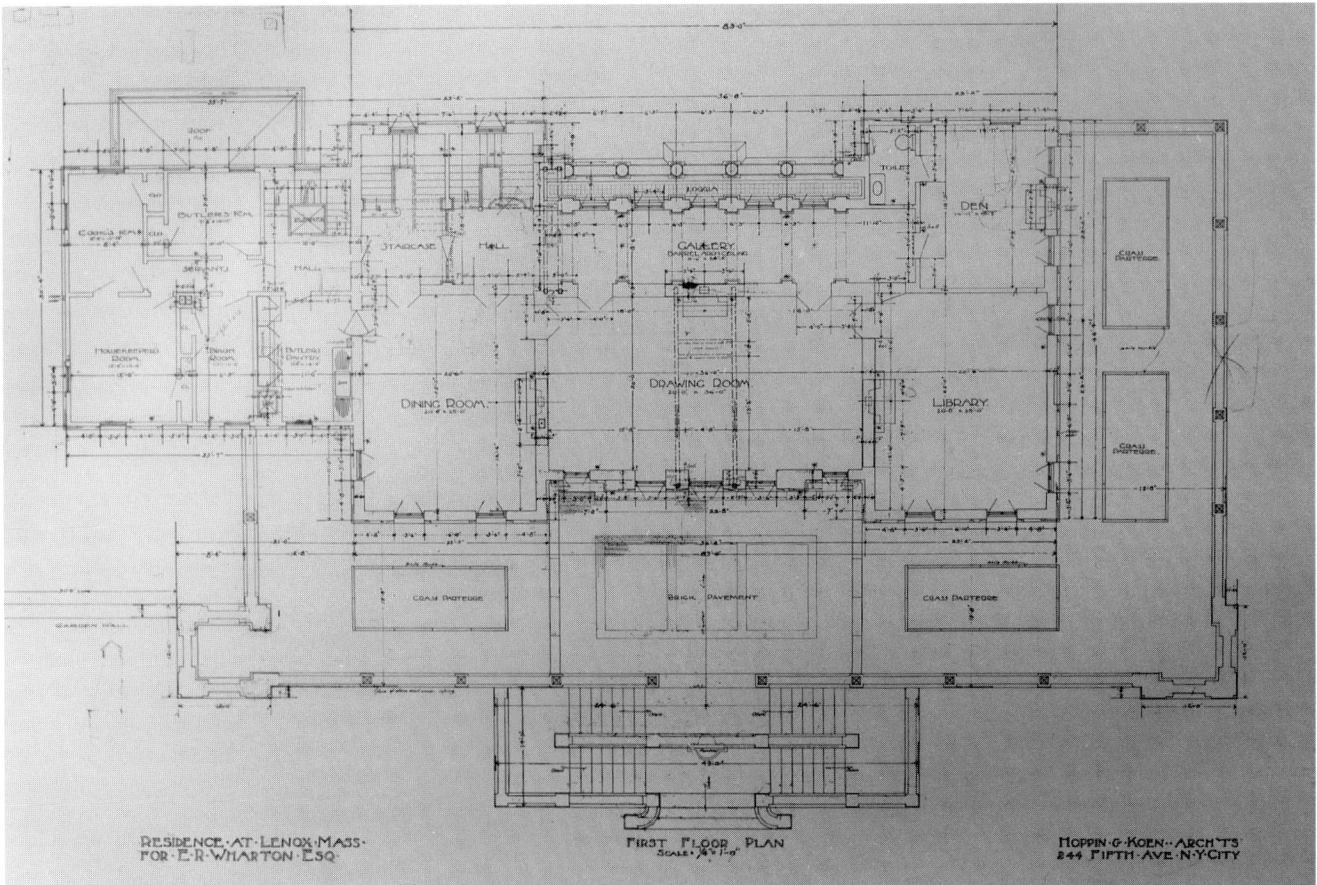

RESIDENCE·AT·LENOX·MASS·
FOR·E·R·WHARTON·ESQ·

FIRST FLOOR PLAN
Scale ⅛"·I'o"

HOPPIN·&·KOEN··ARCH'TS·
244 FIFTH·AVE·N·Y·CITY

Codman's initial drawing for the first story of The Mount indicated an L-shaped hall leading from the hall and stairs on one end to the dining room opposite, with the salon, library, and den opening onto this passage.

As executed by Hoppin & Koen, the principal rooms on the first story also open onto the gallery: the den (on the north end), the library, drawing room, and dining room (from the east), and the staircase hall (and the stairs to the bedroom floor) on the south. The room was designed as one long corridor, rather than an L-shaped hall.

Before construction began, several major modifications were made to Hoppin & Koen's 1901 floor plans. An exterior loggia approximately 4 feet wide, which was to run along the first-floor's west wall, was rejected. Its construction would have made the gallery 8 feet 6 inches wide. In addition, a group of five arched windows on the west wall was reduced to three to preserve the exterior symmetry, with three bays over three bays. Exterior details such as the

balustrade of the loggia, pilasters between the windows, and lunettes between the peaks of the arches were also rejected prior to construction. Finally, curved corners, not shown on Codman's or Hoppin & Koen's plans, were added to the interior of the room. Codman's only surviving elevation for the interior of the gallery represents it without the five arched windows and almost exactly as built.[2]

Edith designed her gallery in the "grand manner,"[3] illustrating the importance of a gallery as set forth in *The Decoration of Houses*. In discussing gala rooms, she noted they were:

meant for general entertainments...therefore to fulfill their purpose, they must be large, very high-studded, and not overcrowded with furniture, while the walls and ceiling — the only parts of a crowded room that can be seen — must be decorated with greater elaboration than would be pleasing or appropriate in other rooms.[4]

Edith and Codman explained that the gallery was "probably the first feature in domestic house-planning to be borrowed from

A 1904 newspaper article noted that the gallery had an "Italian terrazzo floor, panelled in white marble."[7] A veined Italian marble (*fior de pesco carnico*) is used sparingly as a baseboard, and white marble panels from Vermont are also used sparingly for bands and borders. The primary material is terrazzo, a mixture of sand, cement, and marble chips with intervening colored terrazzo panels; the dominant decorative feature of the floor is a circle in the center of bands of terrazzo. This motif recurs in the arched overpanels of the gallery doors and in Edith's boudoir on the bedroom floor.

As spelled out in *The Decoration of Houses*, the floor of the gallery was designed to emulate marble floors in Italian palaces:

The inlaid marble floors of the Italian palaces, whether composed of square or diamond-shaped blocks, or decorated with a large design in different colors, are unsurpassed in beauty; while in high-studded rooms where there is little pattern on the walls and a small amount of furniture, elaborately designed mosaic floors with sweeping arabesques and geometrical figures are of great decorative value.[8]

Edith and Codman also valued such floors as they were easier to keep clean, solid, and durable.[9] In a letter to Mrs. Richard Watson Gilder, probably written in August 1902, Edith stated that the floor in the gallery was still being laid, and the house was inaccessible to visitors: "The floors of the principal floor, including the hall, are being laid in 'terrazzo,' like those one sees in the north of Italy — & this shiny swampy process is now going on . . . I had no idea that it was such a wet business."[10]

Edith was also cognizant of the impact of a well-designed ceiling. In *The Decoration of Houses* she maintained that "In the general effect of the room, the form of the ceiling is of more importance than its decoration. In rooms of a certain size and height, a flat surface overhead looks monotonous, and the ceiling should be vaulted and coved."[11]

The furnishings, as described by *Berkshire Resort Topics* on September 10, 1904, included "terra cotta statues, with three highly prized Italian console tables, and marble columns and

Italy by northern Europe"[5] and became popular as a place for exercise in autumn and winter north of the Alps. Edith adapted her gallery as a showcase for family art treasures, following the examples she observed in Italy.

The room was lighted by two crystal chandeliers. In *The Decoration of Houses*, Edith and Codman stated that "Gala apartments, as distinguished from living-rooms, should be lit from the ceiling, never from the walls."[6] The original chandeliers were changed to the current ones of beaded crystal probably during the Shattucks' occupancy. A heat grate on the east wall provides warmth from the hot-air furnace below. The gallery is the only principal room on the main floor without a fireplace.

vases." [12] In her 1984 analysis of The Mount's furnishings, Amelia Peck describes the gallery as follows:

When entering from the stair-hall, one first came upon two faun-like terra cotta figures, approximately three feet in height, mounted on marble bases. On the window side of the gallery stood two of the three Italian console tables, which were rectangular in shape, and each of which held what appears to have been an oriental carved wood figure. The central window was flanked by two small square stools. The central panel on the wall facing the central window was mirrored, and seems to have been the focal point of the room. A semi-circular Italian console table was placed in front of the mirror, and this table held a variety of objects, including a life-sized terra cotta bust of a woman, two small Chinese jars, and a small footed bowl. The table was surrounded by a number of other objects, including a carved wooden pedestal on either side. Each pedestal displayed a large Chinese jar, decorated with groups of figures. The focus of the two panels that flanked the mirrored panel was a pair of dark marble pillars supporting large stone urns. [13]

Peck surmises that there were at least two more terra-cotta figures on marble bases, like those seen at the south end of the gallery, to enforce the symmetry of the room. [14]

Not much is known about the bas-relief, an oval lunette featuring a child holding a cross, set into the wall above the doors leading into the den. Sally G. Shafto, in her *Room Analysis of The Mount* (1985), identifies the figure as John the Baptist. [15] An amusing anecdote reported by Berkeley Updike, a frequent visitor in the Whartons' time, may apply to this bas-relief: "To a rather impertinent Frenchman who asked to see The Mount and who said somewhat patronizingly as he departed that he approved of it all except a bas-relief in the entrance-hall, she [Edith] replied, 'I assure you that you will never see it here again.'" [16]

In *The Decoration of Houses*, Edith and Codman noted that "The old French decorators relied upon the reflection of mirrors for producing an effect of distances in the treatment of gala rooms." [17] The mirror set into the east wall between the doors to the drawing room creates such an effect, both in the room and from the courtyard looking in.

The original color of the gallery is believed to have been blue green. Later it was painted green. In the early 1980s the room was painted in the present peach color with white trim.

DEN

A door at the north end of the gallery opens into Teddy Wharton's den, which occupies the northwest corner of the main floor. [1] The den could also be reached from the library to the east and through two French doors from the terrace.

In *The Decoration of Houses*, Edith and Codman acknowledged that the word den was now accorded "the dignity of a technical term." [2] A "descendant" of the smoking-room, the den was the personal "lounging-room" [3] of the master of the house. It was there that Teddy planned his day, worked, read, smoked, relaxed, and visited with friends.

Codman's original plans for the first story of The Mount placed the den in the central block of the house — adjacent to the dining room, across the hall from the salon, and across the hallway from the library; coming up the main stairs one would have had to pass by the library and the den.

The final Hoppin & Koen plans contrasted sharply with Codman's initial plan by locating both the den and the library at the far end of the gallery, which ensured more privacy. The fact that these rooms are set side by side and connected by a door (a concealed door on the den side) attests to the nature of Edith and Teddy's relationship at the time that The Mount was designed; each had a private space in which to work or to relax, but the spaces were connected (as were their bedrooms directly above).

The room measures 14 feet 11 inches by 18 feet 5 inches in plan. A French marble mantel flanked by 10-foot-high French doors leading to the terrace dominates the north wall. A waist-high window on the west wall overlooks the forecourt. The south wall has two single doors [4] with painted panels set into the wall above; the left door gives access to and from the gallery while the right one opens into the only bathroom on this floor. The east wall has the concealed door linking the den to the library.

The den illustrates perfectly Edith's and Codman's premise that a small room could be as architecturally correct and comfortable as any of its grander counterparts. As interior designer of the principal rooms, Codman followed carefully the precepts laid forth in 1897 in *The Decoration of Houses*. According to the book, the "best way of obtaining an effect of size is to panel the walls by means of clear-cut architectural moulding: a few strong vertical lines will give dignity to the room and height to the ceiling."[5] The den is dominated by a series of vertical rectangular panels, designed by Codman, with ornamental surrounds alternating with narrower unornamented panels.

The room features four of these large panels — one each on the south and west walls and two on the east wall. The ornament consists of beaded trim and a border of acanthus leaves. The beaded trim is indented in each corner around a flower ornament with six petals and a raised center. This paneling in the den resembles that designed by Codman in the 1890s for the library, hall, and staircase hall at Land's End.

Like the adjacent library, the den has a coved ceiling with an elaborate cornice that reworked motifs from the wall ornament below. The architrave has large acanthus leaves alternating with an upright flower, while in the frieze above, a beaded row supports a smaller row of acanthus leaves.

Codman's ink-on-linen elevations for the den survive[6]; they reveal that construction followed the designs closely. There were some departures: the plasterwork medallion of a head surrounded by swags, situated over the fireplace and mirror on the north wall, was sketched as a woman's head facing east on the Codman elevation. A Roman emperor's head crowned with leaves and facing west was ultimately realized.[7]

The west wall elevation suggests that Codman originally planned a third French door, which might have led to an outside loggia or an exten-

FIG. 52 *Elevation of the north wall of Teddy Wharton's den, Ogden Codman, Jr., c. 1901 (see Figs. 127 and 129). This scheme proposed a medallion of a woman's head above the fireplace mirror; the actual medallion features the profile of a Roman emperor. Edith Wharton added the word "Den."* (EWR)

sion of the terrace. Instead, a window was placed on this wall.

A heat grate with a simple grille is located in the southeast corner of the room. Codman's elevation shows the grate filling an entire wall panel, whereas the actual grate fills only the center portion of the panel.

On the south wall above the two single doors, Codman called for two plain plaster panels. This was later amended to allow for two oil paintings with mythological settings. Both paintings, each measuring 27 inches by 34 inches, are by an unidentified nineteenth-century (or early twentieth-century) artist,[8] although it has been suggested that they may have been painted by Hoppin. An artist who occasionally exhibited his work, Hoppin is known to have executed paintings for his clients' homes.[9] The painting over the hall door shows a male satyr pondering a reclining female satyr, while the one over the bathroom door depicts a woman gazing at a male satyr playing a pipe.

The fireplace in the center of the north wall is of French *rouge* marble. Three insets of black marble form part of the marble hearth. This fireplace is the only one in the house to feature a carved motif — garlands of leaves tied with a ribbon hang from round hooks. A large mirror set in a wooden frame stretches from the marble mantel up to the medallion of the emperor's head and its attendant swags, executed in plaster.

The cast-iron fireback has intact side panels; the central panel depicts an allegory of the sciences, including a globe, map, telescope, and a caduceus, a staff with two entwined snakes and two wings at the top.[10]

The two French doors illustrate the premise in *The Decoration of Houses* that "in the country nothing is more charming than the French window opening to the floor."[11] All the windows and doors in the room retain the original brass hardware in the Louis XV style, which, like the hardware for the principal rooms, was imported from the Paris firm of Sterlin.[12]

In *The Decoration of Houses*, Edith and Codman allowed for the "expedient" of the concealed door, which they employed to link Teddy's den to Edith's library at The Mount. As there was no other opening on the east wall to balance a door into the library, the concealed door was executed for reasons of symmetry. Although the authors acknowledged that some people could never justify such an architectural necessity because it was "deceptive," both felt that, given the average American house (which The Mount was *not*), "every device is permissible that helps to produce an effect of spaciousness and symmetry without interfering with convenience: chief among these contrivances being the concealed door."[13]

The original wall color was cream, and the ceiling and moldings were white,[14] according to the article in *Berkshire Resort Topics* in 1904. *The Decoration of Houses* deemed such colors best for smaller rooms: "The walls should be free from pattern and light in color, since dark walls necessitate much artificial light, and have the disadvantage of making a room look small."[15]

The floor of the den is oak parquet laid in a trellis pattern, the same as in the library. The floor was originally covered with a carpet.[16]

The 1901 Hoppin & Koen floor plans called for four light fixtures: one on either side of the fireplace mirror and two on the south wall between the two single doors. There is no evidence that any of these was actually installed. The plans also specified one bell to summon the staff on the south wall by the door into the gallery; this bell is extant.

Berkshire Resort Topics noted in 1904 that Teddy's den was "very cosily [sic] appointed, the furniture being upholstered in dark leather, which contrasts with the cream-tinted walls and white moulding and ceiling ... There are several pictures" on the walls.[17]

Unfortunately, the den is the only major room on the *piano nobile* of The Mount for which there is no extant photograph. The exact furnishings of the room — and their placement — must, therefore, be somewhat conjectural.

Amelia Peck, in her *Restoration Plan for the Interior of The Mount*, postulates that "rough pencil sketches"[18] on the final Hoppin & Koen floor plan for the room may indicate a furnishing plan by Edith. Using these sketches, Peck hypothesizes the following: a long desk with chair at an angle to the window on the west wall; a small writing-table with chair (all in the same style as the aforementioned desk and chair) in the center of the room; a leather arm-chair with footstool and side table at an angle facing the fireplace and located to the right of it; and a leather upholstered sofa with a side table along the east wall. A cabinet for books and papers may have occupied the west wall to the left of the window; two matching book-cases may have stood against the south wall between the two single doors. A clock and some framed photographs (as in Edith's boudoir directly above) may have adorned the marble fireplace mantel.

Peck reasons that the desks, chairs, book-cases, and cabinet may have been in the Louis XVI style, while the upholstered leather couch and armchair were probably "classic 'men's club' furniture."[19] In *The Decoration of Houses*, Edith and Codman noted that:

Whatever extravagances the upholsterer may have committed in other parts of the house, it is usually conceded that common sense should regulate the furnishing of the den... the master's sense of comfort often expresses itself in a set of "office" furniture — a roller top desk, a revolving chair, and others of the puffy type already described as the accepted model of a luxurious seat. Thus freed from the superfluous, the den is likely to be the most comfortable room in the house; and the natural inference is that a room, in order to be comfortable, must be ugly. One can picture the derision of the man who is told that he might, without the smallest sacrifice of comfort or convenience, transact his business at a Louis XVI writing-table, seated in a Louis XVI chair! — yet the handsomest desks of the last century — the fine old *"bureaux à la kaunitz"* or *"à cylindre"* were the prototypes of the modern "roller-top"; and the cane or leather-seated writing chair, with rounded back and five slim strong legs, was far more comfortable than the amorphous revolving seat.[20]

Peck concludes that Edith probably persuaded Teddy to follow these precepts.

As the marble mantel is reddish in color, and the room contained dark leather furniture, Peck surmises that the draperies in the room were "of a heavy fabric, warm red or reddish-brown in color."[21] The drapes may have been hung on wooden poles and rings like those in Edith's library.

Like Edith's library, the den was furnished to provide a comfortable space for work and relaxation. Teddy was responsible for running the estate, keeping household accounts, and managing his wife's finances and trust funds. A family friend and guest at The Mount, W.K. Richardson, explained that "her husband at that period had charge of most of the house-keeping; and used to drive over to Pittsfield to do the household errands."[22] And although Gaillard Lapsley remembered that Teddy's "idleness... was busy and largely innocent," he did note that Teddy, "as one of her [Edith's] trustees and managing the place at Lenox relieved her of much distasteful responsibility and work."[23]

It is presumed that the Shattucks and the Van Andas continued to use the den as a sitting room, although the 1940 floor plan (for tax evaluation) labeled the room erroneously as "Edith Wharton's Writing Room."

During a part of the Foxhollow School years, the room served as a faculty apartment. The adjoining bathroom was modified to add a bathtub along the west wall, a modern sink, and a new toilet to replace the original pull-chain model. Fortunately, few alterations were made to the den itself.

Problems with the heavy, concealed door on the east wall resulted in the replacement of the original hardware with modern hinges and the loss of the original pieces. The door pulled loose and brought down some pieces of plaster wall in 1987; concealed replacement hardware has been installed recently.

At some point the room was painted yellow-ish-cream, as evidenced by an exposed section of the west wall that had been hidden behind a telephone box. The present green-with-white dates from the early 1980s.

The room is now used for tours and displays.

HOUSE FOR E.R.WHARTON ESQ.
LENOX MASS.

SCALE 1/8
ELEVATION OF LIBRARY.

OGDEN CODMAN JR. ARCH'T
WINDSOR ARCADE NEW YORK

FIG. 53 *Elevation of the north wall of Edith Wharton's library, Ogden Codman, Jr., c. 1901.* (EWR)

LIBRARY

The library, located on the northeast corner of the main floor, measures 20 feet long by 25 feet wide in plan. Two doors on the west wall connect the library to the gallery and to the den. Double doors on the south wall open into the drawing room. Four sets of French doors connect the library to the brick terrace, which wraps around the northeast corner of the building. The fireplace occupies the center of the south wall.

Codman's original plans envisioned the library as the first room a visitor reached when coming up the stairs. He designed two doors opening onto the L-shaped hallway, a third door on the same wall connecting the library to the central salon, and a fireplace on the west wall; to the east, two doors would have opened to a loggia, and three windows on the south wall would have matched the three doors opening into the hallway and salon. The rectangular room would have been balanced by the dining room on the other side of the house.

Hoppin & Koen's floor plans balance the library and the dining room by placing the drawing room in the middle. The library and the dining room have the same square footage, but Hoppin & Koen made both rooms less rectangular. The library was constructed almost exactly as specified by the Hoppin & Koen floor plan. The concealed door connecting Edith's library to Teddy's den, however, was not on the original floor plan; it was added, apparently as an afterthought, and balances the door on the west wall. A second exception is that the shallow closet, perhaps a liquor cabinet, did not appear on the Hoppin & Koen floor plan. It has double doors flanking the fireplace on the left and was apparently added at the time of construction.

Four terrace doors open *into* the library, as specified in *The Decoration of Houses*. The doors of the shallow closet on the south wall open into the room as well, although the doors that balance them to the right of the fireplace open into the drawing room. The concealed door that connects the library to the den opens into the den. Although the flanking door on the

81

west wall is shown on the Hoppin & Koen plan as opening into the library from the gallery, it actually opens into the gallery from the library. The hardware on the interior doors (including the shallow closet) originally had a red-enamel finish, which complimented the ormolu.

Codman's elevations show the room almost exactly as it was built. A minor adjustment was made on the elevation for the fireplace wall; a bronze heating grate, which Codman had placed immediately to the left of the double doors, was located at the bottom of the built-in bookcase to the right of the fireplace.

The room is paneled in oak with elaborate scrollwork and garlands designed by Codman. The north, south, and east walls are dominated by oak bookshelves built into the walls. Edith and Codman wrote that "the plan of building bookshelves into the walls is the most decorative and the most practical... the best examples of this treatment are found in France. The walls of the rooms thus decorated were usually of paneled wood, either in natural oak or walnut... instead of being detached pieces of furniture, the bookcases formed an organic part of the wall's decoration."[1] *Berkshire Resort Topics* in 1904 particularly noted that "the oak book-shelves reach to the ceiling on three sides of the room."[2]

The library floor is laid in the same oak parquet trellis pattern as the den. The oak floor was originally covered with a carpet, which is believed to have measured approximately 15 feet by 12 feet.

The coved ceiling also adheres closely to Edith's and Codman's principles:

In the general effect of the room, the form of the ceiling is of more importance than its decoration. In rooms of a certain size and height, a flat surface overhead looks monotonous, and the ceiling should be vaulted or coved... A coved ceiling greatly increases the apparent height of a low-studded room; but rooms of this kind should not be treated with an order, since the projection of the cornice below the springing of the cove will lower the walls so much as to defeat the purpose for which the cove has been used. In such rooms the cove should rise directly from the walls; and this treatment suggests the important rule that where the cove is not

FIG. 54 *The library, looking southwest, during the Whartons' occupancy, date unknown. Note the fire blazing on the hearth and the striped dog bed to the right of the mantel.* (BL)

FIG. 55 *The library, west wall, during the Whartons' occupancy, with Edith's desk in the foreground.* (BL)

supported by a cornice the ceiling decoration should be of very light character. A heavy panelled ceiling should not rest on the walls without the intervention of a strongly profiled cornice.[3]

Although the library ceiling was not heavily paneled, there is an elaborate and strongly profiled plaster cornice surrounding the room between the coved ceiling and the oak-paneled walls. The top element of the cornice features an acanthus leaf above and an egg-and-dart motif below. A lower section closest to the oak wall appears to be a thin band of intertwined leaves and berries.

Berkshire Resort Topics in 1904 noted that the ceiling was white.[4] Several photographs show a white plaster cornice during the Whartons' occupancy. The cornice has since received a wood stain.[5]

The mantel is a green French marble. Like the mantel in the dining room, it is set almost flush to the wall with no over-mantel. There are three insets of French *rouge* marble on the hearth. The cast-iron fireback features trelliswork and scrolls surrounding an oval crowned

by a bearded head. Within the oval there appears a scene from the Twelve Labors of Hercules, involving Hercules and the Nemean lion.[6] The two side panels feature trelliswork designs.

Berkshire Resort Topics in 1904 stated that "Mrs. Wharton's literary tastes naturally lead to the conclusion that her library must be one of the most interesting rooms in the house."[7] *The Decoration of Houses* advocated that "the

FIG. 56 *The library, looking southwest, in the only known photograph of an interior of The Mount published during the Whartons' occupancy. Entitled "A corner in Mrs. Wharton's library," it appeared in* Berkshire Resort Topics *in 1904. Note the folding screen on the right and, in front of it, a dog ensconced in the striped dog bed.* (BA)

FIG. 57 *The library, west wall, during the Whartons' occupancy, with a tapestry set into the wall. This image shows the folding screen (on the left) behind the chair.* (BL)

FIG. 58 *The library,
northeast corner, during
the Whartons' occupancy
(see Fig. 132).* (BL)

general decoration of the library should be of such character as to form a background or setting to the books, rather than to detract attention from them ... There is no reason why the decorations of a library should not be splendid; but in that case the books must be splendid too, and sufficient in number to dominate all the accessory decorations of the room."[8]

The focal point of the library was Edith's desk, which was located in front of the north wall facing the fireplace.[9] It was a "bureau-ministre," which was highly recommended in *The Decoration of Houses*:

The library writing-table is seldom large enough, or sufficiently free from odds and ends in the shape of photograph-frames, silver boxes, and flower-vases, to give free play to the elbows. A large solid table of the kind called bureau-ministre...is well adapted to the library; and in front of it should stand a comfortable writing-chair.[10]

Several historic photographs reveal the following items on Edith's desk: a blotter, lamp, letter box, books, papers, pen-and-ink stand, framed photographs, boxes, and possibly an ashtray. The desk had extensions that pulled out from the main body. The writing chair for the desk was caned to match the Louis XVI

armchairs and the adjacent Louis XV *lit de repos*, which had flowered cushions that closely matched the *lit de repos* recommended in *The Decoration of Houses*. A spitoon, according to Peck, was located under the desk, perhaps a concession to Teddy or male friends.[11]

Peck's 1984 analysis describes the rest of the room's furnishings, noting that a second focal point was the area before the fireplace. At either side two comfortable matching roll-arm armchairs faced each other; they formed a group with a roll-arm settee, with its back against Edith's desk. All three pieces had fringe and tassels along the bottom. This furniture is no doubt what inspired the *Berkshire Resort Topics* reporter to note, "comfort seems to have been sought in the furnishings."[12]

To the right of the settee was a triangular oak side table. To the left of the fireplace was a rectangular Louis XV side table, while to the right was a round Louis XV side table with ormolu mounts and an inlaid top. Both tables held lamps, dishes or ashtrays, and other items. In front of the hearth was a fur rug and a round dog bed. A bin for logs was located directly behind the round side table. Fire tools leaned against the marble fireplace, which had a transparent firescreen. A fire blazed on the hearth in one of the Wharton-period photographs.

During the Whartons' occupancy, a large painting, in heavy gilt frame, of an unidentified gentleman, hung above the fireplace. A reflection indicates that it was under glass. Codman's original elevation called for a picture to fill the entire wood panel above the fireplace.

A photograph from *Berkshire Resort Topics* in 1904 and another undated view of the west wall both show that a folding screen was at times located behind the round side table and armchair to the right of the fireplace. This screen apparently blocked the view of the drawing room. The screen is not in place in several other photographs (most likely dating after 1904) that show the same corner of the library.

The west wall of the library featured a set-in tapestry measuring approximately 7 feet 8 inches wide by 8 feet 7 1/2 inches high, according to Codman's elevation. Edith and Codman advo-

cated having a tapestry subordinated to the architectural lines of a room by adapting it to fit into a wall panel: "nothing can be more beautiful than tapestry properly used..."[13] The tapestry in the library was a garden scene, perhaps an Aubusson. In a letter to Codman in 1901, Wharton discussed options for the library tapestry: "The change of tapestries you suggest would not do as the two tapestries of which you have sketches are alike in colouring and composition, whereas the one I intend to put in the library is absolutely different."[14]

Immediately in front of the tapestry was a bombe-fronted Louis XV chest with marble top and ormolu mounts. It held a large porcelain figure of a woman from a mythological scene and two porcelain animals, probably dogs.

The chest was flanked by two small matching Louis XVI two-drawer cabinets, decorated with inlay. On top of each was a bust of a child on a marble stand. To the left of the tapestry was an elaborate wall clock. *Berkshire Resort Topics* explained approvingly in 1904: "tapestries, paintings and statuary relieve any appearance of staidness which may be intimated by the long row of books."[15]

Along the east wall of the room there was a table similar to Edith's desk. Several Wharton-period photographs show a lamp on the table surrounded by vases of flowers and many books. *The Decoration of Houses* asserted that such tables should be "large, substantial and clear of everything but lamps, books and papers."[16] This table may well have been "given over to the filing of books and newspapers."[17]

A call-bell was located to the left of the doors that open into the drawing room. The bell, which was specified on the 1901 Hoppin & Koen floor plan, is extant.

A Wharton-period view of the northeast corner of the library shows floor-length draperies hung

FIG. 59 *Edith Wharton at her desk in the library, date unknown. Photograph by Gessford of New York and Lenox.* (BL)

from rings on wooden curtain rods,[18] now painted gold, and with a flower-bud motif on each end. The drapes, which appear to be fairly lightweight, were held open with curtain tie-backs. There were no sheer curtains.

Amelia Peck postulates that if the library rug had a predominantly red background, the color of the draperies and upholstery may have been a deep green. Considering the green marble of the fireplace, this supposition seems well-founded. In *The Decoration of Houses*, Edith and Codman explained how a proper color scheme might be determined:

When the walls are simply paneled in oak or walnut… the carpet may contrast in color with the curtains and chair-coverings. For instance, in an oak panelled room crimson curtains and chair-coverings may be used with a dull green carpet, or with one of dark blue patterned in subdued tints; or the color-scheme may be reversed, with green hangings and chair-coverings combined with a plain crimson carpet.[19]

Edith wrote in bed every morning, although several publicity photographs of the author at her desk in the library give the impression that she indeed wrote there. The library was the most photographed room in the house, which indicates its overall importance in the Whartons' time.

Gaillard Lapsley's memories of Edith in her library in France suggest ways in which the library at The Mount may have been used. Lapsley noted that the afternoon mail was always opened and read in the library prior to tea, after which there would be readings by guests from favorite books (these often included works by Eliot, Brontë, Thackeray, Dickens, and Trollope). Edith would often knit while listening. Animated discussions on a multitude of subjects would follow. Edith wrote fondly of "readings around the library fire"[20] at The Mount with friends such as Henry James, Bay Lodge, Walter Berry, Gaillard Lapsley, Robert Norton, and John Hugh Smith. Lapsley remembered that in conversation, Edith's "standard was high — higher indeed, than I think she always realized. She was herself so abundantly and availably well-informed, so documented and experienced by observation, talk and travel that if her interlocutor's resources brought him as far as her point of departure he was lucky."[21]

As a young child, Edith Jones had spent a great deal of time in her father's library, and she remembered that it was in "the kingdom of my father's library"[22] that she first learned (and was encouraged) to read and write. This early love for such a scholarly room clearly indicates the importance of her own library at The Mount and may well account for her scorn for the "libraries" of others. According to Berkeley Updike, Edith once sarcastically remarked that "The XYZ's have decided, they tell me, to have books in the library."[23]

The library continued in its original usage during the Shattuck and Van Anda years. A

FIG. 60 *The library, north wall, looking toward Edith Wharton's desk, during the Whartons' occupancy. This informal view was probably taken by Edith or Teddy.* (BL)

photograph during the Van Andas' occupancy shows that most — if not all — of the Wharton furnishings had been replaced by several comfortable arm chairs and a couch, tables, and a radio. During the Foxhollow years, the room continued to house a collection of books, some left over from the Van Anda ownership. According to students, the room served at times as a combination library and study hall. Since the late 1970s, the room has been used as a rehearsal space by Shakespeare & Company, though it is used today primarily for tours.

Few alterations have been made to the library. Two sconces were apparently added to the west wall not long after the Whartons left The Mount. At some point the cornice, which was unpainted white plaster during the Whartons' occupancy, was grained to match the oak walls and bookshelves.[24] The tapestry on the west wall was probably sold in the 1935 auction of Mary Shattuck's estate by her heirs. The two side panels of the fireback are missing.

The original hardware of the southernmost door on the east wall was removed during the Foxhollow years; the door had to be rebuilt to open outward to comply with the fire code.

In more recent years, the central cast-iron fireback and the brick hearth cracked when a wood-burning stove was placed in the fireplace by Shakespeare & Company. The marble mantel, which was coming loose from the wall, has been secured.

DRAWING ROOM

The drawing room is located on the main floor in the center of the house, facing east. The room measures 20 feet wide by 36 feet long, which makes it the largest and most spacious room in the house. The fireplace on the west wall is flanked by double doors leading to the gallery. One set of double doors in the southwest corner of the room opens into the dining room. These are balanced by another set of double doors in the northwest corner opening into the library. Three pairs of French doors in the center of the east wall open onto the large brick terrace.

Codman's original drawing for the first story envisioned a large salon in the center of the H-block (also facing east), with the dining room and the library on either side.

The floor plan executed by Hoppin & Koen followed the original Codman proposal very closely, including the placement of the drawing room in the center of the overall floor plan, the fireplace in the center of the west wall, doors on either side of the fireplace leading into the gallery, and doors on either end of the room opening into the dining room and library. The room was constructed as illustrated on the 1901 plan with one major exception: Hoppin & Koen had envisioned five pairs of double doors facing the terrace; Edith chose three pairs. Therefore, inside there are three doors, while on the exterior of the building there appear to be five. Two blind doors flank the others on the exterior. The three central terrace doors open into the room. The four sets of interior double doors that link the drawing room to the dining room, gallery, and library also open into the room. In *The Decoration of Houses*, Edith and Codman noted that "doors should always swing *into* a room. This facilitates entrance and gives the hospitable impression that everything is made easy to those who are coming in."[1]

The ceiling is perhaps the most dominant feature. This is the only room at The Mount to have elaborate ceiling ornamentation. Its decorative plaster ornament consists of a large oval festooned with flowers and fruits and surrounded by floral rosettes.[2]

The floor of the drawing room is composed of the same terrazzo as that in the gallery and is also bordered with white panels of Vermont marble. A large carpet, possibly an Aubusson, covered the terrazzo floor in the Whartons' time.

Another significant feature of the room is the mantel of French marble on the west wall. Part of the largest fireplace in the house, it has three Italian marble insets (*fior de pesco*) on the hearth. As the room was being designed in 1901, Edith wrote Codman concerning the decoration of the wall:

I don't care to have the chimney in the drawing room moved, but surely, as the tapestries match so perfectly in the essentials — i.e. colour and composition — the fact that one is narrower than the other need not matter, since you can put an extra narrow panel on each side of the smaller tapestry. I am dreadfully sorry that the bust can't be recessed over the drawing room chimney. Could it be done by making a small chimney-breast? Of course they did have them in Louis XIV houses —[3]

The surviving cast-iron fireback is the most elaborate one in the house. The central scene represents the sacrifice of Isaac. In addition to the figures of Abraham and Isaac, one can see the angel, a flaming urn (the burnt offering), and the ram, which the angel had commanded Abraham to sacrifice in place of Isaac.[4] Two cupids touch the central oval with a hand; with the other hand each holds a garland of flowers. Another cupid's face crowns the oval, which rests upon abundant foliage. The two side panels have identical elaborate tracery and scrollwork, a bearded figure, and a mythological bird.

FIG. 61 *Drawing room, southeast corner, during the Whartons' occupancy. The tapestry, "Narcissus at the Fountain," was a primary focus (see Figs. 13, 62, 80, and 134).* (BL)

The four interior doors of the room feature elaborate ornamental broken pediments. Adjacent to the interior doors and fireplace, the walls are ornamented with garlands of flowers tied with ribbons and executed in plaster.

The Hoppin & Koen plan called for light fixtures on the east wall and two beside the fireplace. There is no physical evidence that these were ever installed.[5] *The Decoration of Houses* asserted that proper light in the drawing room was supplied by candles:

Nothing has done more to vulgarize interior decoration than the general use of gas and of electricity in the living-rooms of modern houses. Electric light especially, with its harsh white glare, which no expedients have as yet overcome, has taken from our drawing-rooms all air of privacy and distinction.[6]

The original color of the drawing room was reported to be "a bluish-grey tint, with white mouldings and ceiling."[7]

The one Wharton-period photograph of the drawing room looks towards the southeast corner from the center of the room. According to *Berkshire Resort Topics* in 1904, the room was decorated in the English seventeenth-century style: "Flemish tapestries of the period adorn the walls, and attention is especially attracted also by a bust of the last Duke of Parma, by Boudard, and several eighteenth-century French busts. The furniture is chiefly XVIII century Italian."[8] In a letter to a friend dated October 22, 1904, Henry James wrote of some of this furniture: "*Here* I am in an exquisite French chateau perched among Massachusetts mountains — most charming ones — and filled exclusively with old French and Italian furniture and decorations."[9]

The Decoration of Houses described two types of salons: the *salon de compagnie* and the *salon de famille*. Edith and Codman explained that the *salon de compagnie* was a formal room used for special occasions, while the *salon de famille* was a "meeting-place for the whole family."[10] They concluded that

In modern American houses, both traditional influences are seen…the drawing-room is treated as a family

FIG. 62 *"Narcissus at the Fountain," a Brussels tapestry of 1710, was sold after the death of Mary Strong Shattuck. This illustration is from the 1935 auction catalogue.* (EWR)

apartment, and provided with books, lamps, easy-chairs, and writing-tables. In other houses it is still considered sacred to gilding and discomfort, the best room in the house, and the convenience of all its inmates, being sacrificed to a vague feeling that no drawing-room is worthy of the name unless it is uninhabitable. This is an instance of the *salon de compagnie* having usurped the rightful place of the *salon de famille*...[11]

The Wharton-period photograph shows the drawing room as a bit of both. The room was comfortably appointed for conversation, yet, as Amelia Peck notes, there were aspects of the *salon de compagnie* in the placement of the furniture. *The Decoration of Houses* stated: "Circulation must not be impeded by a multiplicity of small pieces of furniture holding lamps or other fragile objects, while at least half of the chairs should be so light and easily moved that groups may be formed and broken up at will."[12]

Peck, in her 1984 furnishing plan, finds that the description of the room by *Berkshire Resort Topics* as eighteenth-century Italian conflicts with the extant photograph, which shows French furnishings. She identifies the sofa in the center of the room as a traditional over-stuffed one, "possibly upholstered in velvet, with deep fringe" at the base.[13] She further identifies the other furnishings in the southeast corner as two Louis XV *bergères* and what appears to be a Louis XVI sofa. The sofa, as well as the wall clock, came from the hallway at Land's End in Newport. The photograph shows a cloth-covered table holding Chinese porcelain and a carved Chinese figure. A large painting in a gilded frame hung on the east wall. The south wall was dominated by a Brussels tapestry (c.1710) entitled "Narcissus at the Fountain,"[14] which was set into the wall.

Other furnishings in the room may have included small bookcases, movable side chairs, side tables, and fire tools.

The use of French and Italian furniture in the drawing room seems to follow Edith's and Codman's precept that the furniture in such a room "should consist of a few strongly marked pieces, such as handsome cabinets and consoles, bronze or marble statues, and vases and candelabra of imposing proportions. Almost all modern furniture is too weak in design and too finikin [sic] in detail to look well in a gala drawing-room."[15] They went on to detail that admirable furniture in the grand style for such a room could be found in both France and Italy.

Edith may have had a bookcase in her drawing room, as recommended in *The Decoration of Houses*: "those who really care for books are seldom content to restrict them to the library, for nothing adds more to the charm of a drawing-room than a well-designed bookcase: an expanse of beautiful bindings is as decorative as a fine tapestry."[16]

The drawing room continued to be used as such by both the Shattucks and the Van Andas. During the Foxhollow School years, the room was used for parents' receptions. According to photographs, it had a piano in the southeast corner, used for piano and singing lessons. Every year a dance was held on the main floor of the house, centering in the drawing room.

Today the drawing room is the site of matinee play performances. The drawing room has also been used by Edith Wharton Restoration for lectures, exhibitions, conferences, meetings, benefits, chamber music recitals, tours, and special events.

Over the years, the terrazzo floors in the drawing room and in the dining room sagged, cracked, and pulled away from the walls. The main floors were resupported in 1986. Leaking pipes from a bathroom in the attic caused the ceiling to collapse in the early 1970s, when the building was boarded up. In 1982, as a tribute to Foxhollow School founder and headmistress Aileen M. Farrell, the ceiling was repaired using rubber and silicon molds and then painted its present shade of white. In the late 1980s, fabric resembling tapestry was installed in the frames on the north and south walls. Otherwise, the drawing room at The Mount is much as it was in Edith Wharton's time.

DINING ROOM

The dining room measures 20 feet 6 inches by 25 feet in plan and is located on the southeast end of the main block on the first floor, adjoining the drawing room on the north and the butler's pantry to the south. Double doors open into the drawing room and face another set that opens into the butler's pantry. Two pairs of doors on the east wall open to the terrace. Directly opposite are two pairs of doors: the south ones lead to the stairs to the bedroom floor, while the north ones connect to the main stair hall. The fireplace is located at the center of the north wall.

On Codman's original plan, the dining room adjoined the salon and the den and was reached by an L-shaped hallway. Doors on either side of the hallway opened into the salon and den. A fireplace was located on the west wall, and an adjacent door led into the butler's pantry. Two doors opposite opened onto a loggia; three windows on the north wall seem to match three doors on the opposite wall. In size and aspect, Codman's plan for the dining room closely resembles that of Hoppin & Koen.

The Decoration of Houses notes that "the walls should be sufficiently light in color to make little artificial light necessary,"[1] and the dining room walls were originally white, according to *Berkshire Resort Topics*.

Berkshire Resort Topics also noted in 1904 that the room was paneled in stucco and ornamented in the eighteenth-century English style of Grinling Gibbons.[2] Codman's elevations for the north and south walls reveal that he designed the large plaster festoons of fruits, vegetables, and fish interspersed with flowers to surround the paintings. Initially the south wall had additional plaster ornaments on either side of the butler's pantry and the French doors. The original treatment of the north wall included plaster ornaments beside the drawing room door and another wall panel.[3]

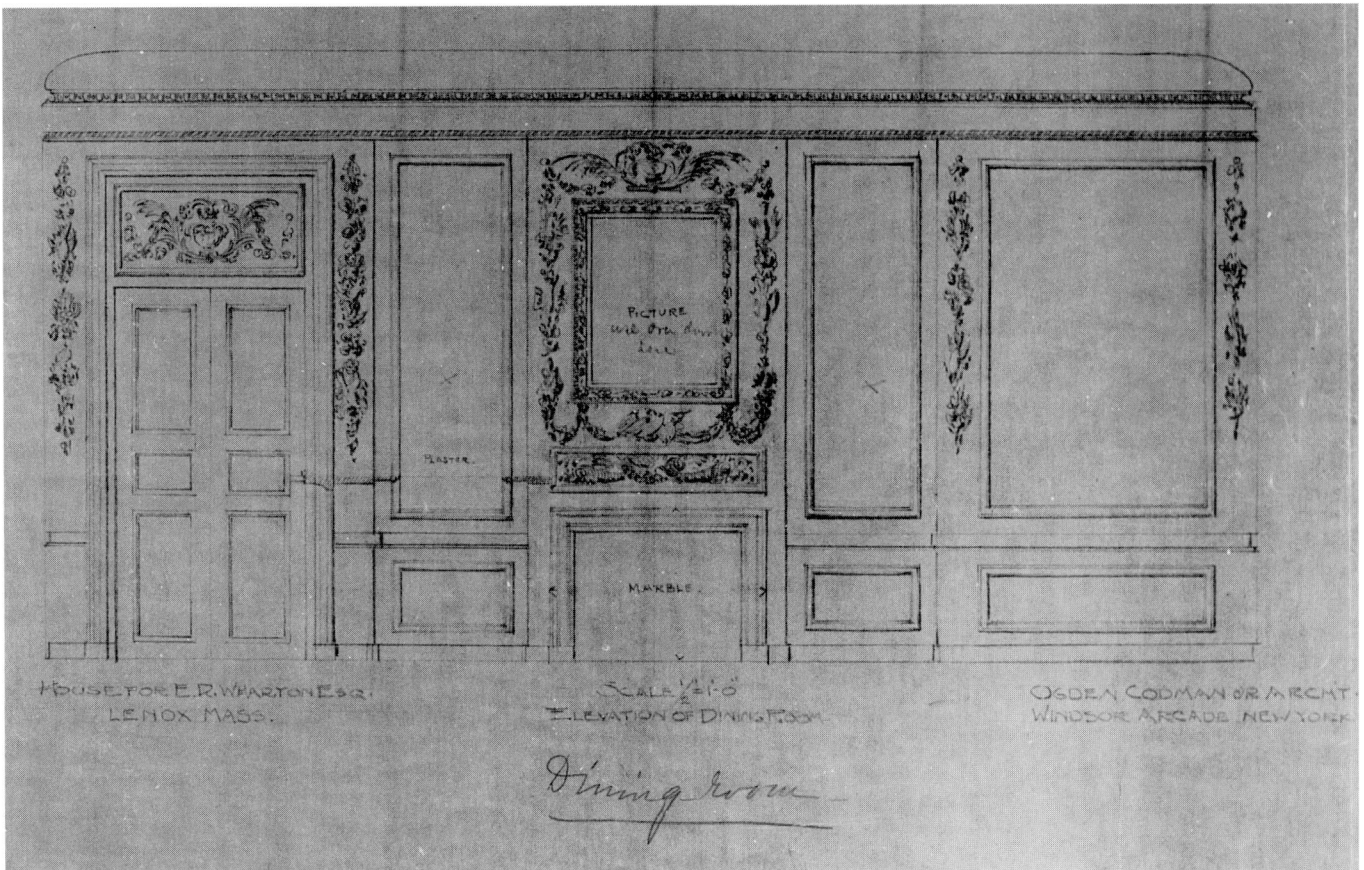

FIG. 63 *Elevation of the north wall of the dining room, Ogden Codman, Jr., c. 1901. A smaller painting was eventually set into the wall (see Fig. 140). Edith Wharton added the words "Dining room."* (EWR)

The interior doors each feature an elaborate plaster over-panel of an urn with stylized fronds and flowers, designed by Codman.

Two paintings in the Flemish style are set into the dining room walls, one above the fireplace and the other on the south wall. Codman envisioned the painting over the fireplace as a vertical rectangle, but the actual painting is a horizontal rectangle 40 inches high by 50 inches wide, featuring two cupids with fruits and flowers. On the south wall is a still life with animals and fruits in a landscape, 50 inches high by 78 1/2 inches wide. The painting over the mantel may date to the eighteenth century, and the painting on the south wall is thought to date from the seventeenth or eighteenth century.[4] Both are set in the wall and framed by ornate moldings. In *The Decoration of Houses*, Edith notes that in dining rooms the walls were often hung with fruit or flower-pieces, or with pictures of fish or game: a somewhat obvious form of adornment which it has long been the fashion to ridicule, but which was not without decorative value and appropriateness. Pictures representing life and action often grow tiresome when looked at over and over again day after day: a fact which the old decorators probably had in mind when they hung what the French call *natures mortes* in the dining room.[5]

The French *rouge* marble mantel is almost flush to the wall with no over-mantel. There are three insets of black marble on the hearth. The cast-iron fireback features an oval surrounded by elaborate scrollwork and crowned by a scalloped shell. Within the oval, two nude children, perhaps Romulus and Remus or Cain and Abel, warm themselves before a fire. At one time, there were two side panels. A Wharton-period photograph reveals that an elaborate firescreen covered the opening at times. A supplementary heat grate for the hot-air furnace is located immediately to the left of the fireplace.

The floor of the dining room is terrazzo with borders of white marble panels. Edith wrote in *The Decoration of Houses* that "a bare floor of stone or marble is best suited to the dining-room,"[6] and that if the floor had a covering, it should be a rug, not a carpet. The Wharton-period photograph shows a rug.

There are four French sconces (two on the north wall and two on the south wall), brought from Land's End. Originally gas fixtures, they were electrified when they were installed at The Mount. A photograph indicates that Edith had four wax candles on the table. In *The Decoration of Houses*, she advocated wax candles in side *appliques* or in a chandelier "since anything tending to produce heat and to exhaust air is especially objectionable in a room used for eating."[7]

A primary cornice borders the ceiling with a secondary cornice below featuring classical egg-and-dart and acanthus-leaf motifs.

The dining room furnishings were transferred intact from Land's End. The dining room table appeared to have been "a heavy late nineteenth-century pedestal table,"[8] apparently an extension table, the type written about somewhat disparagingly by the authors of *The Decoration of Houses*:

Of the dinner-table, as we now know it, little need be said. The ingenious but ugly extension table with a central support, now used all over the world, is an English invention. There seems no reason why the general design should not be improved without interfering with the mechanism of this table; but of course it can never be so satisfactory to the eye as one of the old round or square tables, with four or six tapering legs, such as were used in eighteenth-century dining-rooms before the introduction of the "extension."[9]

The white Louis XIV-style chairs at the dining room table were caned and had cushions of cut velvet. The chair at the east end of the table was an arm chair.

The photograph of the dining room at The Mount also shows that a Louis XV-style china cabinet stood on the west wall between the double doors. A photograph of the Wharton dining room at Land's End suggests that the dining room at The Mount held additional furnishings: four more side chairs; two Louis XV serving tables; and a folding screen, which may have shielded the door to the butler's pantry at The Mount.[10]

Unfortunately, the angle of The Mount photograph does not show the window treatment. In a Land's End photograph, heavy curtains are reflected in a mirror. They appear to be of the same fabric that covered the walls and were topped with an ornate lambrequin. Since Edith and Codman had written that lambrequins and fabric-covered walls were dust-catching and unhealthful, curtains or draperies in the dining room at The Mount were most likely hung from plain rings (perhaps similar to those in the library) and made of lighter fabric than had been used in Newport. In *The Decoration of Houses*, Edith and Codman remarked that dining rooms of the eighteenth century usually avoided "all stuff hangings and heavy curtains."[11]

Little is known of the cuisine served at the Wharton table, although guests repeatedly praised the caring and lavish hospitality of their hosts. Gaillard Lapsley remembered that "Edith herself liked rich and choice food and a good deal of it. She took no shame in discussing it for she thought of cooking as a fine art and used to speak of the marketing as it has been in America of our youth when there was plenty of game and no cold storage, as a

FIG. 64 *The dining room, looking towards the northwest corner, during the Whartons' occupancy (see Fig. 140). Under the table (set for four) is a cushion for a dog. The sconces were moved from the dining room at Land's End (see Fig. 143).* (BL)

lost paradise."[12] Mrs. Walter Maynard, in her reminiscences about visits to The Mount, rhapsodized: "And, oh, such food!"[13] Henry James advised Howard Sturgis in 1904 that "You needn't bring supplementary apples or candies in your dressing bag. The Whartons are kindness and hospitality incarnate…"[14]

The Shattucks and the Van Andas continued to use this space as the dining room. When the Foxhollow School owned The Mount, the dining room was used for Senior Sunday suppers. At an unknown time, a portion of the plaster ornament on the north and south walls was removed. The side panels of the fireback were also removed.

By the late 1970s and early 1980s, the terrazzo floors were sinking and cracking; in 1986 the floors were reinforced. The room was painted bright yellow in the early 1980s.

The two paintings were thoroughly cleaned and restored during the spring of 1996 through the generosity of the Friends of French Art. This non-profit foundation plans to restore other original paintings in the mansion.

Today the dining room is primarily used for tours and for receptions during the Edith Wharton plays and EWR lecture series, as well as for benefits, conferences, and other functions.

STAIRS TO THE SECOND FLOOR

The staircase hall to the bedroom floor — a rectangular area situated at the south end of the main block of the mansion — is located next to the service wing. To the west, the stairs rise to the bedrooms. To the south, a single door opens into the service wing. Double doors on the east give access to the dining room, while on the north double glass doors link the area to the main staircase hall and the gallery.

This design of dividing the staircase hall into two areas with separate stairways allows for greater privacy. By insisting that the main stairs in the house not be a continuous run, Edith was most likely following the precept in *The Decoration of Houses* that stated that "privacy would seem to be one of the first requisites of civilized life, yet it is only necessary to observe the

planning and arrangement of the average house to see how little this need is recognized."[1]

This section of the staircase hall was built more or less as indicated on the 1901 Hoppin & Koen floor plan. Like the adjoining stair hall, the stairs in this area are painted wood, but the walls, instead of having a stringcourse treatment, are decorated with the strong and simple molding found throughout the main floor.

FIG. 65 *The staircase hall, 1942. In the background are the stairs to the bedroom floor. The missing urn finial is visible on the newel (compare to Fig. 146).* (FHS)

93

The black wrought-iron railing is identical to the one at the stairs below. An urn finial crowned the origin of the railing at the foot of the stairs. The stairs cross the window on the west wall in the French manner, allowing them to be fully visible from outside the building.

An oil painting is set into the wall above the single door on the south wall that opens into the service wing. Measuring 29 inches high by 36 inches wide and dating probably from the eighteenth century, it depicts a cupid with flowers. As with the other inset paintings throughout the house, the artist is not known.

A c. 1942 photograph shows carpeted stairs in this area during the Van Anda occupancy. Over the years the urn finial on the staircase railing was lost, and the original door leading into the service wing was replaced with a modern one.

Second Floor (Bedroom Floor)

HALL

An interior hallway approximately 59 feet long runs from the upper stairs at the south end to the door of Edith Wharton's bedroom suite on the north end of the building. To the west, doors lead to the west guest room, small guest room, and one guest bath; on the east are the entrances to the east guest room, Teddy Wharton's room and bathroom, and a service door into Teddy's dressing room. A simple door at the south end of the hallway provides access to the service wing.

In keeping with Edith's precept that the hall was primarily a passageway,[1] the decorative treatment is simple. Clear and vigorous first impressions were most important and best realized by "the use of severe strongly-marked panelling"[2] on the walls. The wall moldings here conform rather closely to the "architectural effect" obtained in "small houses, where an expensive decoration is out of the question... [i.e.] a few plain moldings fixed to the plaster."[3]

There is a classic revival-style wooden arch with a central keystone over the termination of the stairs; a matching one is located about 12 feet north near the doors to Teddy's room. A small, simple arch just north of Teddy's bedroom door concealed chimney flues in the walls and gave the impression of a narrowing effect as the door to Edith's suite is approached.

Codman's original plans for the bedroom area showed a circular glass floor in the attic to allow natural light from the cupola to enter the hallway below. This feature, which would have resulted in less privacy on the bedroom floor

FIG. 66 *Second-story plan, Hoppin & Koen, 1901. The arrangement of Edith's bedroom suite (especially the closet and bathroom) was reworked extensively before actual construction.* (AAFAL)

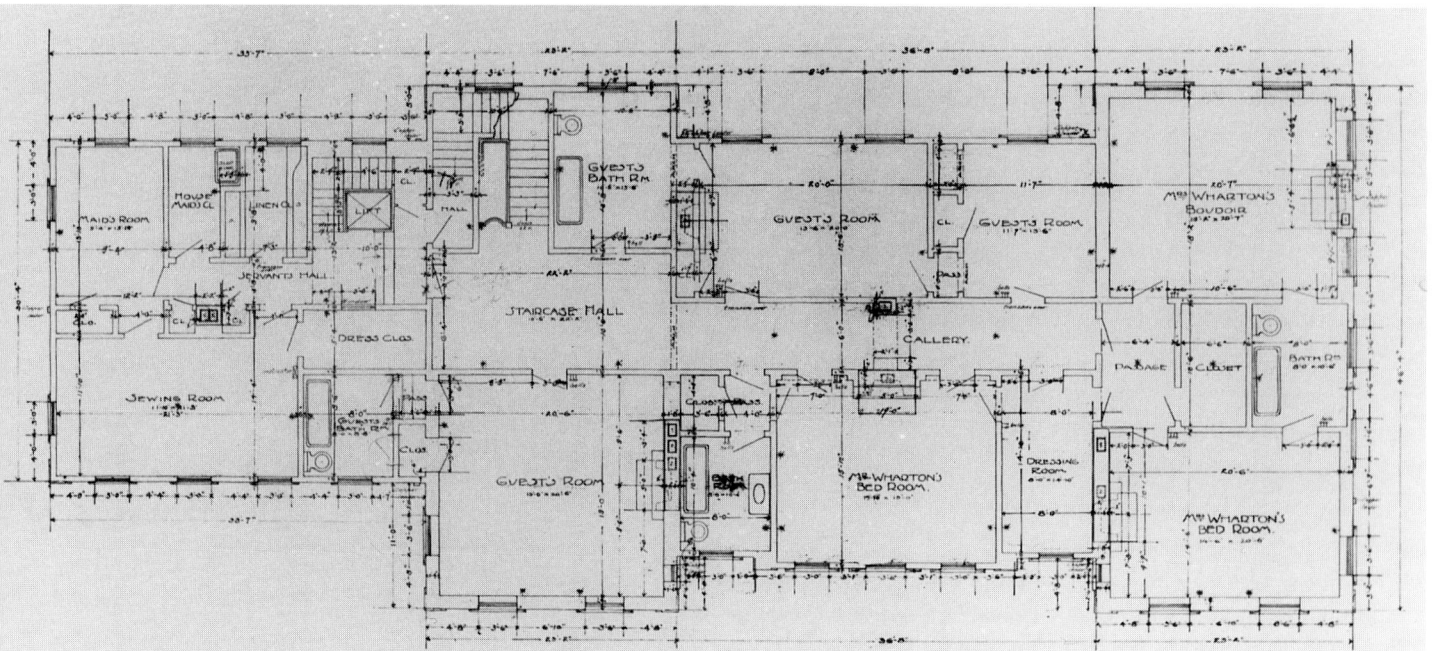

(the servants' rooms were directly overhead), apparently displeased Edith in the earliest stages of house design; it was crossed out with an "X." As executed, the only natural illumination for the hall came from the two windows on the west wall of the stair hall, both of which are bisected by staircases. The Hoppin & Koen floor plan allowed for two ceiling light fixtures[4]; there is no evidence that two wall fixtures specified for the head of the stairs on either side of the door to the east guest room were ever installed. The 1901 floor plan also called for transom windows over the west guest room, small guest room, and guest bath that would have transmitted more light into the hall, but they were not executed.

The hallway is divided into two distinct areas: the staircase hall at the head of the stairs (a rectangular area 22 feet long by 10 feet 6 inches wide) and the narrow gallery onto which the majority of rooms open. No photograph or written documentation about these areas has been located. Since Edith believed that "the hall is not a living-room, but a thoroughfare,"[5] it seems reasonable to assume that there was very little furniture, if any, in the narrower section. However, the staircase hall may well have been furnished with "benches or straight-backed chairs, and marble-topped tables and consoles,"[6] as well as an architectural press "like the old French and Italian *armoires* ... and surmounted with a vase or bust in the centre,"[7] as recommended in *The Decoration of Houses*. The floor is of simple pine planks. If the hall had a carpet, it would most likely have been of "one color, matching that on the stairs."[8]

There would have been some pictures or prints hanging in both parts of the hall. These were probably "few in number, and decorative in composition and coloring. No subject requiring thought and study is suitable in such a position. The mythological or architectural compositions of the Italian and French schools of the last two centuries, with their superficial graces of color and design, are for this reason well suited to the walls of halls and antechambers."[9]

Two photographs of the hall and staircase hall at Land's End may indicate how these

areas at The Mount were treated. A similar strong, simple wall molding is evident, as is a carpet. Only a clock and sconces adorned the walls. The furnishings included a table, straight-backed chairs, and a sofa.[10]

During the Foxhollow School years, two major changes were made to the bedroom-floor hallway. A door was installed[11] at the head of the stairs, and the arch was closed with a plasterboard wall, probably to meet fire-code requirements and to separate the main floor, which was occasionally used for receptions, from the dormitory areas. Additionally, three low, wooden, built-in dressers were added for linens and blankets. These were removed in 1989. The plasterboard wall was taken down in 1990, and the bedroom-floor hallway was painted a shade of blue, believed to have been the original color.

Edith Wharton's Suite

With the completion of The Mount, Edith had a private suite of rooms, which occupied the north end of the bedroom floor.[12] She and Teddy had had separate bedrooms at Land's

FIG. 67 *Edith Wharton, 1905. She sent this photograph to Henry James, who replied: "I must thank you very kindly, with no delay, for the so handsome photograph in which you baissez les yeux so modestly before the acclamations of the world. They are all transcribed for you..., I surely make out, in that compendium you are reading; so that you look thoroughly in possession of your genius, fame & fortune... I take it gratefully...& place it ever so conspicuously among the quaint tributes already beginning to cluster on my mantel shelf" (HJ to EW, December 18, 1905).* (LL)

95

End since the early 1890s.[13] Both suffered from bouts of sleeplessness, nervous irritability, and undiagnosable nauseas and fatigues,[14] making shared quarters undesirable. In addition, they maintained very different schedules. Edith wrote in bed every morning until 11 o'clock or so, seeking privacy for her creative activities; Teddy, an active man who enjoyed hunting, fishing, horseback riding, and golfing and saw to all the household errands and needs, was probably an early riser whose morning ablutions and conversations would have made writing and serious thought impossible.

Edith's suite followed almost exactly the precept laid forth in *The Decoration of Houses* that

of the various ways in which a bedroom may be planned, none is so luxurious and practical as the French method of subdividing it into a suite composed of two or more small rooms. Where space is not restricted there should in fact be four rooms, preceded by an antechamber separating the suite from the main corridor of the house. The small sitting-room or boudoir opens into this antechamber; and next comes the bedroom, beyond which are the dressing and bathrooms.[15]

Codman's original 1901 pencil drawings of a floor plan for The Mount did not have the important antechamber so carefully prescribed in *The Decoration of Houses*.[16] Although the placement of the boudoir and bedroom on the floor plan by Hoppin & Koen corresponds relatively closely to what was built, the antechamber was to open into a large walk-in closet instead of the present bathroom. The plans placed the bathroom on the other side of this closet; the bath was to have entrances from both the boudoir and the bedroom. Although the Hoppin & Koen design adhered more closely in spirit to the dictum in *The Decoration of Houses*, it appears clumsy: the bathroom window was off-center, and the bathroom wall would have bisected one of the two windows on the north wall of the bedroom.

It is easy to see why Edith altered this arrangement by having the closet removed entirely[17] and reoriented the bathroom to have only one door opening into the antechamber. The redesign corrected the window problems and gave more privacy to the small bathroom, which, with a door on either end, would have seemed like a passageway. Correspondingly, Edith's bedroom was enlarged to the size of the adjoining boudoir.

EDITH WHARTON'S BEDROOM

Edith Wharton's bedroom, measuring approximately 17 feet by 20 feet 6 inches in plan, is a very simple room. The plaster walls were originally painted white and are ornamented with only a heavy plaster cornice, the same one found in the hallway and other bedrooms. The floor of the bedroom and boudoir is a simple wooden parquet. The major ornament of the bedroom is a marble mantel of a rare French gray-and-black marble called *melange*.[18] Two full windows on the north wall overlook the terrace and rock garden in the foreground, the flower garden in the mid-distance, and the woods beyond. Two full windows on the east wall provide a view to the terrace and parterres, the meadow and pond, and the distant Laurel Lake and Tyringham mountains. All four windows are slightly recessed with rectangular panels beneath moldings. To the right of the entry a door leads into a dressing room connecting Edith's and Teddy's bedrooms. Also to the right of the door are three mother-of-pearl service bells[19] and a light switch. The room is lit by four sconces, two between the windows on the east wall and two on the west wall spaced far apart, perhaps to accommodate a bedstead.

No photograph or other documentation concerning the furnishings or decorative scheme has been located. From *The Decoration of Houses* it may be surmised that the room may have contained "only the bedstead and its accessories."[20] Edith probably followed her dictates that the "old fashion of painted walls and bare floors naturally commends itself"[21] over unnecessarily elaborate schemes of "heavy window-draperies and tufted furniture,"[22] which she deemed unhealthful. The key to proper bedrooms was, she believed, simplicity: "there is no reason for decorating them in an elaborate manner; and however magnificent the other apartments, it is evident that in this part of the house simplicity is most fitting."[23]

Interestingly, descriptions of Edith's bedrooms in France, by her friend Gaillard Lapsley, revealed that they were decorated and furnished in the same manner; the "scene itself changed only in detail."[24] Each had a "three quarter modern wooden bed painted in some light shade, and flanked by night tables charged with telephone, travelling clock, reading light and such like… I remember her blankets were always rose colour and her sheets of sheer linen."[25]

It seems a reasonable supposition that Edith's bed at The Mount faced the two east windows in order to receive the morning light. Edith, on reaching Berlin during a trip through Germany with Bernard Berenson in 1913, had

a minor fit of hysterics because the bed in her hotel room was not properly situated; not until it had been moved to face the window did she settle down… Berenson thought this an absurd performance; but because Edith never harped upon the physical requirements of her literary life, he did not quite realize that she worked in bed every morning and therefore needed a bed which faced the light. It had been her practice for more than twenty years…and the need was serious one.[26]

Few ever observed Edith working in bed,[27] yet Lapsley has left a vivid impression of an evening encounter that may well describe her writing process:

The room in half darkness and a log smoldering on the little hearth and Edith herself sitting up in bed… she was thinly covered for she had a remarkable circulation and the room was always warm but adequately ventilated. She used to wear a loose silk sacque with short loose sleeves, open at the neck and trimmed with lace and on her head a cap of the same material also trimmed with lace which fell about her brow and ears like the edging of a lamp shade. Her head was large and her hair thick and abundant and as the cap was made generously it was of a size that would have swamped most people's features but Edith's mask only stood out more sculpturally beneath it.

She would have her writing board perilously furnished with an ink-pot on her knee, the dog of the moment under her left elbow and the bed strewn with correspondence, newspapers and books.[28]

Edith dropped the manuscript pages to the floor where her secretary retrieved them and took

them off to be typed for a later proofreading.[29]

Many of the final scenes of Edith's and Teddy's unhappy marriage were played out during July and August 1911 behind the closed doors of her bedroom, away from the servants.[30] On July 24 Edith "dispatched a letter from her bedroom to that of her husband."[31] Although this was a distance of less than 10 feet, it was a psychological gulf that was only to widen until their divorce two years later.

BATHROOM

Edith's bathroom, located between her bedroom and boudoir, opened into the small antechamber making it accessible to the servants, who could draw the bathwater and lay out towels without having to enter her private rooms.[32]

The bathroom measures 7 feet 3 inches wide by 14 feet in plan. The original color of the plain plaster walls is unknown. The floor consists of white marble tiles quarried nearby at Lee, Massachusetts. The room contained a sink, pull-chain commode, and an enamel bathtub with four ceramic feet.

The Decoration of Houses contains only a little information concerning bathrooms. Edith and Codman advocated good design that considered the "harmony of parts,"[33] no matter how costly the materials used in a bathroom, including "precious marbles."[34] They recommended marble because it "gives opportunity for fine architectural effects,"[35] and it is waterproof.[36] A "detached enamel or porcelain bath"[37] was preferred over a built-in metal one.

Edith and Codman complained that the "chief fault of the American bath-room is that, however splendid the materials used, the treatment is seldom architectural."[38] An illustration of a magnificent, late-eighteenth-century bathroom in the Pitti Palace in Florence exemplified how great an effect could be achieved in a very small space. Edith's own bathroom at The Mount was even smaller than this example and appears to have been more functional than decorative or architectural.

The original sink has been removed, as was the pull-chain toilet, leaving only the enamel bathtub, which has had a shower ring added. During the Foxhollow School era, a new staircase was built to provide a second means of egress from the attic. These stairs were dropped into the bathroom from a small servant's room above and exited into the antechamber, compromising the bathroom design.[39]

There is little documentation regarding Edith's bathroom during her occupancy at The Mount, except a 1909 letter to a friend in England in which Edith asked for a "wonderful 'Rose Dentrifice'"[40] from her favorite store, Floris, on Jermyn Street in London.

BOUDOIR

Edith's boudoir, measuring approximately 18 feet by 20 feet in plan, is situated at the northwest corner of the bedroom floor. It adjoins the bedroom and bath[41] and opens to the small antechamber. Two windows facing north afford views of the rock garden, flower garden, the drive to the stable, and the woods beyond. Two windows on the west wall fill the room with afternoon light.

Edith and Codman had a great deal to say about the decoration and the use of a boudoir in *The Decoration of Houses*: "as the boudoir is generally a small room," they wrote, "it is peculiarly suited to the more delicate styles of painting or stucco ornamentation... No detail is wasted, and all manner of delicate effects in wood-carving, marquetry, and other ornamentation [i.e. at The Mount, plaster ornamentation], such as would be lost upon the walls and furniture of a larger room, here acquire their full value."[42] Edith's boudoir, the best documented room on the bedroom floor, followed these ideas closely in design, decoration, and use.

Codman's elevations of the boudoir, recently discovered and now in the collection of Edith Wharton Restoration, reveal that the construction of the room followed his proposal very closely with two interesting exceptions: on the west wall, two slender paintings flanking each of the two windows were replaced by wall panels with circle motifs; three paintings were set into the east wall in place of the two Codman suggested.

FIG. 68 *Elevation for the south wall of Edith Wharton's boudoir, Ogden Codman, Jr., c. 1901.* (EWR)

The boudoir, the most elaborate room on this floor, is dominated by eight paintings of flower arrangements set into the walls. The four windows are recessed and have rectangular panels underneath. There are panels both above and below the paintings, and a low chair-rail surrounds the room. At the center of each wall, just below the cornice, is a medallion with festoons of fruits and flowers executed in plaster. Each corner contains panels and circles. The cornice is decorated in a classical design of modified acanthus leaves. The floor is parquet, matching the adjoining bedroom.

The north wall of the room features a mantel of French *rouge* marble in red and cream. Two mirrors are set into the walls, one over the fireplace mantel, the other across the room. The mirrors may have reflected the firelight across the boudoir.[43]

Although Edith and Codman asserted that the boudoir "is the room in which small objects of art—prints, mezzotints and *gouaches*—show to the best advantage,"[44] the eight paintings in the room were clearly conceived to be part of the wall decor and are representative of a general precept described fully in *The Decoration of Houses*:

Pictures and prints should be fastened to the wall, not hung by a cord or wire, nor allowed to tilt forward at an angle. The latter arrangement is especially disturbing since it throws the picture-frames out of the line of the wall. It must never be forgotten that pictures on a wall, whether set in the panels or merely framed and hung, inevitably become a part of the wall-decoration. In the seventeenth and eighteenth centuries, in rooms of any importance, pictures were always treated as a part of the decoration, and frequently as panels sunk in the wall in a setting of carved wood or stucco moldings. Even when not set in panels, they were always fixed to the wall, and their frames, whether of wood or stucco, were made to correspond with the ornamental detail of the rest of the room.[45]

The eight paintings are still lifes in oil on stretched canvas in the seventeenth-century Dutch manner and may have been executed by nineteenth-century American artists.[46] Six of the paintings are vertical, two are horizontal. The two horizontal paintings, located over the north mantel and on the south wall, have more elaborate frames than the six vertical ones.

Two mother-of-pearl call-bells are located to the right of the boudoir door.[47] Directly below is an original light switch; there are no sconces in the room. The 1901 Hoppin & Koen floor plan called for four electric sconces — two on either side of the fireplace and two more flanking the mirror on the south wall. The heat register, with its original grate, is directly below the light switch.

The original colors of the walls, the plaster ornamentation, and trim, have not been determined.

There is just one known historical photograph of the boudoir; it dates from c. 1905 and is labeled on the back in Edith's handwriting "My sitting-room at The Mount."[48] The photograph shows that she followed her dictate that the boudoir was "really a small private sitting-room for the lady of the house, corresponding with her husband's 'den',"[49] a location for both "work and repose."[50] The modern boudoir, she explained, was often "for the prosaic purpose of interviewing servants, going over accounts and similar occupations."[51] Here Edith planned menus and met with her housekeeper, did correspondence, and worked with her secretary. As a private sitting room, the boudoir rather than her bedroom probably served as the place for discussions with Teddy.

FIG. 69 *Edith Wharton's boudoir, north wall and northeast corner, during her occupancy (compare to Fig. 149; see also Fig. 11). A dog bowl is to the right of the fireplace. Photographs on the mantel include Walter Berry and Teddy Wharton.* (BL)

The furnishings of a boudoir generally included "a writing desk, with pigeon-holes, drawers, and cupboards, and a comfortable lounge or *lit de repos*, for resting and reading."[52] The Wharton-period photograph shows that a *lit de repos* (a day bed) occupied the northwest corner near the fireplace, while a French-style desk was located near the center of the room in front of the fireplace. *The Decoration of Houses* also stated that a boudoir should contain "one or two comfortable arm-chairs."[53] A French sofa was located in the northeast corner near the fireplace. The photograph also shows the edge of a table or chest directly behind the desk chair.

The surface of the desk revealed the following items: a blotter, letter box or stand, ink stand, and a tall vase with flowers. The objects on the mantel were prominent features in the decor. The most arresting piece was an elaborate French-style clock placed in the center against the mirror. Three photographs were located beside the clock. One was of Walter Berry, and another depicted Teddy with three of the family dogs, c. 1898.[54]

A low firescreen and several fire tools are evidence of an active fireplace in this room. A small bowl, perhaps water for the dogs, sat between the fireplace and the sofa. A patterned carpet with a dark border covered most of the floor.

The fireback, still intact, is one of the more elaborate in the house and has a compelling tableau in which a shepherd, with his pipes hanging from his back, is attempting to save his sheep from large birds of prey. He reaches for a bird that has sunk its claws into a sheep as a second bird flies away with another sheep. The side panels have circles containing floral imagery and tracery. Possibly the subject matter is a fairy tale; it seems to be mythological in origin. A vivid and violent scene, it is a startling contrast to the floral wall paintings.

Edith transferred the furnishings and draperies from her boudoir at Land's End. In *The Decoration of Houses* Edith and Codman advised using washable materials, preferably linens or cottons, for draperies in the bedroom suite rather than traditional heavy velvets and brocades. Chintz and *toiles de Jouy* hangings were also recommended.[55] The authors felt that if "the walls are without pattern, a figured chintz may be chosen for the curtains and furniture."[56] The walls of Edith's boudoir, though paneled and decorated with wall paintings, were otherwise without pattern, and the photograph clearly shows that a figured fabric was used for the curtains and much of the furniture. Her desk chair and the corner sofa had the same fabric as the draperies, although the furniture appears to have had upholstery rather than slip covers, as had been advised in the book.

The curtains were hung from large wooden rings attached to wooden poles, similar to the arrangement in the library.[57] These were clearly curtains that could be closed "to exclude light and cold."[58] As recommended in *The Decoration of Houses*, Edith's boudoir was "a simple room, gay and graceful in decoration, but as a rule neither rich nor elaborate."[59]

Edith Wharton's suite continued to be used from 1911-42, first by Mrs. Shattuck and then by Mrs. Van Anda.[60] After 1942 both the boudoir and the bedroom were used as dormitory spaces by the Foxhollow School. Like other rooms on this floor, the boudoir was painted green by the school. The room was repainted in shades of pink by Shakespeare & Company in 1979-80. Since 1978 the bedroom suite has been used by the theater group as a dormitory and occasionally as dressing rooms, guest rooms, and office space. Edith Wharton Restoration plans to restore her bedroom suite to the time of her occupancy.

Teddy Wharton's Suite

BEDROOM

Teddy Wharton's bedroom, in the center of the main part of the mansion over the drawing room, commands a fine view of the gardens, pond, lake, and mountains. Measuring 19 feet long by 15 feet 10 inches wide,[61] it could have space for only "the bedstead and its accessories,"[62] as recommended by *The Decoration of Houses*. Codman's c. 1901 sketch of the bedroom floor plan indicates that while Edith's suite and the two guest rooms would have boudoirs, Teddy would not have a sitting room adjacent to his bedroom.

The room is entered on the west side[63]; directly opposite are three windows filling the east wall. A magnificent mantelpiece of *Negro Marquina* marble (a black-and-white Spanish marble, the only one in the house) is located in the center of the west wall. Next to the entrance are two call-bells,[64] one marked "House Maid."

The original color of Teddy's room is unknown. Unlike Edith's suite, which had parquet floors, this floor is of simple pine.[65]

Although Teddy's room was conceived by the original owners and architects as the master suite, its small size made it less attractive to other male occupants. It is believed that both Albert R. Shattuck and Carr Van Anda used the east guest room instead.[66] The Foxhollow School used Teddy's room as dormitory space for approximately thirty years.

Teddy's bedroom is probably in worse condition than any other bedroom. The settling of the terrazzo floors in the drawing room below resulted in shifting of the walls, doors, and floors. Two bathrooms were located above the bedroom, and leaking water has caused considerable damage.[67] During the summer of 1985, approximately 8 feet of the plaster cornice collapsed.

Beginning in 1978, Teddy's room served as a dormitory for the theater group. During the summer of 1988 it became a dressing room; in the spring of 1994 it was used as a meeting room by Shakespeare & Company.

BATHROOM

The arrangement of Teddy's suite, though far smaller than Edith's, still corresponded in spirit to the recommendation in *The Decoration of Houses* for a "French suite," in which spaces are arranged around the bathroom, where there are "two means of entrance from the main corridor: one for the use of the occupant..., the other opening into the bath-room, to give access to the servants"[68] and also allowing "greater privacy"[69] for the occupant. A small

antechamber connects the bedroom to the bathroom and contains a closet.

The original color of Teddy's bathroom is unknown. The plaster walls are plain, and the same white marble tile floor found in the other bathrooms in the house is still intact.

The room retains its original enamel bathtub and a wide, gray marble-top sink set on decorative legs.[70] The original paneled ceiling also appears to be in place. The tall mirror over the sink, set within a 6-foot-high wooden frame ornamented with carved festoons and stylized acanthus leaves, also survives. The large window in the center of the east wall provides natural light.

DRESSING ROOM

A dressing room, measuring approximately 8 feet by 15 feet, connects Edith's suite to Teddy's bedroom. There were two bells on the south wall to summon the staff. The indicator in the servants' hall one floor below identifies the room as "Mr. Wharton's Dressing Room."[71]

No built-in furniture or cabinets were indicated on the Hoppin & Koen floor plan. *The Decoration of Houses* recommended that the items necessary for "a well-appointed dressing room are the toilet-table, wash-stand, clothes-press and cheval-glass, with the addition, if space permits, of one or two commodes or chiffonniers."[72] Readers were advised to avoid modern furniture in the dressing room, using instead "simple, admirably composed commodes and clothes-presses of the eighteenth-century bedroom."[73] The dressing room would have been one of the most private spaces of any large house.

GUEST ROOMS

Codman's original 1901 floor plans for The Mount called for three guest rooms; two were to have adjoining boudoirs.[74] The 1901-02 Hoppin & Koen plan called for two guest rooms, one of which comprised a suite of two rooms; each guest room had a bathroom. Although the rooms were labeled as guest rooms on the floor plan, the one over the dining room was known to the Whartons as the east guest room.[75] The guest suite across the hallway was called the west guest room and the small guest room by the Whartons.

There are no historic photographs of these rooms and little documentation. One guest, Mrs. Gordon Bell, recalled that "the first time" Edith "showed me my room I remember saying to her, 'What a perfect desk — everything conceivably needed for writing is there'; and I can see her little deprecating smile as she answered, 'Oh, I am rather a housekeeperish person.'"[76] Percy Lubbock summed up the visitor's experience in saying "nobody could deny that to be a guest in a house of Mrs. Wharton's was a deeply, deliciously delicately luxurious experience."[77]

EAST GUEST ROOM

Measuring 19 feet by 20 feet 6 inches in plan, the east guest room is the largest room on this floor. The unornamented plaster walls were originally painted cream, the woodwork and trim were white, and the floor is pine. An elaborate mantelpiece of French *rouge* marble with three black insets on the hearth is located on the north wall. The east wall has two recessed windows that overlook the grass terraces, lime walk, meadow, lakes, and the distant mountains. On the south wall is one window looking down to the walled Italian garden and a door to the bathroom. The Hoppin & Koen floor plan originally called for a narrow window on the north wall adjacent to the fireplace; it balanced a similar window in Edith's bedroom in the north wing. Neither window was realized.[78]

Two original sconces, matching those in Edith's and Teddy's rooms, are located between the two east windows. To the left of the entry are two mother-of-pearl call-bells[79]; one is labeled "Lady's Maid" and the other "Svt's Hall." An original heat grate, which supplemented the fireplace, is located adjacent to it on the north wall. The room is missing its original plaster cornice.

Subsequent owners used the east guest room as the master bedroom.[80] During the Foxhollow School years, the room served as a dormitory for three or four students each year. During this period, the room was painted green. When a

fire escape was built on the east facade, a small flight of wooden steps was added beneath the window in the northwest corner.

Shakespeare & Company used this room as dormitory from 1978-86. The room and the adjoining bathroom were repainted in original colors and used as an apartment and office by Edith Wharton Restoration from 1986-88. In 1988 the room was again used by Shakespeare & Company as an office.

Since 1978, when Shakespeare & Company began to give tours of The Mount to the general public, the east guest room has been known as the Henry James room. While there is no documentation to support this, Edith probably assigned it to James, her most prominent guest, since it is a large room and has fine garden views.

BATHROOM FOR THE
EAST GUEST ROOM

This bathroom is actually located in the service wing. Because the top floor of the service wing is 2 feet lower than the bedrooms, there are two steps down to the bathroom. The steps are located in a small passageway, which retains its original cornice.

The bathroom, measuring 8 feet by 8 feet 6 inches in plan, is the smallest of the four bathrooms for owners and guests on this floor and is the only one that does not have the two entrances recommended in *The Decoration of Houses*. Apparently the Whartons sought to correct this; two schemes for an additional door were presented in 1907 proposals, but neither was carried out. The bathroom became even more cramped when the original design for the door to a closet in the east guest room was relocated to open into the bathroom, rather than into the bedroom.[81]

The room has the same white marble floor tiles as the other bathrooms. A call-bell is located on the door frame to the left of the entry. Adjacent, on the wall, is the only light fixture.[82] One large window faces east. A simple wood-paneled ceiling remains intact.

Although the original pull-chain toilet has been removed, the original enamel bathtub and porcelain sink remain. The pedestal sink was manufactured by the Meyer-Sniffen Company and patented on November 4, 1902.[83] This date suggests that the guest rooms were not ready until the summer of 1903.

WEST GUEST SUITE

The west guest suite consisted of two connecting rooms. The larger, the west guest room, measures 13 feet 6 inches by 20 feet; the small bedroom adjoining it on the north measures 13 feet 6 inches by 11 feet 7 inches.[84] The west guest room opens on the south into a large bathroom.

It is unclear how this particular guest suite functioned. Only the west guest room contains a fireplace. It may have been a bedroom and smaller sitting room, or both may have been bedrooms. The 1901 Hoppin & Koen floor plan labels each room as "Guest's Room."

The Foxhollow School removed the door between the two rooms and erected a solid wall, making two completely separate spaces, each with an original entrance into the main hallway. The rooms served as dormitory spaces. After 1978 Shakespeare & Company used the rooms as dormitories and as offices.

WEST GUEST ROOM

This room has two windows on the west wall. Between them are two original electric sconces, shown on the Hoppin & Koen floor plan. A third fixture for the room, adjacent to the door connecting the two rooms, was either never installed or removed, possibly when the door was walled up.

Two bells to summon the staff[85] are located on the left of the entry-door frame, and an original light switch is adjacent to the bells. The south wall has a fireplace of gray Italian *baridiglio* marble with three grayish-white insets on the hearth. To the left of the fireplace is a closet; to the right is a door leading into the bathroom. The floor is of pine. The original wall color is unknown.

SMALL BEDROOM

This smaller room has a separate entrance to the hallway, probably for the use of servants, in the spirit of the French method of dividing a suite, as described in *The Decoration of Houses*.

Two call-bells[86] and a light fixture are located to the left of the entry from the hallway. Two other light fixtures on the north and west walls either were eliminated or have been removed. There is one window on the west wall.

As in the larger room, the major feature is found on the south wall; here, it is a center closet flanked by two arches. The arch on the east opened into the west guest room; it matches an arch between the west guest room and its bathroom. Within the arch on the west is a built-in cabinet with a marble countertop and surrounds, apparently the only such piece in the house. The floor is pine. The original wall color of the small bedroom is unknown.

BATHROOM FOR THE
WEST GUEST ROOM

Curiously, this is the largest bathroom in the house; at 13 feet 8 inches by 10 feet 6 inches it is larger than Teddy's dressing room or the room for Edith's maid. The bathroom is set within one of the wings; the stairs to this floor and those to the attic are adjacent.

The bathtub and toilet are shown on the Hoppin & Koen 1901 plan; both remain in place, although the original pull-chain toilet was removed many years ago. The sink, not shown on the plan, was located to the west of the arch. The original sink has been removed.

One large window is located on the center of the west wall. There is an electric light fixture on the wall next to the sink; a fixture above the bathtub was either not executed or removed. As in almost all the bathrooms in the house, the floor consists of grayish-white marble tiles. The original wall color is unknown.

The large, built-in, wooden wardrobe now to the north of the door into the main hallway may be original to another area of the mansion, or it may have been brought in from another building since it is stylistically different. A single, unlabeled call-bell is located to the north of the door.

Service Areas

R. W. B. Lewis, in *Edith Wharton: A Biography*, notes that the Whartons "had a great deal of well-organized help"[1] at The Mount. Indeed, given a house of this size, a conspicuously comfortable and luxurious lifestyle, and the steady stream of house guests, a large, attentive, and well-trained staff was a necessity. However, Edith and Codman had nothing to say about service areas in *The Decoration of Houses*.

Lewis explains that Catharine Gross, the housekeeper, and Alfred White, the butler, "divided the general running of the household."[2] Gross had been with Edith since a year before her marriage, and White had joined the Wharton staff soon thereafter in 1888.[3] Under their supervision were housemaids, a footman, a cook, and possibly a laundress and a scullery maid.[4]

Anna Bahlmann, another "indispensable member of Edith's household,"[5] had tutored Edith as a child and in 1904 had become her secretary and "literary assistant."[6] Although Anna was usually at the Wharton home on Park Avenue in New York City, she may have figured occasionally among the staff in Lenox. The

staff also included Thomas Reynolds, the estate superintendent and head gardener, who lived in the gatehouse; William Parlett, the coachman, who lived with his family above the stable; and Charles Cook, the chauffeur, who lived nearby in Lee. There were assistant gardeners, grooms, farm workers, and general laborers, all of whom most likely lived locally, and at least some of whom were employed seasonally.[7]

The problems of keeping a large and well-trained staff were both numerous and constant. In 1904 Edith wrote to her friend Sara Norton: "We had planned to stay in England till nearly the end of June, but I have just heard that *none* of the servants I had are coming back, & to get a household together we shall probably have to sail in about four weeks."[8]

Edith and Teddy generally took their key staff with them on their frequent trips. For example, on one European sojourn in 1907 the Whartons were accompanied by six servants (and two dogs). The traveling staff included Gross, White, Edith's personal maid, a valet for Teddy (possibly White), Charles Cook, sometimes Anna Bahlmann, and possibly a cook.

There was genuine devotion between the Whartons and their staff. One of Edith's friends remembered that

there was real consideration too for the servants and those employed on the place... neither when they [Edith and Teddy] were alone nor when there were visitors at The Mount was any servant required to do more than necessary duty on Sundays or holidays. I once said to Edith, "You are the most considerate person to your servants I ever saw." She replied rather seriously, "Perhaps that is because I was brought up in a household where there was no consideration for them at all." Kindness and helpfulness to those less fortunately placed than themselves were traits that both Edith and Teddy shared equally...[9]

Another friend left a vivid portrait of Edith and Alfred White, the butler:

White was the only one...who stood on an equal moral footing with her. He was Teddy's servant as much as hers and he ruled her household and kept it running smoothly as Gross did after him but he always treated her with a frank though respectful severity which so far

FIG. 70 *Catharine Gross, Edith Wharton's housekeeper from 1884-1933, with Edith's dogs in the Pavillon Colombe gardens. The photograph was probably taken by Edith.* (BL)

from resenting she relied upon. She knew that he was competent where she was not and she had good reason to trust his sound sense and devotion.[10]

As for Edith's four major servants (Cook, White, Gross, and Elise—a later lady's maid), Gaillard Lapsley explained that "with each one she had a human relation deeply rooted in a common experience or understanding and her own respect for the efficiency with which they discharged their several offices and with each there was a personal congeniality that made superficial intercourse easy and comfortable."[11]

Bernard Berenson noted that Edith "was a wonderful housekeeper and understood how to get the best work from her chef and from all her servants."[12]

Staff facilities at The Mount were housed on the three floors of the south service wing and the attic floor of the main house. The laundry room, scullery, wine closet, and a storeroom were located under the terrace.

GROUND FLOOR, SERVICE WING

The ground floor of the service wing contained the kitchen, servants' dining room, scullery and serving area, laundry room, storage space and trunk room, wine closet, lamp room, two servants' toilets, and a large furnace and coal cellar. Most of these rooms opened into a T-shaped servants' hall.

Codman's original drawings for this floor envisioned a smaller service area than the one that was built. He allowed for an L-shaped corridor with the kitchen, scullery, two closets, elevator, and a servants' lavatory on one side of the "L." Opposite were the servants' hall, which doubled as the servants' dining room, cellar, and a coal-storage room. A curving servants' piazza on the east would have overlooked the gardens and afforded the same view enjoyed by the owners.

Vestiges of Codman's original ideas are found in the 1901 Hoppin & Koen plans. Whereas Codman placed the service functions on the north end of the building, Hoppin &

FIG. 71 *The west elevation, service wing, and service porch, c. late 1960s. The forecourt wall, between the courtyard and the service yard, was opened in the mid-to-late 1960s by the Foxhollow School. The piers on the service porch were originally round columns (see Fig. 96).* (FHS)

105

Koen placed them on the south end and in a separate wing. The piazza was transformed into a servants' porch and entrance on the west; the kitchen and scullery were relocated to the east side. The extension of the wing and the new design of the terrace allowed for the addition of the lamp room, laundry room, and other facilities.

The servants' entrance leads directly into a hall and then to the service stairs and service elevator. The stairs begin to the north of the elevator and encircle the elevator cage as they ascend for another two floors. Built of wood and anchored onto the elevator cage, the stairs have a light honey-colored wainscoting approximately 4 feet high. Like the adjacent main stairs, the servants' stairs run across several windows.

The hydraulic elevator was manufactured c. 1901 by the Otis Elevator Company. Water from the main entered an outside casing that contained a piston. When water was pumped into the casing, the pressure forced the piston to rise, which in turn forced the elevator to rise. As the water was let out, the elevator would descend.

The elevator stopped on the main floor and terminated on the bedroom floor. Most likely it carried trunks and luggage, as well as servants with breakfast trays and household equipment.[13] It had a capacity of six hundred pounds. There is a brass flower-shaped light fixture on the ceiling while the front has a sliding gate, and the back of the cab has a large window of opaque wire-reinforced glass. The sides are plain. The roof of the cab, which has a small trap door, is set about 2 inches above the wall, presumably to allow for more illumination.

Behind the elevator and underneath the stairs is a tiny room containing only a toilet for servants. A narrow window provides ventilation and some illumination. The floor is of white marble tiles. The toilet has been removed; it is now a closet.

On the south wall of the hall was the indicator, which rang to summon the staff. It was located next to the servants' dining room and the kitchen. This indicator is not extant.

Also located in the servants' hall was a large built-in refrigerator or ice box, with six compartments.[14]

The original Hoppin & Koen floor plan indicates only one light fixture in this area on the wall next to the indicator-box. A surviving light fixture, which appears to be original, is, however, on the south wall opposite the door into the kitchen. The hall now has a ceiling fixture, which dates from the Foxhollow School years.

The hall floor was most likely the same as that in the connecting back servants' passage, which is of concrete scored to resemble tiles. Currently the area by the servants' entrance has a covering of linoleum tiles. Like the stairs, the service passageways have wainscoting, with plaster walls above. The original color of the walls is not known.

The most significant alteration to this area occurred during the Foxhollow School years, when a new door and a plasterboard wall were installed at the foot of the servants' stairs. This new wall partitions off the elevator, servants' stairs, kitchen, and old servants' dining room from the long servants' passage, lamp room, furnace room, and laundry room. Although probably intended to buffer the furnaces and thermostats from the back door, the new wall destroys the open feeling of the servants' hall and makes the passageway to the laundry gloomy.

SERVANTS' DINING ROOM

A simple room measuring 12 feet 6 inches by 20 feet 4 inches in plan, the servants' dining room, probably also doubled as a sitting room. There are three windows on the west wall and one facing south. One ceiling fixture provided light. Most likely the room would have been furnished with a long table, a number of straight-backed chairs, and a clock.

Here the servants would have had their meals, as well as afternoon tea. In her 1904 short story, "The Lady's Maid's Bell," Edith wrote that "the servants'-hall tea was at six."[15]

Like most of the adjoining rooms and passageways, the room has the same 4-foot-high wainscoting. The original color of the plaster walls above is not known. The floor is of rift pine.

By 1940, when the kitchen had been moved to the main floor, the servants' dining room was moved upstairs adjacent to the kitchen. The 1940 plan labeled the abandoned space "Old Dining Room for Help."

Since 1978 Shakespeare & Company has used this room as a dressing room in summer and for storage in the winter. The company's box office operated out of the northwest corner, with the addition of a partition, until 1988, when it was moved to a trailer adjacent to the stable. The room now has a tile ceiling, linoleum floor, and paint on the wainscoting.

KITCHEN

The kitchen, 13 feet 8 inches by 20 feet 4 inches in plan, is only slightly larger than the adjoining servants' dining room. There are three doors, which open into the servants' dining room, the hall, and to the scullery.

The central feature of the room is a large, built-in range of white encaustic tiles, located on the west wall. A sink with wooden drainboards and built-in cabinet and counter occupied most of the east wall. There are two windows on the east wall and two on the south wall. A ceiling light fixture and a wall fixture were called for in the original design.[16]

The floor is of rift pine, and the walls have 4-foot-high wainscoting with plaster above. The original color of the plaster is not known.

The kitchen would have been the domain of the cook, who, during the Whartons' time, may have been a man.[17] While Edith may not have set foot in the kitchen at The Mount often, it is clear from her writings that she had the greatest respect for a good cook; those of her youth were remembered for "what artists they were!"[18] Although kitchens do not appear as settings in Wharton's fiction, there is a vivid picture of one in the 1937 ghost story, "All Souls."[19]

By 1940 the kitchen had been moved upstairs, leaving this room apparently unused. Not long after the arrival of the Foxhollow School in 1942, the old kitchen was converted into a chemistry lab and classroom; the "initial expenses" of the laboratory were donated by the Class of 1944. A photograph from the 1950s shows the cabinets here and in the

scullery filled with bottles, jars, test tubes, and supplies. A work table occupied the middle of the room, and a blackboard was located on the north wall between the doors.

The room has been used since 1978 as a dressing room for Shakespeare & Company.

SERVING ROOM AND SCULLERY

This is actually one room with the scullery on the east and the serving room to the west. As food was prepared in the kitchen, it was brought to the built-in counter of the serving room. It was then sent upstairs on the dumbwaiter,[20] which connected this room to the butler's pantry above.

Although it was not drawn on the 1901 Hoppin & Koen floor plan, a closet was built into the room on the north wall. The east wall of the scullery has a large sink with drainboards on either side; here all dishes and utensils were washed and dried. The floor is composed of white marble tiles from Vermont. The walls have wainscoting with plaster above; the original color is not known.

The room is dominated by one large, arched window. The 1901 Hoppin & Koen floor plan had originally called for a door to the outside in this location and a window in the adjacent laundry. However, the window was placed in the scullery instead and the door in the laundry. The serving room is located within the structure of The Mount, while the scullery is beneath the Italianate terrace. An iron girder delineating this division is set into the ceiling as reinforcement.

A scullery maid would have worked in this area. She would have been responsible for starting the kitchen fires in the early morning and doing the dirtiest cleaning jobs. She would have been supervised by the cook, who may have also had a kitchen maid or two at his or her disposal.[21]

How this area was used after the kitchen was moved to the main floor is not known. After 1944 it became part of the chemistry laboratory. Shakespeare & Company has used the space as a location for light boards, cables, and generators for outdoor performances. The dumbwaiter was boarded up, and the original sink was covered to hold equipment. Because part of the room is under the deteriorating terrace, the ceiling, walls, and floor of this area have been damaged severely by leaking water and temperature fluctuations.

PASSAGEWAY

The scullery opens into this long, narrow interior hallway, which leads from the servants' porch on the west to the door of the laundry room. The hall is approximately 25 feet long; it is 3 feet 6 inches wide. The walls have wooden wainscoting with plaster above; the original color is not known. The original floor is of concrete scored to resemble tiles.

LAUNDRY ROOM

The laundry room, measuring 17 feet 4 inches by 21 feet 3 inches in plan, was once one of the brightest rooms in the service area, with three large, arched openings — two facing east and an arched door to the south. The floor consists of large, white, marble tiles and smaller black tiles in a simple pattern.

The 1901 floor plan called for two light fixtures on the walls and a round stove that was adjacent to the entrance. The plan also showed the stove in front of an interior window, one of three that would have opened into the furnace and coal room.[22]

Although there is no documentation that the Whartons had a resident laundress at The Mount, the large size of the room suggests that most of the laundry was done here.[23]

There were four built-in "wash trays" along the east wall under the windows, according to the 1901 floor plan (three of the massive wash trays survive and are now in storage). There may have been a barrel washer in the room. Other likely furnishings would have included tables, baskets, irons and ironing boards, and racks for drying clothes.

Presumably the laundry room continued to be used when the Shattucks and the Van Andas lived at The Mount. According to Kergan Davidson, who was in charge of the house and

grounds for many years for the Foxhollow School, the laundry room was used for trunk and luggage storage for the dormitory's residents. Since 1978 it has served as a construction area, scene shop, and storage area for Shakespeare & Company.

Like the scullery, the room has suffered significantly from leaking water from the terrace above and from temperature fluctuations. Most of the plaster ceiling and the lath are down, and the brick vaulting for the terrace is exposed.

SERVANTS' TOILET/STOREROOM

A small (8 feet by 8 inch square) room adjoining the laundry room was originally designated on the 1901 floor plan as a storeroom, although pencil markings indicate that the Whartons wished that it be a servants' toilet instead.[24]

The floor of the room is the same pattern as in the laundry room: white marble and smaller black tiles. There is one narrow slit of a window in the east wall. The thick walls of this square room were originally conceived to support an elaborate terrace gazebo above, which was never realized.

It is unknown whether the room had a sink, as well as a toilet; certainly the space was large enough, and one was needed, since the other servants' toilet room on this floor had only a toilet.

The 1940 floor plan labels the room as a toilet, so it was apparently still in use. The toilet was removed at some point, and the room has been used by Shakespeare & Company for storage.

TWO LAUNDRY-ROOM CLOSETS

Two doors open into the laundry room on the north wall. The original floor plan had called for a single space, labeled a "Trunk Room," which measured 11 feet 8 inches by 17 feet 4 inches in plan; two smaller rooms were actually constructed.[25]

These two small closets were among the least finished parts of The Mount. The floors are poured concrete. The dividing wall consists of the same wood used for wainscoting, but here it extends to the ceiling. Some of the walls, particularly in the east closet, may never have been plastered; the walls are the same rustic stone used in the terrace and foundations.

WEST CLOSET/TRUNK ROOM/ BASKET CLOSET

The west closet was probably used to store the trunks for both the Whartons and their guests. Considering how frequently Edith and Teddy traveled, a large amount of storage would have been necessary. By 1940 this area was being used by the Van Andas as a basket closet. Since 1978 it has been used to store tools and other items for Shakespeare & Company.

EAST CLOSET/WINE CLOSET OR WINE CELLAR

The east closet was apparently the Whartons' wine cellar.[26] It would have been well-secured and was probably presided over by the butler, Alfred White, who reported on this matter to Teddy rather than Edith. R. W. B. Lewis notes that it was Teddy

who was in charge of the wines. Edith attributed her dislike of wines to her brothers' premature attempt to develop her interest in them; but though she took the occasional glass of Cointreau or Dubonnet and liked champagne (she always had a bottle ready for guests arriving after a long railroad journey), she had in fact little discernment in this matter. Teddy's taste was superb, and the finest wines were served at the table.[27]

Apparently the Shattucks and the Van Andas continued to use the space as a wine cellar.[28] Its function after 1942 is not known. For several years it has served as a storage room for Shakespeare & Company.

Today both small closets are in very poor condition, having lost plaster from the ceilings and walls due to leaking water and temperature fluctuations.

LAMP ROOM

Located at the end of the servants' hall, this small room, measuring 10 feet 10 inches by 11 feet 9 inches in plan, has one window facing west, wainscoting, and plaster walls (original color unknown), and a floor of concrete scored to resemble tiles.

The exact purpose of this room is unclear. Although electricity was installed when the house was built, other illumination was also used. This room may have been a storage area for all items relating to illumination, as well as general storage. The room also houses part of the machinery for the hydraulic elevator.

In 1940 the room was identified as having an "electric meter and motor." Now used for storage, it also contains telephone switching systems, the primary fuse box, and (since 1988) a smoke-detection and fire-alarm system.

FURNACE AND COAL ROOM

Entered from the servants' hall (and also originally from the laundry room), the furnace room is located just opposite the lamp room. It stretches behind the entrance hall and terminates behind the coat room.

The original floor plan called for a much smaller furnace and coal room that ended at the wall aligned with the north wall of the staircase hall. Pencil markings on the 1901 floor plan indicate that the Whartons wanted to have another large area to the north excavated. This change extended the area 36 feet, completely reconfiguring it into a long rectangle directly behind the entrance hall.

The additional area was divided into two rooms by a brick wall, creating several distinct spaces. A large penciled-in circle in the northernmost space on the 1901 plan may indicate a separate furnace for the main house. The center area would most likely have been used for coal storage[29]; the south room housed the hot-water boiler and a "heater." This area originally was to have had a set of three interior windows opening into the trunk room and the laundry room, but apparently only one (actually a door to the laundry room) was built. It has since been sealed.

Heating The Mount has been a problem since its construction. Edith complained in 1907: "we found last autumn that the hot-water furnace which heats the servant's wing was inadequate in really cold weather, & they suffered very much in Dec.; so this year we shall have to spare them that, & *next* year put in a new 'system'. Oh, the imbecility of the U.S. architect!"[30]

By 1940 the floor plans submitted by Carr Van Anda to the Lenox tax assessors indicate that a new heat-and-air-conditioning plant costing $1000 was housed in the northernmost area of the furnace room and that a water heater had replaced the "old hot water boiler" in the first room. Van Anda's accompanying statement further explained the earlier arrangement:

The fault, discovered only after purchase, was in the system of heating. There were two furnaces, one supplying hot air to a part of the house, the other operating a hot-water circulation through pipes to other parts of the house. It was known that the existing furnaces were worn out and the one which sent hot air through the family rooms was replaced. It was found to be useless to replace the other unless the walls of the house were cut open to replace the worn and rusted pipes. This involved tearing up the principal rooms of the house (the drawing room would have had to be cut open in four places) and afterward restoring them, because this system, primarily designed to heat the service quarters, was insanely, as we think, extended through all the family part of the house to reach and heat the bathrooms there.[31]

He decided that he would not expend an estimated $7,300, to replace the antiquated system. In 1940, therefore, The Mount had no heat in the service wing, the basement, the attic, or any of the bathrooms. The servants at this time had to get on "as best they can with small portable coal-oil stoves in their rooms."[32] The Van Andas occupied The Mount only during the summer.[33]

When the Foxhollow School purchased The Mount in 1942, the building was, for the first time, pressed into year-round use as a dormitory. Presumably at this point the hot-water system was reactivated so that regular heat was available throughout the house.

Today The Mount uses the original two-furnace system: hot air for the principal rooms on the main and bedroom floors and hot-water radiators for the rest of the building.

FIRST FLOOR, SERVICE WING

The service area on the main floor of The Mount measures approximately 30 feet wide by 33 feet long. The service stairs and elevator are at the north end of a servants' hall, which runs most of the length of the area. All of the rooms originally opened onto this hall: the butler's pantry, brush room, housekeeper's room, cook's room, and butler's room. A door on the north wall adjacent to the elevator and stairs opens directly into the staircase hall of the mansion.

Codman's original pencil drawing for this area contained only one service room, which would have been a butler's pantry next to the dining room. The service elevator and stairs would have occupied a small area to the right of the pantry. Clearly, far more service rooms were necessary, and the service wing that was planned and built by Hoppin & Koen was about six times larger.

SERVANTS' HALL

The servants' hallway was approximately 23 feet long. As its narrowest point it was 3 feet 8 inches; it widened somewhat at the foot of the servants' stairs and the elevator. This wider area has the same wainscoting as the rest of the service areas. The walls above are of plaster; the original color is unknown. The narrower portion of the hallway has full plaster walls without wainscoting.

An indicator-box is located on the east wall between the doors to the brush room and the housekeeper's room.[34] It was manufactured under "Holtzer's Patent" by Berkshire Electric Company in Pittsfield, Massachusetts. There are twelve slots for the different locations to which a servant could be called: Mrs. Wharton's bedroom, Mrs. Wharton's boudoir, Mrs. Wharton's bath, Mr. Wharton's bedroom, Mr. Wharton's bath, Mr. Wharton's dressing room, East Guest Room, East Guest Room bath, West Guest Room bath and Small Guest Room.[35]

A number of changes have occurred over the years, including a reconfiguration of rooms and doors. The original door on the north wall that led to the main staircase hall has been removed, and a shorter door has been installed. The door from the hall into the butler's pantry was recreated in the spring of 1995 when that room was restored.

A partition and door have been constructed near the door leading into the butler's pantry, dividing the hall in two. The original floor plan called for a swinging baize door in this location; it is unclear whether this was actually installed. It would have provided somewhat more privacy to the three staff rooms beyond the bustle of the hall stairs and elevator.

A fuse-box is set into the north wall west of the door to the butler's pantry. An identification sheet attached inside the box reveals that it was known as the "Butler's Pantry Cutout Box"; it lists the number of lights in each room and identifies the rooms controlled by the eight fuses. The names of the rooms (and their inferred uses) indicate that this list dates to the Whartons' occupancy.

BUTLER'S PANTRY

Opening directly onto the main hall, the butler's pantry was the busiest and most important room in this part of the service wing. A small room, measuring 11 feet by 14 feet 4 inches in plan, it adjoined the dining room. It contained the dumb waiter, which delivered the food from the kitchen below before it was served to the Whartons and their guests, probably by a footman.

On the north wall is a large sink with a marble countertop and drainboards.[36] There are built-in cabinets above the sink. An indicator-box above the sink and adjacent to the dining-room doors was called for on the original 1901 floor plan.[37] The plan also specified a swinging door between this room and the dining room; instead there appear to have been two sets of double doors.[38]

A built-in cabinet was located west of the dumbwaiter. Next to the cabinet was to have been a closet. The original floor plan had called for this closet to have been the safe, the repository for the Whartons' finest china and silverware. The safe was, however, constructed into the northwest corner of the room.[39]

The room has one window on the east wall, and there were two light fixtures, one near the window and one above the sink.[40]

The original floor plan specified a refrigerator under the cabinet on the south wall. As the main refrigerator was downstairs, this supplementary one probably helped keep items cold before being served at table. A butler's pantry often included a warming oven; although none is indicated on the 1901 floor plan, it is possible that there was one in this room.

The original color of the plaster walls was green.[41] The walls also have wooden wainscoting; all of the wainscoting, doors, and trim are oak. The original floor was of rift pine.

Until 1942 this room functioned as a butler's pantry for the Shattucks and the Van Andas. During the Foxhollow School years, it and the adjacent brush room were combined into a kitchen. When the wall between the two rooms was taken down, the dumbwaiter was also removed. The rift pine floor was covered with linoleum.

During the winter of 1994 and spring of 1995, the area was restored to be seen on tours and for use as a kitchen for the many events that take place in the mansion.

The project was made possible through the generosity of GE Plastics, Formica Corporation, and architect Robert Orr & Associates, of New Haven, Connecticut. A key participant was Wood-Mode, Inc., which donated new cabinetwork. In addition, Rejuvenation Lamp & Fixture Company contributed wall and ceiling fixtures; Sherwin-Williams contributed wall and ceiling paint to recreate the original color scheme; Baldwin donated brass hardware plates; Joanna, Inc., contributed appropriate shades for the two windows; and Howard Miller, Inc., donated a wall clock. Edith Wharton Restoration estimates that $100,000 worth of services, materials, appliances, labor, and funding were given.

Most of the original features of the room were restored under the guidance of contractor David Andersen, of New Marlborough, Massachusetts. The work included stripping five coats of paint from cabinets, wainscoting, doors, and trim and restoring the original finish to all these surfaces. The original hardware was cleaned and polished and loose cabinetry resecured. Following repair and restoration of the plaster ceiling and side walls, the original colors were restored (green for the walls, white for the ceiling). Three layers of linoleum and plywood flooring were removed before a new floor could be installed; the deteriorated original was retained as a sub-floor. Period-style ceiling lamps and push-button fixtures were installed, the original marble countertop and splashback were cleaned and polished, and the original porcelain sink was resurfaced. In addition, the missing white oak door to the hall, measuring 3 feet by 8 feet, was recreated.

In order to incorporate modern conveniences, such as the GE dishwasher and cooking facilities, an island for appliances was designed for the center of the room, where the original historic fabric would not be disturbed. The island did not attempt to copy the historic features; in fact, it was designed to clearly delineate what was original from what was added. A new counter-top surface by Formica, "Nuvel," is featured both on the island and on an original cabinet surface.

The kitchen restoration is the first major work to take place inside the mansion.

BRUSH ROOM

This small room, 6 feet 9 inches by 14 feet 4 inches in plan, probably housed cleaning utensils for the household staff and would have been controlled by the housekeeper and the butler. It had one closet on the south wall, one window facing east, and one light fixture to the right of the window.[42] The floor was of rift pine. The original color of the walls was green.

By 1940 this room was being used as a pantry by the Van Andas. It was combined with the butler's pantry during the Foxhollow School years to become a kitchen.

HOUSEKEEPER'S ROOM

According to the 1901 Hoppin & Koen floor plan for the service wing, the large room (12 feet by 14 feet 4 inches) on the southeast corner was to be the housekeeper's room. If so, it probably served as a combination office and sitting room[43] for Catharine Gross.

However, there is some evidence that this room may have been the cook's room.[44]

According to the butler's pantry cutout box, the housekeeper's room, the cook's room, and the butler's room, as indicated on the 1901 floor plan, actually may have been used as the cook's room, the chef's room, and the butler's room.

This is the largest of the three staff rooms on the main floor. There are two windows, one facing east and the other south. The original color of the room may have been a reddish gray.[45] The floor was of rift pine.[46] There is one closet on the north wall.

According to the 1901 floor plan, this room opened into the cook's room to the west. The 1940 floor plans also show an opening here, as does a photograph from the Foxhollow School years.

By 1940 this room was the main kitchen for the Van Andas. A photograph taken in the early Foxhollow School years shows the kitchen was still intact: a long sink and a table were on the east wall, the refrigerator was on the north wall, a stove on the south wall, and a kitchen table in the center of the room.[47]

The opening between this room and the cook's room was later closed, and a new floor was laid.[48] These changes were evidently necessary to create dormitory space.

In recent years Shakespeare & Company has used this room to house the light and sound equipment for performances on their outdoor Mainstage.

COOK'S ROOM

A far smaller room than the housekeeper's room, this room (measuring 8 feet 4 inches by 13 feet 10 inches in plan) may have served as a combination office and sitting room for the Wharton's cook. Evidence from the butler's pantry cutout box also suggests it may have been the chef's room.[49]

Located on the southwest corner of the service wing, this room has two windows, one facing south and the other west. The original color of the plaster walls may have been cream.[50] The floor was of rift pine.[51] There was one closet on the north wall.[52]

By 1940 this room was the dining room for the Van Andas' servants. The Foxhollow School used it for home economics classes, including sewing classes. Apparently, the room was also used as a supplemental kitchen at this time; there were stoves against the south and west walls.

The Foxhollow School later reconfigured the room, possibly in the mid-1960s. The north wall and the two closets were removed, thereby connecting this room to the original butler's room for use as dormitory space.

Currently this room serves as an office/ dressing room for Shakespeare & Company.

BUTLER'S ROOM

The butler's room, measuring 9 feet 8 inches by 10 feet 11 inches in plan, was the smallest of the three staff office/sitting rooms on this floor.[53] It was located across the hall from the butler's pantry.

The room had one window facing west, one light fixture on the wall, and a closet. The floors were of rift pine. The original color of the plaster walls is unknown.

Alfred White, the Whartons' butler, most likely used this space only as an office and sitting room, not as sleeping quarters, since he may have had a small cottage elsewhere on the grounds.[54]

From this small office White oversaw the household, including the activities of the footmen. In 1913 Edith spoke of a departing footman as "a very good servant, but he needs the discipline of a man like White, who keeps a firm hand over all his footmen."[55] The footmen at The Mount wore livery.[56] A reporter visiting The Mount in October 1907 observed that "With the exception of a slightly oppressive butler and a fool of a footman in livery, Mrs. Wharton's presence was not at all formidable."[57]

The 1940 floor plan indicates that this room was still serving as the butler's sitting room for the Van Andas. It is not known how it was used during the early days of the Foxhollow School. The room was combined with the adjacent cook's room, possibly in the mid-1960s. The northwest corner was converted into a bathroom with a sink and toilet but no bathtub.[58]

With reconfigured walls, dropped ceilings, and new floors, there are only a few traces of the original space.

SECOND FLOOR, SERVICE WING

In Codman's original plan for the second floor of The Mount, the service area contained only a maid's room and service stairs. In contrast, the plan prepared by Hoppin & Koen called for a number of service rooms. As built, this floor contained the linen closet, housemaid's closet, maid's room, sewing room, dress closet, and several other closets. This part of the house was largely the province of three key female staff: the housekeeper, the housemaid, and Edith's personal maid.

The floor plan is similar to that of the main floor: the northwest corner of the wing contains the service stairs, as well as the service elevator. All rooms open onto an interior hall.

A skylight above the interior hall could be opened for ventilation.[59] The hall has the same 4-foot-high wooden wainscoting found in the other service areas. The original color of the plaster walls is unknown. The two small closets on the east wall, located on either side of a flue coming up from the kitchen, have hooks around the upper walls, possibly for uniforms, aprons, and other clothing. All floors in this area are of rift pine.[60]

LINEN CLOSET

A narrow room measuring 9 feet 8 inches long by a few feet wide, the linen closet held the sheets, towels, blankets, and other linens needed by the Whartons.

On the south wall are two sets of built-in shelves reaching from floor to ceiling. The shelves are on rollers, and each has two handles. At the center of each set of shelves is a pull-out shelf to serve as a counter, presumably for counting or folding.

On the north wall are nine drawers, each with two curved brass handles. The three drawers near the door have tiny round plates engraved with the numbers 20, 21, and 22; the other drawers are not numbered.

The tops of the drawers form a counter running the length of the room. Above this are four shelves supported by brass brackets. The first three shelves curve in to meet the wall by the window, terminating in the window frame. The uppermost shelf does not curve.

The original color of the plaster walls is unknown. The floor is of rift pine. There is one window, which fills almost all of the west wall. There was one light fixture in the room.[61]

Edith mentioned the importance of the linen room to the household arts in *A Backward Glance*. Having discussed with evident fondness the food served at her family's table as a child, she remarked bitterly:

I have lingered over these details because they formed a part — a most important and honorable part — of that ancient curriculum of housekeeping which, at least in Anglo-Saxon countries, was so soon to be swept aside by the "monstrous regiment" of the emancipated: young women taught by their elders to despise the kitchen and linen room, and to substitute the acquiring of University degrees for the more complex art of civilized living. The movement began when I was young, and now that I am old, and have watched and noted its results, I mourn more than ever the extinction of the household arts.[62]

The Van Anda floor plan indicates that this room continued as a linen closet up to 1940 and probably through the Foxhollow School years. From 1978-87 it served as a storage closet. In 1988 it was converted into an office for Edith Wharton Restoration; it now serves as storage for the organization.

HOUSEMAID'S CLOSET

The housemaid's closet, 4 feet 8 inches by 9 feet 8 inches in plan, approximately the same size as the linen closet, probably contained the servants' cleaning equipment.[63] The room had a slop sink, with a surround of polished white-and-gray marble. There is one window facing west and one light fixture.[64] The original color of the plaster walls is believed to have been cream. The original floor may have been rift pine; at present there is an old red linoleum.

Prior to 1940 this room had been converted into a servants' bathroom by the Shattucks. A porcelain bathtub on four claw feet appears to date from this period. A more modern sink has replaced the original slop sink, and there is a flush toilet on the south wall. The room now serves as storage for Edith Wharton Restoration.

MAID'S ROOM

Edith's personal maid lived in this small room at the southwest corner of the top floor of the service wing, which is aligned to the bedroom floor of the mansion. Measuring 9 feet 4 inches by 13 feet 10 inches in plan, the room has two windows, one facing south and the other west. There is one extant light fixture on the south wall. Next to the closet on the east wall is a door into the sewing room. The original color of the plaster walls is believed to have been gray; the ceiling was a golden yellow. All woodwork had a clear finish instead of paint. The floors are of rift pine.

Edith's personal maid was the only servant to sleep on the bedroom floor. With the push of a button, Edith could summon the maid to her bedroom suite in only a few seconds. The maid would have been on call almost 24 hours a day, seven days a week. The indicator-box is still located in the sewing room.

The room was furnished most likely with a single bed, a chair, and a dresser with a bowl and wash basin. In Wharton's 1904 short story, "The Lady's Maid's Bell," the narrator (a lady's maid) describes her quarters as "a neat room, nicely furnished, with a picture or two on the walls."[65] It opened "into a square hall at the end of the passage,"[66] much like the placement of this maid's room at The Mount.

By 1940 the Van Andas had converted the maid's room into a servants' sitting room. It apparently served as both dormitory and faculty housing for the Foxhollow School from 1942 through the early 1970s. During this period, a small alcove to the east of the entry was blocked off to create a separate closet for the sewing room.

Shakespeare & Company used the room as a dormitory after 1978. In 1988 it became part of an apartment for an Edith Wharton Restoration staff member. The wallboard partition was removed, restoring the original opening to the sewing room. In 1990 the room became part of the office of Edith Wharton Restoration; it currently serves as storage.

SEWING ROOM

The sewing room on the southeast corner is the largest room on the top floor of the service wing, measuring 11 feet 10 inches by 21 feet 3 inches in plan. It is the only room to have four windows, three facing east and one south. Two light fixtures were called for on the 1901 floor plan.[67] The room has one large closet, the dress closet, on the north wall. The floor is of rift pine.

An indicator[68] is located on the north wall to the right of the door to the dress closet. The box, which is extant, has three slots labeled for Edith Wharton's boudoir, bath, and bedroom.[69]

The original color of the plaster walls is believed to have been cream and the ceiling gray. The woodwork has been painted over, except for a small area of the base molding covered over when interior stairs to an exterior fire escape were built. The original sash window was also removed at this time, and a window that opened out was added. The steps were removed later.

Edith's personal maid used the sewing room as a work area and sitting room. She may have also shared it with the housekeeper, Catharine Gross.[70] It was in the sewing room, according to Wharton's short story, "The Lady's Maid's Bell," where a lady's maid would settle down to an afternoon's sewing while her mistress was out or involved with the day's activities. The story makes clear that the sewing room was a fixture of a large house.[71]

Furnishings in the sewing room would have included a table or two, a sewing machine, and several comfortable chairs.

By 1940, the sewing room had become the butler's living quarters, which he used in conjunction with his own office/sitting room one floor below. This room also served as dormitory space and faculty housing for the Foxhollow School from 1942 through the early 1970s. Shakespeare & Company used it as a dormitory

from 1978-88. In 1988 the room became part of a private apartment for an Edith Wharton Restoration staff member, and in 1990 it became the office for Edith Wharton Restoration. It currently serves as storage.

DRESS CLOSET

The dress closet is a small interior space measuring 5 feet 4 inches by approximately 10 feet in plan. It was used to store Edith's dresses, wraps, coats, furs, shoes, parasols, and other accessories.[72] Her clothes were cared for by her personal maid, who would bring them back and forth along the hallway as needed.

The room has an interior window with frosted glass high on its west wall, probably for ventilation. One light fixture was called for on the floor plan.[73] The floor is of rift pine. The original color of the plaster walls is believed to have been cream.

Brass hooks were originally attached to a strip of molding approximately 6 feet 6 inches high on the north, east, and west walls; most hooks remain.

In 1940 the room was labeled a closet, perhaps used by the Van Andas' butler. The Foxhollow School converted it into a bathroom. In early 1988 the fixtures were removed, and the room became a small kitchen for an Edith Wharton Restoration staff member. A sink, stove, and refrigerator were added, along with built-in counters and wall cabinets on the east wall.

STAIRS TO THE ATTIC FLOOR

To reach the stairs to the attic floor, one had to climb two steps adjacent to the service elevator, as the top floor of the service wing is approximately 2 feet below the mansion's bedroom level. A door to the north connects the service wing to the bedrooms and hallway.

To the west are a small closet[74] and doors leading to the stairs to the attic floor. A light fixture remains at the foot of the stairs. Like all other staircases, it crosses a window.

Changes have concealed the original circulation patterns. A wall now divides the north end of the hall from the sewing room, maid's room, housemaid's closet, and linen closet, which are currently storage areas. A second wall and door block the elevator and stairs from the bedroom floor of the mansion and the continuation of the stairs to the attic; the doors leading to the attic stairs have been removed.

ATTIC FLOOR

Codman's original attic plan for The Mount bears little resemblance to the actual plan that was devised and executed by Hoppin & Koen. Codman envisioned ten tiny rooms for servants (all approximately the same size), one bath for the servants, and, in one-third of the space, a guest suite with bedroom, boudoir, and bath. Hoppin & Koen provided for nine servants' rooms (amended before construction to eight rooms) of varying sizes and one bathroom. There was no guest suite on the attic floor, allowing for somewhat larger servants' rooms. The steep slope of the roof above is clearly evident in each room. The south stairhall may have also functioned as a sitting area for the female staff. A central hall ran the length of the building from south to north; all rooms open onto this interior passageway. The proximity of the rooms and the shared bath suggest that only the female staff resided on this floor.

As was customary, all of the servants' rooms are relatively plain. The original colors of the plaster walls are unknown. The floors are of rift pine. The doors to each room have bull's-eye moldings,[75] as well as transom lights.[76] The dormers help to define the spaces. Each room has at least one window; half of the rooms have two. Every room has a closet.

The 1901 floor plan locates an indicator in the stairhall on the north wall.[77] A second indicator was specified for the center room on the west side of the hall[78]; there is an existing indicator not called for on the floor plan located on the west wall in the southeast corner room.[79]

The original floor plan called for nine servants' rooms. Pencil markings on the 1901 plan indicate that the Whartons combined two west bedrooms, resulting in five good-sized rooms and three much smaller ones. The central room on the east has only a tiny oculus window in the center of the exterior pediment.

The servant's bedroom at the southeast corner opens directly into the stairhall and may have been the most important. Pencil markings on the 1901 floor plan sketched in a fireplace.[80]

The servants' rooms were probably furnished simply but comfortably. There would most likely

FIG. 72 *Attic plan, Hoppin & Koen, 1901. The two servants' rooms on the west side were crossed out in favor of one larger room.* (AAFAL)

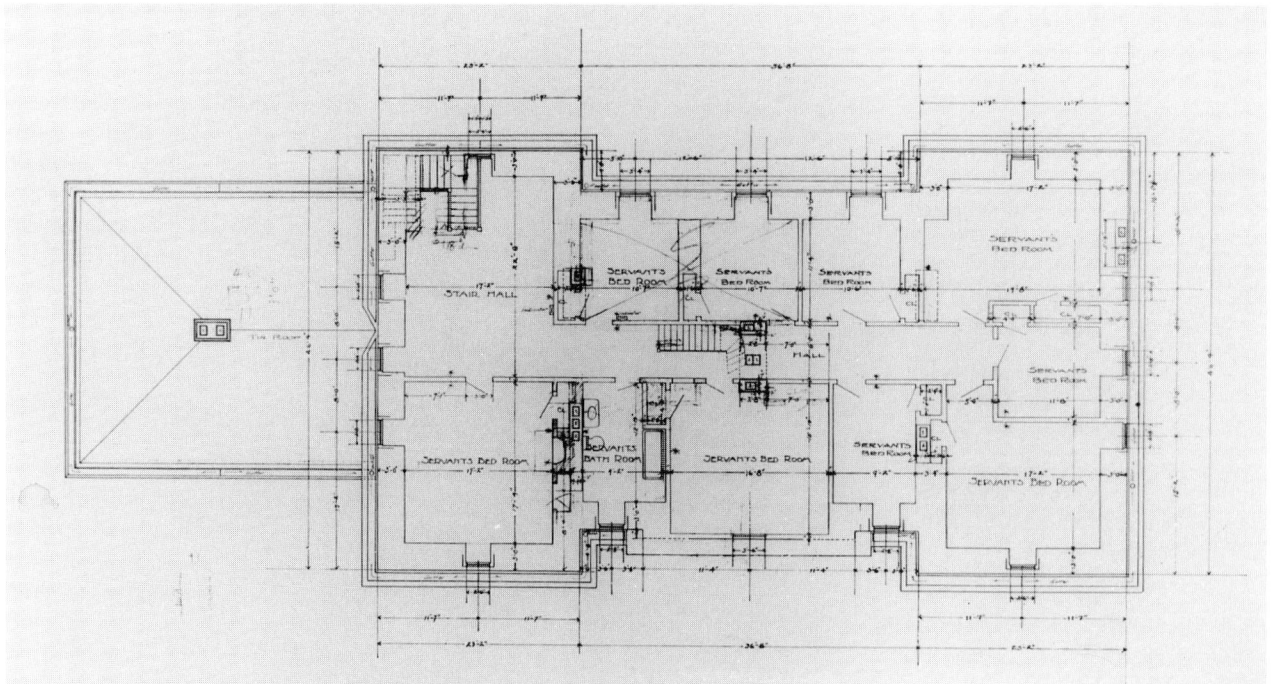

116

have been a bed with iron headboard, bedside table, dresser, a chair or two, and washstand with bowl and basin. A few pictures, a small throw rug, and curtains might have been the only decorative touches.

The servants' bathroom with toilet, sink, and bathtub[81] measures 9 feet 2 inches by 12 feet 8 inches in plan. The floor is of the same white Vermont marble found in the other bathrooms throughout The Mount. The one window faces east. The room was slightly reconfigured from the 1901 floor plan when a closet for the adjacent room to the north was not built.

A short, narrow flight of stairs on the west wall of the hall leads to the cupola. A small door on the east wall above the stairs opens into a crawlspace under the roof and may have provided ventilation. The original water system (a large tank) is located in this crawlspace below and to the north of the cupola. The cupola also illuminates the attic floor.

The 1940 floor plan reveals that the stairhall was used as a trunk storage area by the Van Andas and that the large servant's room on the southeast corner had been a servants' sitting room. Although it is not known if the Van Andas had enough staff to fill all the rooms on this floor (most likely they did not), the rooms were still labeled on the plan as bedrooms for staff.

In 1942 the Foxhollow School converted this floor into a dormitory with one, two, or three girls to a room. The stairhall served as a lounge and study area with chairs and table.

The school made two major changes to this floor to provide better egress. A staircase was inserted in the small servant's room at the northern end of the hall, running down through Edith's bathroom into the vestibule of her suite. Three fire escapes exiting from the attic floor were erected at varying intervals on the east facade soon after 1943.[82] They were removed in the early 1980s.

The school also added a bathroom in the bedroom behind the pediment. Unfortunately it caused significant water damage to the ceiling of the drawing room in the early 1970s. The

fixtures have been removed, and the room now serves as a closet.

From 1978-95 the attic served as year-round offices for Shakespeare & Company, with the stairhall as a reception area.

CUPOLA

The octagonal cupola of The Mount was copied almost exactly after the one at Belton House in Lincolnshire, England. Doors on the north and south sides open onto the balustraded walkway on the roof.

The cupola served a practical as well as ornamental purpose. A flue in a narrow chimney runs through the space, and the exhaust exited through the elaborate ironwork of the crown directly beneath the weathervane. The flue is not visible from below.

The weathervane and cupola were restored in 1982.

Conclusion

The service wing was planned by Hoppin & Koen to meet the needs specified by Edith and Teddy Wharton, as well as those of their staff. Hoppin & Koen prided itself on exactly this type of work; in a 1911 article the firm explained that "To build a symmetrical house, planned on the most modern principles of house planning, involves the conveniences of the owners and the conveniences of the servants. This firm seeks to arrange the necessaries of domestic life in the house with the least care in maintenance for the mistress and the domestics; to divide properly and practically the living part from the service..."[83] Although Edith was unhappy about the need to install another heating system for the service wing in 1907, there is little evidence that she or Teddy was unhappy with Hoppin & Koen's work. The fact that the Whartons chose the firm to design an extension to the wing speaks of their satisfaction with their architect, particularly in respect to this part of The Mount.

CHAPTER 7

Proposed Alterations in 1907

In September 1907 Hoppin & Koen prepared a series of elevations and floor plans for the alteration of the service wing. Although each was somewhat different with regard to room sizes, arrangements, and placements, the basic idea was simple: to extend the length of the entire service wing from basement to roof for approximately 26 feet (an extension of two bays on the southern end of the existing wing).[1]

Most of the alterations were intended to provide the Whartons with more space and increased comfort for their current staff, space for additional servants, and more efficient functioning of the household. In addition, several spaces in the enlarged wing would be used for Edith Wharton's own activities and for more guests.

Proposed Alterations to the Exterior of the Service Wing

The proposed extension would have the same rusticated stone base as the existing wing and the same white stucco upper walls. Identical window treatments and marble lintels over windows on the basement level would tie the new addition to the existing wing. Quoins delineating each side of the two-bay extension were to link it visually to the same quoins on the two projecting wings of the main part of the mansion.

To accommodate the new interior arrangement, the two southernmost windows on the first and second stories would be moved approximately 2 to 3 feet further south, placing them at the center of six windows across the new facade. The kitchen would have a new set of three connected windows (versus the two existing windows spaced 4 feet apart), and there would be a new entrance on either the east or west side of the wing, with a flight of outside stairs descending to a newly excavated cellar.

The two elevations differed significantly in their treatment of the roof.[2] The east elevation indicated a relatively flat roof, similar to the existing one.[3] This elevation reinforced the subservience of the service wing to the mansion: set back, lower, and less ornamented.

The alternate elevation would affect the appearance of The Mount radically. A more elaborate scheme, it called for a full attic floor running the entire length of the wing, with dormer windows punctuating the roofline. The height of the service wing would be raised to the level of the main part of the house, with the exterior decorated with raised rectangular panels similar to those above the windows on the bedroom floor of the mansion. The cornice and brackets on the main part of the house would extend the length of the building on the east (and presumably west) side. Although the first two floors of the wing would retain an austere character, the grander pretensions of the upper two floors of the alternate elevation — nearly identical in treatment with the main house — would effectively merge the service wing into the mansion, when viewed from a distance.

New Cellar Floor

Two schemes survive for the creation of a new cellar floor beneath the existing basement floor.[4] Both plans called for a coal bin, a wood bin, a new furnace or heater, and interior and exterior stairs.

Both schemes are further evidence that the Whartons were seeking to correct grave deficiencies in the heating plant of the service wing. A letter from Edith to Sara Norton on November 1, 1907, not long after the proposed alterations were presented, explained the problem:

Don't put your visit off too late, for we have decided to sail on Dec. 5th, so we shall have to leave here on the 1st. I hate to go so early, but we found last autumn that the hot-water furnace which heats the servant's wing was inadequate in really cold weather, & they suffered

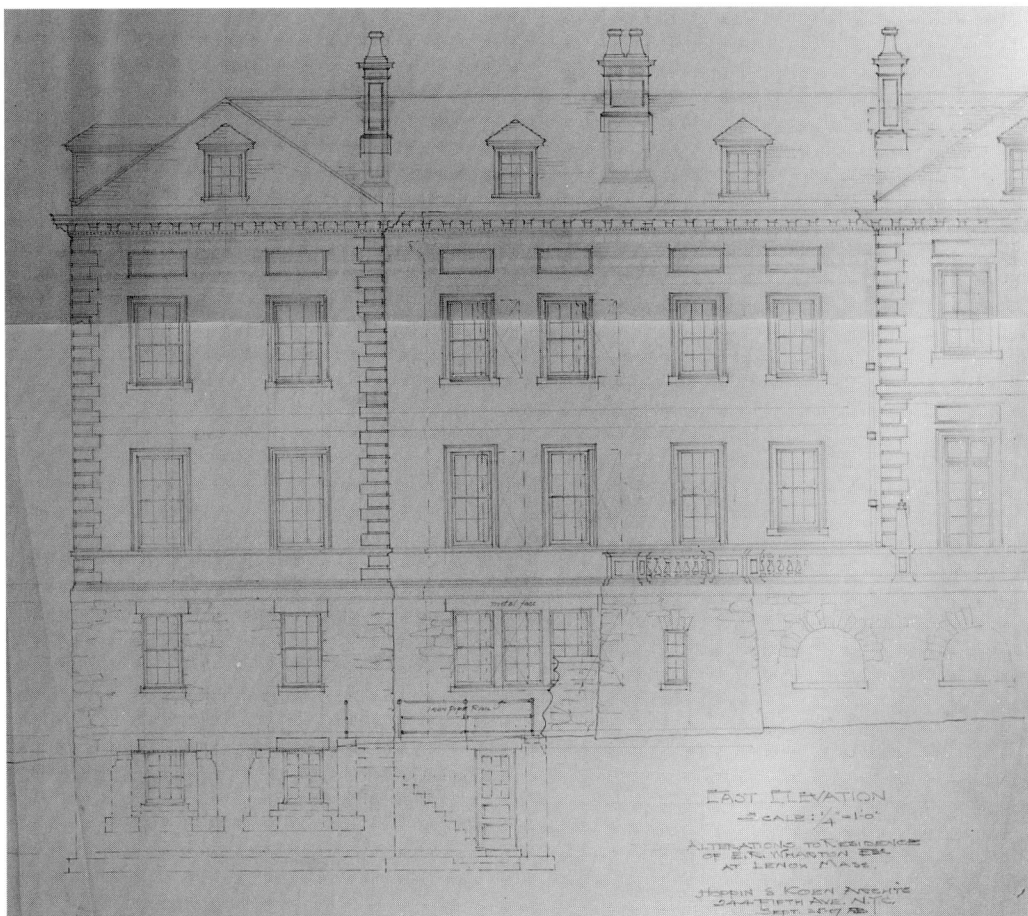

FIG. 73 *Alternate elevation for the east elevation, Hoppin & Koen, September 25, 1907. This unrealized scheme would have extended the service wing two bays to the south and added an attic floor with chimneys and dormers, incorporating the wing into the main block of the house.* (EWR)

very much in Dec.; so this year we shall have to spare them that, & *next* year put in a new "system." Oh, the imbecility of the U.S. architect![5]

Scheme No. 1 called for an L-shaped unexcavated space in the southwest corner of the cellar. Scheme No. 2 would have excavated that area, almost doubling the available space. The sizes of the coal bin and the wood bin were likewise doubled, and there would have been several additional cellar rooms, including one with a sink. Instead of a "furnace" in the first scheme, the second proposed a "heater" almost twice the size.

The cellar areas were to have been partly illuminated by natural light, with below-grade windows with lightwells covered by iron gratings. Scheme No. 1 proposed three such lightwells, with an exterior flight of stairs to the east side of the wing. Scheme No. 2 offered seven lightwells, with the exterior entrance to the cellar on the west side of the building adjacent to the servants' porch.

Alterations to the Basement Floor Plan

Only one plan for the extension of the basement floor survives.[6] The entrance from the servants' porch on the west would remain the same. No changes were contemplated for the existing lamp room, furnace room, passage, laundry room, refrigerator, scullery, and serving room. The major alterations would have involved moving the service elevator and stairs, enlarging the kitchen and the servants' dining room, and adding a new refrigerator and storage area.

The entire service elevator and the servants' stairs that surround it for three floors would move 26 feet south into the new extension, allowing the tiny servants' toilet room under those stairs to be enlarged and a sink to be added. The entrance to the bathroom, adjacent to the outside door, would be moved to a more convenient position opposite the existing

FIG. 74 *Second-floor plan, second scheme, Hoppin & Koen, September 25, 1907. This unrealized plan proposed an additional guest room and guest bath, a bedroom for staff, and a cedar closet. The sewing room would have gained a fireplace, and the maid's room and the dress room would be enlarged. The guest bath for the east guest room (lower right corner) would have opened onto a passage, as prescribed by the authors of* The Decoration of Houses. *(EWR)*

refrigerator. The addition of an interior sash door just inside the door of the porch would help to keep the cold air out of the service wing.

A new storage room (9 feet by 14 feet 6 inches) was to be located within the area currently occupied by the existing servants' dining room. The 1907 alterations provided for much-needed space throughout the service areas.

The servants' dining room was doubled in size and renamed the servants' hall and included a fireplace and a built-in dresser (or cabinets) on the opposite wall.

The existing kitchen would be enlarged 3 feet on the south end; a built-in dresser would be added on that wall. On either side of the dresser doors, the room would connect with the new servants' hall on the west, and on the east with a new kitchen storage area and a huge new walk-in refrigerator almost three times the size of the existing one. The larger kitchen, refrigerator,

and storage areas in this configuration would make meal preparations at The Mount easier.

Alterations to the First Floor

Three different schemes, incorporating the same features with different sizes and arrangements, were prepared by Hoppin & Koen to alter the first floor of the service wing.[7] The existing floor has a central passage with the service elevator and the servants' stairs wrapping around it on the north end of the corridor. The butler's pantry, a brush room, the housekeeper's room, the cook's room, and a room for the butler open onto the passage.

The new schemes called for a flower room in place of the elevator and stairs; the latter would move 26 feet to the south. In the new flower room Edith could arrange freshly cut flowers from her gardens and greenhouse. Other addi-

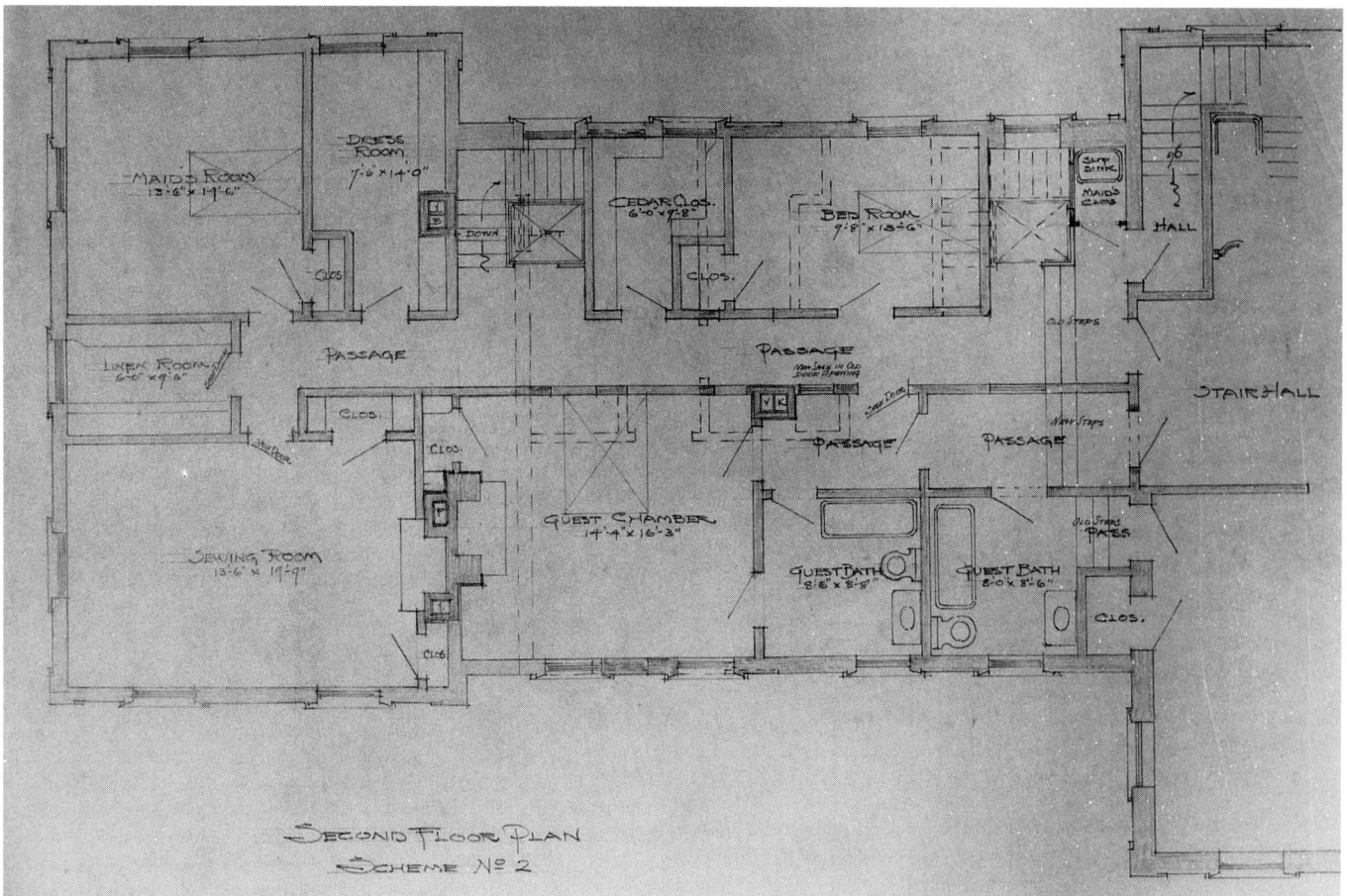

120

tions included a valet's room, a hot closet, a good-size sitting room for the staff whose rooms were located on this floor, and a new men's bath to be shared by the butler, valet, and cook.[8] The housekeeper's room[9] would move up one floor to an area occupied by Edith's personal maid.

This plan would have segregated male and female employees better. Even more important, all of the principal staff — butler, valet, cook (and housekeeper upstairs) — would enjoy larger rooms, more closet space, a new communal sitting room with a fireplace, and a new full bath. Apparently the servants on the first floor were using the bathrooms on the other floors of the service wing and had no proper sitting area of their own.

In all three schemes the cook had the largest room,[10] which may indicate something about the hierarchy of the staff, as well as the Whartons' own priorities. The butler had the next largest space of the three male staff, the valet having the smallest.

Alterations to the Second Floor

Two Hoppin & Koen schemes for alterations to the second floor of the service wing survive.[11] These schemes proposed the same new features, enlargements, or changes but provided alternate ways to achieve them.

The existing floor plan incorporates a central passage that includes the termination point for the service elevator. The sewing room, the linen closet, a dress closet, a housemaid's closet (with slop sink), and Edith's personal maid's room open onto this passage, which is lit by a skylight. Also in the wing, but not accessible from this passage, is a bathroom for the east guest room.[12]

Both schemes would add several new features for the staff, including a new room for the housekeeper[13] and a cedar closet.[14] The sewing room would be enlarged and improved with the addition of a fireplace; it probably also would then serve as a combination work area and sitting room for the housekeeper and the

personal maid. The former dress closet would be doubled in size to become a dress room for Edith's clothing. The personal maid's room would also be enlarged. The linen closet and the housemaid's closet would be slightly smaller in their new locations.

Both schemes added a new guest room (with fireplace) and a connecting guest bath. The existing guest bath would be made accessible to staff from the outside hallway, as were the other existing baths on the bedroom floor. Scheme No. 1 proposed one central passage; Scheme No. 2 suggested two passages side-by-side, one for guests, the other for servants. In the first scheme, the service part of the wing began immediately after the entrance to the new guest room and was separated from the rest of the house by a closed door. While keeping the existing servants' passage, the second scheme would make a new passage through the former dress closet; the existing guest bath (with its new access), the new guest room, and the new guest bath would open onto it.

New Attic Floor

Unfortunately, no floor plans survive (if, indeed, any were ever drawn) for the new attic floor on the alternate elevation of the wing; it probably would contain additional servants' rooms, another servants' bath,[15] and a sitting area.

Why the 1907 Alterations Were Not Realized

There is no documentation concerning why the Whartons decided not to undertake the proposed alterations. Until they sold The Mount in 1911, they maintained an interest in improving the estate. Judge Robert Grant, a frequent visitor, remembered: "My last visit to The Mount [1911] seemed the happiest at the moment, for each of my hosts gave the impression of being in love with what they built, and Edith spoke gleefully of hoping to pay for a new terrace with the profits of her next book. Within three weeks I heard that they had decided to uproot themselves and live abroad."[16] The major problem — and Judge Grant hints at this — seems to have been financial, although Edith probably had a very personal reason as well.

The year 1905 had been tremendously successful financially for Edith, owing mainly to her first real bestseller, *The House of Mirth*. On Thanksgiving Day 1905, Edith noted in her diary that she and Teddy had given thanks "for the best period of their lives."[17] At the same time, she also added with some satisfaction that *The House of Mirth* was still selling "at a tremendous rate."[18] As R.W.B. Lewis explains:

Altogether, in the course of that year, Edith Wharton's literary earnings amounted to more than $20,000… It is next to impossible to translate the meaning of income from one period to another with any accuracy; but given the absence of income tax in the United States of 1905 and the rate of inflation in our own time, one should probably multiply the figure of $20,000 by eight or nine to get some sense of its dollar value today. Edith Wharton's annual expenses, it may be added, were almost always identical with her income.[19]

As *The House of Mirth* continued to sell, Edith and Clyde Fitch were preparing a theatrical version of the novel. Edith was also working on a volume of "motor-flight articles" of the French countryside, several short stories, the novella *Madame de Treymes*, and a novel, *The Fruit of the Tree*, for which she and her publishers had the highest of hopes. It was against this background that Edith and Teddy Wharton contemplated the expansion of the service wing of The Mount.

In October 1906 the theatrical version of *The House of Mirth* failed in New York, but Edith was probably not too concerned, as she had never really believed that there was a play in her novel. More alarming were the sluggish sales of *The Fruit of the Tree*, published in October 1907.[20] Edith's "literary earnings in 1907 … were less than half those of the preceding year": $32,000 in 1906, $13,500 in 1907.[21] This sharp drop probably caused the Whartons to rethink their expansion plans.

By 1907 Edith began to transfer her allegiance from America to the Faubourg section of Paris. For the newly emerging and "observant American novelist of manners,"[22] this part of Paris with its "sense of continuity and the sense of personal freedom"[23] held a strong attraction; it became the milieu for her work-in-progress, *Madame de Treymes*. Edith rented 58 rue de Varenne, the George Vanderbilts' apartment, and over the next several years spent more and more time in Paris.

In October 1907 Edith hosted Morton Fullerton at The Mount. It was during this visit that Edith began to fall in love with him; with Fullerton's departure for France Edith began a diary of her thoughts about him. Only days later, she "advanced her sailing date to France from early January to December 5, giving it out that with autumn's unusually heavy snow and the long cold spell, the servants' quarters were too chilly to be occupied."[24]

Teddy was, as usual, unwell; his "numbness of spirit combined with Edith's uncertainty about Morton Fullerton to provide a serious distraction from writing."[25] By February 1908, the relationship between Edith and Morton Fullerton had taken "a definite turn,"[26] and for the next several years, her attentions were directed towards him.

CHAPTER 8

History of The Mount, 1911 and After

The Whartons Sell The Mount, 1911-12

Edith Wharton spent her last extended period of time at The Mount several years before the house was sold; she was in residence for approximately five months from late May through most of October 1908, when she worked on a new novel, *The Custom of the Country*.

On October 30 Edith sailed for Europe, accompanied by Walter Berry. For the next two years she would divide her time between France and England, not returning to The Mount until July 2, 1911. Although Teddy visited Lenox in April 1909, they rented The Mount for the summers of 1909 and 1910 to Albert R. Shattuck, his wife, Mary, and her mother, Mrs. William Strong.[1] The Shattucks purchased The Mount from the Whartons in the fall of 1911.[2]

Edith gave different accounts of how she came to sell The Mount. In *A Backward Glance* she discussed her decision twice: "There for over ten years I lived and gardened and wrote contentedly, and should doubtless have ended my days there had not a grave change in my husband's health made the burden of the property too heavy."[3] She also explained:

But much as I loved the place…it was all darkened by my husband's growing ill-health. Since the first years of our marriage his condition, in spite of intervals of apparent health, had become steadily graver. His sweetness of temper and boyish enjoyment of life struggled against the creeping darkness of neurasthenia, but all the neurologists we consulted were of the opinion that there could be no real recovery; and time confirmed their verdict…

The care of The Mount had been my husband's chief interest and occupation, and the place had now to be sold, for much as I loved it the burden would have been too heavy for me to carry alone.[4]

The actual sequence of events may best be understood from Edith's letters to her friends and from several other sources.

On July 2, 1911, Edith arrived at The Mount after an absence of almost three years. The next day she wrote Morton Fullerton of her "mingled emotions,"[5] which included her pleasure in being back and the great beauty of the place — particularly the many improvements in the landscaping and gardens achieved by her "admirable head gardener,"[6] Thomas Reynolds, who had, however, given his notice some months before. Already there had been some discussion of selling The Mount: Teddy had agreed, but at the last moment "he had made a sudden volte-face and raised an obstacle, trifling in itself, which had put off the purchaser. Et violà!"[7]

In July Edith presided over the last gathering of her inner circle at The Mount — Henry James, John Hugh Smith, and Gaillard Lapsley were in attendance. With the departures of Smith and Lapsley, Wharton and James had time to talk at length about her personal concerns. James felt that she should sell The Mount and separate from Teddy, but Edith was not yet able to take such drastic action.[8] James wrote her on July 19 that "2 things surely emerge clear: 1st that it's vital to get rid of the absolutely unworkable burden & complication of the Mount; & 2d that with the recurrence of scenes of violence you must insist on saving your life by a separate existence… But settle the Mount question first, & the rest will offer itself in much simpler form."[9]

Teddy arrived at The Mount by July 13, and husband and wife continued to try to live together until the night of July 22, when the situation worsened. After a long talk, in which Teddy apologized convincingly for his behavior of the past ten days, Edith decided not to sell The Mount and to return its management to Teddy. The loss of control over the estate — Teddy's primary occupation since 1902 — had been a major factor in their deteriorating relationship. Ever since Teddy had embezzled and recklessly spent monies from her trust funds in 1909, Edith had kept him away from controlling her funds and property. Allowing Teddy to manage The Mount (towards which she would deposit $500 a month in an account for him) once again was a major concession for Edith, although she demanded that Teddy resign from his position of trustee of her estate and "thus rid his mind of business preoccupations which have for the last few years been only a source of useless distress to him." [10]

Edith planned to stay at The Mount until the middle of September, when she would return to Europe. Teddy was to join her there in March. They would then return to Lenox for the summer of 1912 "if all goes well." [11]

Edith wrote a long letter to Teddy's brother, William F. Wharton, explaining the terms. She showed the letter to Teddy and asked him to verify its accuracy. Teddy was angry and stated, according to Edith, that unless she would allow him to act as trustee of her estate, "it was useless for us to try to live together either here or elsewhere, & that for his part he thought there had better be a final break between us at once, as he should take no interest in managing The Mount & running the household..." [12]

Edith resolved to take Teddy at his word and wrote him of her decision the next day. Yet two weeks later, on August 6, she wrote to John Hugh Smith that an offer to sell The Mount had been rejected because she had hoped that Teddy might "improve & really benefit by the life here." [13] She also noted that "our purchaser, as soon as he found me indifferent, expressed a readiness to wait!" [14] The identity of this purchaser is unknown.

But everything changed again two weeks later when Mr. and Mrs. William Pollock expressed interest in buying The Mount. [15] On August 22, William D. Curtis, a Lenox real-estate agent,

showed the property to the Pollocks, who offered $180,000 for it. Curtis had an evening meeting with Teddy, who agreed to give a decision the next day.

On August 23, Teddy and Mrs. Pollock began meeting to arrange the details of the sale. Edith wrote Sara Norton on August 26:

We have had a *very* large offer for The Mount since I last wrote you, & have very suddenly decided to sell it. The reasons are partly economic, and partly based on Teddy's condition. The place is *very* expensive, so much so that it requires constant care & adjustment to keep it from being *too* much so; & with a big country place you know how hard it is to maintain that balance! —[16]

Edith had felt inclined to keep The Mount, she continued, if Teddy were willing to manage it, but with the departure of their head gardener, Teddy did not feel "well enough & dreaded the constant responsibility." [17] She had left the entire matter up to Teddy to decide, as she felt he was well enough to deal with the situation calmly.

According to Curtis, on August 29 the Whartons refused to sign an agreement with the Pollocks, who then called the deal off. Curtis met with both parties the following day in an attempt to reconcile their differences, but he was unsuccessful.

The following night Teddy telephoned Curtis and asked him to sell The Mount for $180,000; yet when Curtis met with him the next day (September 1), Teddy made a new demand—that The Mount be sold unfurnished for $160,000. Although Curtis met for the next two days with Pollock, no deal could be effected. The reasons for the Whartons' decision to cease negotiations with the Pollocks (whose large offer had obviously pleased Edith one week before) are unknown. [18]

On September 2 Albert and Mary Shattuck entered the picture; they had rented The Mount in 1909 and 1910 while the Whartons were abroad. Curtis met that day with Mrs. Shattuck, who asked for first refusal on the property, a request that both Edith and Teddy (who met later with Curtis) declined.

On September 7 Edith sailed for Europe in anticipation of a long-awaited rest cure at

Salsomaggiore. She gave Teddy power of attorney to complete the sale of The Mount, but she apparently did not expect him to proceed as quickly as he did. She angrily wrote to Morton Fullerton on September 22:

Yes — he *promised* not to sell the Mount to any one, at any price, till after I had reached Paris & he had communicated with me; & to remind him, I sent back a line to the same effect by the pilot [of the ship]… Yet when I landed I found his cable saying he had sold! And today comes a letter; he is apparently much pleased with what he has done, & makes *no* allusion to the agreement made when we parted![19]

The day after Edith left for Europe, Teddy and Albert Shattuck met several times with Curtis, and Mrs. Shattuck revisited The Mount. On September 9 there were several more meetings, including one in which Teddy exempted certain articles of furniture and personal belongings from the sale. That evening a written agreement for a purchase price for $180,000 was signed, and a check for $10,000 was given to Teddy as a deposit.

According to *The Berkshire Evening Eagle* of September 11, 1911, it

was well known that Mr. Shattuck had made an offer for the Mount, and his being the purchaser of the property, after the end of negotiations by Mr. and Mrs. Pollock, is no surprise in Lenox to those who have been kept informed as to the trend of events with regard to the sale. One matter has come out regarding the value of the property, and that is that The Mount cost Mr. and Mrs. Wharton close to $250,000, and the purchase price was not far from $180,000.[20]

On September 12 Curtis received a commission of $4,500; on September 28 the deed and a final bill of sale were sent by registered mail to Edith in Italy.

Unaware that the sale had just taken place, James wrote sympathetically to Edith on September 19 about "the great business of parting with the Mount," worrying about "that gorgeous millstone of the Mount—hanging around your atlantean neck, yet helping too it would after all seem to turn the wheel of poor Teddy's fortune."[21]

Edith continued to blame Teddy for breaking

his word to her. To her sister-in-law Mary Cadwalader Jones she wrote: "Of course this business of selling the Mount while I was at sea, after promising me *not to do so*, is proof that his purposes are still vague & vacillating, & that he forgets, or re-arranges in his memory, the most definite & emphatic agreement, half an hour after it is over."[22] Yet she sounded a cautiously optimistic note by concluding: "But, for all ordinary 'rapports' of life he is now possible for the first time in nearly three years — & that's a good deal to be thankful for!"[23] The Whartons' unhappy marriage dragged on for almost two more years until Edith filed for a French divorce in Paris in 1913.

The deed to The Mount was signed in Paris by Edith and Teddy in January 1912.[24] A few months later, writing to her friend Gaillard Lapsley, who visited regularly with his relatives in nearby Stockbridge, Massachusetts, Edith pleaded: "Write me soon, dear Gaillard. But don't tell me anything about the Mount, for there's a great ache there still."[25]

Mary and Albert R. Shattuck, Owners, 1912-38

For the next quarter of a century, The Mount was owned by Mary and Albert R. Shattuck or their heirs. Albert Shattuck was born in New York City in 1854[1] to parents from Louisiana.[2] Little is known about the first thirty years of his life.[3] He went into the banking business and "accumulated his fortune in New Orleans,"[4] before moving to New York City, where for many years he was associated with the British & American Mortgage Company.[5] In 1890 he married Mary U. Strong (1868-1935), of New York City. Her father, William L. Strong (1827-1900), accumulated a large fortune in the dry goods business and capped his career by serving as Mayor of the City of New York from 1895-97.[6]

Around 1885, William B. Shattuck, Albert's father, commissioned architect James Renwick[7] to build a summer house in Lenox, Massachusetts, for his family, who lived in New Orleans the rest of the year.[8] Known as Brook-

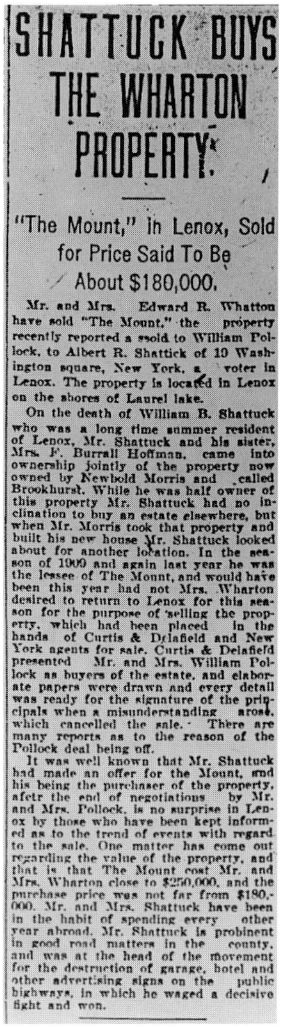

SHATTUCK BUYS THE WHARTON PROPERTY.

"The Mount," in Lenox, Sold for Price Said To Be About $180,000.

Mr. and Mrs. Edward R. Wharton have sold "The Mount," the property recently reported a sold to William Pollock, to Albert R. Shattuck of 19 Washington square, New York, a voter in Lenox. The property is located in Lenox on the shores of Laurel lake.

On the death of William B. Shattuck who was a long time summer resident of Lenox, Mr. Shattuck and his sister, Mrs. F. Burrall Hoffman, came into ownership jointly of the property now owned by Newbold Morris and called Brookhurst. While he was half owner of this property Mr. Shattuck had no inclination to buy an estate elsewhere, but when Mr. Morris took that property and built his new house last year he was about for another location. In the season of 1909 and again last year he was the lessee of The Mount, and would have been this year had not Mrs. Wharton desired to return to Lenox for this season for the purpose of selling the property, which had been placed in the hands of Curtis & Delafield and New York agents for sale. Curtis & Delafield presented Mr. and Mrs. William Pollock as buyers of the estate, and elaborate papers were drawn and every detail was ready for the signature of the principals when a misunderstanding arose, which cancelled the sale. There are many reports as to the reason of the Pollock deal being off.

It was known that Mr. Shattuck had made an offer for the Mount, and his being the purchaser of the property, aftctr the end of negotiations by Mr. and Mrs. Pollock, is no surprise in Lenox by those who have been kept informed as to the trend of events with regard to the sale. One matter has come out regarding the value of the property, and that is that The Mount cost Mr. and Mrs. Wharton close to $250,000, and the purchase price was not far from $180,000. Mr. and Mrs. Shattuck have been in the habit of spending every other year abroad. Mr. Shattuck is prominent in good road matters in the county, and was at the head of the movement for the destruction of garage, hotel and other advertising signs on the public highways, in which he waged a decisive fight and won.

FIG. 75 *The sale of The Mount was first reported in* The Berkshire Evening Eagle, *September 11, 1911.* (BA)

hurst, the property, which was located between West Street and Hawthorne Street, consisted of the main house, a stable, a gatehouse, and other outbuildings, all in an eclectic Queen Anne style. On the death of their father, Albert and his sister, Lucy, came into joint ownership of Brookhurst.[9] Around 1908 the house burned to the ground, and Albert and Lucy sold the property to Newbold Morris, of New York City, a cousin of Edith Wharton.[10]

Mary and Albert Shattuck moved from New Orleans to Manhattan around 1899[11] and settled at a handsome townhouse, No. 19 Washington Square North. Albert quickly became "one of Wall Street's shrewdest investors."[12] The Shattucks were soon well-respected members of New York society[13]; Albert was said to have "an appreciation of beautiful things,"[14] to surround himself with books and pictures,[15] and to be of "a literary turn."[16] Mary and Albert spent their summers and falls in Lenox, where he was admired as one of the resort's "most public spirited summer residents."[17]

Shattuck figured prominently in news accounts at the turn-of-the-century; he was associated with a group of well-to-do men who early on recognized the importance of the automobile and worked to make it an invaluable part of everyday American life.[18] By 1900 Shattuck owned four automobiles and motored in them daily.[19] According to *Lenox Life*, acclimating horses to the new horseless carriage was "the table talk of the cottagers at breakfast, lunch and dinner"[20] at the turn-of-the-century. From the beginning Shattuck maintained a keen interest in this issue. For several years, along with several other prominent Lenox men, he offered his services to help accustom the horses of his friends and neighbors to the sight and sounds of the automobile.[21]

By 1901, Shattuck's passion for automobiling led to his election as president of the Automobile Club of America, which included "in its membership all of the prominent automobilists of the east"[22]: William K. Vanderbilt, Jr., Col. John Jacob Astor, Harry Payne Whitney, David Wolfe Bishop, Cortlandt Field Bishop, Alfred

C. Bostwick, George Isham Scott, Whitney Lyon, and Dr. W. Seward Webb, among others. During Shattuck's two-year term, he was instrumental in early efforts to improve automobiles and roads.

In 1902 Shattuck was involved in efforts to have the highway between East Lee and Chester, Massachusetts, designated a state road, creating a state highway from the Berkshires to Springfield.[23] In the fall of 1902, he publicly "expressed himself as heartily in favor of the license system for automobile drivers,"[24] a controversial issue in New York. According to *Lenox Life*, Shattuck believed that "license laws should be state laws and not pertain solely to individual cities, or a tourist would have to take out a license in every city through which he had occasion to pass."[25] *The Berkshire Evening Eagle* in 1911 also stated that "Mr. Shattuck is prominent in good road matters in the county, and was at the head of the movement for the destruction of garage, hotel and other advertising signs on the public highways in which he waged a decisive fight and won."[26]

During the 1890s Mary and Albert Shattuck stayed at Brookhurst when they visited Lenox. After the death of his parents (both were dead by 1899[27]), the Shattucks rented local cottages for their summers and falls in Lenox, presumably renting Brookhurst to other tenants.[28] According to *The Berkshire Evening Eagle*, before Newbold Morris purchased the Brookhurst property in 1908, "Mr. Shattuck had no inclination to buy an estate elsewhere, but when Mr. Morris took that property and built his new home, Shattuck looked about for another location."[29]

During the summers of 1909 and 1910, Mary and Albert Shattuck rented The Mount while Edith and Teddy Wharton were in Europe.[30] In September 1911 the Shattucks entered into negotiations with the Whartons to purchase The Mount. By September 9, with Edith at sea, Teddy agreed to a sale and accepted a check for a down payment of $10,000. The final deed was signed by the Whartons in January 1912; for $180,000, Mary and Albert

FIG. 76 *Albert R. Shattuck,* Lenox Life, *May 19, 1900.* *His photograph from* Automobile Magazine *was published because of his prominence as an early automobilist.* (BA)

Shattuck purchased The Mount and most of its furnishings.

In May 1912 *The Berkshire Evening Eagle* reported that Albert Shattuck was staying at the Curtis Hotel and "superintending changes and alterations at his estate, The Mount."[31] According to an obituary, "Mr. Shattuck greatly improved the property with formal gardens and winding drives by doing whatever was needed, regardless of expense, to make it an ideal gentleman's estate."[32] Another account noted that after acquiring The Mount, "the Shattucks spent more than $200,000 on alterations and additions, including a new swimming pool, elaborate stable, tennis courts and new road..."[33]

The Shattucks renamed the estate "White Lodge," as "The Mount" was no doubt too closely associated with the Whartons. They stayed regularly at White Lodge, along with Mary's mother, Mrs. William L. Strong, and Albert's sister, Lucy E. Hoffman, and her four sons, William, F. Burrall, Albert, and Murray.[34]

For the next few years the Shattucks appear to have led a quiet life. However, in 1917 they were thrust into the news when their butler[35] stole $12,600 worth of Mrs. Shattuck's jewels from their New York home and disappeared. Five years later, early on the morning of Sunday, April 2, 1922, the former butler returned, bringing four accomplices.[36] Well-versed in the layout of the house and the schedules of its inhabitants, he knew that the Shattucks would be resting in their rooms and the household staff of eight would be having lunch in the servants' dining room. All were forced at gunpoint down into the cellar and locked into the wine vault. As *The New York Times* explained: "Electric wires had been cut, with the result that ten persons were left in the darkness in a small airtight chamber."[37]

While the criminals selected Mrs. Shattuck's most valuable jewelry upstairs, in the dark wine cellar Mr. Shattuck

fumbled at the heavy oak door until he found the lock. With a small gold penknife from his watch chain and a dime he scraped at the rusty screws. It was desperate work for that 69-year-old man there in the dark, using improvised tools, his hands trembling... The air grew staler and staler. Within half an hour all were uncomfortable from the lack of oxygen. Fifteen minutes later they were all suffering. All knew that if the door could not be opened they would die. One by one the screws yielded until, after an hour's feverish work, the lock fell off and the door opened.[38]

Although the robbers fled with $80,000 worth of jewelry, several were captured soon after. The trails of two others, including the former butler, pointed to France. Mary and Albert closed the Washington Square house and went to Europe. She was concerned to rebuild her health, and he, fired by a desire for vengeance, began a relentless search for the criminals.[39] Rewards were offered, heads of police departments were visited, posters were distributed in many countries, and the Pinkerton Agency was retained.[40]

Eventually the former butler was arrested in Paris; Shattuck appeared before a French court to testify, and the butler was sentenced to death at the guillotine. Both Shattucks begged the court and the President of France for mercy,[41] and the former servant was instead sent to Devil's Island in 1926 to serve a life sentence for robbery and imprisonment.[42]

In June 1925 Mr. Shattuck arrived in Lenox from London; in late July he suffered a severe heart attack and "a nervous breakdown."[43] Mrs. Shattuck rushed to White Lodge from Paris, arriving during the first week of August, and remained at his bedside day and night as he was kept alive by oxygen and attended by nurses around the clock. During this period White Lodge was kept under constant guard.[44] Albert Shattuck died in his bedroom at White Lodge of heart disease on November 4, 1925,[45] at age 72. His funeral was held on November 6 at Trinity Church in Lenox,[46] with interment in the Strong family vault in Woodlawn Cemetery in New York City.

Mary Strong Shattuck became a very wealthy woman. Her father had been a millionaire, and her husband left her all of his money and property (including the New York City townhouse and White Lodge).[47] At Albert's death, a trust established by his father amounted to $500,000.[48]

For the remaining ten years of her life, Mary Shattuck apparently divided her time between Europe, occasional visits to 19 Washington Square North in New York City, and White Lodge.[49] She died in Lenox at White Lodge on March 1, 1935, and was buried in Woodlawn beside her husband, her father, and her mother.[50]

In October 1935 the American Art Association Anderson Galleries held a three-day auction of her jewelry, furniture, and objets d'art in New York City, netting a total of $84,687. It seems likely that the majority of the Wharton/Shattuck furnishings at The Mount were dispersed at this time. Among the items sold were "a Louis XV occasional table stamped with the name of Nicolas Petit [$1,300]..., four Louis XV carved and parcel-gilded walnut armchairs for $520 each..., a Brussels tapestry of the eighteenth century depicting Narcissus at the fountain [$900], $850 paid...for another Brussels tapestry of the same period showing Bacchus and Ariadne...and $800...for a pair of Louis XV walnut fauteuils and...for a tulipwood commode of the eighteenth century."[51]

Soon after Mary Shattuck's death, her Lenox estate was offered for sale. The listing under its original name in an issue of *Country Life* magazine in 1936 read as follows:

French chateau, unusually fine country estate in Berkshires, Lenox, Mass.; 155 acres; house elevation 1,200 feet; 5 master bedrooms, 4 master baths, personal maid's room and bath, 9 servants' rooms and bath. Eight-room gatehouse, garage and stable for 10 cars with 4 box stalls, 7-room apartment. Greenhouse, farmhouse, other farm buildings. Estate free and clear.[52]

It seems likely that The Mount was being offered for sale without any furnishings. The advertisement contained a photograph of the east elevation of the mansion, including the lime walk, taken from the meadow. Apparently the advertisement drew no purchasers.

Mary Shattuck's heirs sold The Mount to Louise D. Van Anda on October 20, 1938, for $25,600.[53] If an account of her husband, Carr V. Van Anda, is correct, The Mount remained unoccupied from 1935-38.

Louise and Carr V. Van Anda, Owners, 1938-42

Carr Vattel Van Anda was born in 1864 in Ohio, the son of an attorney.[1] He evinced an early interest in newspapers; at age six he apparently compiled an entire publication on his own and sold it to relatives. While in his early teens he purchased a printing press for $5 and published his own gazette. At age sixteen, Carr attended Ohio University[2] in Athens, where he studied mathematics and physics while working as a correspondent for Cleveland and Cincinnati newspapers. He left college to work full time as a foreman for *The Auglaize Republican*, a Wapakoneta weekly, where he learned about the mechanical aspects of the trade. By 1883 he was a typesetter and reporter for *The Cleveland Herald*. His success led to a promotion to telegraph editor. In 1885 the *Herald* was sold to the *Cleveland Plain Dealer*; Van Anda stayed with the new publication briefly, then went to *The Cleveland Evening Argus* for a year or so until that paper failed. By the time he was 21, Van Anda had learned the newspaper business thoroughly.

In 1885 Van Anda married Harriet L. Tupper in Cleveland, Ohio. They soon moved to Baltimore, where he worked for *The Baltimore Sun* as a night editor for two years. A daughter, Blanche, was born in Baltimore in 1887; Harriet Van Anda died in December of that year.

Van Anda moved to New York City in 1888, working as a reporter and copy editor with *The Sun*. In 1893 he was promoted to night editor, a position he held for 11 years. "In that capacity he distinguished himself for his initiative and enterprise in handling the news of such events as the Spanish-American War and the Philippine uprising."[3]

In 1898, when he was thirty-three years old, Van Anda married again; his second wife was Louise Shipman Drane, of Frankfort, Kentucky. A son, Paul Drane Van Anda, was born in 1899.

Van Anda was hired by Adolph S. Ochs to be managing editor of *The New York Times* in early

1904. Ochs, who had purchased the paper in 1896, was determined to build a daily that was reliable, honest, and trustworthy in a period known for its sensationalism and "yellow journalism." By the time Van Anda was hired, circulation was up, and advertising revenues were improving. Ochs gave Van Anda a free hand; "V.A.," as he became known at *The Times*, soon galvanized the staff with his prodigious energy and enthusiasm. He had unusual intellectual powers, a strong curiosity, and an unfailing intuition about the news and how to present it. He was also known to be fair, thorough, and extremely well organized.

V.A. was a hard worker, working 12-hour days, seven days a week, rarely taking a vacation or even a day off. He repeatedly scored a "clear beat" over the other New York papers on many major stories of the day, including the Japanese naval victory over the Russians during the Russo-Japanese war; the sinking of the *Titanic*; Marconi's experiments; the discovery of the North Pole by Admiral Peary; and Amundsen's discovery of the South Pole, followed by Scott's arrival there a few days later. *The Times* led the world in coverage of subjects of particular interest to Van Anda: advances in science, aviation, wireless telegraphy, and exploration. He loved to organize the details of a story; "he saw it in pages instead of columns."[4]

World War I gave Van Anda his "greatest opportunity to display his astonishing catholicity of interests. Few developments in either the military or the diplomatic aspects of the war escaped his attention, and he was quick to recognize the significance of many events that to other newspapermen had little or no interest."[5] *The Times* again led the world in coverage of documents, speeches, and "the publication in full of the arguments of the various European governments — the White Papers, Yellow Books, Orange Papers, and so on, consisting of the diplomatic correspondence leading up to the war."[6] *The Times* was the first recipient of the Pulitzer Prize for "disinterested and meritorious service" by a newspaper in 1918 "for publishing in full so many official reports, documents and

FIG. 77 *Louise D. Van Anda (?) in the drawing room, probably c. 1940.* (FHS)

speeches by European statesmen relating to the progress and conduct of the war."[7]

Van Anda continued full coverage of the stories that most interested him, including trans-Atlantic flights by Lindbergh and others. Van Anda, "more than any other individual, was responsible for the attention devoted by the American press to such events as the exploration of Tut-ankh-Amen's tomb, and the upholding of Einstein's theory of relativity through the astronomical observations of 1919."[8] Anecdotes concerning Van Anda's knowledge of Egyptology and hieroglypics and his correction of a mistake by Einstein in one of the scientist's own theories have become legendary at *The New York Times*.[9]

His article, "The Unsolved Riddle of the Solar System," written in 1931, was published in the magazine *Science*. Van Anda "criticized certain theories that had been advanced by Sir James Jeans, the eminent British astrophysicist, and Dr. Harold Jeffreys of Cambridge University, a leading geo-physicist." *The New York Times* noted: "Sir James and Dr. Jeffreys subsequently accepted the corrections suggested by Mr. Van Anda." [10]

In 1925, due to ill-health, Van Anda took a long leave of absence from *The Times*. In fact, he never returned to work as managing editor, although he retained his title and did not formally retire until 1932. For some years the Van Andas spent time at their country home, Tory Trail, in Onteora Park near Tannersville, New York. Their city residence by this time was an apartment at 1170 Park Avenue. What brought them to the Berkshires is not known, but on October 20, 1938, they bought The Mount at auction (in Louise D. Van Anda's name) for $25,600 from the heirs of Mary Strong Shattuck. [11]

It may have been that the Van Andas purchased The Mount as a retirement home since he was just months away from his seventy-fourth birthday. On Van Anda's application for the abatement of taxes, submitted in September 1940, he commented that The Mount "was bought in the expectation of all-year occupancy." [12] But it soon became clear to the new owners that the furnace system was a more serious problem than they had imagined. It seems the Van Andas occupied The Mount only during the summers for the four years they owned it. [13]

Some repairs were made to the property soon after purchase. In 1939, $3,768 was spent on the mansion and the greenhouse. Van Anda found that repairs were also needed to the defective heating system (estimated cost $7,300), the exterior of the house ($3,280 estimated), the terrace walls and balustrade (estimated at $1,800), and the walls of the Italian walled garden. Additionally, $1,276 was needed for the first-floor rooms, $1,196 for the second-floor rooms, and $1,457 for the third-floor rooms. Many thousands of dollars were believed necessary to repair the service areas.

The outbuildings also had problems. The hen house, piggery, ice house, and wagon shed were not being used and were in disrepair. The nearby barn was used only for hay storage (to fill the pools in the gardens during the winter), and The Mount's elegant stable was being used to store the Van Andas' car and the cars of their employees. The greenhouse was in the worst condition, requiring $868 to put it in working order. In 1939, $168 was spent to keep the brick foundation from complete collapse.

It clearly came as a shock when the property (157 acres of land and all "improvements," i.e. buildings thereon) was assessed for taxes of $2,240 for the year 1940. The total valuation of the land and buildings was estimated by the Town of Lenox at $70,000 (land, $23,500; buildings, $46,500). Van Anda submitted an application and accompanying statement in September 1940, arguing for the tax to be reduced by half to $1,104 (land, $12,060; buildings, $22,438, for a total of $34,498).

Van Anda compared the neighboring estates of Bellefontaine, owned by Giraud Foster, and the Foxhollow School, on the former Westinghouse property, to The Mount. He was able to demonstrate that The Mount had been overassessed. His attorney secured a reduction of $30,000 for the property, about $7,500 more than Van Anda had argued for but a considerable decrease. However, in 1941 the town of Lenox assessed The Mount at $71,500, an increase of $1,500 above the figure Van Anda had already contested. [14] He was apparently in the midst of dealing with this problem when Louise Van Anda died of bronchial pneumonia on February 17, 1942, in New York City. [15] Van Anda spent the summer of 1942 alone at The Mount, except for the staff.

During that summer Aileen Farrell, the headmistress of the adjoining Foxhollow School, expressed interest in purchasing The Mount. The school's stables had burned to the ground on December 11, 1941, and during the spring of 1942 the girls had to be driven to Pittsfield for horseback riding, a difficult undertaking during wartime and gas rationing. The Mount would provide a stable, a dormitory, and study and classroom space for the growing school. According to Miss Farrell, Van Anda, her "friendly neighbour,"[16] was tiring of living alone at The Mount.[17] Throughout the summer of 1942 he considered her proposal.

On September 12, 1942, The Mount was sold to the school[18] for $18,000 for the mansion, outbuildings, and grounds and $5,659 for furniture.[19] Miss Farrell later wrote that Van Anda had been "delighted to sell his property to us... Needless to say these easy prices [for purchase] were an expression of Mr. Van Anda's confidence in me & in Foxhollow's educational value."[20] Van Anda moved out of The Mount on September 19, and two days later the first students moved in.

Van Anda returned to 1170 Park Avenue in New York City and lived quietly for the next few years. He died of a massive heart attack at age 80 on January 28, 1945, after learning that his only daughter Blanche Van Anda, age 58, had been found dead in her New York apartment.[21] A double funeral for father and daughter was held several days later, followed by cremation; the ashes were sent to Frankfort, Kentucky, to be buried next to Louise Van Anda.

Van Anda was publicly mourned by *The New York Times*, which published a lengthy obituary, several other articles lauding his diverse interests, and an editorial. The paper noted his contributions during the momentous years of its development into the world's best-known and most admired daily, his influence on typography and composition, and his strong belief in training staff for the future. As the January 30, 1945, editorial concluded:

His signature is written large across *The Times* today... It is not easy to write of him in the usual terms of an obituary, for this newspaper is proud to feel that the Van Anda touch has not vanished from its pages and will not do so... He had an insatiable curiosity and an unabatable eagerness. He lived life intensely, lived it to the full, and left behind a memory which is an inspiration to every member of this newspaper's staff.[22]

The Foxhollow School, Owner, 1942-76

The Foxhollow School, which purchased The Mount in September 1942, was founded by Aileen Mary Farrell. Born in London in 1898 to Irish parents,[1] she was educated in a Benedictine convent in Warwickshire and at Oxford.[2] She came to America in 1923 and taught at Marymount-on-the-Hudson in Tarrytown, New York, and the Foxcroft School in Middleburg, Virginia."[3] Her dream was to found a school for girls based on an interdisciplinary curriculum, a revolutionary concept in American education at the time.

In 1930, not long after turning down a position at Mount Holyoke College, Farrell was living in Rhinebeck, New York, on the estate of Tracy Dows, where she was employed as a tutor to his daughter. When Dows decided to sell the 100-acre property overlooking the Hudson River, he suggested to Farrell that she lease the white Colonial-revivial mansion and grounds, known as Foxhollow Farm, for a school.

FIG. 78 *Aileen M. Farrell (center), founder and longtime headmistress of the Foxhollow School, talking to students on the Lenox campus, date unknown. At left is her associate, O. Meigs Fowler. Photograph by Clemens Kalischer.* (FHS)

Assisted by a friend, Isabel R. Moore, Farrell opened the Foxhollow School in October 1930, with eight students and eight faculty (two more students were added during the year).[4] She also taught English history and English literature. The school prospered for five years. In 1935, the Dows family decided to sell the property to the Astors, and the school moved to the adjoining estate of Helen Crosby, a young woman who attended Vassar and occupied the top floor of the mansion only on her vacations. The Crosby property of 700 acres included a large brick mansion, a stable, and attractive gardens. By 1939 the enrollment had reached 36; the number of faculty remained at eight.

In 1938 the Crosby estate was offered to Farrell for purchase, but she declined because "I recognized that most of my time would have to be spent as a restoring farmer."[5] On the advice of a teacher, she came to the Berkshires to examine Holmwood, the former estate of Margaret Emerson Vanderbilt.[6] This large property, situated on the Lenox and Lee town lines, had been the 1890s summer estate of George Westinghouse, known as Erskine Park. By 1938 it consisted of a neo-Colonial mansion (built 1919), a large array of outbuildings from the Westinghouse era — stables, gymnasium built for George Westinghouse, Jr., ice house, and others (all c. 1893) — and gardens on approximately 400 acres.

At the same time Farrell was shown The Mount, which abutted Holmwood to the south. The property was then for sale by the heirs of Mary Strong Shattuck. Although she loved the house, Farrell decided to buy Holmwood, because it "had a gymnasium and lots of flat lawn for playing fields,"[7] even though at $65,000 it was much more costly than The Mount. Negotiations for the purchase money took many months.[8] Extensive and costly repairs were necessary, and the mansion was largely unfurnished. Funds were eventually obtained, contracts were completed in April 1939, and the move to Lenox took place that May. *The Berkshire Evening Eagle* reported that

Farrell "hopes to have things in readiness for opening the school in the Berkshires next fall."[9]

Soon after opening on the Lenox campus, Farrell decided to incorporate the school with not-for-profit status. A board of trustees was formed and purchased what had been Miss Farrell's own proprietary venture for $39,091.[10]

On December 11, 1941, a major disaster struck the fledgling school. At 1:30 a.m., an intoxicated groom, searching for his kittens in the old Westinghouse stables, dropped several lighted matches into tons of loose hay. The raging fire burned the building to the ground and almost destroyed the gymnasium, which stood only 15 feet away. Firemen from three towns managed to save the gymnasium, as well as the horses. During the spring of 1942, the girls from Foxhollow had to be driven to Pittsfield regularly for their riding, a difficult feat during the wartime years. As Farrell explained, "Needing a stable and extra space for increasing enrollment...I approached a friendly neighbour Mr. Carr Van Anda...Left alone after the death of his wife he was delighted to sell his property to us."[11]

The impending sale was reported in mid-August 1942. *The Berkshire Evening Eagle* noted that the Van Anda property included "a 29-room mansion, gate house, garage and stable, caretaker's house, barns, ice house, boat house and poultry buildings" on 155 acres.[12] "The property is assessed for more than $100,000...The grounds are beautifully landscaped with lawns, terraces, rustic walks, formal gardens and other features...Additional ski and bridle trails and lake-front facilities are made available through the purchase of The Mount."[13] The entire school campus — with the addition of The Mount property — then totalled 365 acres.[14]

In order to dispel delusions of grandeur, Farrell told the media, "The students will still be trained to help in the upkeep of the grounds and care of the house, and definite courses of cooking, sewing, typewriting and shorthand will be added as a complement to the college preparatory courses. Those girls not headed for college will receive a diploma for efficient work completed in these subjects, while the college candidates will have some training along these lines." [15]

The sale took place in September 1942. The Foxhollow School purchased The Mount for $18,000 and the furniture in the mansion for $5,659.[16] Van Anda moved out of the house on September 19, 1942, and the students moved in two days later. As Farrell explained years later: "As a mover of furniture I think I graduated with honors in those two days." [17]

The Berkshire Evening Eagle carried a brief story on the sale and conversion of The Mount on September 12, 1942. The piece illustrated several interiors of The Mount as they looked during the Van Andas' occupancy. The caption for a photograph of the library noted that the school had acquired the entire collection of books in this "well equipped room." [18] Other text alongside explained that the drawing room "is largely and readily adaptable for the school's purposes." [19] There was also a photograph of the entrance hall. The article further stated that: "While her intention is to avoid palatial surroundings for the students Miss Farrell felt the opportunity to buy this property at a low figure should be accepted." [20] The article also noted that the purchase included "stables to replace those destroyed by fire a year ago." [21] The school gained a variety of other structures, including the barn, ice house, wagon shed, hen house, piggery, greenhouse, and the gatehouse on Plunkett Street.

Soon after the sale and the move, the Town of Lenox conducted a hearing in Land Court in May 1943, concerning the zoning status of the new school property.[22] School attorneys discussed other private schools located nearby and questioned whether a "municipality had a right to permit a public school in a zoned area and excluded therefrom [sic] a private school." [23] They stated that "unless it could be shown that the use of the Van Anda property would jeopardize public health, morals or welfare, an effort to prevent such a use by applying the zoning regulations would constitute...a deprivation of the rights of private property." [24] Farrell testified

about the status of the school, noting that "if it had not been for a combination of circumstances including the war and the fire in December 1941, which destroyed the school's teachers' dormitory building...she would not have bought the Van Anda property." [25] In conclusion, Farrell explained that "since the school has been incorporated, it has been exempt from real estate taxation by the town of Lenox... Before the school was incorporated, it paid taxes to the town." [26] The zoning variance for the property was eventually granted.

Farrell's notes and manuscripts chronicle the history of the school over the next 35 years, often citing physical improvements or construction of new buildings. One of the first changes to The Mount was the addition of stairs as a fire exit between the attic and bedroom floors of the mansion, occupying one former servant's room and portions of the bathroom in Edith Wharton's bedroom suite. Fire escapes on the exterior of the building were also erected around this time — several across the east facade and the service wing and one on the north end of the house.

The attic and bedroom floors became dormitories for juniors and seniors. The library was also used as a study hall/meeting space, while seniors had dinners in the dining room every Sunday evening. The den was converted to a private apartment for Farrell's use. The drawing room — which then had a piano — was used for entertaining. At the end of every year the senior class held a dance on the main floor. The class of 1944 donated the initial funds to convert the old kitchen on the basement floor into a chemistry laboratory. Home economics classes were held during the mid-1940s in the former Van Anda kitchen on the main floor.

A mid-1950s school publication described The Mount as Foxhollow's "Junior and Senior House," housing thirty students and five teachers. It stated that since the original kitchen had been converted into a laboratory, an additional kitchen had been created for senior Sunday suppers. The stable was said to have been converted for use as a studio.[27]

FIG. 79 *Foxhollow students, c. 1950s, in The Mount's original basement-floor kitchen, which was converted into a chemistry laboratory.* (FHS)

According to Farrell's notes, few physical changes took place at The Mount from the 1940s through the 1950s. In 1960 the sum of $35,000 "partly subscribed & partly taken from current funds was spent on 'shoring' up the terrace at The Mount."[28] At the same time, the drawing room, dining room, and library were refurnished by Mr. and Mrs. Dudley Ingraham, who "generously expended a great deal of money in re-newing the furniture."[29] In June 1965 several major changes occurred. Farrell recorded that the "larger part of the kitchen at The Mount was transformed into two extra bedrooms,"[30] no doubt reflecting increasing enrollment. In addition, the only new construction on the grounds since 1902 took place: "A house was built for Davidson [the school's facilities manager] on the drive of The Mount."[31]

As the school grew and matured, enlarging the physical plant and providing for the future were major concerns for Farrell and the board of trustees. In 1963 the board approved the building of a house for Farrell and her assistant, Ona Meigs Fowler. Each of the two women paid one quarter of the cost, the school paid a portion, and additional funds were provided by

a state award for the taking of ten acres of woodland by eminent domain in order to widen Route 7. The new house was built along the drive leading to the administration building on the main campus (not on The Mount property). Both Farrell and Fowler were nearing retirement, and each had spent many years living near the dormitories. The new house allowed them to retire with life tenancy yet to keep an eye on the school.

An effort to establish an endowment and development fund was discussed by the board in 1967 and begun the following year. Farrell and the board were concerned that a new head would be less effective in fundraising in the beginning and would require a larger salary.

In late 1969 Hilda Mumford visited the school as the prospective replacement for Farrell. After a second visit, Farrell recommended Mumford to the head of the search committee. Mumford had taught history at the Bryn Mawr School for girls in Baltimore from 1955-63; she currently headed the history department at Garrison Forest School outside of that city.

"Foxhollow's Miss Farrell to Retire as Principal" announced *The Berkshire Eagle* on August 8, 1970. According to this account, Mumford "was selected from among 23 candidates interviewed over a three-year period."[32] Farrell "said that she will stay on as president of the Foxhollow School Corp., would continue to reside on the 450-acre property, and would do some teaching...Miss Farrell said she would stay close to the school to help Mrs. Mumford in her 'first year's adjustment' but then may 'pick [sic] up my heels and travel a bit.' "[33]

Farrell noted that Mumford "arrived for duty"[34] in August 1970 too late for the school to hire English or science teachers, so Farrell and Fowler stayed on in their respective positions, instead of retiring. Farrell also continued "to administrate business affairs"[35] for the school.

At an October meeting of the board of trustees, Farrell announced that for the first time in its history the school had a deficit of $29,036.60. An even larger deficit was predicted for 1970-71, as enrollment had fallen to 45 students. The daily life of the school was also affected by a subtle struggle for power between Farrell and Mumford. After a February 1971 board meeting, Farrell wrote there was a "strong movement to hand entire control [of the school] to Mrs. Mumford which I thought was premature."[36] In March Mumford went to a series of meetings with alumnae without informing Farrell of the participants. By May a former student suggested to Farrell that she not attend an alumnae meeting on campus because the alumnae wished to discuss the school's current problems in privacy.

At a June 1971 meeting of the trustees, the practicality of continuing the Foxhollow School was discussed. One month later, in an effort to forestall the closing of the school, the trustees offered a 14-acre parcel of land bordering Laurel Lake for sale at $100,000. Farrell, in her notes, observed that she had "lost all confidence in [the] financial acumen of [the] Trustees."[37] A year later, on May 19, 1972, the land (known as the "Lake Field") was purchased jointly by the towns of Lee and Lenox (with the help of federal funds) for use as a town recreation center. The area was then designated "Edith Wharton Park."

In 1972 the school closed The Mount as a dormitory. On September 6, 1972, without Farrell's knowledge, the school sold the furniture in the main rooms of the mansion to a New York auction house.[38] When the building closed, it was left unheated as another cost-saving measure. A burst pipe in an attic bathroom caused so much water damage that the plaster ceiling in the drawing room—ornamented with garlands of fruit and flowers and stylized rosettes — collapsed. At the same time, heavy rains resulted in the collapse of the north wall of the forecourt, and the statue of Apollo, which Edith Wharton had brought from Land's End in Newport, fell to the ground from its niche,[39] fortunately without damage.

As the contents of the house were sold and the buildings and grounds deteriorated, Farrell met with "a bright young Wharton enthusiast,"[40] Mary Pitlick, who was involved as a researcher for the 1975 Wharton biography by R.W.B.

FIG. 80 *The drawing room, c. 1960. Aileen Farrell's inscription on the photograph reads: "The drawing room, with furnishings bought by the Foxhollow School from Carr Van Anda in 1942, was redecorated by Mr. and Mrs. Dudley Ingraham in 1960." The furnishings were sold by the school's trustees in 1972.* (FHS)

135

Lewis. Pitlick, according to Farrell, "resuscitated my interest in Edith's writings and her [Pitlick's] interest inspired me to work for the restoration of The Mount." [41] In November 1972, Farrell and Fowler returned from an overseas trip to the rumor that The Mount would be sold "in favour of building new buildings up near the Main House" [42] on the school campus. Shut out from the operation of the school that she had founded and directed for so long, Farrell turned her prodigious energies towards saving The Mount.

On November 11, 1971, The Mount had been designated a National Historic Landmark [43] through the efforts of Hilda Mumford and the school, making it eligible for federal and state funding. In addition, a newly organized Committee for the Restoration of The Mount was formed, with Dr. Walter Muir Whitehill as honorary chairman. [44] At this point, restoration was estimated to cost $400,000 over a period of four or five years. [45] Plans for the use of The Mount included "cultural workshops, literary seminars and salon concerts." [46] The restoration group was "an outgrowth of a subcommittee chartered" by the Foxhollow trustees. [47]

Farrell was coordinating chairman; the committee of 19, which she selected, included William Miles, executive director of the Berkshire County Historical Celebrations Committee; Amy Bess Miller, president of Hancock Shaker Village; Susie Malevsky-Malevitch, representing the Lenox Garden Club; Stephen B. Hibbard, a Pittsfield attorney and former trustee of the Foxhollow School; and Cornelia Brooke Gilder, Peter Cusick, Walter Wheat, and F. Brooks Butler. The honorary chairman, Dr. Whitehill, had for many years served as librarian and historian of the Boston Athenaeum and was a trustee of both the National Trust for Historic Preservation and the Massachusetts Historical Commission.

Farrell worked hard to advance the restoration through personal speeches and writings; in one appeal she wrote:

We therefore have no reticence in seeking financial help from our Alumnae and their parents who so much enjoyed the atmosphere of The Mount; from our Berkshire County neighbours who pride themselves on the historical validity of this district; from the reading public who value Edith Wharton as one of the shrewdest recorders of her times and lastly from those Foundations interested in keeping alive the architectural and literary traditions of the country. [48]

In mid-summer 1976, the school placed The Mount and 130 acres of its property on sale "in order to raise endowment money," [49] according to Headmaster Thomas Ryan, who had succeeded the retiring Hilda Mumford in 1974. Because Foxhollow had no endowment, Ryan stated that the sale was "to insure long-term financial stability of the school." [50] One of Ryan's annual goals was to raise $30,000 to $40,000 to balance the budget. Two alternatives were examined: a capital campaign (ultimately abandoned due to poor economic conditions) and the sale of the 130 acres of "excess land… not necessary to the overall operation of the school." [51]

At this time the school was leasing The Mount to the Lenox Arts Center, Inc., to house its professional staff. [52] Renovation was proceeding, funded by grants made possible by The Mount's designation as a National Historic Landmark. In March 1974, The Mount had qualified for a $6,300 state grant; at the time Mumford had announced that the funds would be used to restore the courtyard and for masonry work on the outside of the building. [53] Additional grants were approved in 1976 and 1977 by the National Park Service of the United States Department of the Interior. In January 1976, The Mount was awarded $8,070 in federal funds, [54] which were used for masonry repairs to the courtyard wall and the terrace, and in December 1977, $10,130 was approved to "stabilize and replace existing materials," [55] particularly cornices, gutters, and leaders and to do work on the cupola. The federally funded project was to be administered by the Massachusetts Historical Commission.

Only a few weeks after the sale of The Mount had been publicized, Ryan announced on August 24, 1976, that the Foxhollow School would close: "The board of trustees of Foxhollow School, Inc., voted at a recent meeting to cease operation of the secondary girls' boarding school effective immediately...A reason cited for the unanimous vote of those trustees present included enrollments, which while increasing slightly each year, were inadequate to generate enough cash to meet operating expenses. Also cited was the fact that with the impending sale of The Mount, the upper campus could not house enough girls to keep the school financially viable."[56] According to Ryan, the enrollment problem was complicated by the impending sale of The Mount, for which he had recently received a serious offer from a prospective buyer.

Without The Mount, Foxhollow can only "comfortably" house 55 students, Ryan said, which is at least 10 below the number needed to keep the school operating. He added that Foxhollow now only has a small mortgage on the property and school officials decided to close for this fall rather than mortgaging the property "to the hilt" if new dormitories were built. "The school is not heavily in debt and cash resources are immediately available to pay all existing obligations as well as to provide housing on campus for faculty and staff for several months," Ryan added. He said the board of trustees will meet soon to decide what to do with the property.[57]

Farrell "expressed deep regret...over the closing of the school...'We are all very, very sad about it,' she commented."[58] The Mount had housed 29 classes of seniors and juniors from 1942-71 as "a lovely refuge from their arduous studies and activities,"[59] she later wrote. The school immediately began to place its current students and faculty in other schools and other jobs, while prospective buyers examined the entire property, including The Mount. *The Berkshire Eagle* noted that "Foxhollow is the last of the schools that date back to the time when Lenox was a major center for private, secondary education. The other major private schools of that period — Cranwell, Lenox School and Windsor Mountain — have all closed within the past five years for reasons similar to those that are closing Foxhollow."[60]

As work toward the restoration of The Mount commenced, the longest ownership of the property, almost 35 years by the Foxhollow School, had come to a melancholy conclusion.

The Center Incorporated, Owner, 1977-80

In August 1976, soon after the Foxhollow School had offered The Mount for sale, the property was described in a local newspaper as a "sickly white elephant...a monument to neglect...the stone and stucco mansion is crumbling and the grounds, once diligently cultivated,...are densely overgrown."[1] To Aileen Farrell, the seventy-eight-year-old retired headmistress of the Foxhollow School, efforts to restore the house had begun to seem hopeless: "They might as well put a powder keg under it," she said. "There really isn't any hope that we can get going again...It grieves me terribly to see it going to wrack and ruin."[2] Options being discussed included tearing The Mount down to build economical housing or converting it into a restaurant or hotel.[3]

A month later, *The Berkshire Eagle* reported that The Bible Speaks, a fundamentalist religious corporation that had already purchased considerable acreage in Lenox, would purchase the former Foxhollow School property for about $600,000.[4] The group planned to use the campus for classrooms and dormitories.[5]

By mid-October, however, the sale was "definitely off,"[6] according to Andrew T. Campoli, attorney for the religious group. Instead, the trustees of the Foxhollow School had "verbally accepted an offer by Connecticut developer Donald I. Altshuler."[7] Altshuler, president of Altshuler Enterprises in New York and of Georgetown North of Connecticut, Inc., proposed converting the school to a conference and crafts center similar to the Silvermine Guild in Connecticut. Under his plan, The Mount would become an inn.[8]

On January 15, 1977, The Center Incorporated purchased the Foxhollow School property, including The Mount, for $650,000.[9] The deed noted that the board of trustees of the Foxhollow School, Inc., had met on October 16, 1976, and approved the sale unanimously. The sum of $650,000 consisted of a cash payment of $150,000 and the balance of $500,000 in the

THE MOUNT *Part One*

form of a note and a first mortgage. The sale included the acreage of the property and a first mortgage, as well as "all tangible personal property of the [Foxhollow] corporation."[10]

Soon after the purchase, Altshuler began his plans to transform the main campus overlooking Laurel Lake into a condominium/time-share resort, hotel, and conference center. In December 1977, Altshuler was reported to be planning to renovate The Mount if his organization could "obtain about $150,000 in federal funds to do half of the project"[11]; he estimated that "a complete renovation of The Mount would cost about $300,000."[12] His plan was to "renovate the building sufficiently to use it as a French restaurant in the summer…The Mount could also be used for meeting rooms and special events and as a museum in the winter."[13] In mid-1977 The Mount and about 60 surrounding acres were put up for sale for $250,000, but Altshuler said he would not sell it if he could obtain partial outside funding for its renovation.[14] There were no offers, although The Center advertised The Mount and the 60 acres in *New York* magazine and other publications.[15]

Shakespeare & Company at The Mount, 1978-Present

In the spring of 1978, Tina Packer, an English actress-turned-director, visited the Berkshires in search of a location for a theatrical company dedicated to performing Shakespeare according to her philosophies. While directing a Molière production at Smith College, Packer met Mitchell Berenson, a former longshoreman who was then a real-estate developer, and he persuaded her to consider the Berkshires. After inspecting the former gymnasium on the Foxhollow property, Packer and Berenson drove through the woods and by The Mount. Packer felt that her search was over: "I knew I wanted *this* house. It had a real identity."[1]

Altshuler was amenable to renting The Mount to Packer's group for the summer of 1978, with an option to buy after that.[2] The company agreed to pay rent of $8,000 and provide $4,000

worth of labor to clean and repair The Mount. A $5,000 grant to Packer from the Ford Foundation helped to underwrite the project.

On May 22, 1978, the theater company arrived to find the house was in desperate need of work. Some ceilings were down, plaster was falling off walls, there was water damage throughout, and the place was filthy. No one had lived at The Mount since it was closed by the Foxhollow School in 1972 except for the summer of 1976, when the cast and staff of the Lenox Art Center had been housed there.[3]

As the company began to clear debris, paint, plaster, and clean windows, the Lenox building inspector ordered them to be evicted, as the building had no functioning septic or electrical systems. After these problems were corrected in mid-June, the inspector approved occupancy by up to thirty people. The company lived a spartan existence, sleeping on mattresses, sharing several bathrooms, and using one communal kitchen.

Several weeks later, Shakespeare & Company opened The Mount to the public with weekend tours of the mansion and gardens. Six actors trained to work as guides and showed approximately one hundred local residents through the property that first weekend.

The company's first production that summer, *A Midsummer Night's Dream*, was received warmly by both audiences and critics. This success cemented Packer's plans to rent The Mount during the fall and to attempt to purchase the property. On September 1, 1978, Shakespeare & Company announced that it would buy the mansion for $200,000. The Company was to sign a contract with Altshuler on September 15 when it would be required to pay $12,000; another payment of $24,000 by January 10 would give them title. In addition, the company would assume an existing 15-year mortgage.[4]

The company had paid Altshuler $12,000 for use of The Mount from May 1 to September 1 and agreed to pay $2,000 a month during the winter. According to Dennis Krausnick, the company's director of restoration, Shakespeare & Company had plans to raise $6,000 from individuals and to borrow $6,000 more to avoid interest payments. The remaining $24,000 would be raised or borrowed.[5]

By November 3, 1978, *The Berkshire Eagle* reported that Altshuler and Shakespeare & Company had signed a "tentative contract"[6] for the purchase of The Mount. However, approval was necessary from the trustees of the Foxhollow School, who held the first mortgage on the 285-acre property. The property was to change hands on March 15 after the theater group made a payment of $65,000. Krausnick said that Shakespeare & Company had raised half of the $65,000 payment [on the total of $200,000 for the property], explaining: "It is a fairly ineffective contract until we get a written agreement from the Foxhollow trustees that they will honor it… There are still many problems to be ironed out."[7]

The November 3, 1978, article disclosed for the first time that The Mount would not, however, be owned by the acting company. A separate corporation, Edith Wharton Restoration, Inc., would own the property and be responsible for maintaining the house.

Throughout the fall and the winter of 1978-79 the company instituted a series of regular workshops to teach Shakespeare to a wider audience. They also began an active program of Shakespeare in the Schools. Several Edith Wharton evenings and afternoons (readings, plays, and similar projects) were developed. The 1979 summer season brought continued success with a production of *The Winter's Tale*. A new stage was constructed on the edge of the lawn and the woods to the southeast of the mansion, adjacent to the walled garden. Audiences were enthusiastic, but expenses continued to grow. By the fall of 1979 the company was $150,000 in debt.[8]

FIG. 81 *Shakespeare & Company on the Palladian staircase, 1979. In the front row (from left) are founding members Tina Packer, Kristin Linklater, and Dennis Krausnick. Photograph by Clemens Kalischer.* (S&C)

Shakespeare & Company
1979

Photo: Clemens Kalischer © '79

Edith Wharton Restoration, Inc., Owner, 1980-Present

In the spring of 1979, Lila W. Berle, a resident of Stockbridge, Massachusetts, a graduate of the Foxhollow School, and a member of Shakespeare & Company's board of directors, was invited to lunch at Brookhurst, the Lenox home of Stephen Morris, where she met John Frisbee, head of the Endangered Properties Fund of the National Trust for Historic Preservation.[1] Much of the discussion focused on The Mount, and within days Frisbee was invited to visit the property. According to Berle, negotiations with the National Trust "consumed the autumn and the winter."[2] As she explained, the Trust was interested in becoming involved "only if a separate community-based corporation was established, with a board membership that they approved of."[3] Shakespeare & Company had previously incorporated Edith Wharton Restoration, Inc.; as Berle explained, "it was a paper entity until the autumn of '79 when I assumed the role of making it what the Trust demanded."[4] Berle became Edith Wharton Restoration's first chairman and began building a board of directors in accordance with the National Trust's specifications.

Among the National Trust's requirements were that Edith Wharton Restoration raise $120,000 towards the purchase price of The Mount and that a preservation-oriented board of directors for the new organization be activated. By April, Berle wrote to Frisbee that "the Board of Edith Wharton Restoration, Inc. clearly understands and accepts its responsibility to the National Trust to purchase and maintain the property known as The Mount. Though Shakespeare & Company is, and most likely will always be, the primary tenant of the property, Edith Wharton Restoration, Inc. views its responsibility to be primarily to the purchase, maintenance, and restoration of the buildings and grounds, and secondarily to Shakespeare & Company or whomever its tenant may be."[5] Berle, who had personally raised over $100,000,

reported that "Total monies received or pledged to Edith Wharton Restoration, Inc. as of April 9, 1980 amount to $110,607.41 . . . In addition we have received word informally that the Trustees of the Foxhollow School will support Edith Wharton Restoration Inc's purchase of The Mount in the amount of $10,000."[6] To date there were eight board members of EWR, including Berle as chairman; several were directors of Berkshire preservation organizations.[7]

On April 16, 1980, *The Berkshire Eagle* announced that with the expiration of its option of April 15 the National Trust would buy The Mount and its 49 acres with funds from its Endangered Properties Program.[8] The sale of The Mount property was approved by the Lenox Zoning Board of Appeals in late May.[9] On July 1, 1980, the National Trust purchased The Mount for $290,000 from Altshuler and subsequently resold it to Edith Wharton Restoration, Inc., "for the same amount."[10] Shakespeare & Company was to continue on the property as a tenant, leasing it from its new owner, Edith Wharton Restoration. Frisbee stated that the Trust gave Altshuler a check for the full amount and then sold the property to Edith Wharton Restoration, which had "paid $100,000 down and taken a $190,000 mortgage at the Trust's preferential six percent rate."[11] The balance of the funds had to be raised in three years. The Trust retained conservation restrictions on the land and architectural restrictions on all the buildings on the property: mansion, stable, gatehouse, and cottage. The restrictions specified that no exterior changes could be made without the prior consent of the National Trust.

By early July *The Berkshire Eagle* reported that Edith Wharton Restoration had raised $131,000 towards the downpayment and for maintenance.[12] About $20,000 was to be used immediately for repairs, and additional funds were granted by the Massachusetts Historical Commission for roof repairs on the mansion. The Commission retained preservation restrictions on both the interior and the exterior of the building specifying that no alterations could be made without the prior consent of the Massachusetts Historical Commission.

Edith Wharton Restoration's board of directors had its first meeting on May 2, 1980.[13] A June 1980 roster of the new organization included Lila Berle as board chairman; Paul Ivory, director of Chesterwood in Stockbridge; Mrs. Lawrence K. Miller, founder and director of Hancock Shaker Village in Pittsfield; George Wislocki, director of the Berkshire Natural Resources Council; plus Kelton Burbank; Mrs. Nat King Cole; Lester Collins; Dr. Milos Krofta; and Stephen V. C. Morris, a distant relative of Edith Wharton. The board also included several founders of Shakespeare & Company: Tina Packer, Dennis Krausnick, and Mitchell Berenson.[14]

In late July, the Lenox Zoning Board unanimously approved a variance "authorizing the conversion of buildings at The Mount into living quarters, the use of an outdoor amphitheater for public theatrical productions, to permit public tours of The Mount and to establish an Edith Wharton library."[15] The approval was "contingent upon the construction of a new sewage disposal system to serve the estate's main building"[16] by June 1, 1980, and other restrictions.[17]

Prior to Edith Wharton Restoration's purchase of The Mount, work had been done by Shakespeare & Company to clean the building, repaint interior walls and exterior shutters, and repair plumbing and electrical systems. Some clearing of overgrowth on the grounds and in the formal gardens had also been done. In addition, the group had adapted many of the rooms in the mansion for offices, rehearsal space, and living quarters. Most of the work had been necessary for the property to operate, but it consisted of repairs, not restoration.

At the end of January 1981, Edith Wharton Restoration named Robert E. Brolli project director of The Mount.[18] Formerly a teacher of English and theater arts at Monument Mountain Regional High School in nearby Great Barrington, Brolli was in charge of restoration and maintenance of the entire Mount property and

of coordinating all work and activities with Shakespeare & Company.[19]

In 1981 Brolli oversaw the repainting of several of the principal rooms at The Mount and solicited donations of new drapes for the library, drawing room, and dining room. The current dining room drapes were remade for Edith's boudoir. Brolli obtained furnishings on loan from the Albert and Mary Spalding collection of the Berkshire Museum in Pittsfield. The majority of these came from the turn-of-the-century Spalding estate, Aston Magna, in Great Barrington and were placed in The Mount's gallery, den, library, drawing room, dining room, and boudoir.

During the early 1970s, The Mount's elaborately detailed drawing room ceiling had suffered significant damage from burst pipes in an overhead bathroom. About one-fourth of the ceiling had already collapsed onto the floor; most of the rest was "dipping" and in danger of collapse.[20] Hilda Mumford, then headmistress, was considering replacing what remained with Sheetrock-type plaster boards. Dorothy Carpenter, a Foxhollow alumna, volunteered to remove the surviving plasterwork, code all pieces, and store them in the former chemistry laboratory downstairs. The ceiling was also documented in photographs before it was dismantled.

In order to duplicate the elaborate plaster rosettes and garlands, local contractors used a silicone mold from a product developed at General Electric in Pittsfield.[21] The drawing room was then repainted in a creamy color.

In October 1983, at a special service, the drawing room work was dedicated in memory of Aileen Farrell.[22] A plaque was unveiled in the southeast corner of the room, reading: "This restoration is completed as a tribute to Aileen M. Farrell, M.A. Oxon., Founder and Principal of Foxhollow School, 1930-1970, for her success in vivifying education for young women, her lifelong commitment to excellence and her foresight in preserving 'The Mount.'"

Dorothy Carpenter and her family contributed $5,000 toward the ceiling restoration[23]; financial assistance also came from the Massachusetts Council on the Arts and from GE in Pittsfield, which had donated an estimated $2,000 of the silicone molding material.

In 1982 a challenge grant from the Massachusetts Historical Commission awarded $50,000 to Edith Wharton Restoration to restore the roof of The Mount and the cupola. Edith Wharton Restoration raised matching funds totalling $124,000. A new septic tank was also installed at a cost of $26,000.

Brolli's tenure as project director was marked by increasing tensions between Shakespeare & Company and Edith Wharton Restoration. A magazine profile of The Mount in the early 1980s described the relationship as an "uneasy but productive alliance…Naturally the efforts of both actors and curators to work side by side at restoring the property have not always been harmonious…"[24] In 1983 Brolli left Edith Wharton Restoration, which was run from this time until mid-1984 by the chairman of the board, Lila Berle, and the executive secretary, Mary Misch.

In spring 1984, Thomas S. Hayes, of Longmeadow, Massachusetts, was hired by the EWR board of directors as its first executive director beginning that June.[25] He was to be responsible for "planning, promotion, fundraising and directing historic preservation at The Mount."[26] According to board president Lila Berle, "the naming of a director represents a financial and spiritual 'threshold' for the organization,"[27] which had worked for three years to pay off a mortgage on the property and other debts. Although substanial payments remained, the board chose to make " 'an investment' in Hayes. 'We wanted to operate more like a normal non-profit organization.' "[28]

Hayes and his family moved into the gatehouse, which had been used for several years as a dormitory for Shakespeare & Company. Edith Wharton Restoration's board raised and expended approximately $27,000 to renovate the building; $2,500 was later spent in 1986 for landscaping. The Edith Wharton Restoration office (previously located in the tiny original coat room on the ground floor of the mansion) was moved to the first floor of the gatehouse, and Joy Hayes was hired to assist her husband.[29]

During 1985 the Massachusetts Historical Commission awarded a challenge grant of $53,000 for restoring the roofs on the stable and the gatehouse. Matching funds of $36,000 were raised ($18,000 was announced to establish an endowment fund for maintenance). The asphalt-shingled roofs on the two original outbuildings were removed, and new cedar-shingled roofs were installed to match the originals. The cupola and weathervane on the stable were also restored. The Massachusetts Historical Commission placed preservation restrictions on the stable and gatehouse as a result of the challenge grant.

The entrance hall of the mansion was repainted the original color in 1985. The following year, the terrazzo floors in the dining room and the drawing room were resupported at a cost of $6,800. The concealed jib door between the den and the library, which had fallen from the wall, was reinstalled in 1988 for $1,000. A new staff apartment costing $5,000 was created on the third floor of the service wing in 1988. In 1990 the main stairhall and bedroom-floor hallway were repainted in their original colors; new stair carpet was laid; the bedroom-floor hallway was cleared of school-era built-in furniture and an added partition wall; and the bedroom-floor hallway was redecorated.

In addition, new tapestry-like panels were installed in the library and the drawing room, and work was done on the marble fireplaces in the den, library, and Edith Wharton's bedroom. Furnishings secured on long-term loan from the Clark Art Institute in Williamstown were placed in the library, gallery, and dining room; several items recalling the original furnishings were added to Edith Wharton Restoration's permanent collection.

The collection was enhanced by several items that had belonged to Edith Wharton: oil portraits of her father, George Frederic Jones, and of her two brothers, and a painting by her friend Robert Norton of the garden at her French home, Pavillon Colombe (all four

FIG. 82 *Restoration of the stable roof and cupola, 1985, funded by a matching grant from the Massachusetts Historical Commission. The asphalt shingles were replaced by wood shingles similar to those on the original 1902 roof.* (EWR)

paintings were donated by the King Family). In addition, Edith Wharton's christening cup was given by her godson, Colin Clark. In October 1988, with the death of O. Meigs Fowler, long-time friend and colleague of Aileen Farrell, a significant collection of original historical material — known as the Foxhollow School Archives — was donated by alumnae Dorothy Carpenter and Catha Grace Rambusch.

The vista from the house to Laurel Pond (approximately 7 acres) was restored during 1983-86 with volunteer assistance. In 1986 the east garden was cleared and the outlines of the garden relaid. As a temporary measure, the former flower beds were planted with wild flowers, and the former gravel walkways were seeded with grass.

In 1987, the two sets of lawn terrace steps and the three sets of stairs leading into the walled garden were restored, and connecting gravel paths were laid between them. Beginning in 1987, the masonry walls of the walled garden, some in danger of imminent collapse, were repointed. The original rock garden on the north end of the house was cleared and redefined.

Hayes formed three board committees to plan and approve the restoration work on the house, gardens, and grounds. In 1986, work on a historic structure report for The Mount was initiated with the firm of Mesick•Cohen•Waite Architects (now John G. Waite Associates, Architects), of Albany, New York. Under the guidance of John G. Waite, the firm documented existing conditions of the mansion. Edith Wharton Restoration staff prepared a history of The Mount, its design, construction, outbuildings, architects, and other historical material.

Staff at The Mount was supplemented by summer interns. In 1985, Scott Marshall, a student in the Graduate School of Architecture, Planning, and Preservation at Columbia University, became The Mount's first intern and in 1986, upon graduation, its first assistant director. An architectural historian and Wharton authority, Marshall was selected to research and write the historical sections of The Mount's historic structure report. Mary Hart Parker, Foxhollow School '49, became The Mount's first landscape intern through *Yankee Magazine* during the summer of 1986. Parker, a graduate student in the Department of Landscape Architecture and Regional Planning at the University of Massachusetts at Amherst, prepared a report as a site design for Edith Wharton Restoration and for the adaptive re-use of The Mount property by a cultural organization. Parker also oversaw the design of the flower beds and walkways for the east garden.

George Darey, a Lenox selectman who had been doing work on the property since the early 1980s for both Edith Wharton Restoration and Shakespeare & Company, was made superintendent of the house and grounds early during Hayes's tenure.

The book and gift shop was moved into the former coat room and expanded; the gross increased from $4,500 in 1984 to $50,000 per year in 1991. Membership in the Friends of Edith Wharton Restoration increased significantly. Its newsletter, *Vista from The Mount*, was revamped, expanded, and published several times per year. A large corps of volunteers was developed to help with tours, the shop, benefits, and other activities. Brochures and other printed literature were redesigned. In June 1987 the first-ever Edith Wharton conference, co-sponsored by the Edith Wharton Society and Edith Wharton Restoration, was held at The Mount. Interpretative tours of The Mount were expanded and redefined, and more in-depth guide training was instituted. Additional displays about Wharton's life and her work were installed. New programming included the Berkshire Cottages Tours, a walking tour of Wharton's Old New York, lectures, seminars, and concerts. In 1985 Edith Wharton Restoration produced the Edith Wharton matinee plays; for several years following, the plays were co-produced with Shakespeare & Company until monies owed to Edith Wharton Restoration by the theater company and other problems resulted in a major rift on this issue.[30]

In mid-May 1992 Hayes resigned as president of Edith Wharton Restoration.[31] In late 1992 the board hired Stephanie W. Copeland, of New York City, as executive director. Copeland, an independent development consultant and most recently an executive search and placement consultant, had an extensive background in theater, including work as a producer and consultant to the NEA. In the early 1980s she had worked as director of development and later as managing director for Shakespeare & Company. Copeland recruited Scott Marshall, who had left The Mount in 1989, to return as Edith Wharton Restoration's deputy director.

Edith Wharton Restoration's programming now focused on recognizing the unique achievements of significant women. Several new lecture series were initiated, including the "Edith Wharton Women of Achievement Lecture Series." A grant of $20,000 from the Macmillan Publishing Company to underwrite a new mail-order catalogue helped to provide year-round revenue through the sale of books by and about Edith Wharton.

John G. Waite, of John G. Waite Associates, Architects, in Albany, New York, was named The Mount's consulting architect for all restoration work. A grant of $25,000 from the Florence Gould Foundation was secured by Copeland in 1994, making possible the publication of *The Mount, Home of Edith Wharton: A Historic Structure Report*.

The Mount's present kitchen (originally the butler's pantry and the brush room) was renovated/restored during the winter of 1994-95 through an innovative initiative project involving corporate gifts from GE, Formica, Robert Orr & Associates Architects, of New Haven, Connecticut, and other donors. The value of the work donated was estimated at approximately $100,000.

In the spring of 1996, the two original dining room paintings were restored through the generosity of the Friends of French Art, a non-profit foundation. Cleaning and conservation were done by conservator Katrina de Carbonnel. In late fall of 1996, the Friends began restoring the eight original paintings in Edith Wharton's boudoir, under the supervision of de Carbonnel. The foundation plans to restore the five remaining original paintings in the mansion during the next several years. The restoration of the 15 original paintings is a gift valued at approximately $100,000.

CHAPTER 9

Outbuildings

The Mount originally consisted of 113 acres to which Edith Wharton later added approximately 15 more.[1] The property is bordered on the north by Plunkett Street (then Cross Road), on the west by Kemble Street (now Route 7), by the vast estate of George Westinghouse (since 1976 the Foxhollow Resort) on the south, and by Laurel Lake and the Chapin estate (today known as Seven Hills Inn) to the east. The estate included woods, pastures, orchards, manicured lawns, formal gardens, and at least ten outbuildings.

Outbuildings to the east of the drive contrast with natural woodlands on the west; this design is attributed to Edith and her niece, landscape architect Beatrix Farrand (then Beatrix Jones). The entrance sequence acknowledged European estates, where visitors passed by an array of outbuildings that reflected the working life of an estate long before arriving at the house.

Front Gate

The front gate is located on Plunkett Street (then Cross Road), at the north end of the property. The original gate consisted of a white wood fence and gateway of simple construction but elegant design. The fence had two concave sections framing the gateway and additional straight sections parallel to the street; one section was to the west of the gateway, and there were six sections plus a garden gate to the east.[2] Square

FIG. 83 *Superintendent's lodge (the gatehouse) from Cross Road (now Plunkett Street), c. 1942, and the original gateposts with urn finials.* (FHS)

wood posts linked by a thin top rail and a wider bottom rail were connected by vertical dowels.

The gate was among the last features to be executed at The Mount. *Berkshire Resort Topics* in September 1904 mentioned that "a gate at the main entrance"[3] was a prospective addition. Presumably the gate was designed by Hoppin & Koen.

Originally, the four wood posts comprising the concave sections of the entrance were topped by wooden urn finials, which added a classical note. It also seems likely that the west portion of the fence consisted of six sections to balance the east side; the missing five sections were probably removed and destroyed when Route 7 was relocated in 1926, and the State of Massachusetts took this land from the Shattucks by eminent domain. The front gate would have mirrored the scheme in the forecourt more closely: tall gateposts flanked by concave sections and linked by equidistant straight sections. Urn finials, which were rejected by the Whartons in several Hoppin & Koen schemes for the forecourt, were employed only on the entrance gateposts.

A c. 1942 photograph shows the gates were intact and swung in toward the drive. The gateposts, fence, and gate leaves will be restored once a new entrance to the property is constructed.

The gateposts and fence were completely reconstructed around 1960 by carpenter Joseph Bartini. The raising of Plunkett Street soon after resulted in drainage problems, which caused damage to the gate. An automobile accident in February 1985 destroyed the concave section on the left side. EWR board member David H. Bennett has prepared working drawings for the restoration of the gateposts and fence, including the urn finials.

Superintendent's Lodge (Gatehouse)

The superintendent's lodge is located to the left of the drive on entering, adjacent to the gate and to Plunkett Street. The Georgian Revival-style house is two-stories high, plus an attic. It has wood-frame construction, finished in stucco, and is painted white with dark green shutters flanking the double-sash windows topped with ornamental keystones. It sits on a raised basement with a brick foundation; the roof is of cedar shingles. The structure is three-bays wide and has a pedimented central projecting bay inset with an ocular attic opening for ventilation. This central bay features a Classical entrance porch with pedimented roof supported by four Doric columns. There are two chimneys, one on either end of the building. The south one is a dummy stack; the north one vents the furnace in the basement and originally vented the stove in the kitchen. The quoins at the corners of the house and the central bay are similar to those on the mansion. The rear facade consists of three simple bays, a central ventilation dormer with an ocular opening, and a curved roof that terminates in volutes.

The lodge was designed and constructed by Hoppin & Koen in 1901-02, along with the mansion and stable. Identified by the architects as the "Lodge," it functioned as a gatehouse and as the home of the superintendent for the estate, who doubled as head gardener, therefore the adjacent greenhouse.

During the Whartons' tenure, the house was occupied by their superintendent, Thomas Reynolds, and his family.[4] In a letter to Morton Fullerton on July 3, 1911, Edith wrote glowingly of Reynolds as "my devoted and admirable head gardener,"[5] whom she feared might leave The Mount soon for "the prospect of a secure future and unlimited sway over some millionaire's orchids!"[6] Reynolds at first agreed to stay indefinitely, but by the end of August he was gone. His departure may have been an important factor in the Whartons' decision to sell The Mount later that year.[7]

The structure was clearly built as a family residence. Its plan is simple: four rooms over four. The first floor consists of living room, dining room, kitchen, and office (a pantry adjacent to the kitchen was converted to a bath); upstairs are four bedrooms and a bath.

From 1912 to 1942 the gatehouse presumably

continued as the estate superintendent's home. During most of the Foxhollow years it was faculty housing or a rental property.[8] Shakespeare & Company used the gatehouse to house actors and theater staff from 1978-83. In 1984 it was renovated as a residence for the president of EWR and his family. The gatehouse now serves as the EWR office.

The gatehouse remains largely intact. The entrance porch was enclosed in glass after 1942. The roof was restored to cedar shingles in 1985.

Greenhouse and Potting Shed

This structure is located to the left of the drive immediately adjacent to the gatehouse. The front of the greenhouse is aligned with the rear wall of the gatehouse.

The one-story greenhouse has a brick-and-concrete foundation with concrete floor and a frame of glass, wood, and iron. The attached potting shed to the east is of brick finished in stucco and painted white.

Estate greenhouses usually supplied flowers and plants for the owners' rooms and terraces. Edith also depended on her greenhouse for the arrangements she submitted at flower shows. In 1904 she won one first prize, five second prizes, and two third prizes at the Lenox Horticultural Society's Annual Exhibition. In 1905 she received seven first prizes.[9] Although many of the flowers must have come from her outdoor gardens, the Marguerite carnations that she included each year would have been cultivated in the greenhouse.

During a 1905 Christmas visit to the Vanderbilt chateau, Biltmore House, in Asheville, North Carolina, Edith "found much to interest her in the expansive shrubberies and nurseries which she explored."[10] In *The House of Mirth* (1905), Judy Trenor complains to Lily Bart that one of the guests "made Gus take her all through the glass-houses yesterday and bothered him to death by asking the names of the plants."[11] It is reasonable to assume that guests at The Mount visited its greenhouse.

A hot-water heating plant in the cellar of the potting shed provided the means to grow plants. By 1939, Carr Van Anda, the new owner of The Mount, wrote that he had spent $168 to keep the greenhouse from falling down and that $868 was necessary to put it in working order. A photograph, c. late 1940s, shows that the greenhouse was functioning during the early days of the Foxhollow School. The chimney on the potting shed was removed at an unknown date.

At present the greenhouse is in total disrepair. It was stabilized by contractor David Andersen in the summer of 1996. The landscape and grounds committee of the board of directors of EWR has voted to restore the building for income-producing purposes.

Modern Cottage

This one-and-one-half story building located to the left of the drive next to the greenhouse was erected in 1965 by the Foxhollow School. Headmistress Aileen M. Farrell wrote that a "house was built for [Kergan] Davidson on the drive of The Mount."[12] It is the only major structure on the grounds that does not date to the Whartons' tenure.

Stable

The stable is located to the left of the drive approximately 400 feet from the entrance gate. It occupies a key location where the formal allee ends and the curving woodland section of the drive begins.

A two-story Georgian Revival structure (plus attic), seven-bays wide, the stable is finished in white stucco to harmonize with the mansion and the gatehouse. On the south elevation, the center section contains a large, arched doorway, which is topped by an ornamental Flemish gable. All windows have double-hung sash. Second-story dormer windows pierce the roof edge and are capped by gabled roofs, while the center of the Flemish gable has a round window. Two oval windows flank the

FIG. 84 *The stable,*
February 1943. Note the
shutters and trellis. Photo-
graph by Marylou Kieckhefer,
FHS class of 1943. (FHS)

central section in the attic. The new cedar-shingle roof (1985) features a central cupola that is octagonal in plan and is topped by a gilded weathervane. The cupola (which was used for ventilation) is flanked by two smaller ones that also functioned as ventilators.

The stable was designed and constructed by Hoppin & Koen in 1901-02. *Berkshire Resort Topics* in 1904 noted "Mr. Wharton's pride is the stable, which is indeed one of the finest in Lenox. The plan was of his own execution, and architecturally the building is a copy of the stables at 'Belton,' "[13] an estate in Lincolnshire, England. The building served as a stable (east section), as carriage storage (the carriage room was on the west end, closest to the drive), and quite possibly as a garage for the Whartons' Pope-Hartford motorcar.[14] *Berkshire Resort Topics* explained that "in the center is a large wash-box ... A corridor leading from the wash-box to the stables divides the cleaning-room from the harness-room. The stables [areas] are particularly fine, consisting of a large box-stall in each corner, with a row of hitching stalls along the north side. Every convenience for feeding and cleaning has been adopted."[15] Most of these original features remain.

An examination of stable plans published in *The Architectural Review* in 1902 shows the stable to be typical of its time.[16] Most stables also had a carriage wash in the center or at the entrance to the building. Likewise, the carriage rooms and the stalls were often on opposite ends of a structure, as they are at The Mount.

The Whartons' stable housed a pair of carriage horses, Duchess (a seven-year-old chestnut mare in 1902) and Dowager (an aged brown mare); Don (an aged bay gelding); Dobbins (an eight-year-old gray gelding in 1902); horses suitable for pulling a phaeton or surrey; and Frank, Edith's own mount, (a lady's saddle horse), an eight-year-old chestnut gelding in 1902.[17]

The exact number and type of carriages kept by the Whartons is unknown. Gaillard Lapsley describes Edith in one of her Lenox carriages:

I can see her again this time in less detail on a radiant summer day at Lenox. We had driven to the post-office where I got down to send a telegram for her and as I returned I saw her in the trim, two-seated open carriage with a light fringed cover like an old fashioned pony phaeton, her coachman in front and a pair of smart cobs.[18]

The second story of the stable contained "the coachman's apartments": a "parlor, dining-room, kitchen, five bedrooms and bath."[19] A large hayloft was located directly above the stalls and stable area.

William Parlett was the Whartons' coachman during their residence at The Mount. Born in England, Parlett and his wife, Emma, emigrated to America in 1895. By 1897 they were employed by the Whartons at Land's End. While in Newport, Parlett received a gold pocket watch from his employer; the inscription read: "To William Parlett, from Mrs. Edward Wharton, June 14, 1897."[20] The significance of the date is unknown. By the time that the Parletts moved to Lenox with the Whartons in 1901, they had a growing family. A son, Charles, had been born in 1897, and in 1901 a daughter, Cicely, was born in Lenox. Marjorie was born in 1908 while the family was living above the stable at The Mount.

Edith once mentioned Parlett (though not by name) in a letter to Morton Fullerton. On June 11, 1908, having heard a rare cuckoo-call while in the walled garden, she wrote: "my bird-books informed me that there is a cuckoo who 'ranges' as far north as this; but he must be rare, for our coachman, who is a savant ornithologist, told me he *thought* he had heard the note once, in his seven years here, but was not even sure of that! —"[21]

The other important staff member whose work centered on the stable was Charles Cook, a native of Lee, Massachusetts, who was hired by the Whartons as a chauffeur when they purchased their 1904 Pope-Hartford motorcar. It is believed that the motorcar (and any subsequent ones purchased by the Whartons) was parked in the center carriage-wash area.[22]

The stable may have drawn prospective owners to The Mount. Albert R. Shattuck, who purchased the property in 1911, was an enthusiastic collector of automobiles. His executors advertised in 1936 that the stable could hold ten cars.

By 1938 the stable was described as "in large part a useless relic of the obsolete customs of a bygone age."[23] The Van Andas used it as a garage. A 1940 floor plan shows the carriage room and stable area being used for storage.

The stable at the adjoining Foxhollow School burned on December 11, 1941, and students were being driven to Pittsfield in the spring of 1942 for their regular riding. As Miss Farrell, headmistress of the school, explained: "Needing a stable and extra space for increasing enrollment...I approached a friendly neighbour Mr. Carr Van Anda..."[24] The school purchased the property in 1942, and the building again became a working stable. The former kitchen

FIG. 85 *Edith Wharton on her horse, "Fatty," date unknown.* (LL)

FIG. 86 *Teddy Wharton on horseback holding Jules, date unknown.* ((LL)

FIG. 87 *William Parlett (right), the Whartons' coachman from 1897 to 1911; his brother, Frederick; and William's wife, Emma, who holds the hand of their son, Charles. The photograph was taken c. 1900 at Land's End in front of trelliswork designed by Ogden Codman, Jr. Jules, a Wharton dog, is at Mrs. Parlett's feet. William Parlett and his family lived above the stable at The Mount during the Whartons' occupancy. Photograph courtesy of William Parlett's granddaughter, Virginia Agar. (EWR)*

garden adjacent to the stable was converted to a riding paddock.

According to Kergan Davidson, who was in charge of the buildings and grounds for many years, the first floor of the stable served for a time as an art studio for the school.

Since 1978 Shakespeare & Company has used the stable for rehearsals and performances, and for storage. Performances have been given in the former carriage room beginning in the summer of 1990. The second-floor apartment became residential space in the summers; currently, it houses storage areas and dressing rooms. The attic of the stable contains a number of architectural elements from the three major original buildings, including shutters, French windows, pilasters, columns, and pediments (for the mansion's drawing room).

During the 1940s, the facade of the stable was covered with a latticework trellis; it is not known if this feature was original. The building did have pairs of dark green shutters at each window, similar to those on the mansion and the gatehouse. In 1985 a matching grant from the Massachusetts Historical Commission made possible the restoration of the cedar-shingled roof and of the cupola, along with work on the central Flemish gable. Soon after, the cupola weathervane was restored and re-gilded.

Spring-House

Located south of the stable on the east side of the drive, the ruins of this structure mark the beginning of the curved section of the drive at the point where it enters the woods.

There is little documentation concerning this structure, and its original function is not clear. The spring-house has "symbolic impor-

tance as the source of the meandering brook which crisscrosses the drive, disappears under the formal garden (where it may have fed the three fountains), and reappears in the meadow, ultimately spilling into Laurel Lake Pond."[25] It was not included on the 1940 Van Anda tax assessment.

The spring-house may be glimpsed at a distance in two photographs of the grounds. One photograph, c. 1905, of the east garden (looking northwest) shows the roof; a second photograph, possibly dating to the Whartons' tenure, was discovered in 1989 in the Foxhollow School Archives. This view (looking north from the mansion and possibly from Edith's boudoir window) reveals that the open landscaping allowed her to look from her bedroom suite directly north to the stable, kitchen garden, superintendent's lodge, and the gate. The spring-house may be discerned in the center distance; it appears to have been a rustic, gazebo-type structure. The photograph indicates that from its vantage point the Whartons and their guests could look down across manicured lawns and rock outcroppings to the mansion and the flower garden; in the distance one could also see the pond, the lake, the farm buildings, and the Tyringham mountain range.

Restoration of this structure would have to be somewhat conjectural, but it could recreate some of the sense of drama on approaching the mansion.

Pond Building

There is little documentation regarding the character of this vanished building, its function, or its exact location on the far (east) side of Laurel Pond.

A photograph, c. winter 1942, by a Foxhollow student, reveals that there was a small building on the edge of the pond, possibly a boathouse. There is no trace of the structure along the edge of Laurel Pond today. It was not included in the 1940 tax assessment, and it is unclear if it existed during the Whartons' tenure. In an article of August 17, 1942, in *The Berkshire*

Evening Eagle, a "boathouse" was listed as one of the structures on the property.

Farm Buildings

These buildings are located southeast of the mansion and Laurel Pond, on a rise overlooking a meadow and Laurel Lake. The complex of six wood-frame, vernacular, farm-style structures, faced with stone and shingles, included a quadrangle of barn, ice house, and wagon shed; a hen house and piggery to the north; and a farmhouse across the road from the quadrangle.

The majority of buildings that comprised the Whartons' working farm predated the purchase and creation of The Mount in 1901. Apparently they belonged to the Sargent family, from whom Edith Wharton purchased the land.

The scant documentation for these buildings is at times contradictory. The 1940 tax assessment for Carr Van Anda stated that the main barn, ice house, wagon shed, and piggery were each forty-four years old (constructed in 1896). The hen house was noted to be thirty-five years old and constructed in 1904, which was reported on the accompanying plan and elevation. A c. 1940 photograph states that it had a living apartment. The farmhouse across the road is not mentioned in this assessment — possibly the property had been previously sold to a separate owner.[26]

It is very difficult to date vernacular farm buildings. Gaillard Lapsley suggests that the Whartons constructed the piggery:

Long ago at Lenox when he and Walter Maynard were walking behind Edith, Teddy pointed to her saying "Look at that waist! No one would ever guess that she had written a line of poetry in her life." He could respect her gifts, however, for on the same visit he told Walter that when they wanted but could not afford a new piggery, she had solved the problem by publishing a set of verses.[27]

Berkshire Resort Topics adds to the confusion by noting in 1904 that "among the prospective additions are those of a farm barn and a gate at the main entrance."[28] *The Berkshire Gleaner*, a local journal in the nearby town of Lee,

announced in the spring of 1905 that "Edward R. Wharton is to build a large farm barn at his place near Laurel Lake and proposes to keep a herd of registered Jerseys."[29]

Apparently, many of the structures were in place when the Whartons purchased the property. Because of their location away from the central quadrangle, the hen house and the piggery are believed to have been added by the Whartons around 1904.

The house across from the quadrangle appears to have been the home of a farm superintendent. R.W.B. Lewis notes that the Whartons' butler, Alfred White, had a small house on the grounds,[30] but it is unclear whether this farmhouse was his residence. A 1915 tax assessment for the Town of Lenox does not include this house, although the adjacent farm buildings are listed.

The farm complex, like the main stable, was Teddy's domain. According to Lewis, tender-hearted Teddy "loved all the cows, sheep, ducks, and hens at The Mount so much that he could not stand to slaughter any of them."[31] Still, the farm complex no doubt existed mainly to supply the Whartons with meat, bacon, eggs, and other food.

Period photographs show the complex in full view from the terrace and east windows of the mansion. Edith remembered the farm in *A Backward Glance*: "There was a big kitchen-garden with a grape pergola, a little farm, and a flower-garden outspread below the wide terrace overlooking the lake."[32]

The Shattucks probably maintained the farm complex for a while, but by the time the Van Andas took over in 1938, it had fallen into disrepair. In 1940, Van Anda noted that "no use whatever is made of the chicken house, the piggery or the ice house. The open shed exposes to the weather for further decay, if that is possible, a lot of junk . . . The farm barn is of no use except to store a few tons of hay used chiefly to fill the two fish pools [in the formal gardens] during the winter."[33] He sought to have the "obsolete and abandoned buildings"[34] exempted from taxation.

FIG. 88 *The farm buildings: barn and stable for farm horses (center) and ice house (right), c. 1942. The corner of the wagon shed is at the extreme right. A low shingle wall enclosed the compound. Not shown are the hen house and piggery.* (FHS)

The complex was used again by the Foxhollow School mainly for storage, although the barn may have housed some of the school's horses. During the school's ownership the house across from the quadrangle was again part of the property. In a scrapbook of photographs, it is labeled "Farm Dwelling/Lake Cottage."

In the early 1980s the quadrangle was transformed radically by Donald Altshuler, the developer of the Foxhollow Resort, into a private residence (then called "FarmBarns"). The ice house was converted to a residence and the wagon shed to a garage with living space above. The main barn (which still retains its Palladian window—possibly an addition from the Whartons' time) remains in its original use.

Unfortunately the hen house was demolished. It and the other farm buildings are all fully documented in the 1940 tax assessment records with plans and elevations. At present the piggery is in a sad state of decay. The "FarmBarns" complex was purchased from Altshuler in 1992 by Michael and Annette Miller, who plan to stabilize the piggery.

The complex also includes at least three sets of gates and rustic stone gateposts — one in front of the quadrangle, another in front of the farmhouse, and a third along the road near the piggery. A c. 1942 photograph (taken for the realty firm of Wheeler & Taylor) discovered in 1989 in the Foxhollow School Archives, shows that the quadrangle of main barn, ice house, and wagon shed was originally enclosed by a solid, waist-high wall, faced in shingles like the three buildings, to keep ducks, chickens, and other animals within. The original wall has been replaced by a split-rail fence.

About the Author

SCOTT MARSHALL has been associated with Edith Wharton Restoration at The Mount since 1983. Currently EWR's deputy director, historian, archivist, and Wharton authority, he was EWR's assistant director from 1986-89 and its first intern in 1985. He lectures frequently on Edith Wharton and The Mount and is the author of several articles on Wharton, published in *The Edith Wharton Review* and other publications, and of a walking tour, "Edith Wharton's Old New York." In 1991 he organized a session on "Edith Wharton and Film" for the first international Wharton conference in Paris, followed by a similar session in 1995 at Yale University for the conference "Edith Wharton at Yale," both sponsored by the Edith Wharton Society. His article, "Edith Wharton and Kate Spencer," appeared in the Norton Critical Edition of *Ethan Frome* (1995), edited by Kristin O. Lauer and Cynthia Griffin Wolff. An essay, "A History of Edith Wharton on Film," was published in Japan in *The World of Edith Wharton: New Essays on Edith Wharton* (Yumi Press, 1996), edited by Keiko Beppu.

From 1990 to 1993 Marshall was the executive director of the Greenwich Village Society for Historic Preservation in New York City. He received a B.A. in English from New York University and an M.S. in historic preservation from the Graduate School of Architecture, Planning, and Preservation at Columbia University in 1986.

Acknowledgments

I began researching the history for The Mount's historic structure report in 1987, completing the text in mid-1990. The report is finally being published in the summer of 1997, thanks to a generous grant from the Florence Gould Foundation.

The following friends and colleagues generously contributed information and assistance that significantly enriches this report: Virginia Agar, granddaughter of the Whartons' coachman, William Parlett; David H. Bennett, EWR board member and landscape authority; Shari Benstock, Wharton biographer, for material on Wharton and her architects; Lila W. Berle, Foxhollow School '54 and founding member of EWR; Julia Bowers, for material on Francis Hoppin; Dorothy Carpenter, Foxhollow School '68; Kergan J. Davidson, facilities manager for the Foxhollow School; Ruth Degenhardt, director, the Local History Room, the Berkshire Athenaeum; Jonas Dovydenas, chair and president of the EWR board of directors; Eleanor Dwight, EWR board member and Wharton biographer; Mary Law Evans; Bonnie Fuller; Cornelia Brooke Gilder, for material from *The Berkshire Gleaner* and information regarding Edith Wharton's original drawing-room tapestries; Terry Hallock, Terry F. Hallock Architects; Bryce Hill; William Brice Hobbs, for Edith Wharton's letter to his great-aunt, Helen Brice; Dr. Regina M. Kellerman, for information on nineteenth-century New York City rowhouses; Deborah Krulewitch, for the 1936 article from *Country Life*; the staff of the Lenox Library; Nancy Lewis and R. W. B. Lewis, Wharton biographer and together the editors of *The Letters of Edith Wharton*; Grace McMahon, librarian, *The Berkshire Eagle*; Nancy D. Marasco, former president of the Lenox Historical Society, for the diary entries of William Derbyshire Curtis relating to the 1911 sale of The Mount; Samuel N. Martin; Pauline C. Metcalf, EWR board member and authority on the life and work of Ogden Codman, Jr.; Lori Misura; Melodye Moore, historic-site manager, Mills Mansion State Historic Site; Tina Packer, artistic director, Shakespeare & Company; Mary Hart Parker, Foxhollow School '49; Mrs. Leonard Peters, for the 1935 auction catalogue of the Shattuck estate, including Edith Wharton's original drawing-room tapestries; Pauline Pierce, head, Stockbridge Historical Room; Catha Grace Rambusch, Foxhollow School '54; Stuart Siegel, for providing his unpublished thesis on the life of Francis Hoppin and the work of Hoppin & Koen; Sally Torodash, for supplying turn-of-the-century copies of *Lenox Life*; John G. Waite, Douglas Bucher, and Michael Curcio, principals, John G. Waite Associates, Architects; Dr. Patricia Willis, curator of American Literature, the Beinecke Rare Book and Manuscript Library, Yale University; Richard Guy Wilson; and Cynthia Griffin Wolff, Wharton biographer. I wish to acknowledge my gratitude to them all, especially David H. Bennett and Pauline C. Metcalf for their extraordinary assistance and support throughout this decade-long effort. My appreciation also to the EWR staff who worked on various aspects of this report over many years: Genet Cunningham, Laura Qualliotine, and Allison Whitmarsh. Without the computer expertise of Susan M. Hanson, this report would probably not have seen the light of day.

Beginning in the early 1980s, several reports were commissioned that focused on particular aspects of The Mount's history. This historic structure report acknowledges the earlier research of Wendy Baker, David H. Bennett, and Diane Dierkes in their 1982 landscape architectural analysis; William Hickman in his 1985 paint analysis; and Amelia Peck in her 1984 furnishings analysis of the main floor's principal rooms.

Edith Wharton Restoration gratefully acknowledges the Edith Wharton Estate and the Watkins/Loomis Agency, Inc., for permission to quote from manuscripts and correspondence by Edith Wharton (both published and unpublished) in archives and in private collections.

For assistance with permissions and copyrights, Edith Wharton Restoration and the author thank the following: Robert Behra, curator of special collections, Redwood Library and Athenaeum; George Braziller, George Braziller, Inc.; Lorna Condon, curator of library and archives, Society for the Preservation of New England Antiquities; John Donahue, Copyright and Permissions, Harvard University Press; Wayne Furman, Office of Special Collections, The New York Public Library; David R. Godine Publishers, Inc.; HarperCollins Publishers, Permissions and Copyrights; Ron Hussey, Consumer Permissions, Simon & Schuster; Denis J. Lesieur, director, the Lenox Library Association; Gloria Loomis and Lily Oei, Watkins/Loomis Agency, Inc.; Nancy D. Marasco, curator, the Lenox Historical Society; Henry Hope Reed, president, Classical America; Elena Smilevich, Rights & Permissions, Harry N. Abrams, Inc.; Patricia Willis, curator of American Literature, the Beinecke Rare Book and Manuscript Library, Yale University; Richard Guy Wilson, the Parrish Art Museum, and Alicia Longwell, registrar; and M. Joan Youngken, deputy director and curator, the Newport Historical Society.

Special thanks to Jonas Dovydenas for taking all of the present-day photographs of existing conditions in Part II. For assistance with illustrations in this report, the author wishes to thank the following: Robert Behra, curator of special collections, and Maris S. Humphreys, special collections librarian, the Redwood Library and Athenaeum; Joanna Britto, Office of Rights and Reproductions, National Portrait Gallery, Smithsonian Institution; Douglas Bucher and Michael Curcio, principals, John G. Waite Associates, Architects; Ann Clifford, assistant archivist, Society for the Preservation of New England Antiquities; Michael and Sunny D'Amore, Sunshine Photographics, Pittsfield, Massachusetts; Ruth Degenhardt, director, the Local History Room, the Berkshire Athenaeum; Angela Giral, director, and Janet Parks, curator of drawings and archives, Avery Library, Columbia University; Christopher Gray, director, Office for Metropolitan History, New York City; Denis J. Lesieur, director, the Lenox Library Association; Dan McCleary, Shakespeare & Company; Lisa Nelson, AP/Wide World Photos; Yvonne Schofer, University of Wisconsin Memorial Library; Nancy Seaman; Eileen Sullivan, Photograph and Slide Library, the Metropolitan Museum of Art; Saundra Taylor, curator of manuscripts, the Lilly Library, University of Indiana; Peter Tomlinson, Culver Pictures, Inc.; Patricia Willis, curator of American Literature, and the staff of the Beinecke Rare Book and Manuscript Library, Yale University; and M. Joan Youngken, deputy director and curator, the Newport Historical Society.

I am also greatly indebted to the very skillful and patient editor of this report, Diana S. Waite, of Mount Ida Press, and for the help of her managing editor, Patricia Gioia. I also want to acknowledge Constance Timm, of The Market Street Group, and her associate, Adrienne Beaver, the designers of the report.

Mostly importantly, my appreciation to Thomas S. Hayes, former president of Edith Wharton Restoration, who commissioned the report and asked me to research and write it; and to Stephanie W. Copeland, executive director of Edith Wharton Restoration, who oversaw its completion, format, illustrations, and finally, publication.

SCOTT MARSHALL
The Mount
February 1997

Notes

Key to Notes

Frequently cited sources appear in this key; other sources are cited in the notes.

BOOKS

ED, *EW:AEL*
Eleanor Dwight, *Edith Wharton: An Extraordinary Life* (New York: Harry N. Abrams, 1994). All rights reserved.

EW, *ABG*
Edith Wharton, *A Backward Glance* (New York: Appleton-Century Company, 1934). Copyright (c) 1933, 1934 by Charles Scribner's Sons; Copyright (c) 1961, 1962 by William R. Tyler. Used by permission of Scribner's, a Division of Simon & Schuster.

EW, *IVG*
Edith Wharton, *Italian Villas and Their Gardens* (New York: The Century Press, 1904).

EW and OC, *DH*
Edith Wharton and Ogden Codman, Jr., *The Decoration of Houses* (New York: Charles Scribner's Sons, 1897).

L and L, *LEW*
R. W. B. Lewis and Nancy Lewis, eds. *The Letters of Edith Wharton* (New York: Charles Scribner's Sons, 1988). Copyright (c) 1988 by R. W. B. Lewis, Nancy Lewis, and William R. Tyler. Used by permission of Scribner's, a Division of Simon & Schuster.

PCM, "FLL," *OCDH*
Pauline C. Metcalf, "From Lincoln to Leopolda," *Ogden Codman and the Decoration of Houses* (Boston: David R. Godine, 1988).

PL, *PEW*
Percy Lubbock, *Portrait of Edith Wharton* (London: Jonathan Cape, 1947).

RGW, "EO:WDA," *OCDH*
Richard Guy Wilson, "Edith and Ogden: Writing, Decoration, and Architecture," *Ogden Codman and the Decoration of Houses* (Boston: David R. Godine, 1988).

RWBL, *EW*
R. W. B. Lewis, *Edith Wharton: A Biography* (New York: Harper & Row, 1975). Used by permission of HarperCollins, Publishers.

SB, *NGC*
Shari Benstock, *No Gifts from Chance: A Biography of Edith Wharton* (New York: Charles Scribner's Sons, 1994). Copyright (c) 1994 by Shari Benstock. Used by permission of Scribner's, a Division of Simon & Schuster.

WAC, "GC," *DH*
William A. Coles, "The Genesis of a Classic," Introduction to the Classical America edition of Edith Wharton's and Ogden Codman's *The Decoration of Houses* (New York: W. W. Norton & Company, 1978). Used by permission of Classical America.

PERIODICALS/ARTICLES

"ARSD," *BEE*
"Albert R. Shattuck Dies at his Villa in Lenox," *The Berkshire Evening Eagle*, November 5, 1925, 15.

"ARSD," *NYT*
"Albert R. Shattuck Dies of Heart Attack," *The New York Times*, November 5, 1925, 23.

"AT," *LnLf*
"Automobile Topics," *Lenox Life*

BE
The Berkshire Eagle

BEE
The Berkshire Evening Eagle

BRT
Berkshire Resort Topics

"CVA-E," *NYT*
"Carr V. Van Anda," editorial, *The New York Times*, January 30, 1945, 18.

"CVA, NTE," *NYT*
"Carr V. Van Anda, Noted Times Editor, Dies Here, Aged 80," *The New York Times*, January 29, 1945, 1, 13.

"DTT," *LnLf*
"Dinner Table Talk," *Lenox Life*

EW, "ALGNY"
Edith Wharton, "A Little Girl's New York," *Harper's Magazine* 176 (March 1938): 356-364.

H&K, "SCCR," *NYA*
Hoppin & Koen, "Some City and Country Residences," *The New York Architect* V (July 1911): 149-156.

LnLf
Lenox Life

"ML," *BRT*
"The Mount in Lenox," *Berkshire Resort Topics* II (September 10, 1904): 1-2.

NYT
The New York Times

"SBWP," *BEE*
"Shattuck Buys the Wharton Property," *The Berkshire Evening Eagle*, September 11, 1911, 6.

STW, "EQ," *NYT*
S.T. Williamson, "The End of a Quest — Stranger than Fiction," *The New York Times*, November 15, 1925, IX, 2.

UNPUBLISHED MATERIALS

AMF, "EWatM,"
Aileen M. Farrell, "Edith Wharton at the Mount." Foxhollow School Archives, Edith Wharton Restoration.

AMF, "EW-M"
Aileen M. Farrell, "E. W. — Mount." Handwritten notes, 3-14, Foxhollow School Archives, Edith Wharton Restoration.

AP, *RPI-TM*
Amelia Peck, *Restoration Plan for the Interior of The Mount, Lenox, Massachusetts*. Thesis for the Division of Historic Preservation, Graduate School of Architecture and Planning, Columbia University, 1984.

BBD, *ALAAMP-TM*
Wendy Baker, David Bennett, and Diane Dierkes, *A Landscape Architectural Analysis and Master Plan for The Mount*. Prepared for the Massachusetts Council on the Arts and Humanities, Edith Wharton Restoration, Inc., and Shakespeare & Company. Harvard Graduate School of Design, 1982.

CVA, "SRAAAT"
Carr V. Van Anda, "Statement of Reasons for the Attached Application for Abatement of Taxes on the Property of Louise D. Van Anda," Lenox, Massachusetts, September 26, 1940. Lenox Library Association.

DBU, "Memories"
Daniel Berkeley Updike, "Memories of E. W.," May 1938. Yale Collection of American Literature, Beinecke Rare Book and Manuscript Library, Yale University.

EW, "LAI"
Edith Wharton, "Life and I." Yale Collection of American Literature, Beinecke Rare Book and Manuscript Library, Yale University.

GL, "EW"
Gaillard Lapsley, "E.W." Yale Collection of American Literature, Beinecke Rare Book and Manuscript Library, Yale University.

"LSR," H&K, RL
"Lodge, Stable and Residence, E. R. Wharton, Lenox, Mass." Unpublished account books of the Hoppin & Koen firm. The Redwood Library and Athenaeum, Newport, Rhode Island.

PP, *PWDDPA-TM*
The Preservation Partnership, *Project Work Documentation for Development Project Application — The Mount*, 1981.

RWG, NYPL
Richard Watson Gilder Papers, Rare Books and Manuscripts Division, The New York Public Library, Astor, Lenox, and Tilden Foundations.

SS, *AHK*
Stuart Siegel, *The Architecture of Hoppin & Koen*. Graduate thesis for the Department of Architectural History, University of Virginia, 1980.

ARCHIVES AND ORGANIZATIONS

BL
Beinecke Rare Book and Manuscript Library, Yale Collection of American Literature, Yale University

EWR
Edith Wharton Restoration Archives, The Mount

FHS
Foxhollow School Archives, Edith Wharton Restoration

LnL
Lenox Library Association, Lenox, Massachusetts

S&C
Shakespeare & Company

SPNEA, CFMC
Society for the Preservation of New England Antiquities, Codman Family Manuscripts Collection

PERSONAL NAMES

AMF	Aileen M. Farrell
ARS	Albert R. Shattuck
CVA	Carr Van Anda
EW	Edith Wharton
FH	Francis Hoppin
GL	Gaillard Lapsley
HJ	Henry James
H&K	Hoppin & Koen Architects
MCJ	Mary Cadwalader Jones
MF	Morton Fullerton
MTC	Margaret Terry Chanler
OC	Ogden Codman, Jr.
SBC	Sarah Bradlee Codman
SN	Sara Norton
TW	Teddy Wharton
WB	Walter Berry
WCB	William Crary Brownell
WFW	William Fisher Wharton

Edith Wharton Restoration gratefully acknowledges the Edith Wharton Estate and the Watkins/Loomis Agency, Inc., for permission to use quotations from manuscripts and correspondence by Edith Wharton (both published and unpublished) in archives and in private collections.

PREFACE

A Passion for Houses

1. EW, *ABG*, 44.

2. Ibid., 106.

3. RWBL, *EW*, 461. EW to Elisina Tyler, c. 1924.

4. EW, *ABG*, 363.

5. RWBL, *EW*, 421. EW to Royall Tyler, c. 1921.

6. RGW, "EO:WDA," *OCDH*, 160. EW to OC, August 1, 1900, SPNEA, CFMC (also in SB, *NGC*, 114).

7. EW, *ABG*, 125.

8. Ibid.

CHAPTER 1

Edith Wharton: Designing a Life

1. "Edith Wharton: Designing a Life," written in 1989, draws most heavily on *Edith Wharton: A Biography* by R. W. B. Lewis (1975). More recently, two biographies of Wharton have added significant new material and interpretations of her life, particularly relating to the 1890s: *No Gift from Chance: A Biography of Edith Wharton* by Shari Benstock (1994) and *Edith Wharton: An Extraordinary Life* by Eleanor Dwight (1994).

CHAPTER 2

Edith Wharton and Design: A Study of Her Earliest Homes and Influences

1. EW, "LAI," 1.

2. EW, *ABG*, 2.

3. EW, "LAI," 2.

4. EW, *ABG*, 28.

5. Ibid., 27.

6. Ibid., 28. According to other sources, the name of the house was "Wyndcliff."

7. Ibid.

8. Ibid., 29.

9. Ibid., 32.

10. Ibid., 33.

11. EW, "LAI," 7.

12. Ibid.

13. Ibid., 41.

14. EW, *ABG*, 54-55.

15. R. W. B. Lewis in his 1975 biography describes the house on West 23rd Street as a "three-story brownstone" with "the inevitable Dutch stoop" (*EW*, 22). The one surviving photograph of the house (see Note 17) shows that the building was four-and-one-half stories and had no Dutch stoop.

16. The Fifth Avenue Hotel would later figure in some of EW's fiction, including "New Year's Day" from *Old New York* (1924) and *The Buccaneers* (1938).

17. This description is based on the one known surviving photograph of 14 West 23rd Street. The photograph, which is in the collection of the New-York Historical Society, was published in *Literary New York — A History and Guide* by Susan Edmiston and Linda D. Cirino (Boston: Houghton-Mifflin Co., 1976). The photograph is actually of 12 West

23rd Street, the building next door. The eastern one-third of the Jones home, including the entrance on the street level, is clearly visible. The date of the photograph is unknown, but most likely it was taken during the final years of the family's occupancy, i.e. prior to 1882. After the family moved, the brownstone residence was converted into a retail store; a cast-iron facade was added in the 1890s. 14 West 23rd Street still stands but in a greatly modified form.

18. EW, "ALGNY," 357.

19. R. W. B. Lewis assumes this in *EW*, 22.

20. EW, "ALGNY," 361.

21. EW, "LAI," 26.

22. EW on the "gentleman's library" of the time:

"In my grand-parents' day every gentleman had what was called 'a gentleman's library.' In my father's day, these libraries still existed, though they were often only a background; but in our case Macaulay, Prescott, Motley, Sainte-Beuve, Augustin Thierry, Victor Hugo, the Brontes, Mrs. Gaskell, Ruskin, [and] Coleridge, had been added to the French and English classics in their stately calf bindings" (*ABG*, 52).

"my father read sermons, & narratives of Arctic exploration. But at that time every gentleman, whether he was a reader or not, possessed what was known as 'a gentleman's library'; that is, a fair collection of the 'standard' works in French and English" ("LAI," 25).

"Most of the little brownstone houses in which the Salvator Rosas and Domenichinos gloomed so incongruously on friendly drawing-room walls still possessed the surviving fragments of 'a gentleman's library' — that is, the collection of good books, well written, well printed, well bound, with which the aboriginal New Yorkers had beguiled their long and dimly lit leisure" ("ALGNY," 361).

23. EW, *ABG*, 43.

24. Architectural historian Dr. Regina M. Kellerman suggests that most likely the billiard room and the conservatory were on the ground floor, based on similar house plans of the period. The kitchen would have been located in the basement. Most New York townhouses in this style had a full basement, accessible from the street by a flight of stairs and lit by large windows with the aid of lightwells between the building and the sidewalk. See *ABG* (58-59) for EW's memories of the family's cooks and the marvelous foods they prepared during her childhood years.

25. EW, "ALGNY," 361.

26. EW, "LAI," 20.

27. EW, "ALGNY," 361.

28. Ibid., 358.

29. Ibid.

30. Ibid., 360.

31. Ibid.

32. EW, "LAI," 20.

33. EW, *ABG*, 44.

34. Ibid., 45.

35. The date of construction of Pencraig is not known but may be presumed as c. 1860-65. EW remarked in "LAI" that the family went to Europe in 1865 to economize, and one way of doing so was to rent the "newly-built country-place at Newport" (2).

36. EW, "ALGNY," 360-361. The use of Colonial furniture at Pencraig is also interesting in that it parallels OC's interest in Colonial furnishings and interior design and his love for

the Codman family's ancestral home, The Grange, in Lincoln, Massachusetts. It seems that EW developed similar tastes while living at Pencraig.

37. Ibid., 360.

38. Ibid.

39. EW, "LAI," 25.

40. EW, *ABG*, 53.

41. Ibid., 54.

42. Ibid., 79-80.

43. Ibid., 90.

44. Ibid.

45. EW, "LAI," 1-2.

46. In *EW*, Lewis describes Pencraig Cottage as "a compact frame building of no particular style" (54).

47. EW, *ABG*, 91.

48. Ibid., 92.

49. Ibid., 93.

50. RGW, "EO:WDA," *OCDH*, 136-138. As Wilson explains, "For Edith, Winthrop's interiors were a revelation" (138).

51. EW, *ABG*, 92.

52. GL, "EW," 21. Pencraig Cottage still stands, although altered, as a private home; Pencraig was demolished in 1956, according to the Newport Historical Society.

53. RWBL, *EW*, 68.

54. Ibid.

55. RGW, "EO:WDA," *OCDH*, 138.

56. EW, *ABG*, 106.

57. Ibid.

58. Ibid.

59. PCM, "FLL," *OCDH*, 9.

60. EW, *ABG*, 106-107.

61. Ibid., 106.

62. Ibid., 107.

63. RGW, "EO:WDA," *OCDH*, 140.

64. Wilson, however, finds that the results retreated "into the overdone Rococo scroll work and still-cluttered interiors of the 1890s." RGW, "EO:WDA," *OCDH*, 140.

65. EW, *ABG*, 14. If these andirons were taken by the Whartons to The Mount, they may have been placed in the drawing room, TW's den, or EW's bedroom. Period photographs indicate that they were not located in the library or the dining room at The Mount.

66. RGW, "EO:WDA," *OCDH*. 140-141. The design is illustrated on 142.

67. EW, *ABG*, 106.

68. Ibid. Land's End still stands, although altered, as a private home.

69. *BRT*, June 13, 1903, 7.

70. RWBL, *EW*, 67.

71. EW, *ABG*, 143.

72. Ibid.

73. HJ to MCJ, January 13, 1905. Leon Edel, ed. *Henry James — Letters Volume IV 1895-1916* (Cambridge, Massachusetts: The Belknap Press of Harvard University Press, 1984), 338. Copyright (c) 1984 by Leon Edel, Editorial; Copyright (c) 1984 by Alexander R. James, James Copyright material. Used by permission of Harvard University Press.

74. Leon Edel, *Henry James — The Master: 1901-1916* (New York: Avon Books, 1972), 262. Copyright (c) by Leon Edel. Used by permission of HarperCollins, Publishers.

75. RGW, "EO:WDA," *OCDH*, 146. EW, in fact, had disliked the dark red color of the upper wall panels, preferring a uniform pink shade. Whatever the color of the panels at 884 Park Avenue, this design scheme reappeared in a new guise, including striped cushions on the sofa and chairs to match.

76. Elsie de Wolfe, *After All* (London: William Heinemann Ltd., 1935), 35.

77. DBU, "Memories," 7.

78. PL, *PEW*, 36.

79. Ibid., 37.

80. Ibid., 38-39. The Wharton home at 884 Park Avenue was demolished c. 1920s. At some point during the Whartons' ownership, OC made a drawing that would have united the front elevations of 882-884 Park Avenue into one, cohesive, French-style townhouse (illustrated in Theresa Craig, *Edith Wharton — A House Full of Rooms: Architecture, Interiors, and Gardens*, The Monacelli Press, 1996, 82). The work was apparently not realized. The elevation is at AAFAL.

81. EW, *ABG*, 107.

82. RWBL, *EW*, 76 (see Note 1, Chapter 1).

83. Ibid.

84. EW, "LAI," 41.

85. WAC, "GC," *DH*, xxix.

86. EW, *ABG*, 108.

87. PCM, "FLL," *OCDH*, 9.

88. EW, *ABG*, 107.

89. Ibid., 110. For a further discussion of the writing of *The Decoration of Houses*, see RGW, "EO:WDA," in *OCDH*.

90. In a later letter, EW lamented to OC: "it seems to me that the bogey we had been fighting had long since been destroyed, though only to be replaced by worse things" (EW to OC, April 21, 1937, SPNEA, CFMC).

91. OC to EW, April 18, 1937, SPNEA, CFMC.

92. Ibid.

CHAPTER 3

A House of Her Own Making: The Design of The Mount

1. EW to OC, July 1900, SPNEA, CFMC. From the lecture "From the Ground Up" by David H. Bennett. Lewis in *EW* states that EW had visited Belton House, "which she had inspected and greatly admired during one of her visits to England" (100).

2. EW and OC, *DH*, Chapter I, 4 (Note 1). It should be added that despite the problems with the northern climate that EW and OC envisioned for Italian villas in the United States, other architects were able to adapt this form successfully. Charles Platt often used villa precepts in his designs, while in Lenox, Massachusetts, architects Peabody and Stearns designed Wheatleigh in such a style for the Count and Countess de Heredia in 1893. EW's feelings about the Georgian style are clearly delineated in an 1896 letter she wrote to the editor of the *Newport Daily News*, entitled "Newport's Old Houses." The letter is reprinted in *Edith Wharton: The Uncollected Critical Writings*, edited by Frederick Wegener (Princeton University Press, 1996), 55-57.

3. RGW, "EO:WDA," *OCDH*, 164, 182 (Note 100).

4. Ibid. Though EW and OC may have thought so at the time, Wren was not the architect of Belton House. Various architects have been mentioned for this honor; it may best be left unattributed. Grinling Gibbons did do some of the ornamental carvings at Belton.

5. The plate in *Vitruvius Britannicus*, as well as period paintings of Belton, shows that such a staircase was a part of the English house at some point; later photographs indicate that the stairs were changed, possibly by the turn-of-the-century. If so, the plate in *Vitruvius Britannicus* would have been the direct source for The Mount's staircase.

6. Pauline C. Metcalf, "Elegance Without Excess; Ogden Codman in New York," *Newsletter — Preservation League of New York State*, Winter 1986, 5.

7. Ibid.

8. RGW, "EO:WDA", *OCDH*, 165.

9. Bennett, "From the Ground Up," 12.

10. BBD, *ALAAMP-TM*, 53.

11. PCM, "FLL," *OCDH*, 5-7. The majority of all the information on OC is drawn from this definitive book on the architect.

12. Ibid., 9. It is unclear what OC's bill for work on the Wharton house refers to; it could have been work for 884 Park Avenue in New York or, as suggested here, on Pencraig Cottage in Newport before the Whartons purchased Land's End in 1893.

13. EW, *ABG*, 106. Ironically, the original architect of Land's End in 1864 was John Hubbard Sturgis, OC's uncle.

14. Ibid.

15. PCM, "FLL," *OCDH*, 9.

16. Ibid., 12. OC to SBC, December 1893, SPNEA, CFMC.

17. Ibid.

18. PCM, "FLL," *OCDH*, 15.

19. Ibid.

20. RGW, "EO:WDA," *OCDH*," 149.

21. PCM, "FLL," *OCDH*, 15-16.

22. Ibid., 16.

23. OC to SBC, February 7, 1901, SPNEA, CFMC.

24. OC to SBC, February 17, 1901, SPNEA, CFMC.

25. OC to SBC, February 25, 1901, SPNEA, CFMC.

26. Ibid.

27. Ibid.

28. Ibid.

29. OC to SBC, March 9, 1901, SPNEA, CFMC.

30. OC to SBC, March 11, 1901, SPNEA, CFMC.

31. OC to SBC, March 13, 1901, SPNEA, CFMC.

32. OC to SBC, November 26, 1900, SPNEA, CFMC.

33. OC to SBC, February 7, 1901, SPNEA, CFMC.

34. ED, *EW:AEL*, 90.

35. SB, *NGC*, 118.

36. ED, *EW:AEL*, 90-91.

37. Ibid., 90.

38. OC to SBC, April 7, 1901, SPNEA, CFMC.

39. OC to SBC, April 16, 1901, SPNEA, CFMC.

40. SB, *NGC*, 119. WB to EW, Spring 1901.

41. There was, however, a flare-up of the old disagreement between OC and the Whartons in early February 1905 over an earlier bill submitted by the architect for the painting of EW's boudoir. OC charged a commission on this; the Whartons contended that the work had not been done under his supervision or had not been connected in any way to the work he had done for them on The Mount. Annoyed at the bill for $85, which she had never seen before, EW then charged that OC had made measurements for the boudoir panels while in her presence but that when the panels arrived, they were the wrong size. This necessitated repainting the room. She claimed that OC had admitted that his office was at fault and that there would be no charge. An original bill was submitted by OC on September 1, 1903 — various letters passed back and forth between the principals involved, including WB, acting as the Whartons' lawyer, and OC's attorneys. OC blamed the entire matter on H&K's contractor, Robert Curry, whom he claimed had taken his (OC's) correct measurements and proceeded to cut the panels the incorrect size. EW continued to insist in a subsequent letter that OC had promised her (and TW) that his office would absorb the cost of the mistake. Eventually the matter was settled — or dropped. The letters are in the archives of SPNEA, CFMC.

42. There is confusion over the year of FH's birth — 1866 or 1867. Richard Champlin in "Col. Hoppin's Newport" (*Newport History*), the obituary in *The New York Herald Tribune* (9/10/41), and the FH entry in the *National Cyclopedia of American Biography* assert that the architect was born on October 7, 1866. On the other hand, the FH entry in the *Macmillan Encyclopedia of Architects* (by Stuart Siegel), the FH entry in Withey's *Biographical Dictionary of American Architects (Deceased)*, and the thesis by Stuart Siegel all assert October 7, 1867.

43. SS, *AHK*, Chapter 1, n.p. Used with the kind permission of the author. Siegel has thoroughly researched FH's background and early years and had access to unpublished family letters that can no longer be located. FH later named his Newport home (1929 and after) "Auton House," presumably for his uncle's 1882 book.

44. In 1898, at the beginning of the Spanish-American War, FH enlisted in the 12th Regiment, New York National Guard, serving for nine months. Subsequently he rejoined the regiment with the rank of captain. He became a major, saw service on the Mexican border, and was appointed military secretary to former Governor Charles S. Whitman, of New York. In December 1918, Governor Whitman promoted him to colonel ("Col. Hoppin, 74, Architect and Painter, Dead," *New York Herald Tribune*, September 10, 1941).

45. Although some sources (including Withey's *Biographical Dictionary of American Architects (Deceased)* state that FH studied in Paris at the Ecole des Beaux-Arts, this is apparently not true. Richard L. Champlin in "Colonel Hoppin's Newport" (*Newport History*) explains: "Richard Chafee, joint author of *The Architecture of the Ecole des Beaux-Arts* (New York: Museum of Modern Art, c. 1977) failed to find FH's name on the student list at Ecole des Beaux-Arts, but believes he might instead have studied at a Paris architect's *atelier*" (Note 1, 35). Siegel, in his thesis, asserts that FH took the entrance examination for the Ecole des Beaux-Arts and passed on March 8, 1888. He apparently did not attend classes and later that year returned to America, where he worked in Providence, Rhode Island, for his brother Howard's firm (SS, *AHK*, 6).

46. SS, *AHK*, Chapter 1, 6. Siegel further explains in a footnote that "even though Hoppin left them [Hoppin, Read & Hoppin] after a short period of time, he still maintained a

professional relationship with the firm which lasted most of his career" (Chapter 1, Note 20, 5). One example of this continued collaboration was the Van Wickle Gates for Brown University.

47. H&K, "SCCR," *NYA*, 148-157. The dates cited here are confusing. Hoppin and Koen started their own firm in 1894 and left McKim, Mead & White at the same time. The article — in 1911 — asserts that they left McKim, Mead & White "eleven years ago." It further states that Koen worked in the service of McKim, Mead & White for 18 years; Siegel writes that Koen "entered McKim, Mead & White in 1880, just one year after the firm was started" (SS, *AHK*, Chapter 1, n.p.).

48. Very little is known about Koen — Siegel quotes Egerton Swartout, who worked in the McKim, Mead & White office at the same time and knew Hoppin and Koen, as stating that many people assumed from his name that Koen was Jewish, but that in fact he was Irish (SS, *AHK*, Chapter 1, Note 31, n.p.).

49. H&K, "SCCR," *NYA*, 149.

50. Ibid.

51. Ibid.

52. Ibid.

53. Ibid.

54. EW to OC, June 30, 1897, SPNEA, CFMC. I am indebted to Julia Bowers for bringing this letter to my attention.

55. See Chapter 4.

56. There are two exceptions: 1) EW to SN in 1907 about the problems with heating the service wing of The Mount: "Oh, the imbecility of the American architect!" (see Chapter 7), and 2) EW to WCB, June 11, 1903: heavy rains came and The Mount had a "big leak" (Firestone Library, Princeton, University). (SB, *NGC*, 138). I am indebted to Shari Benstock for bringing this to my attention.

57. L and L, *LEW*, 277. EW to GL, August 19, 1912. FH was married twice; following a divorce from Sarah Carnes Weekes by 1906, he married Mary Latham Gurnee in 1910.

58. Barr Ferree, "Talks with Architects: Mr. F. L. V. Hoppin on the House and Garden," *Scientific American Building Monthly* 35 (March 1903): 47.

59. Ibid.

60. Ibid., 61.

61. Ibid.

CHAPTER 4
Construction of The Mount

1. EW, *ABG*, 124-125. The history of the earlier Mount has been chronicled by the author in an article, "The 'Original' Mount in Astoria, N.Y.," in *Vista from The Mount*, Winter 1988-89.

2. Ibid., 14. EW discussed her great-grandfather and his home, The Mount, in *ABG* (11-14).

3. RWBL, *EW*, 100. Georgiana Sargent was a distant relative of the famous portrait painter John Singer Sargent and was "a local watercolorist of no little freshness and grace" (100). Miss Sargent represented the estate of her father, John O. Sargent, in the transaction. EW, in a letter of March 12, 1902, wrote to SN: "We have bought the Sargent farm at Lenox — I think when you were here we were negotiating for it, as Miss Sargent herself would say..." (L and L, *LEW*, 45).

4. OC to SBC, February 7, 1901, SPNEA, CFMC.

5. OC to SBC, February 17, 1901, SPNEA, CFMC.

6. L and L, *LEW*, 45. EW to SN, March 12, 1901.

7. RWBL, *EW*, 100.

8. OC to SBC, July 1, 1901, SPNEA, CFMC.

9. ED, *EW:AEL*, 91.

10. OC to SBC, July 1, 1901, SPNEA, CFMC.

11. *LnLf*, May 25, 1901, 3. The article reported that "building operations are active" in Lenox, noting, in addition to The Mount, the construction of "Blantyre" for Mr. R. W. Patterson, of New York, new houses for Dr. Jacques and Mr. George Turnure, a new hotel [The Aspinwall], and an addition to the Curtis Hotel. EWR is indebted to Sally Torodash for supplying a large number of copies of *Lenox Life*, an invaluable resource concerning turn-of-the-century society life in the Berkshires.

12. Unpublished original deed, dated June 29, 1901 (John O. Sargent by Trustees to Edith N. Wharton). Berkshire County Registry of Deeds, Pittsfield, Massachusetts. EW purchased 113 acres, to which she later added "about fifteen acres more," for a total of approximately 128 acres (RWBL, *EW*, 100). By the time the Whartons sold it in 1911, the property had grown to approximately 150 acres. EW wrote to SN of the benefit to TW of not having "150 acres to look after" (*LEW*, 255. EW to SN, August 26, 1911).

13. "Among the Cottagers," *LnLf*, July 6, 1901, 1.

14. "At Curtis Hotel," *LnLf*, July 6, 1901, 1. Robert W. Curry was a builder "whom Hoppin came to rely on for other work" (Richard Lawrence Champlin, "Colonel Hoppin's Newport," *Newport History* 59 (Winter 1986): 28-35. Curry worked with FH as early as 1900 in Newport on "Armsea." He is also known to have done "Brookhurst," the Lenox home of Newbold Morris, with the H&K firm.

15. "LSR," H&K, RL, n.p.

16. EW to OC, July 29, 1901, SPNEA, CFMC.

17. RWBL, *EW*, 102. Concerning the Whartons' departure for Europe at this time, *LnLf* reported: "The Lenox cottagers will regret the departure" of Edith and Teddy Wharton, who were sailing on July 31. "They have remained in Lenox to look after the many details incident to the building of their new residence, which is to be a very handsome one." (*LnLf*, July 27, 1901, 1).

18. "Mr. Wharton's New House," *LnLf*, August 17, 1901, 8.

19. OC to SBC, October 27, 1901, SPNEA, CFMC.

20. "LSR," H&K, RL, n.p.

21. RWBL, *EW*, 105.

22. Ibid. (Full letter in *LEW*, 55-56).

23. Ibid. Mimi was the first of several beloved dogs to be buried in the small pet cemetery at The Mount. The inscription on the gravestone reads: "Mimi Died January 1902." As Mimi no doubt died in New York, it seems likely that her gravestone is a commemorative one, testifying to EW's deep affection for this particular pet.

24. OC to SBC, January 1, 1901, SPNEA, CFMC.

25. Ibid. The Frenchman's name is unknown.

26. *Disintegration*, set in turn-of-the-century New York and on Long Island, was abandoned by its author after 74 typed pages and a dozen or so more by hand. As Lewis notes, it was "an invaluable rehearsal for *The House of Mirth* three years later. It was her first large-scale look at social change and social pressure, and at the wounding effect both could have upon the young and sensitive" (RWBL, *EW*, 107).

Around the same time EW was completing a poem for *Harper's*, an article on George Eliot for *The Bookman*, a sketch on Parma for *Scribner's Magazine*, and a ghost story, "The Lady's Maid's Bell."

27.   OC to SBC, January 27, 1902, SPNEA, CFMC.

28.   Ibid., March 14, 1902, SNEA, CFMC.

29.   RWBL, *EW*, 100.

30.   OC to SBC, March 24, 1902, SPNEA, CFMC.

31.   ED, *EW:AEL*, 92. Dwight notes that this is a *1901* letter from EW to OC.

32.   SB, *NGC*, 126. OC to SBC, January 5, 1914.

33.   Ibid., 126-127. OC to SBC, March 3, 1902, SPNEA, CFMC.

34.   OC to SBC, April 26, 1902, SPNEA, CFMC.

35.   EW to RWG, April 1902, NYPL.

36.   TW to OC, May 11, 1902, SPNEA, CFMC. There was an unpleasant argument between OC and the Whartons concerning wall decorations of EW's boudoir, which lasted into 1905 (Chapter 6, 3. Bedroom Floor).

37.   L and L, *LEW*, 64. EW to MTC, May 17, 1902.

38.   *LnLf*, June 7, 1902, 1.

39.   RWBL, *EW*, 111.

40.   Ibid., 110. Lewis further explains that "in her insistence on installing the latter amenities [electric lights and plumbing], it should be remarked, Edith Wharton was well ahead of her time." Electricity was extremely easy to come by at The Mount as EW's neighbor to the south was George Westinghouse, of Westinghouse Electric Company. At the time that his estate, "Erskine Park," was constructed in 1893, Westinghouse had included a power plant near Laurel Lake. This plant supplied power to the town of Lenox. During the period that The Mount was under construction, Westinghouse added new gas engines and additional dynamos to give the town more service. As *LnLf* admiringly reported: "The Westinghouse place uses more light when it is opened than any other consumers in the village." (*LnLf*, June 21, 1902, 4). Electricity for The Mount was both practical and, no doubt, relatively inexpensive to come by at that time.

41.   "LSR," H&K, RL. Only occasional expenses for the stable and lodge were recorded after the fall of 1902.

42.   *LnLf*, August 9, 1902, 1. Bourget, the famous French novelist, and his wife, Minnie, first visited the Whartons at Land's End, in Newport, in the autumn of 1893. Many visits to each other's homes and trips through France and Italy together ensued. Bourget exerted a profound and early influence on EW: "With the Bourgets, literature and thought entered her living room almost for the first time, and on an imposing scale," according to Lewis (*EW*, 68).

43.   Ibid.

44.   L and L, *LEW*, 70. EW to WCB, September 12, 1902.

45.   Ibid., 72. EW to SN, September 30, 1902. The passage is from *Faust* by Goethe: "Two souls, alas, do dwell within my breast." Lewis notes that *Meine* should read *meiner* (*LEW*, 73, Note 1).

46.   "Among the Cottagers," *LnLf*, September 20, 1902, 5.

47.   Ibid. September 27, 1902, 1. Egerton Winthrop (his third cousin once removed, Grenville Winthrop, was then in the process of establishing a Lenox summer estate, "Groton Place") was the older friend who had helped to form and establish EW's tastes in the arts, interior decoration, travel, and things Italian during the early years of her marriage. William D. Sloane was one-half of W. & J. Sloane; his wife

was the former Emily Vanderbilt. Colonel William Jay was the founder of the New York Yachting Club. Reginald C. Vanderbilt was a dashing young playboy (often mentioned in the society papers), who had only recently become engaged to Miss Neilson.

48.   RWBL, *EW*, 111.

49.   OC to SBC, October 8, 1902, SPNEA, CFMC.

50.   RWBL, *EW*, 114.

51.   Ibid.

52.   SB, *NGC*, 133-34. OC to SBC, December 19, 1902, SPNEA, CFMC. As Benstock notes in *NGC*, OC's letter was "virtually a case history" of TW's "mental and physical health" at that time (133).

53.   L and L, *LEW*, 85. EW to SN, June 5, 1903.

54.   Ibid, 84.

55.   "LSR," H&K, RL. The only entry after the fall of 1903 is a payment to R. W. Curry (in full) on February 13, 1905.

56.   Ibid.

CHAPTER 5

Life at The Mount

1.   RGW, "EO:WDA," *OCDH*, 160. EW to OC, August 1, 1900, SPNEA, CFMC (also in SB, *NGC*, 114. Pine Acre, TW's family's Lenox home, had been acquired by his mother, Nancy Spring Wharton, as a country retreat in 1892, seven years after it had been built by Mrs. M. E. Rogers, of Philadelphia.

2.   EW, *ABG*, 106.

3.   Ibid., 124.

4.   *LnLf*, July 6, 1901, 4.

5.   "Editorial," *LnLf*, June 30, 1900, 4.

6.   "DTT," *LnLf*, June 2, 1900, 1.

7.   *LnLf*, August 17, 1901, 4.

8.   RGW, "Picturesque Ambiguities: The Country House Tradition in America," *The Long Island Country House 1870-1930* (Southampton, New York: The Parrish Art Museum, 1988), 13. As Wilson explains, the country house, with its English origins and associations, has always stood for something quite intangible: "The American fascination with country houses, both our own and the English, retains a firm hold on our imagination as an exemplary, if not *the ideal* way in which to live. The notion of the country house has provided a freedom for Americans they could not find in the city... One can claim that the American country house with all its ambiguities, variety, problems of definition, Anglophilic origins, and uncertain location somewhere in the landscape, is a central feature of American identity and culture."

9.   Ibid., 24.

10.   Ibid., 15.

11.   Ibid., 29.

12.   Paul Goldberger, "Edith Wharton Home: An Unusual Rescue," *NYT*, August 7, 1980, n.p.

13.   PL, *PEW*, 33.

14.   RWBL, *EW*, 111.

15.   Ibid., 148.

16.   *BRT*, July 4, 1903, n.p.

17.   PL, *PEW*, 27-28.

18.   HJ to Howard Sturgis, October 17, 1904. Leon Edel, ed. *Henry James — Letters Volume IV 1895-1916*

(Cambridge, Massachusetts: The Belknap Press of Harvard University Press, 1984), 325 (see Note 73, Chapter 2 for copyrights and permission).

19. Millicent Bell, *Edith Wharton & Henry James: The Story of Their Friendship* (New York: George Braziller, 1965), 92. HJ to MCJ, October 1904.

20. Ibid., 91.

21. PL, *PEW*, 29.

22. Ibid., 35.

23. Ibid., 51.

24. Mrs. Walter Maynard, unpublished memories on her stationery, 501 Fifth Avenue, New York, n.d., n.p., BL.

25. PL, *PEW*, 129-130. (also in Bell, *Edith Wharton & Henry James*, 80).

26. Ibid., p. 34-35.

27. RWBL, *EW*, 170. For a list of all the guests who stayed at The Mount from 1902-11, see Note 77, Chapter 6, 3. Bedroom Floor.

28. Maynard, unpublished memories, BL. "My most vivid memory of Edith Wharton — greeting us in that lovely house in Lenox — usually holding a little dog in her arms."

29. EW, *ABG*, 316.

30. GL, "EW," 17.

31. PL, *PEW*, 30.

32. EW, *ABG*, 125.

33. PL, *PEW*, 82.

34. W.K. Richardson, "Informal Memories of Edith Wharton," 44, unpublished material, BL.

35. PL, *PEW*, 30.

36. "The Lenox Cottagers," *BRT*, August 6, 1904, 6.

37. RWBL, *EW*, 147.

38. EW, *ABG*, 125.

39. RWBL, *EW*, 149.

40. Ibid., 136.

41. "The Lenox Automobilists," *BRT*, July 9, 1904, n.p.

42. *BRT*, August 13, 1904, 7.

43. According to a September 10, 1937 article, in *BE* in the Wharton file at the Berkshire Athenaeum in Pittsfield, Massachusetts ("Mrs. Wharton's Chauffeur First Person to Climb Greylock in Car"), EW supposedly left money to her former chauffeur, Charles Cook, mentioning that he had been the first to accomplish this feat. However, *BRT* records that the first automobile ascent of Greylock took place in July 1902 — it was not a motor driven by Cook; indeed, the Whartons did not have a car at this time. A letter from EW to SN on September 16, 1907 (BL), appears to note the first time the Whartons went by car to the top of the state's highest mountain: "It has been glorious here lately, & yesterday we went to the top of Greylock by the road — a really beautiful excursion."

44. Bell, *Edith Wharton & Henry James*, 92-93. HJ to William James, July 1905.

45. EW, *ABG*, 177.

46. Ibid., 153. EW explained that her two New England novellas, *Ethan Frome* and *Summer*, were results of such explorations by motorcar of sleepy backwoods villages and their inhabitants.

47. See PL, *PEW*, 85-86.

48. Ibid.

49. GL, "EW," 4.

50. See *LnLf*, October 5, 1901, 4, and *LnLf*, September 20, 1902, n.p.

51. EW to Helen Brice, August 13 [1903], on The Mount stationery, unpublished. EWR is indebted to William Brice Hobbs for supplying a copy of this letter to his great-aunt.

52. PL, *PEW*, 46.

53. Ibid., 27-28.

54. "Social Life in Lenox," *BRT*, October 15, 1904, n.p.

55. See "Berkshire Resort News" in *The Pittsfield Sun*, July 27, 1905, 2, and August 10, 1905, 2.

56. Records of the Lenox Library, Lenox Library Association, Lenox, Massachusetts.

57. For the Lenox Village Improvement Society: *LnLf*, July 19, 1902, 1. For the Lenox Educational Society: *The Berkshire Gleaner*, March 18, 1903, n.p. EWR is indebted to Cornelia Brooke Gilder for providing the information from *The Berkshire Gleaner*.

58. PL, *PEW*, 28.

59. Ibid., 51.

60. L and L, *LEW*, 102. EW to SN, February 21, 1906.

61. Ibid., 107. EW to Mrs. Alfred Austin, August 14, 1906.

62. Ibid., 252. EW to Bernard Berenson, August 6, 1911.

63. Ibid.

64. EW, *ABG*, 125.

CHAPTER 6

History of the Exterior and Interior of The Mount

Exterior: Forecourt

1. EW, *ABG*, 106.

2. EW noted that the successive owners of the property had promptly effaced her entrance scheme at Land's End (*ABG*, 106).

3. One of the proposed schemes for the forecourt by H&K noted that the contractor should "verify all measurements at bldg," proving that the building was already far along as the forecourt was being planned and dating this feature to 1902.

4. The center section on the south side of the courtyard was opened up during the Foxhollow School years. This diminished the strict separation between the principal and the service entrances, although it may be advantageous for present-day management of the property.

5. BBD, *ALAAMP-TM*, 66. EW and OC did not discuss the forecourt of the country house in *The Decoration of Houses*, beginning their discussion of the proper entrance sequence at the front door.

6. Carole Palermo-Schulze, *Summary for the Restoration of the Formal Gardens at The Mount*. Unpublished report, 1985, n.p., EWR.

7. BBD, *ALAAMP-TM*, 53.

8. Ibid.

9. OC to SBC, October 8, 1902, SPNEA, CFMC.

10. "ML," *BRT*, 1. As landscape architect Carole Palermo-Schulze notes, these plantings created an effective "transition between the wall and flooring by adding color and texture" in the style of a carpet, thereby reinforcing the area's close

relationship with the interior of the house (*Summary for the Restoration*, n.p.). Palermo-Schulze has prepared plans and working drawings for the future restoration of the forecourt.

11. "ML," *BRT*, 1. Photographs of the statues in the forecourt of The Mount c. 1960s (Foxhollow School period) and of the gardens at Land's End in Newport in the 1890s make it clear that EW moved the two statues — one male and the other female — from Land's End to the forecourt of The Mount. According to Foxhollow School headmistress AMF, one statue was of Apollo and the other of Diana; the back of a school photograph, c. 1960s, names the female statue as "Egeria." Photographs and written documentation place "Apollo" in the north niche and "Diana/Egeria" in the south one (see also Chapter 8 on the Foxhollow School years). The statues were sold by the Foxhollow School in the early 1970s.

12. Repairs made to the forecourt walls in the mid-1970s were "inadequate," stated an angry AMF. "In replacing a garden [forecourt] wall, she noted, the contractor left out two niches that had housed statuary. Farrell seems aware that only she will know or care very much that the niches are missing. But similar omissions, she feels, would destroy what remains of The Mount's individuality as surely as a bulldozer." (Dee Siegelbaum, "National Landmark in Lenox a Sickly, White Elephant," *The Albany Times-Union*, August 2, 1976, n.p.). The location of the two niches is substantiated by Kergan J. Davidson, who oversaw the house and grounds for many years for the Foxhollow School.

13. The fountain design eventually found its way into the lion's-head fountain on the Palladian staircase on the east terrace side of The Mount, although in a much more modest realization.

14. EW, *IVG*, 26.

15. EWR. The two schemes by H&K are neither dated nor numbered.

Exterior: Terrace

1. Although the Palladian staircase appears in the drawing that was published in *Vitruvius Britannicus*, historical and present-day photographs of the north elevation of Belton House show a very different staircase. It is not known whether the Palladian staircase was built and later removed or intended but never executed. Assuming that EW and/or OC visited Belton House — and that the Palladian staircase was not in place around the turn-of-the-century — it seems reasonable to conclude the one at The Mount was inspired directly from the plate in *Vitruvius Britannicus*.

2. According to Eleanor Dwight in *EW:AEL*, such a plan would have been similar to the grotto effect at the Villa Cetinale near Siena, Italy (95).

3. There is no evidence to support the premise that the basement sequence of passages and grotto on OC's original sketches was not executed because the solid rock of the hillside prevented successful blasting or excavation. The 1901 H&K plans, which were most likely completed before construction, retain no vestiges of such a sequence.

4. EW, *IVG*, 83.

5. Ibid., 19.

6. EW to OC, December 17, 1897, SPNEA, CFMC. This letter was supplied to the author by Julia Bowers. After she left The Mount in 1911, EW had two permanent homes in France: Pavillon Colombe outside of Paris and Ste. Claire in Hyères, overlooking the Mediterranean. Both had large terraces that stretched along the entire sides of each house

with views of gardens and/or vistas and, therefore, were reminiscent of the terrace at The Mount.

7. Some examples (with modifications) include Blithewood (1899-1902, Barrytown-on-Hudson, New York); Armsea Hall (1900-04, Newport, Rhode Island); and Sandhurst, Hopelands, and the F. S. Taylor Residence (all c. 1902, Aiken, South Carolina). Later H&K houses for which terraces, loggias, and large porches were particularly distinctive include Sherwood (1906-08, Newport, Rhode Island); Brookhurst (1909-11, Lenox, Massachusetts); and Ashintully (1909-12, Tyringham, Massachusetts).

8. An opening in the balustrade allowed access from the terrace to the adjacent rock garden.

9. PP, *PWDDPA-TM*, n.p. In addition to the holes in the marble panels of the balustrade, there are small gutter spouts protruding at intervals on some parts of the stone foundation wall of the terrace. According to the Preservation Partnership report, originally the brick "was laid on sand, and both the sand layer and its surface were separately drained."

10. The marble railing, steps, etc. were tooled to give a rusticated, slightly weather-beaten, aged effect.

11. PP, *PWDDPA-TM*, n.p.

12. Ibid.

13. The obelisks were to have been placed on every post that was not a part of the north or south piers or partially engaged to the house. There would have been one on the south railing (between the wall of the service wing and the south pier), eight on the east railing (four on either side of the Palladian staircase), and six along the north railing of the L-shape alongside the library and TW's den, for a total of 15.

14. H&K elevations, EWR. There may have been a precedent of belvedere-like structures at Belton House in Lincolnshire. According to *Belton House*, a guidebook published by The National Trust of England in 1985, "...Sir Matthew Digby Wyatt, who had worked for Lady Marian Alford at Ashridge, might have brought about a radical change in the appearance at Belton. Plans submitted by him in 1867 proposed the building of two enormous domed pavilions linked to the house at either end" (61). These pavilions were not built at Belton, but it is possible that EW and/or H&K were aware of the plans and based the proposed belvederes for The Mount on them.

15. The belvederes were never constructed. Presumably cost was a major factor, although their elaborate design may have been at odds with the white simplicity of the east elevation. In addition, the belvederes would not have appeared quite symmetrical because the one on the south end would always have been viewed (from the east vantage point) against the service wing, while the north one would have appeared freestanding. Even on the 1901 elevations this dichotomy results in an odd feeling of imbalance.

16. The lion's-head fountain set within the Palladian staircase on the east elevation is perhaps all that remains of an elaborate plan by H&K for the entrance forecourt on the west. A surviving blueprint indicates that a lion's-head fountain would have been an elaborate centerpiece on the north wall of the forecourt (Chapter 6, Exterior: Forecourt).

17. Unfortunately, the belt-course paneling was stuccoed over at an unknown date, sometime after the mid-1940s.

18. The two semicircular openings in the marble landing for these planters were not indicated on the 1901 H&K first-floor plan.

19. An outside service-bell to the left of the drawing room's center French doors was called for on the 1901 floor plan. If installed, there is no trace of it today.

20. PL, *PEW*, 28.

21. Ibid., 35.

22. EW, *ABG*, 125.

23. L and L, *LEW*, 251-252.

24. ED, *EW:AEL*, 101.

25. EW, *ABG*, 181.

26. Ibid., 192.

27. Ibid., 193.

28. Ibid., 193-194.

29. RWBL, *EW*, 273.

30. PL, *PEW*, 28-29.

31. "Pendennis," "The Thinking Heart: An Impression of Mrs. Edith Wharton at Close Range," *The Book News Monthly* 26 (November 1907): 173.

32. "Mrs. Wharton in Lenox," unsigned letter to the editor of *BE*, handwritten date of August 20, 1937, n.p. In the files of the Berkshire Writer's Room in the Local History Department of the Berkshire Athenaeum, Pittsfield, Massachusetts. The terrace itself was occasionally the location for luncheon or dinner. "Mrs. Edward R. Wharton has been entertaining the Misses Helen and Ethel Brice of New York at 'The Mount,' which is one of the gayest of the country seats in Lenox this year. A dinner was given by Mrs. Wharton for her guests on Tuesday, on the large veranda, and there were handsome decorations of orchids and roses." *BRT*, July 11, 1903: 6-7.

33. RWBL, *EW*, 182.

34. Ibid.

35. Ibid.

36. L and L, *LEW*, 243.

37. PL, *PEW*, 28. The speaker was Berkeley Updike.

38. The framing of the awning is clearly visible in an early color-tinted postcard in the collection of FHS.

39. Unfortunately, a different color-tinted postcard (c. 1905?) in the collection of LnL shows the color of the awning as a solid olive green, which was clearly inaccurate, as the awning was striped.

40. One photograph (date unknown) of one of the Whartons' dogs crossing the north terrace from the rock garden and heading toward the house does indicate some furniture on the terrace, including a piece of wicker in the far left corner. A photograph of EW with HJ and Howard Sturgis (probably 1904) taken adjacent to the terrace shows EW seated on a light-colored or tan wicker chair with armrests.

41. "Mrs. Wharton in Lenox," *BE*, August 20, 1937, n.p.

42. In *DH*, EW and OC rejected rattan furniture in the house "as the models are too bad" (see Note 1, 26). Instead they advocated "willow-chairs with denim cushions and solid tables with stained legs and covers of denim or corduroy." They were referring to furniture in living rooms in general, yet porch furniture of EW's choice might have been goverened by these thoughts.

43. CVA, who had many complaints to make about the condition of the house in his 1938 tax-abatement application, noted that $1,800 was then needed to repair the terrace walls and balustrade.

44. AMF," EW-M," 6.

45. According to the Preservation Partnership in *PWD-DPA-TM*: "This had the effect of eliminating all previous sub-surface drainage, and water is now definitely being trapped within this inflexible yet brittle structure" (n.p.).

Interior: Ground Floor

ENTRANCE HALL

1. The H&K plan for the ground floor of The Mount noted that the ceiling of the entrance hall is constructed with the Gustavino arch.

2. EW and OC, *DH*, 104.

3. Known as "The Pan of Rohallion," the piece was the first of a series of fountain statues by Frederick MacMonnies (1863-1937). The original bronze stood 8 feet tall and was created for an estate, Rohallion, of Edward Adams in Seabright, New Jersey. It has been described by Loredo Taft in *The History of American Sculpture* (New York: Arno Press, 1969) as "a boy standing upon a globe in a mock heroic attitude, and laughing as he plays upon a double reed... The globe upon which the mischievous little chap poises a-tiptoe is in turn supported by eight able-bodied fishes which stand upon their tails and spout water with commendable diligence. The other slight accessories...along with the smile...transform an excellent 'academy' into a real work of art." (341). The figure was popular and was cast many times in smaller versions; EW's stood approximately 2 feet tall. It is currently on loan to the Berkshire Museum in Pittsfield, Massachusetts. Future plans call for its reinstallation as a working fountain in the entrance hall.

4. In 1981 the coat room was converted into an office for EWR. Since 1985 it has served as a book and gift shop, selling publications both by and about EW, as well as items of related interest.

5. EW and OC, *DH*, 104.

6. Ibid.

7. "ML," *BRT*, 1.

8. EW and OC, *DH*, 105.

9. Ibid., 103.

10. Ibid., p. 104-105. Several of EW's friends have written of her consideration for the needs of her staff.

11. EW and OC, *DH*, 103.

12. Plans of other H&K country houses examined include: Blithewood (1899-1902); the George B. McClellan House (1905-06); Brookhurst (1909-11); Fahnestock (1909-12); the residence of George Rose (c. 1911); Ashintully (1909-12); and Hopeland House (1913-16). Although the McClellan house in Princeton, New Jersey, was a villa, and the entrance hall of Hopeland House was "designed in the Italian feeling" ("SCCR," H&K, *NYA*, 151), the similarities of marble floors and other features are superficial to the entrance hall at The Mount. H&K placed the entrance hall on the same floor as the main rooms of their country houses and did not favor the carefully thought-out European-style entrance sequence recommended by EW and OC in *DH*.

STAIRCASE HALL

1. EW and OC, *DH*, 112.

2. Ibid., 115.

3. Ibid., 117.

4. A door (for staff use only) leading into the service areas of the basement floor of The Mount is located directly at the foot of the main staircase.

5. In *DH*, EW and OC expounded on iron as "the more suitable material" (113). There were some instances where marble, stone, or wood were judged satisfactory, but the authors were vehement in their dislike of steel as opposed to

wrought iron. *DH* included two illustrations (plate XXXI — the staircase of the Hotel de Ville, Nancy, and plate XXXII — the staircase in the palace at Fontainbleau) markedly similar to the basic design of the staircase at The Mount.

6.   EW and OC, *DH*, 117.

7.   Ibid., 114.

8.   Ibid., 119.

9.   Ibid., 117.

10.   Similar curving French-style staircases with wrought-iron railings and paneled stringcourses for the walls were distinctive features in the halls of several OC houses, including the Berkeley Villa in Newport (1910); 7 East 96th Street (1912), and 3 East 89th Street (1915) in New York City; and the architect's own home, the Villa Leopolda in France (1929). By comparison, H&K tended to favor the grander English-style staircase, which they found more in keeping with the classical neo-Georgian features of the country estate. EW's and OC's genius lay in their understanding, application, and assimilation of several different classical styles into an exquisitely harmonious whole.

11.   EW and OC, *DH*, 118.

12.   Research in 1987 by Douglas Bucher, of John G. Waite Associates, Architects, Albany, New York.

13.   Although there is no known photograph of the stairs at The Mount during EW's occupancy, there is an existing photograph of the stairs at Land's End in Newport, Rhode Island, after it was redecorated in 1893 by EW and OC. The carpet, a deep solid color (possibly red), was attached to the wooden stairs with carpet rails.

14.   EW and OC, *DH*, 119.

15.   Ibid., 115.

16.   Ibid. Plans for other country houses by H&K indicate that the halls were generally designed for lounging, with open fireplaces and tables with lamps, easy-chairs, books, and magazines. Such design was exactly opposite to that recommended by EW and OC.

17.   "ML," *BRT*, 1.

18.   This was the case with a piece of sculpture near the stairs of OC's La Leopolda, and the design of the hall at The Mount indicates the need for prominent artwork in this space. H&K originally planned for the stairs to begin to ascend on the wall directly adjoining the entrance hall. EW may well have deemed this arrangement too cramped and ungracious for the entrance sequence; in any case, the stairs were then placed on the opposite wall from the glass doors connecting the entrance hall.

19.   "ML," *BRT*, 1.

20.   Ibid.

First Floor (Main Floor)

GALLERY

1.   From the gallery looking north, the double doors appear to be real, although the left one is a false door, while the right door opens into the den. The back of the false door is part of the south wall of the den.

2.   The whereabouts of the original elevation is unknown. A photocopy is in the appendix of Amelia Peck's report on the furnishings at The Mount (AP, *RPI-TM*).

3.   EW and OC, *DH*, 136.

4.   Ibid., 135.

5.   Ibid., 137.

6.   Ibid., 140.

7.   "ML," *BRT*, 1.

8.   EW and OC, *DH*, 99.

9.   Ibid.

10.   EW to Mrs. Richard Watson Gilder, August 16, 1902(?), NYPL (courtesy of David H. Bennett).

11.   EW and OC, *DH*, 93.

12.   "ML," *BRT*, 1.

13.   AP, *RPI-TM*, 69-70. The oriental carved wood figure on the console table in the Wharton-period photograph of the gallery may be the same figure visible in a photograph of EW's drawing room at the Pavillon Colombe a number of years later (see ED, *EW:AEL*, top illustration on page 215).

14.   Ibid., 70.

15.   Sally G. Shafto. *A Room Analysis of The Mount*. Unpublished guides training material for EWR, June 1985, 7.

16.   PL, *PEW*, 31-32.

17.   EW and OC, *DH*, 141.

DEN

1.   On the gallery side, this entrance appears to be a set of double doors. However, the one on the left is a false door; on the den side, there is only one single door. The rationale was a visual symmetry: double doors match on either end of the gallery, and two single doors balance on the south wall of the den.

2.   EW and OC, *DH*, 152.

3.   Ibid., 151-152.

4.   See Note 1 above.

5.   EW and OC, *DH*, 153.

6.   EWR. All four wall elevations survive; EW's handwriting on one identifies it as the "Den."

7.   OC designed a similar head surrounded by swags for the Land's End library. As Wilson notes in "EO:WDA," *OCDH*: "The decoration of several of The Mount's rooms especially the den and her [EW's] boudoir, closely followed Codman's designs at Land's End" (168). The plaster ornament of a head within a medallion was one of OC's design trademarks.

8.   According to the Williamstown Regional Art Conservation Laboratory, Inc., after a 1985 inspection.

9.   From "SCCR," H&K, *NYA*: "The house of Mr. R.T. Wilson, at 15 East Fifty-seventh Street, New York, is designed in the pure Adam style. Mr. Hoppin went to London to study the work of the Adam Bros. before designing the interiors... Mr. Hoppin himself painted some of the ceilings in this house" (152).

10.   This is one interpretation; the panel may also represent imperial Roman imagery.

11.   EW and OC, *DH*, 66.

12.   Much of the hardware in the house has the initials "ST" for Maison Sterlin, Paris. OC often used this supplier.

13.   EW and OC, *DH*, 62.

14.   "ML," *BRT*, 1.

15.   EW and OC, *DH*, 153.

16.   "ML," *BRT*, 1: "The oak floor has a rug upon it..."

17.   Ibid.

18. AP, *RPI-TM*, 61.

19. Ibid., 63.

20. EW and OC, *DH*, 152.

21. AP, *RPI-TM*, 65.

22. W.K. Richardson, "Informal Memories of Edith Wharton," unpublished memories submitted to PL for the book *PEW*, 44.

23. GL, "EW," 15-16.

LIBRARY

1. EW and OC, *DH*, 148-149.

2. "ML," *BRT*, 1.

3. EW and OC, *DH*, 93.

4. William Hickman, in his 1985 paint analysis, asserts that the original color of the library ceiling was a "pinkish gray."

5. Based on the lack of a layer of soot between the white plaster and the wood stain, John G. Waite Associates, Architects, suggest that the graining on the cornice may have been applied during EW's years at The Mount.

6. Hercules was the son of Jupiter and Alcemena. As Juno was always hostile to the offspring of her husband by mortal mothers, she declared war against Hercules from his birth. She sent two serpents to destroy him as he lay in his cradle, but the precocious infant strangled them with his own hands. He was, however, by the arts of Juno, rendered subject to Eurystheus and compelled to perform all his commands. Eurystheus enjoined upon him a succession of desperate adventures, which are called the "Twelve Labours of Hercules." The first was the fight with the Nemean Lion. The valley of Nemea was infested by a terrible lion. Eurystheus ordered Hercules to bring him the skin of this monster. After using his club and arrows against the lion in vain, Hercules strangled the animal with his hands. He returned carrying the lion on his shoulders.

The fireback in EW's library does portray a figure with a club in one hand and in what may be a lion's skin (it appears to have paws). Unfortunately, this fireback is the most damaged one in the house. The information from *Bulfinch's Mythology* was furnished to EWR by Samuel N. Martin.

7. "ML," *BRT*, 1.

8. EW and OC, *DH*, 150.

9. According to Lewis in *EW*, it was "a surprisingly small desk — at which, however, Edith Wharton wrote nothing but letters" (135).

10. EW and OC, *DH*, 151.

11. AP, *RPI-TM*, 49.

12. "ML," *BRT*, 1.

13. EW and OC, *DH*, 39-40.

14. ED, *EW:AEL*, 92. EW to OC, 1901, SPNEA, CFMC.

15. "ML," *BRT*, 1.

16. EW and OC, *DH*, 150.

17. Ibid., 151.

18. The present wooden poles and curtain rings in the room are the original ones, according to Douglas Bucher, of John G. Waite Associates, Architects. In "ALGNY," EW wrote that she had "scandalized my Bostonian mother-in-law... by the banishment from our house in the country [The Mount] of all the thicknesses of muslin which should have intervened between ourselves and the robins on the lawn" (358). In this reminiscence, Wharton described the heavy draperies of Victorian homes as symbolizing "the

super-imposed layers of under-garments worn by ladies of the period — and even, alas, by the little girls."

19. EW and OC, *DH*, 29.

20. EW, *ABG*, 192.

21. GL, "EW," 8.

22. EW, *ABG*, 43.

23. PL, *PEW*, 26.

24. John G. Waite Associates, Architects, postulate that the lack of a layer of soot on the cornice may indicate that the stain was applied prior to 1911 by the Whartons.

DRAWING ROOM

1. EW and OC, *DH*, 61. In the spring of 1996, the center set of doors to the terrace was removed and stored in the hope of future reinstallation. Contractor David Andersen made a new set of doors (with panic hardware) that swing *out* to the terrace in order to meet current safety codes.

2. The ceiling was heavily damaged in the early 1970s by leaking water from the burst pipes of a bathroom above. Much of it came down and other parts were destroyed. Restoration work in 1982, using sculpted molds, recreated some of the damaged sections of the ceiling.

3. ED, *EW:AEL*, 92.

4. "And Abraham stretched forth his hand and took the knife to slay his son. And the angel of the Lord called unto him out of heaven and said 'Abraham, Abraham' and he said, 'Here I am.' And He said, 'Lay not thine hand upon the lad, neither do thou any thing unto him: for now I know that thou fearest God, seeing thou hast not withheld thy son, thine only son from me.'" (Genesis 22:10-12).

5. An electrical outlet set into the floor in the center of the room may be an original one. The one photograph of a corner of the drawing room during the Whartons' occupancy does not show any electric light fixtures in the room.

6. EW and OC, *DH*, 126.

7. "ML," *BRT*, 1. William Hickman's 1985 paint analysis (which is clearly at odds with the historical material) asserts that the walls, panels, windows and doors, and surrounds were a cool cream color; all other surfaces, including cornice and modillions, he judged to have been an off-white.

8. "ML," *BRT*, 1.

9. Leon Edel, ed., *Henry James — Letters Volume IV 1895-1916* (Cambridge, Massachusetts: The Belknap Press of Harvard University Press, 1984), 329. HJ to Jessie Allen from The Mount, October 22, 1904 (see Note 73, Chapter 2 for copyrights and permission).

10. EW and OC, *DH*, 124.

11. Ibid.

12. Ibid., 125.

13. AP, *RPI-TM*, 80.

14. The 1935 auction catalogue (*French Furniture of the Eighteenth Century, Queen Anne and Georgian Silver, Chinese Porcelains: Property of the Estate of the late Mary Strong Shattuck*, New York: American Art Association, Anderson Galleries, Inc., October 17, 18, 19, 1935), described EW's tapestry, "Narcissus at the Fountain:" "View of an undulating wooded landscape with an Ionic temple in the middle distance on the farther shores of a stream; in the right foreground is an ornamental fountain with a sculptured lion. The youthful Narcissus in golden yellow robe and crimson cloak, attended by a hound, is

gazing at his reflection in the water, while a kneeling Cupid aims his bow at the youth. Behind him at the foot of a rock is seated an adoring nymph, who gazes after him hopelessly. Particolored *tete de negre* and tan border, with clusters of roses, pinks, narcissus, and other blossoms, tied with bowknots. The whole woven in a rich variety of colors, including a beautiful mauve and crimson, the highlights in silk." The measurements of the tapestry, which is illustration number 514 in the catalogue, were given as "height, 10 feet 2 inches; width, 10 feet 1 inch."

The flanking tapestry on the north wall of the drawing room must have been "Bacchus and Ariadne," also a Brussels tapestry of c.1710 with a "border very similar to that of the preceding" ["Narcissus at the Fountain"]. "Bacchus and Ariadne" was described in the catalogue as: "The edge of a wood with a view of tall cliffs and a sheet of water in the distance; in the foreground, an amor holding a torch appears hovering above the seated figure of Ariadne with rosy fawn robes and crimson cloak. Bacchus, wearing a leopard skin tunic and rich blue cloak and with russet vine leaves in his hair, stands before her protesting his love." Measuring 9 feet ll inches high by 8 feet 1 inch wide, it was illustrated in the frontispiece of the catalogue. At the 1935 auction, "Narcisus at the Fountain" was sold for $900 to the Darsa Company; "Bacchus and Ariadne" sold for $850 to W.P. Pickhardt (undated and unattributed news clipping, "Shattuck Art Collection Nets $84,687 in Sale," placed inside the catalogue.) EWR is indebted to Mrs. Leonard Peters and Cornelia Brooke Gilder for providing a copy of the 1935 auction catalogue, which had been saved by Jane Peters Heathfield.

15.   EW and OC, *DH*, 125-126.

16.   Ibid., 130.

DINING ROOM

1.   EW and OC, *DH*, 160. The paint analysis in 1985 by William Hickman found the following: the dining room walls were an off-white and the ceiling, enriched panels, and frieze were warm gray.

2.   The dining room of Belton House in Lincolnshire, England, contains similar carvings and moldings by Grinling Gibbons on which OC based those that he executed at The Mount.

3.   These additional moldings, some of which are documented in the one existing Wharton-period photograph, were removed at an unknown date.

4.   According to a report by the Williamstown Regional Art Conservation Laboratory in 1985.

5.   EW and OC, *DH*, 160.

6.   Ibid. Amelia Peck surmises that the dining room rug was an oriental one.

7.   Ibid.

8.   AP, *RPI-TM*, 57.

9.   EW and OC, *DH*, 161.

10.   A photograph of the Wharton dining room at Land's End shows at least seven matching chairs in the room — four at the table and the others around the walls of the room. Most likely the set of chairs numbered eight.

11.   EW and OC, *DH*, 159.

12.   GL, "EW," 17.

13.   Mrs. Walter Maynard, unpublished memories on her stationery, 501 Fifth Avenue, New York, n.d., n.p., BL.

14.   Leon Edel, ed., *Henry James - Letters Volume IV 1895-1916* (Cambridge: The Belknap Press of Harvard University Press, 1984), 325. HJ to Howard Sturgis, October 17, 1904 (see Note 73, Chapter 2 for copyrights and permission). In addition, Lubbock in *PEW* noted, "'I must warn you,' Henry James had said to me, in thoughtful reminiscence, on the eve of my first visit to the Rue de Varenne [Wharton's Paris apartment after The Mount], 'against the constant succession, in our dear Edith's hospitality, of succulent and corrupting meals.' They were his words, and I couldn't improve them" (83).

STAIRS TO THE BEDROOM FLOOR

1.   EW and OC, *DH*, 22.

Second Floor (Bedroom Floor)

1.   EW and OC, *DH*, 117.

2.   Ibid.

3.   Ibid., 118.

4.   It seems that the existing third ceiling fixture in the "Stair-case Hall" area was substituted instead of the two wall sconces on either side of the door into the east guest room. Today this third ceiling fixture has an institutional globe from the Foxhollow School era. According to Douglas Bucher of John G. Waite Associates, Architects, the other two ceiling globes may be the original ones.

5.   EW and OC, *DH*, 119.

6.   Ibid., 117.

7.   Ibid.

8.   Ibid., 118.

9.   Ibid., 119-120.

10.   Both the sofa and the clock were moved from the hallway at Land's End to The Mount, where they were among the furnishings of the drawing room in Lenox.

11.   The door that was put in place at the head of the stairs was original to the service wing of The Mount.

12.   RWBL, *EW*, 135. Lewis locates EW's bedroom suite on the "eastern end" of The Mount. Though her bedroom is on the eastern corner of the building, the suite (i.e. bedroom, bathroom, and boudoir) actually occupies the northern end of this floor of the house. Lewis explains that after several years of marriage, the "unbroken proximity with Teddy... [had become] a source of great and growing distress, especially since, though the relationship was a sexless one, she had to share a bedroom with him in their small New York and Newport homes" [i.e. 884 Park Avenue and Pencraig Cottage].

13.   The plan of the bedroom floor for Land's End in Newport, Rhode Island, designed by OC, was recently published in *Edith Wharton: A House Full of Rooms: Architecture, Interiors, and Gardens* by Theresa Craig (The Monacelli Press, 1996), 85. EW had her own bedroom with a boudoir that connected to TW's bedroom. Both EW and TW also had separate bathrooms. EW's and TW's bedrooms both faced the ocean, with two guest rooms on the other side of the house. Many elements of OC's Land's End bedroom floor plan, which is at AAFAL, are similar to the the bedroom floor of The Mount.

14.   These were symptoms that EW had suffered for close to 15 years (approximately from the time of her marriage to TW in 1885). TW's health problems were only just beginning. Although for EW these were indications, as

Lewis surmises, of a "severe identity crisis" (76), they were probably psychosomatic symptoms of a very unhappy and unfulfilled marriage (RWBL, *EW*, 74-76).

15. EW and OC, *DH*, 169-170.

16. OC's original rough floor plan placed EW's bedroom and bath in the center block of the house, an area that corresponds to the location of TW's bedroom as built. One entered directly into her bedroom from a side hallway. The bathroom and a closet were on the left; these were flanked on the right by the boudoir (which would have been located approximately where the major guest room [the east guest room] was actually built.

17. Presumably the adjoining dressing room of the suite and the dress closet in the service wing served EW's requirements (and held the items that would have been stored in the closet that was removed from her bedroom suite). It should be kept in mind that one of the problems addressed in the plans for alterations to The Mount in 1907 (never carried out) was the lack of enough closet and storage space (Chapter 7).

18. The word means "mixture" in French. Marble identifications at The Mount were done by an expert in 1985.

19. The H&K plan of EW's bedroom, which was altered, showed three bells on the left side of the door upon entering; in actuality they were placed on the right side. Of the three bells, two are labeled: the top one summoned the "House Maid" while the bottom button rang the "Servant's Hall." The unmarked center bell probably called EW's personal maid.

20. EW and OC, *DH*, 171.

21. Ibid., 170.

22. Ibid.

23. Ibid.

24. GL, "EW," 2.

25. Ibid. The bedroom in Paris faced north, and the one at St. Brice had a view of the garden, according to Lapsley. EW's bedroom at The Mount did both — it faced north and east *and* overlooked the principal flower garden.

26. RWBL, *EW*, 353-354.

27. EW's early morning writing routine rarely varied throughout her life. Vivienne de Watteville (Mrs. Gerard Goshen), herself an author, wrote in February 1938 to Lubbock that: "Writing is a habit, she many times told me, and one should acquire this daily habit" (1). Lewis in *EW* explains her routine (in 1922) this way: "around noon, dressed and buckled, combed and manicured, she went downstairs to the library" where her house guests awaited (4). Berkeley Updike in PL's *PEW* said, "At Lenox her writing was done early in the day, though very little allusion was made to it, and none at all to the infinite pains that she put into her work or her inexhaustible patience in searching for the material necessary to perfect it. By eleven o'clock she was ready for friends and engagements, for walking or garden work" (30). The following other memories of EW working in bed are from unpublished fragments sent to Lubbock for the compilation of his "tribute" in 1947. All are in original manuscript form at the Beinecke Library, Yale University:

John Hugh-Smith: she would work in the morning to "write her books, order dinner and answer the telephone. Interruptions, which would drive any man mad, were nothing to her" (2).

W.K. Richardson: "At Lenox she used to get up early and work all the morning, being accessible to her house-party at lunch and thereafter" ("Informal Memories of Edith Wharton," 44).

Mrs. Winthrop Chanler: EW's mornings were "jealously guarded"; she came downstairs about 12:15 to check the garden before luncheon (III).

EW, who apparently did her best thinking in bed as well as finding it restfully therapeutic, once confided to SN in a letter of February 13, 1902: "I know so well the value of a day in bed that I am glad to think of you being able to permit yourself such an interlude" *LEW*, 57.

28. GL, "EW," 2-3.

29. See RWBL, *EW*, 4. Among the published volumes on which EW worked at one point or another in her bedroom at The Mount are: *Sanctuary* (1903), *Italian Villas and Their Gardens* (1904), *The Descent of Man and Other Stories* (1904), *The House of Mirth* (1905), *Italian Backgrounds* (1905), *Madame de Treymes* (1907), *The Fruit of the Tree* (1907), *A Motor-Flight Through France* (1908), *The Hermit and the Wild Woman and Other Stories* (1908), *Artemis to Actaeon* (1909), *Tales of Men and Ghosts* (1910), and possibly parts of *Ethan Frome* (1911). Much of the early work on *The Custom of the Country* (1913), which she began in 1908, took place at The Mount that summer. It is not difficult to surmise that accidents must have occurred while EW wrote in bed. Gordon Bell remembered that once, while staying with Howard Sturgis at his home in Windsor, EW was working in bed and "inadvertently spilled a bottle of ink all over Howard Sturgis' beautiful coverings." Gordon Bell, unpublished memories sent to Lubbock during the preparation of *PEW*, Beinecke Library, Yale University, 47. Lapsley noted that EW would "put her slippers at her bedside toes out so that they [hobgoblins] could not stand in them and overlook her while she was asleep" (GL, "EW," 37). Such an observation is interesting, given EW's own life-long terrors of the supernatural and the overwhelming choking fears of her youth, which she drew on to produce several superlative volumes of ghost stories, including *Tales of Men and Ghosts* in 1910.

30. See RWBL, *EW*, 304-306.

31. Ibid., 306.

32. See EW and OC, *DH*, 170.

33. Ibid., 172.

34. Ibid.

35. Ibid. All of the bathrooms at The Mount, including the one for the servants on the attic floor, employed the same white marble floor tiles.

36. Ibid.

37. Ibid. When EW did over her new apartment at 53 rue de Varenne in 1909, she visited several Paris bazaars and antique shops in the Faubourg in search of the necessary furnishings and "keeping an eye out, too, for that most urgent necessity, a porcelain bathtub" (RWBL, *EW*, 258).

38. EW and OC, *DH*, 172.

39. A report prepared by the Preservation Partnership in 1981 found that the stairs were not structurally supported and that their load had pitched the surrounding floors towards the unsupported corners. Removal of these stairs is necessary for proper restoration of EW's bedroom suite. PP, *PWDDPA-TM*, n.p.

40. L and L, *LEW*, 175.

41. The boudoir should be a "part of the bedroom suite" (130); the boudoir "usually adjoined the bedroom" (131). *DH*, 130-131.

42. EW and OC, *DH*, 131-132.

43. The idea that EW used these mirrors to check her hem lines or to dress by is not in keeping with their placement in

the room or her use of the boudoir. The cheval-glass in the nearby dressing room perhaps fulfilled such needs.

44.   EW and OC, *DH*, 132.

45.   Ibid., 46.

46.   Inspection record of the Williamstown Regional Art Conservation Laboratory, Inc. for EWR, 1985.

47.   Three bells were originally called for on the 1901 H&K floor plan.

48.   The original photograph is located at the Beinecke Library, Yale University.

49.   EW and OC, *DH*, 131.

50.   Ibid., 132.

51.   Ibid., 130.

52.   Ibid. See 130-131 for the suitability of the *lit-de-repos*.

53.   Ibid., 171.

54.   The person in the third photograph is an unidentified older gentleman. Occupying such a prominent place in her private suite, along with photographs of TW and WB, it must have been a person who was particularly important to EW. Possible identities of the gentleman include Charles Eliot Norton, Egerton Winthrop, HJ, her father, or her brother Henry, among others.

55.   According to Pauline C. Metcalf, the toile fabric used in EW's boudoir was a pattern designed in 1806 by Huet in Jouy, France. (See 164-171 in *DH* concerning fabrics for the bedroom or boudoir). EW's toile pattern was identified using the collection at SPNEA. According to Schumacher, which has had a long history with this particular fabric design, the subject, "Le Meunier, son fils et l'ane" [the miller, his son, and an ass], was taken from the eighteenth-century illustrations by Oudry for the French classic, *The Fables of Fontaine*. EW and OC mentioned the appropriateness of the La Fontaine fables as subject matter in *DH*, 169.

56.   EW and OC, *DH*, 171.

57.   Of all of the historical photographs of interiors at The Mount, only three show windows and the type of hangings used in the decor: the library, boudoir, and gallery. The three arched windows in the gallery had no curtains, but both the library and the boudoir employed the wooden curtain poles and rings.

58.   EW and OC, *DH*, 165.

59.   Ibid., 131. The design and execution of the boudoir proved to be a matter of lingering acrimony between the Whartons and OC as late as 1905. Both parties resorted to communicating through their lawyers over OC's claim that he was owed several hundred dollars for repainting. The Whartons claimed that the boudoir panels had been made the wrong size, necessitating the repainting, although OC had taken the measurements in EW's presence. OC's lawyers asserted that the mistake was that of R. W. Curry (the builder in charge) who "made the setting inaccurately, and not in accordance with Mr. Codman's measurements." Edwin D. Worcester, Jr., to EW, February 7, 1905, 3, SPNEA, CFMC. Mr. Worcester, of the firm of Saunders, Webb & Worcester, was an attorney for OC. One thing that the dispute makes clear is that although OC was the interior designer of The Mount, "the painting of our house was not done under his supervision" (EW to Messrs. Saunders, Webb, & Worcester, February 2, 1905, 2, SPNEA, CFMC). Items under dispute included "Painting boudoir, $85," another item for $175, as well as "Commission of Curry painting" (amount unknown). The matter was eventually resolved or dropped.

60.   The annunciator-box in the sewing room of the service wing still contains labels for the bells indicating "Mrs. Shattuck's Boudoir," "Mrs. Shattuck's Bath," and "Mrs. Shattuck's Bed Room," which were placed over the identical labels for EW. Floor plans submitted in 1940 with "Valuation of Property of Louise D. Van Anda" labeled the rooms as "Madam's Bed Room," "Bath," and "Boudoir."

61.   TW's bedroom was smaller than EW's bedroom, her boudoir, and the east guest room.

62.   EW and OC, *DH*, 171.

63.   A second door entering the room was initially proposed to the north of the fireplace on the 1901 H&K floor plan. It was never built. It is unclear why a second door into this room would have been necessary here; it certainly would have meant considerably less privacy for the occupant, if built according to plan.

64.   Three bells were called for on the 1901 H&K floor plan.

65.   Much of the pine used for ceilings and floors at The Mount was identified on the 1940 "SRAAAT" as North Carolina pine.

66.   The floor plan for the 1940 "SRAAAT" labels TW's room as "Guest Room" and the former Wharton east guest room as "Master's Bed Room."

67.   A report prepared in 1981 for Shakespeare & Company concluded that: "During the dubious stewardship of the Center at Foxhollow [which followed the school in 1975], pipes were repeatedly allowed to freeze, so that the Teddy Wharton bedroom has a badly damaged cornice and ceiling, and extensive water-staining." PP, *PWDDPA-TM*, n.p.

68.   EW and OC, *DH*, 170.

69.   Ibid.

70.   The bathtub has a primitive shower ring attached to the wall above. The original pull-chain toilet was removed many years ago. A cabinet built into the east wall to the right of the sink is probably not original to the Whartons' occupancy.

71.   The dressing room of Mr. and Mrs. Brympton is the scene of the tragic denouement in EW's 1904 ghost story, "The Lady's Maid's Bell," when Mr. Brympton interrupts a visit to his wife from Mr. Ranford, and the lady's maids (one real, the other a ghost) also intervene.

72.   EW and OC, *DH*, 171-172.

73.   Ibid., 172.

74.   One guest room with boudoir and one guest room without an adjoining boudoir were envisioned for the bedroom floor of the house. The second guest room with boudoir would have been located on the attic floor, along with the servants' rooms.

75.   The name "East Guest Room" was first discovered on a sheet of paper found in 1985 in a fusebox in the service wing opposite the service elevator on the main floor of the house. The paper, entitled "Butler's Pantry Cutout Box," is a checklist of which lights were controlled by various fuses. The names for rooms on this list correspond closely to those on the H&K 1901 floor plans for The Mount, most likely dating this document to the Whartons' occupancy. The majority of rooms listed were located in the service wing or on the southeast corner of the mansion; the area constituting the west guest suite was not included on this list. The servants' call-boxes on the first floor and the attic floor, in which the original Wharton-period labels remain intact, verify that the guest rooms were known as the east guest room, west guest room, and small guest room.

76.   PL, *PEW*, 35.

77. Ibid., 33. Although there were only two guest rooms, EW and TW managed to entertain a large number of distinguished close friends. Henry Jones (EW's brother), Mary Cadwalader Jones, Beatrix Jones (later Beatrix Farrand), Berkeley Updike, Henry James, Howard Sturgis, Judge and Mrs. Robert Grant, Gaillard Lapsley, Clyde Fitch, Mr. and Mrs. Gordon Bell, Walter Berry, Morton Fullerton, Mr. and Mrs. Walter Maynard, Mr. and Mrs. George Cabot Lodge, Sara Norton, Elizabeth Norton, Egerton Winthrop, Moncure Robinson, Ralph Curtis, Edward Robinson, Eliot Gregory, Johnson Morton, Mr. and Mrs. Bayard Cutting, Mr. and Mrs. Brook Adams, William King Richardson, Paul and Minnie Bourget, Langdon Mitchell, William Buckler, Herman Edgar, Florence LaFarge, Carl Snyder, John Hugh Smith, Margaret Terry Chanler, Robert Minturn, Robert Norton, the Jusserands from Washington, James J. Van Alen, Mr. and Mrs. Cass Canfield, the Misses Helen and Ethel Brice. The following sources were used to compile this list: RWBL, *EW*; L and L, *LEW*; EW, *ABG*; PL, *PEW*; SB, *NGC*; and issues of the periodical *BRT* for 1903 and 1904.

78. There were no such corresponding narrow windows on the west facade on the bedroom floor in the west guest suite or in EW's boudoir. The only other location on the building where such windows were realized was on the west facade of the main floor. One window gave light into and ventilated the bathroom off TW's den; the other on the opposite flanking wing was a "blind window."

79. Three bells were called for on the original floor plan.

80. On the floor plan accompanying the "SRAAAT" in 1940, this room was labeled "Master's Bed Room." Although there is no definite evidence that ARS used this room (or TW's) as his bedroom, he was on oxygen for the final weeks of his life and was accompanied by several nurses, possibly necessitating a larger room. He died in bed at The Mount on November 4, 1925.

81. It is unclear why this change was made, although the penciled changes are clearly visible on the 1901 H&K floor plan. This is the only instance at The Mount of a closet opening into a bathroom and is an awkward arrangement.

82. The light fixture is apparently original and of a less ornamental design than that found in the bedrooms. Similar fixtures are also found throughout the service wing and service areas.

83. The company name and patent date are still clearly legible under the bowl of the sink.

84. These two rooms no longer are connected. The 1940 floor plan for "SRAAAT" shows them connected; presumably sometime after 1942 the Foxhollow School walled up the door between the rooms to create two separate spaces.

85. Three bells were called for on the original floor plan. Of the two bells that were installed, one is missing, and the other was for the "Svt's Hall."

86. Three bells were called for on the original plan. Of the two bells that were installed, one was for the "House Maid," and the other for the "Svt's Hall."

SERVICE AREAS

1. RWBL, *EW*, 149.

2. Ibid. In his biography, Lewis refers to White as "Arthur White." Both Shari Benstock and Eleanor Dwight in their biographies note that his name was "Alfred White."

3. According to Gaillard Lapsley, Gross "had been for more than half her life in Edith's service and had in fact made her the object of a life that had been cruelly emptied. She was an Alsatian who at seventeen or so had been seduced, put her child out to nurse and taken service in England. She came to Edith not long after and never served anyone else... Edith seldom failed in compassion and if she accepted the selfless devotion of Gross's remaining years she repaid it with deep and true affection. She treated her as a friend or kinswoman, advised with her as long as Gross remained active and when she grew infirm surrounded her with attentions petted and laughed at her when she was at home and when she was travelling always sent a telegram or a picture post-card every day or so. If you had seen Edith with her in these last years when Gross had to look to her for everything you could measure the depth and bitterness of the loneliness that she had to live with" after Gross died in 1933 (GL, "EW," 27-28). Lewis notes that Gross was "a buxom, round-faced, placidly competent Alsatian woman" who was in her early thirties when she came to work for Edith in 1884: "they seem to have communicated largely in French; Edith, who invariably called the other woman Gross or Grossie, would grow fonder of her than of almost anyone else in her life" (RWBL, *EW*, 54). Lubbock in *PEW* also had some penetrating comments about the close relationship between EW and Gross (84-85, 200-203).

Lewis notes that Alfred White (see Note 2 above) was an Englishman with a marked Cockney accent who was in his late twenties when he joined the Whartons in 1888 (RWBL, *EW*, 54). Lubbock called him "White the great" (*PEW*, 200) and explained that he was "a kindly master, with very distinct views as to the manner in which Edith should be served and her establishment ordered. They were old friends of many years; they had studied their art and matured in it together; so she always said; but one felt that it was he who watched over her progress and had seen to it that she never swerved from the perfect way. He served her, as G.L. [Gaillard Lapsley] put it, with respectful severity; and she very well knew she could rely on him, not only to keep her taste true to the highest mark, but to safeguard and help her, to lift trouble off her back, in every way that appertained to his department and I don't know in how many more" (PL, *PEW*, 84). He outlived EW (RWBL, *EW*, 532) and had continued to assist her through her final years. Lapsley noted that she "provided for him generously in her will" (GL, "EW," 27).

4. RWBL, *EW*, 149.

5. Ibid., 150.

6. Ibid.

7. Local directories for the towns of Lee and Lenox, for the years 1907-12 at the Berkshire Athenaeum in Pittsfield contain "A General Directory of Citizens, a Classified Business Directory, Street Directory, Town Officers, Churches, Societies, Census Tables, and other valuable miscellaneous information." The directories revealed the names of local residents who were thereby designated as "Employee E.R. Wharton." In addition to Thomas Reynolds (the estate superintendent) and William Parlett (the coachman), other workers at The Mount, most of whom were general laborers on the estate, were John Burz, Patrick Connelly, James Connors, Jean Ster, Jerry Welch, and two brothers, Joseph and William Winters. No house staff were listed; the Federal Census for 1910 did not count the Whartons or their staff as they were overseas at that time. (Scott Marshall, "Employee - E.R. Wharton," VISTA newsletter, Spring/Summer 1987).

8. L and L, *LEW*, 89. EW to SN, May 5, 1904.

9. PL, *PEW*, 29. The speaker was Daniel Berkeley Updike.

10. GL, "EW," 26-27.

11. Ibid., 26.

12. Bernard Berenson, unpublished memoirs, n.p., BL.

13. A Lenox resident in his eighties, who did plumbing work at The Mount for both the Shattucks and the Van Andas, told the author that he well remembered the staff riding up and down constantly in the elevator.

14. There is a small compartment with a hinged door in the center of the refrigerator at floor level. It can no longer be opened; it may have given access to some of the machinery for repairs. The built-in refrigerator also has three cabinets of varying sizes on the south side facing the door into the kitchen. As they have small holes with screens, they may have served to store breads and baked items, much as an old "pie safe" would have. The manufacturer is unknown.

15. EW, "The Lady's Maid's Bell," *The Descent of Man and Other Stories* (New York: Charles Scribner's Sons, 1904), 247.

16. The wall fixture on the plan was indicated for the left side of the range. There is no evidence today that it was placed there.

17. See Note 8, Chapter 7.

18. EW, *ABG*, 59. EW pointed out that in the old New York of her youth: "to know about good cooking was a part of every young wife's equipment" (58). She remembered fondly her mother's favorite "cookery books," the many elaborate dishes that graced the family table of her youth and their "two famous negro cooks, Mary Johnson and Susan Minneman," who were, to her, "great artists" (58).

19. "All Souls'" was her last completed short story, sent to her agent in February 1937, and published after her death. See RWBL, *EW*, 523. All of the servants in the household have vanished overnight, leaving the mistress of the estate, Mrs. Clayburn, who has recently injured her ankle, all alone. In her search for another person in the building, Mrs. Clayburn drags herself toward the servants' quarters and the kitchen: "some indefinable instinct told her that the kitchen held a clue to the mystery. She still felt strongly that whatever had happened in the house must have its source and center in the kitchen. (263-264). When she finally reaches it, she is terrified to hear an unknown voice speaking softly in a foreign language; it turns out to be a "portable wireless" sitting "in the middle of the carefully scoured table" in the "orderly and empty" room (264).

20. The section of the dumbwaiter in the scullery was sealed up some years ago; it could be restored to its original appearance as the doors still remain in the room. They have been placed behind some pipes and wires on the north wall. The section of the dumbwaiter in the butler's pantry on the main floor was completely removed many years ago.

21. See EW, "Afterward," *Tales of Men and Ghosts* (New York: Charles Scribner's Sons, 1910), 357. Servants such as the scullery maid or the kitchen maid were never to be seen outside of these work areas. In this 1910 ghost story, EW imagined the tragic implications of a situation where the kitchenmaid, for lack of proper staff at the moment, is sent by the cook out of the back passages and into the main part of the house to open the door to a mysterious stranger. Later in the story, after the inexplicable disappearance of the master of the house who went out with the unknown stranger, the kitchenmaid is interviewed by the mistress of the house and the housekeeper. But the poor servant is unable to help: "The obligation of going to the front door to 'show in' a visitor was in itself so subversive of the fundamental order of things that it had thrown her faculties into hopeless disarray" (357).

22. The three interior windows were never built. One assumes that they might have been similar to the interior windows that were constructed between the entrance hall and the furnace room. Only a door was constructed between the laundry room and the furnace room, and it has since been completely closed up. Perhaps it was planned to assist in activities that took place in the laundry room, such as drying.

23. In *ABG*, EW remembered that on one of HJ's visits to The Mount he became extremely agitated (in the midst of a heat wave) at the thought of changing his plans and returning to England sooner than he had planned. Along with numerous complaints, she quoted him as worrying, "And [what about] his wash, which had been sent to the laundry only the afternoon before?" (189). Presumably she was speaking of the laundry room of The Mount.

24. The letters "W.C." were penciled in on the plan, along with a freehand drawing of a toilet bowl against the south wall. The Butler's Pantry Cutout Box lists one light in the "Laundry W.C.," verifying its existence.

25. Pencil markings indicating a partition wall, and two entrances for two rooms are visible on the 1901 H&K floor plan.

26. The Butler's Pantry Cutout Box lists one light each in the "wine closet," in the area of the laundry W.C., the laundry, and the scullery.

27. RWBL, *EW*, 149. Lewis also adds later: Teddy "was much more knowledgeable than she [EW] about fine wines; after a discourse with Berenson concerning some rare vintages, Edith wrote with wan pride that was something Teddy really did know" (272). GL on EW and wine: "she positively disliked still wines, however fine; she regretted this and thought it might be due to her brothers' premature attempts to develop in her a taste for them. She liked champagne (half a sherry glass at most) and Cointreau and Dubonnet on occasions. But she took great pains to furnish her table with good and sometimes with fine wine..." (GL, "EW," 17).

28. The 1940 floor plan labels the room the "wine cellar."

29. The 1940 floor plan labels the center section as "Fuel."

30. EW to SN, November 1, 1907, BL. (Also see Chapter 7.)

31. CVA, "SRAAAT," 4.

32. Ibid.

33. See "SRAAT." Under Post Office Address it is noted: "Summer — Lenox, Mass.; other times, 1170 Park Ave., N.Y. City."

34. The H&K floor plan shows an indicator on the east wall to the right of the door into the butler's pantry. The indicator may have been moved to its present location, although that seems unlikely. Probably the location was changed prior to the actual installation.

35. The original labels are intact. The last slot has no label.

36. The marble countertop and its drainboards are intact. EWR has been informed by a marble expert that the marble is from Carrera, Italy. The sink bears the name of the Ideal Co. and the date 11-4-01.

37. There is no evidence that an indicator was located in this position.

38. Only the dining room doors remain in place today. The doors that would have opened into the butler's pantry are missing, although holes in the door frame indicate where the earlier hinges were located.

39. The location of the safe (as built) is indicated on the floor plan by some pencil markings. The 1907 floor plans for proposed alterations to the service wing label this closet the "safe."

40. There is no physical evidence for either light fixture (the room now has several ceiling fixtures); the Butler's

Pantry Cutout Box also states that there were once two lights in this room.

41.   The study done by William Hickman in 1985 also did not take into account that the "kitchen" had originally been two rooms. His finding of a cream color was incorrect for this entire area.

42.   There is no physical evidence of a light on the wall by the window. The Butler's Pantry Cutout Box agrees that the brush room had one light.

43.   A conclusion supported by John G. Waite, of John G. Waite Associates, Architects. Waite postulates that often servants would have had beds in their combination office/sitting rooms to rest on or to spend the night if they lived off the property and their presence was required late or unusually early. In addition, the fact that there was no bathroom on this floor for these important staff is further evidence that these rooms were not bedrooms for the servants in question.

44.   The Butler's Pantry Cutout Box indicates that this was the "Cook's Room," if one follows the order listed on the sheet. In addition, all schemes for the proposed 1907 additions to the service wing place the "Cook's Room" in this location.

45.   In his 1985 paint analysis, William Hickman worked without an original floor plan for The Mount. Presumably he was referring to this room as "Pantry" when he made the analysis of "reddish gray."

46.   The floor has been changed. It is now a wooden parquet that appears to be laid over the original rift pine.

47.   The photograph, c. 1943-44, shows a home economics (or cooking) class in progress. Four girls were preparing a meal; several wear aprons that were made from the same fabric used for the window curtains of this room. FHS.

48.   Notes by AMF suggest that this may have been done as late as 1965. The notes seem contradictory but indicate that work was done in this area: "In June 1965 the larger part of the kitchen at The Mount was transformed into two extra bed-rooms" (AMF, "EW-M," 7).

49.   Following the listing of rooms in order.

50.   It is not clear if William Hickman meant this room as the "Office" when he did his analysis.

51.   See preceeding note. The same wood parquet was laid in this room as well.

52.   The closet is not extant since the room was combined with the adjacent butler's room.

53.   The Butler's Pantry Cutout Box agrees that this was the butler's room.

54.   See RWBL, EW, 136. The whereabouts of this cottage, as well as the "several small cottages" cited by Lewis, are unclear.

55.   L and L, LEW, 302. EW to Mary Berenson, May 20, 1913.

56.   The letter states that the servant in question had "allowed White to order a new livery for him last week" (see Note 55).

57.   "Pendennis," The Book News Monthly 26, (November 1907): 172.

58.   The dates for this conversion are unknown.

59.   Directly below the skylight were two interior windows with angled slats that provided ventilation to the attic crawlspace above.

60.   In EW's 1904 short story, "The Lady's Maid's Bell," this part of the service wing was carpeted: "Then I heard a footstep hurrying down the passage toward the main house.

The floor being carpeted, the sound was very faint, but I was quite sure it was a woman's step" (260).

61.   The floor plan called for the light to have been located to the left of the window. There is no physical evidence that it was. The ceiling fixture in the room appears to be the original one.

62.   EW, ABG, 59-60.

63.   The housemaid is not to be confused with the "maid" nearby: EW's lady's maid.

64.   As in the linen closet, the original fixture appears to have been placed on the ceiling and not on the wall to the right of the slop sink.

65.   EW, "The Lady's Maid's Bell," 247.

66.   Ibid, 246.

67.   One was a ceiling light fixture; the other was to have been on the north wall. There is no evidence that the one on the north wall was installed.

68.   This indicator might be called the lady's maid's bell for the author of "The Lady's Maid's Bell."

69.   The labels, which are still extant, are from the Shattucks' occupancy; they read (from left): "Mrs. Shattuck's Boudoir," "Mrs. Shattuck's Bedroom," and "Mrs. Shattuck's Bath."

70.   If the room one floor below was the chef's room, there may have been no housekeeper's room unless she shared the sewing room with the lady's maid. In addition, the 1907 proposed alterations to the service wing placed a room in close proximity to the sewing room. That room, which is unlabeled on the proposed schemes, is hypothesized to have been the housekeeper's room.

71.   EW, "The Lady's Maid's Bell," 250. The servant, Hartley, explains: "I had no fault to find with my place or my mistress, but I thought it odd that in so large a house there was no sewing room for the lady's maid..."

72.   A closet had been planned within EW's bedroom suite, but with the reconfiguration of those rooms, it was not built.

73.   The ceiling fixture appears to be original; the floor plan indicated a light on the west wall to the left of the interior window.

74.   The original use of this closet is unknown; most likely it was used by the housekeeper or the housemaid.

75.   The same bull's-eye moldings are also found in the superintendent's lodge (gatehouse) and on the second floor of the stable, which was the coachman's apartment.

76.   The transoms (or transom lights) were not indicated on the original 1901 floor plan.

77.   If it was located there, it is no longer extant.

78.   This indicator is also not extant.

79.   The labels in this indicator are from the Whartons' occupancy: "East Guest Room," "West Guest Room," and "Small Guest Room."

80.   A shallow fireplace and wooden mantel — which may be original — are extant in this position. Possibly they housed a wood-burning stove.

81.   The bathtub and its original fixtures are still intact.

82.   In her handwritten and untitled notes about the history of The Mount, Foxhollow headmistress AMF noted that "very soon [after the purchase of the building in 1942] we erected the fire-escapes, and new staircase" (AMF, "EW-M," 4). These alterations may be dated c. 1942-44.

83.   H&K, "SCCR", NYA, 149.

CHAPTER 7

Proposed Alterations in 1907

1.   The plans are dated over a three day period: September 24, 25, and 26, 1907. Most are initialed by an "AEB," and were probably executed after consultation between the Whartons and the original architect, FH. In H&K, "SCCR," *NYA*, the firm explained that a primary aim was "to design a house as to facade which can be easily added to, if it should be desired, yet maintain a symmetry and pleasing appearance to the facade" (149).

All of the surviving schemes are in the archives of EWR. None have been previously published. The majority are titled: "Alterations to Residence of E. R. Wharton, Esq., Lenox Mass." The following comprise the collection and are dated as indicated:

Exterior	East Elevation	September 25, 1907
	Alternate Elevation	no date
		(overlay for above)
Cellar Plan	Scheme No. 1	September 25, 1907
	Scheme No. 2	September 26, 1907
Basement Plan		September 25, 1907
First Floor Plan	Scheme No. 1	September 24, 1907
	Scheme No. 2	September 24, 1907
	Scheme No. 3	September 24, 1907
Second Floor Plan	Scheme No. 1	September 24, 1907
	Scheme No. 2	September 25, 1907

The elevations and schemes are all pencil on trace paper; the interior schemes are also in colored pencil (blue = new stone work; red = new brick; yellow = new wood; green = existing). The different schemes recall OC's observation to his mother that FH had had "to make three sets of plans" for the construction of The Mount in 1901-02.

2.   Both, however, would have added a new chimney.

3.   There would have been a slight peak in the new roof over the two-bay extension, though it would not have been visible from the ground, as there was a low parapet wall originally running around the roofline of the service wing. The rest of the roof of the wing would have remained as built, with only a slight slope.

4.   Scheme No. 1 was dated September 25 and Scheme No. 2 on the following day. The latter is the only scheme dated September 26, 1907. Scheme No. 1 matched the exterior elevation known as the east elevation.

5.   EW to SN, November 1, 1907, BL. Lewis postulates that the real reason behind the earlier departure was EW's desire to see Morton Fullerton in Paris, rather than the comfort of her servants. Her letter — and the 1907 plans for the alterations — make it clear that her concern for the comfort of her staff was also real.

6.   Dated September 25, 1907. With the cellar stairs on the east descending outside of the kitchen, it matched Scheme No. 1 for the new cellar floor and the east elevation of the exterior.

7.   Scheme Nos. 1, 2, and 3 were all dated on September 24, 1907.

8.   The Wharton's cook was — as these plans indicate — a man. EW did employ a male cook in France (RWBL, *EW*, 494).

9.   Catharine Gross, who had come to work for EW soon after her marriage to TW in 1885.

10.   Possibly the cook was married and needed additional space.

11.   Scheme No. 1, dated September 24, 1907, and Scheme No. 2, one day later.

12.   The largest guest room, the east guest room (sometimes known today as the "Henry James Room"). All of the other guest baths, as well as those for EW and TW, opened onto the hallway for access for the servants to draw the bath water and lay out towels. The bathroom in question was the only one on the bedroom floor that did not allow for this kind of service for the occupant, and both schemes sought to remedy this.

13.   Not labelled as such, but the housekeeper's room was removed from the first floor by all three new alteration schemes; no doubt it was changed to this location. The plans both labelled it as a "Bedroom."

14.   A cedar closet (a room lined in that particular wood) facilitated winter clothes storage.

15.   The one existing bath on the attic floor served eight servants' rooms there, in addition to other staff on the first and second floors.

16.   PL, *PEW*, 51.

17.   RWBL, *EW*, 159.

18.   Ibid.

19.   Ibid., 151-152.

20.   Ibid., 180.

21.   Ibid.

22.   Ibid., 176.

23.   Ibid.

24.   Ibid., 191 (see also Note 5).

25.   Ibid., 193.

26.   Ibid., 203.

CHAPTER 8

History of The Mount, 1911 and After

THE WHARTONS SELL
THE MOUNT, 1911-12

1.   List of Cottagers. Printed by Louis Regnier, Newsdealer and Stationer. Dated by hand "July 1909." LnL. Also, "SBWP," *BEE*, 6.

2.   According to the September 11, 1911, article, the Shattucks would have leased The Mount again in 1911 "had not Mrs. Wharton desired to return to Lenox for this season for the purpose of selling the property, which had been placed in the hands of Curtis & Delafield and New York agents for sale." "SBWP," *BEE*, 6.

3.   EW, *ABG*, 125.

4.   Ibid., 326.

5.   L and L, *LEW*, 242. EW to MF, July 3, 1911.

6.   Ibid.

7.   Ibid.

8.   RWBL, *EW*, 303.

9.   Lyall H. Powers, ed. *Henry James and Edith Wharton Letters: 1900-1915* (New York: Charles Scribner's Sons, 1990), 182. HJ to EW, July 19, 1911. Copyright (c) by Lyall H. Powers. Used by permission of Scribner's, a Division of Simon & Schuster.

10. L and L, *LEW*, 246. EW to WFW, July 22, 1911.

11. Ibid.

12. Ibid., 248. EW to WFW, July 23, 1911.

13. Ibid., 253. EW to John Hugh Smith, August 6, 1911.

14. Ibid.

15. William Derbyshire Curtis, "A Daily Reminder of Important Matters." Unpublished notations in his diary for the year 1911, collection of the Lenox Historical Society. EWR is indebted to Nancy D. Marasco, curator and former president of the Lenox Historical Society, for supplying this important information. Most of the information dealing with the Pollocks, Shattucks, Curtis, and the sale of The Mount is drawn from this material. No further information about Mr. and Mrs. Pollock is known.

16. L and L, *LEW*, 254. EW to SN, August 26, 1911.

17. Ibid.

18. According to the September 1911 article, the sale of The Mount to William Pollock had been "recently reported... Curtis & Delafield presented Mr. and Mrs. William Pollock as buyers of the estate, and elaborate papers were drawn and every detail was ready for the signature of the principals when a misunderstanding arose, which canceled the sale. There are many reports as to the reason of the Pollock deal being off." "SBWP," *BEE*, 6. The reasons remain unknown.

19. L and L, *LEW*, 255-256. EW to MF, September 22, 1911. According to Lewis in *EW*: "On September 2, before sailing for Europe, Edith signed a document making her husband her 'true, sufficient, and lawful Attorney' for any action involving The Mount; giving him 'full power to rent said real estate and personal estate on such terms and for such times as he may see fit'; and 'especially' granting 'full power to negotiate a sale of said real and personal estate, at his sole discretion.' Teddy was legally entrusted with absolute authority" (313).

20. "SBWP," *BEE*, 6. (Also reported in *The Pittsfield Journal*, Pittsfield, Massachusetts, September 11, 1911, 6).

21. Powers, ed. *Henry James and Edith Wharton Letters: 1900-1915*, 190-191. HJ to EW, September 19, 1911 (see Note 9).

22. L and L, *LEW*, 259. EW to MCJ, September 23, 1911.

23. Ibid.

24. RWBL, *EW*, 313. Deed of Sale for The Mount, vol. 368, Berkshire Probate Court, received and recorded from the original on May 16, 1912. The "legal evasion" of "One dollar and other valuable considerations" was paid by Albert L. Richardson, of Greenwich, Connecticut, who may have been ARS's uncle; Richardson was the party to whom the deed was formally made out. ARS's mother's maiden name was Elizabeth C. Richardson. It may be that ARS's middle name was Richardson; only the initial "R" is given in all press accounts pertaining to him, including his obituary. It is unknown why Albert L. Richardson served as a purchasing agent for Mr. and Mrs. Shattuck when they bought The Mount.

25. L and L, *LEW*, 277. EW to GL, August 19, 1912. EW's final years and her death are well documented in several biographies. Less is known about TW after the formal divorce in 1913, although he spent considerable time in Lenox for another 15 years and was buried there after his death in New York City on February 7, 1928. See article by Scott Marshall, "Whatever Happened to Teddy Wharton?" (Vista from The Mount, Winter 1987-88) for information about TW's final years.

MARY AND ALBERT R. SHATTUCK, OWNERS, 1912-38

1. According to his obituary, "ARSD," *BEE*, 15: "Mr. Shattuck was born in New York." His birthdate was November 30, 1854. The Thirteenth Census of the United States: 1910 population — Lenox, Massachusetts, stated his place of birth as Louisiana.

2. ARS's father was William B. Shattuck and his mother was Elizabeth C. Richardson. A sister, Lucy Evelyn (later Mrs. F. Burrall Hoffman), was born on February 11, 1857 (from her grave marker at St. Ann's Cemetery, Lenox Massachusetts). Although the Shattuck family, including William B. Shattuck, was from Louisiana, the following should be noted: "The Shattuck family, many of whom have become distinguished in New England life, have a common ancestor, William Shattuck, who was born in England and died in Watertown, Massachusetts in 1672" (Malone, Dumas, ed. *Dictionary of American Biography XVII* (New York: Charles Scribner's Sons, 1935), 31.

3. Unfortunately ARS never appeared in any volume of *Who's Who*; *Who's Who in New York*; or *Who's Who in New England*. Nor can he be found in the *National Encyclopedia of Biography*, the *Dictionary of American Biography* or any such volume. His obituary hardly mentions his early years.

4. "ARSD," *NYT*, 23. Also see "ARSD," *BEE*, 15.

5. "ARSD," *BEE*, 15.

6. William Lafayette Strong, born on an Ohio farm in 1827, moved to New York in 1853. He established his own business — a dry goods firm known as W.L. Strong & Co. — at age 42; by the time of his death he was a millionaire. Among his many positions, he was president of the Central National Bank and of the Homer Lee Bank Note Company, vice-president of the New York Security and Trust Company, and a director of other banks, insurance companies, and railroad companies. He also served as president of the Union League and of the Business Men's Republican Association. In 1882 Strong ran for Congress and lost. In 1895 he was elected Mayor of New York City and had the distinction of being the last mayor of Old New York, when the city consisted only of the island of Manhattan. Among his achievements were the appointment of Theodore Rooselvelt as Police Commissioner, consolidation of the New York Public Library, and some major building projects. His term as mayor was extremely unhappy, as he spent most of his time battling Tammany Hall and many prominent Republicans in his own party. According to the *Dictionary of American Biography*, "under him the City was honestly governed for the first time in many years, and in some departments there was great improvement in efficiency" (vol. IX, 156). Strong declined to serve more than one term, stepping down in 1897 and supporting Seth Low, the independent candidate for mayor, versus Thomas Collier Platt, the Republican boss and party nominee. Strong died on November 2, 1900. He was buried in Woodlawn Cemetery in New York City. Strong married the former Mary Aborn, of East Orange, New Jersey, and had one son, P. Bradlee Strong (later a lawyer in Washington, D.C.) and one daughter, Mary, who married ARS. His New York City residence was at 12 West 57th Street and his office was at 75 Worth Street. (*Dictionary of American Biography* and other sources).

7. James Renwick was a prominent New York City architect whose work included churches (Grace Church, St. Patrick's Cathedral, Calvary Church on Park Avenue and 21st Street — all in New York City) and public buildings (the original Smithsonian Institution building on the mall in Washington, D.C.), as well as private residences.

8. "Mr. Shattuck first came to Lenox with his father who in 1883, bought the Dr. E.J. Danning property and built a new house costing $30,000." "ARSD," *BEE*, 15.

9. "SBWP," *BEE*, 6.

10. Morris hired the firm of H&K, architects of The Mount, to design and construct a neo-Georgian brick mansion c. 1909 on the site of the previous Shattuck house. The estate continues to be known as Brookhurst, and the original Shattuck stable and gatehouse still survive.

11. According to the *Social Register, 1899*. The Shattucks are not listed as city residents until 1899, except for occasional visits to 12 West 57th Street, Mary Shattuck's father's house, according to previous *Social Registers*.

12. "ARSD," *NYT*, 23. His Berkshire obituary stated that "he retired a number of years ago." Also see "ARSD," *BEE*, 15.

13. Ibid.

14. STW, "*EQ*," NYT, 2.

15. Ibid. According to his Berkshire obituary, "He was a connoisseur of art and quite a collector." "ARSD," *BEE*, 15.

16. "ARSD," *NYT*, 23. Shattuck was a member of the Metropolitan Club and the New York Yacht Club.

17. In 1911, "Mr. and Mrs. Shattuck have been in the habit of spending every other year abroad." "ARSD," *BEE*, 15.

18. Cleveland Armory, *Who Killed Society?* (New York: Harper & Brothers, 1960), 492.

19. "DTT," *LnLf*, May 26, 1900, 2.

20. "DTT," *LnLf*, July 19, 1902, 1.

21. "DTT," *LnLf*, July 21, 1900, 1. Almost every morning ARS could be found driving on Main Street in Lenox, along with other prominent men in their motors; they would meet various cottagers and "proceed with the education of the horses." These efforts continued for several seasons as a training school or morning clinic. The program included driving horses alongside and around a standing and a moving automobile until the horses became accustomed to it. See "AT," *LnLf*, August 2, 1902, 7, and July 26, 1902, 7; also "DTT," *LnLf*, July 19, 1902, 1.

22. "AT," *LnLf*, September 8, 1900, 3.

23. "AT," *LnLf*, August 30, 1902, 1 and 7.

24. "AT," *LnLf*, September 27, 1902, 5.

25. Ibid.

26. "SBWP," *BEE*, September 11, 1911, 6. His Berkshire obituary also noted that: "Mr. Shattuck was much interested in the preservation of Berkshire scenery. He abhorred conspicuous and glaring billboards and frequently, in his drives over the rural roads, he carried a hatchet and personally chopped down signs illegally placed along the highway." "ARSD," *BEE*, 15.

27. William B. Shattuck died in New Orleans on November 18, 1894; his wife, Elizabeth, died at Brookhurst in Lenox on July 13, 1899. See the *Social Register* for 1894 and 1899 respectively.

28. Lists of Cottagers in 1900, 1901 and 1902 indicate that Brookhurst was rented to Mrs. Max Fleischmann. In 1904 it was rented by Mr. and Mrs. William A. Read (*BRT*, October 8, 1904).

29. "SBWP," *BEE*, 6.

30. See Notes 1 and 2 for Chapter 8, "The Whartons Sell The Mount."

31. "Lenox," *BEE*, May 17, 1912, n.p.

32. "ARSD," *BEE*, 15.

33. "Mrs. Albert Shattuck, Once Imprisoned in New York by Robbers, Dies" *BEE*, March 1, 1935, n.p. The Shattucks did not build a new stable; this is the only known mention of a swimming pool on the grounds.

34. The Shattuck's four nephews were William Wickham Hoffman (1880-1966), Francis Burrall Hoffman (1882-1980), Albert L. Hoffman (1887-1981), and L. Murray Hoffman (1891-1982). F. Burrall Hoffman, Jr., was the architect of the Vizcaya estate of John Deering in Miami, Florida. In addition, he was the architect of St. Ann's Church (1911-12) in Lenox, Massachusetts. The four brothers, their wives, and their parents are buried in St. Ann's cemetery. Mrs. Strong died in 1921; Lucy Hoffman died on February 8, 1925.

35. *The New York Times*, November 5, 1925, gave the butler's name as Gabriel Alphonse Mourey; another article on December 26, 1926, called him Alphonse Gabriel Mourey and asserted that he had been employed by the Shattucks under the name of "Henri Bollet." The majority of the robbery account is drawn from two articles in the *NYT*: STW's "EQ," and also "ARSD."

36. *NYT*, December 26, 1926, 3.

37. STW, "EQ," *NYT*, 2. See also "Every Saturday-Shattuck Robbery-Inside Story Told," *BEE*, March 9, 1935, n.p.

38. STW, "EQ," *NYT*, 2.

39. "ARSD," *NYT*, 23. See also STW, "EQ," *NYT*, 2.

40. "Every Saturday-Shattuck Robbery-Inside Story Told," *BEE*, March 9, 1935, n.p. ARS met with the Pittsfield Chief of Police and obtained a permit to carry a revolver. According to the report, he then became "a crack shot." He also had guards who "were expert pistolmen."

41. STW, "EQ," *NYT*, 2. See also "Every Saturday-Shattuck Robbery-Inside Story Told," *BEE*, March 9, 1935, n.p.

42. Ibid.

43. "ARSD," *BEE*, 15.

44. Ibid.

45. ARS's obituary noted: "Many of Mr. Shattuck's friends believe that the shock of the robbery at his New York home…undermined his health and hastened his death, but one who was close to him said tonight that was not true. He said Mr. Shattuck had dismissed the robbery entirely from his mind." ("ARSD," *NYT*, 23).

46. "Funeral of A.R. Shattuck," *NYT*, November 7, 1925, 15. The body was then taken to New York City for burial at Woodlawn Cemetery "in a special car attached to a New York, New Haven & Hartford railroad train at Stockbridge." ("Body will be taken to New York." *BEE*, November 6, 1925, 24).

47. According to the will of ARS (Berkshire County Probate Court, #36721, probated in New York, March 5, 1926; filed in Berkshire County, November 1, 1926), an inventory of The Mount was evaluated as follows (no contents were listed):

Residence	$ 50,000.	
Gardener's Cottage	3,500.	
Greenhouse	400.	
Farm-barn	4,500.	
Ice-house	900.	
Shed	600.	
Hen-house	900.	
Piggery	100.	
Farm-house	3,000.	[opposite farm complex]
Garage	8,000.	[The Mount's stable]
110 acres of land at $350 per acre	38,500.	
	$110,400.	[Total]

Mary Shattuck's residence was given as 19 Washington Square North. F. Burrall Hoffman and Murray Hoffman both had addresses at 147 East 51st Street; William Wickham Hoffman lived at 24 East 95th Street. Albert L. Hoffman was noted as living for more than a year in Brussels, Belgium.

48. "Shattuck Heirs Divide $500,000 Trust Fund," *NYT*, November 20, 1926, 23.

49. CVA, "SRAAAT," 3-4. CVA stated that the preceding owner [Mrs. Shattuck] had resided in Europe near the end of her life.

50. Mary Strong Shattuck died at The Mount on the morning of March 1, 1935 (see her obituary, "Mrs. Albert R. Shattuck, Once Imprisoned In New York By Robbers, Dies" in *BEE*, March 1, 1935).

Mrs. Shattuck left substantial bequests totalling $490,000; her estate was then estimated at several millions. Among the bequests were: $25,000 each to The House of Mercy, Pittsfield, Massachusetts; the Massachusetts Society for the Prevention of Cruelty to Children in the Berkshire District, Lenox; the Women's Hospital in the State of New York; the New York Police and Fire Relief Funds; and to "various New York institutions for the aged and the blind." Bequests of $10,000 each went to the Lenox Fire Department; the Berkshire County Home for Aged Women of Pittsfield; the Lenox Library Association; the Seamen's Church Institute; and to various New York institutions. Trinity Church of Lenox and the Lenox Visiting Nurse Association each received $5,000. "The residuary estate was bequeathed to trustees for distribution to charitable and benevolent associations they will select." In addition, she left life incomes from $50,000 trust funds to Jeane Fisher, a personal maid, and to Charles Zang, a butler, both of The Mount. She left a life estate in $50,000 to Gershon C. Buch, a valet and butler, of Lenox, "the principal of which will go to his wife and children." "Berkshire Institutions Given Sizeable Bequests by Mrs. Shattuck's Will," *BEE*, March 6, 1935, n.p.

The Strong Family Vault — which contains the graves of Albert and Mary Shattuck — is located on Ravine Avenue in Woodlawn Cemetery. Sadly, it is untended today. Notables buried in close proximity include R. H. Macy, Admiral Farragut, and Herman Melville.

51. "Sale of Jewels, Furniture and Objets d'Art of the Late Mrs. Shattuck of Lenox Brings $84,687," *BEE*, October 22, 1935, n.p.

52. *Country Life*, 1936, month unknown, page unknown (American or British version unknown). The advertisement advised prospective buyers to consult their brokers or to contact Cadwalader, Wickersham & Taft, a New York City law firm, on Wall Street. A copy of the advertisement was kindly supplied to the author by Deborah Krulewitch.

53. The papers listed Thomas B. Gilchrist, William Wickham Hoffman, and the U. S. Trust Co. as executors.

LOUISE AND CARR V. VAN ANDA,
OWNERS, 1938-42

1. "CVA, NTE," *NYT*, 1, 13. A major part of the following account of CVA's life is taken from his impressive and lengthy obituary. CVA was born in Georgetown, Ohio, on December 2, 1864, the son of Frederick C. Van Anda, an attorney, and Mariah E. (Davis) Van Anda.

2. The Ohio University School of Journalism presents a "Carr V. Van Anda Award" to students (*BE*, May 19, 1969, n.d., n.p.).

3. "CVA, NTE," *NYT*, 1, 13.

4. Ibid., 13. Also see "CVA-E," *NYT*, 18.

5. Ibid.

6. Ibid.

7. Ibid. *The New York Times* was quoting here from the text of the award itself. According to the paper, CVA's "coverage of the First World War made journalistic history" ("CVA-E," *NYT*, 18).

8. Ibid.

9. Russell Owen, "Van Anda A Savant in Diverse Fields," *NYT*, January 30, 1945, 20. Also see "CVA, NTE," *NYT*, 13.

10. "CVA, NTE," *NYT*, 13.

11. Unfortunately little is known about the circumstances of this auction. On page 1 of the "SRAAT," it is noted: PROPERTY ACQUIRED *1938* HOW *At Auction*. The application states the costs of the property as $25,062*; the asterisk explains "Part of total price $25,600 applicable to Lenox tract."

12. CVA, "SRAAAT," 4.

13. The "SRAAAT" lists the Van Andas' post office address as "Summer — Lenox, Mass.; other times, 1170 Park Avenue, N.Y. City."

14. "Van Anda Estate to Appeal Value Placed on 'Mount,'" *The Springfield Republican*, March 19, 1942, n.p. This article suggests that the Van Andas returned the name "The Mount" to the property after the Shattuck ownership and the previous change of name to "White Lodge." CVA's statement and the accompanying application only refer to the place as "the property of Louise D. Van Anda"; the article in *The Springfield Republican* in 1942, CVA's obituary in *NYT* in 1945 and Louise Van Anda's will in 1942 refer to it as "The Mount."

15. "Mrs. Van Anda Dies in New York," *BEE*, February 18, 1942, n.p. Mrs. Van Anda's will, drawn on December 30, 1940, left all of her property to her husband. According to *The Springfield Republican* on March 19, 1942: "The bond filed with the will by Atty [Attorney] Donaldson shows real estate in Massachusetts of $30,000 [The Mount] and personal property of only $100." The will, probated on March 18, 1942 (#49756), in Berkshire Probate Court, noted $20.00 worth of clothing and $50.00 worth of books among her personal items at The Mount at the time of her death.

16. AMF, "EW-M," 3.

17. AMF, typewritten essay, "Edith Wharton and the Mount," unpublished manuscript, 10, FHS.

18. Berkshire County Registry of Deeds.

19. AMF, "EW-M," 4.

20. Ibid. As the Foxhollow School was a non-profit corporation, it seems possible that by selling the property to the school, CVA may have seen it removed from the tax rolls for the town of Lenox, no doubt a form of revenge after his past and pending tax struggles with the town assessors.

21. *The New York Times*, usually exact in the cause of deaths in its articles and obituaries, is vague about the exact cause of death of Blanche Van Anda, who was found dead in bed at age 58. Her recent life appears to have been a sad one — living alone for four years in a one-room apartment in the Hotel Fairfax. CVA suffered a massive heart attack, brought on by the sudden shock of the news of his daughter's death. He was survived by his son, Paul D. Van Anda, a lawyer in the firm of Spence, Windels, Walser, Hotchkiss & Angell, who lived at 1 Glenwood Road in Scarsdale, New York.

22. "CVA-E," *NYT*, 18.

THE FOXHOLLOW SCHOOL,
OWNER 1942-76

1. "Foxhollow's Miss Farrell to Retire as Principal," *BE*, August 8, 1970, n.p. Her birthdate was May 8, 1898.

2. Ibid. At Oxford she was awarded the degree of MA Oxon.

3. "Foxhollow School Buys The Mount, Lenox," *The Springfield Daily Republican*, Springfield, Massachusetts, August 18, 1942, n.p.

4. Most of the early history of the school is drawn from a booklet published by the school, c. 1950s. The booklet is incomplete and has no title page. The material drawn upon comes from a section entitled "History," 7-11, FHS.

5. AMF, "EWatM," 10.

6. Margaret Emerson Vanderbilt was the widow of Alfred Gwynne Vanderbilt, who died in the "Lusitania" maritime disaster in 1915. She was the daughter of Isaac Emerson of Baltimore, the inventor of Bromo-Seltzer.

7. AMF, "EWatM," 10.

8. One source of money for the purchase of the property was Sarah Delano Roosevelt, the mother of President Roosevelt, a friend and neighbor in Hyde Park, New York.

9. "Fox Hollow, For Girls Aged 13 to 18," *BEE*, April 3, 1939, n.p. Also see "Fox Hollow School to Move From Rhinebeck to Holmwood," *BEE*, c. April 1939, n.p. (files of *BE*).

10. *Plans For the Future of Foxhollow School*, c. mid-1950s, n.d., n.p., FHS.

11. AMF, "EW-M," 3-4.

12. "Foxhollow School Buys Mount To Use With Present Buildings," *BEE*, August 17, 1942, n.p.

13. Ibid. In "Van Anda Estate Sold," *NYT* reported at the same time that "the assessed valuation four years ago was $114,400. It is now $41,200" (August 1942).

14. "Foxhollow School Buys The Mount, Lenox," *The Springfield Daily Republican*, August 18, 1942, n.p.

15. Ibid.

16. The figures are from AMF's notebooks. An article in *BEE* on August 21, 1942 ("Foxhollow Pays $18,000 for the Van Anda Place"), states that CVA "has petitioned through his attorney, Frederick M. Myers of this city [Pittsfield], the Probate Court for authorization to sell at private sale to the Foxhollow School, Inc., for $18,000 certain property Mrs. Van Anda owned in Lenox and Stockbridge at the time of her death." The sale was handled by Wheeler & Taylor in Great Barrington.

17. AMF, "EWatM," 11.

18. "Foxhollow School Has Spacious Rooms in New Building," *BEE*, September 12, 1942, 4.

19. Ibid.

20. Ibid.

21. Ibid.

22. "Foxhollow School Petition Being Heard by Land Court," *BEE*, May 20, 1943, n.p. The hearing was to determine "whether [the] town, under zoning rules, can prevent [the] school from using [the] Van Anda property." Attorneys Frederick M. Myers and Stephen B. Hibbard represented the School; the Town was represented by its counsel Cornelius J. Broderick, of Lenox and Pittsfield attorney James M. Rosenthal. Myers argued that the newly expanded Foxhollow School was located in the same area as the original Foxhollow campus, the Lenox School for Boys, and the nearby Cranwell

School. AMF testified that the Foxhollow School was a boarding school, not a day school and was not endowed; its expenses were paid from the tuition fees from students. There were five or six scholarships offered by the school to qualified students but no agreement or understanding "between the school management and Lenox officials about admitting any specified member [sic-number] of Lenox students; anyone who had the required fee and educational qualifications could become a student there," she said.

23. Ibid.

24. Ibid.

25. Ibid.

26. Ibid.

27. *Plans for the Future of Foxhollow School*, c. mid-1950s, n.d., n.p., FHS.

28. AMF, EW-M," 6.

29. Ibid.

30. Ibid., 7.

31. Ibid.

32. "Foxhollow's Miss Farrell To Retire as Principal," *BE*, August 8, 1970, n.p. For information about Mrs. Mumford and her background, see "A Time of Transition at Foxhollow: The Second Headmistress Takes Over," by Ralph Conroy, *BE*, October 27, 1970, n.p. Hilda Thomas Mumford (Mrs. Thomas D.; born 1909) died in February 1996. She retired as headmistress of the Foxhollow School in 1974 at age 65.

33. Ibid.

34. AMF, "EW-M," 10.

35. Ibid.

36. Ibid, 11.

37. Ibid., 13.

38. The items included a Savonnerie rug from the drawing room, which AMF speculated might have belonged to EW (*note* — the one photograph of the drawing room in the Whartons' time indicated that the Savonnerie rug would have belonged to the Shattucks or the Van Andas — not the Whartons). Also included in the sale (which realized approximately $15,000) was a Meissonier painting, which had been placed within the molding above the fireplace mantel in the drawing room and which Farrell believed belonged to EW. At the time of the sale, AMF was asked how much she would pay for the statue of Pan by MacMonnies that stood in The Mount's entrance hall, which she in particular wished to have. The sale of the statue did not come to pass, and the valuable Pan was eventually removed for safekeeping to the Berkshire Museum in Pittsfield, Massachusetts.

39. AMF, "EW-M," 13.

40. Ibid.

41. Ibid., 12.

42. AMF, "EW-M," 14.

43. *Directory of National Historic Landmarks - Northeast Region:* A Preservation Program of the Heritage Conservation and Recreation Service, U.S. Department of the Interior, 34. According to a later article, "The Mount, Home of Edith Wharton, Eligible to be National Landmark," by Alexander Hawes, Jr. (*BE*, February 11, 1972, n.p.), the designation of The Mount was announced on February 10 or 11, 1972, through the office of Congressman Silvio O. Conte. According to a spokesperson for Conte, Secretary of the Interior Rogers C. B. Morton "has found the mansion to possess national significance in commemorating United

States history." The estate was already listed on the National Register of Historic Places, according to the article. The designation of The Mount as a National Historic Landmark was approved by the Foxhollow School, which was interested in applying for federal funds for maintenance, according to then-headmistress, Hilda Mumford.

44. Ralph E. Brown, "Committee Planning Restoration of Edith Wharton House in Lenox," *BE*, March 11, 1975, n.p.

45. Ibid.

46. Ibid.

47. Ibid.

48. AMF, "The Mount," text for a brochure for the restoration of The Mount, 4, FHS. In a speech to alumnae, she stated: "I would exhort all of you to re-read dear Edith's works and come down to see her lovely house then ask yourselves how you might help to save it for its inherent beauty and as a well kept memorial of Edith Wharton's literary distinction and of her friends who gave it so distinguished a life some seventy years ago." AMF, "EWatM," 12.

49. "Foxhollow Puts Mount on Market to Raise Funds," *BE*, July 1, 1976, n.p.

50. Ibid.

51. Ibid.

52. The Mount was used by the Lenox Arts Center, headquartered at Citizen's Hall in nearby Interlaken, Massachusetts, as housing for their "professional staff of artists, writers and musicians." Foxhollow headmaster Thomas P. Ryan stated that the lease agreement ran from June 1 to August 31, 1976, and that the school was no longer using The Mount because "it was too expensive to heat" ("Lenox Arts Center to Lease The Mount," *BE*, April 13, 1976, n.p.).

53. "Lenox Building Qualifies for $6,300 State Grant," *BE*, March 13, 1974, n.p.

54. Susan Besaw Walsh, "U.S. Grant of 410,130 set for The Mount," *BE*, December 6, 1977. Also see "Grant Obtained for Work on Edith Wharton's Home," *BE*, January 22, 1976, n.p.

55. Ibid.

56. Susan M. Besaw, "Foxhollow School Closing Because of Rising Costs," *BE*, August 24, 1976, n.p.

57. Ibid.

58. Ibid.

59. AMF, "EWatM," 11.

60. Susan M. Besaw, "Foxhollow is Placing Students, Teachers," *BE*, August 31, 1976, n.p.

THE CENTER INCORPORATED,
OWNER, 1977-80

1. Dee Siegelbaum, "National Landmark in Lenox a Sickly, White Elephant," *The Albany Times Union*, August 2, 1976, n.p.

2. Ibid.

3. "Novelist's Former Home in Need of an Underwriter: Wharton Mansion Future a Financial Problem," *The Albany Times Union*, August 2, 1976, n.p.

4. Susan M. Besaw, "Bible Speaks Pays $600,000 to Buy Foxhollow Site in Lenox," *BE*, September 20, 1976, n.p. Walter L. Wheat, a Foxhollow trustee and vice-president in charge of the First Agricultural National Bank's trust department in Pittsfield, confirmed that the School's trustees had accepted The Bible Speaks's offer at a recent meeting.

5. Ibid.

6. "Two New Offers Made for Foxhollow: Bible Speaks Won't Buy," *BE*, October 13, 1976, n.p. The Foxhollow School returned the deposit made by The Bible Speaks, which had bid $600,000 to purchase the property.

7. Ibid.

8. Ibid.

9. Berkshire County Registry of Deeds, Book 985, 13-19 (#197639-40). Parcels III, IV and V constituted The Mount property as it had belonged to the Shattucks and the Van Andas. The Center Incorporated was an organization created by Donald I. Altshuler — president and sole director — with a post office box and principal office at 251 Kemble Street, Lenox, Massachusetts.

10. Ibid., 22.

11. "Renovation of The Mount Considered," *BE*, December 7, 1977, n.p.

12. Ibid.

13. Ibid.

14. Ibid. In a December 6, 1977, article in *BE*, it was reported that "Altshuler at one time had considered converting it [The Mount] into conference rooms and a gourmet restaurant but apparently scrapped those plans because of the high cost of renovations, particularly to the interior of the mansion." Susan Besaw Walsh, "U.S. Grant of $10,130 Set for The Mount," *BE*, December 6, 1977, n.p.

15. Linda Carman, "Resort Selling Wharton Mansion," *BE*, October 8, 1977, n.p.

SHAKESPEARE & COMPANY AT
THE MOUNT, 1978-PRESENT

1. Helen Epstein, *The Companies She Keeps — Tina Packer Builds a Theater* (Cambridge, Massachusetts: Plunkett Lake Press, 1985), 67.

2. Susan Besaw Walsh, "Theater company leases The Mount," *BE*, June 2, 1978, n.p. "Under its lease agreement with the Center at Foxhollow, Shakespeare & Company also has an option to buy The Mount. It was placed on the market last fall at a price of $250,000."

3. Linda Carmen, "100 Visit The Mount," *BE*, July 3, 1978, n.p. From a Shakespeare & Company press kit entitled "The Mount and The Company." According to Dennis Krausnick, the company's "temporary general manager...the 25 staff members now in residence at the resort [Foxhollow] are doing extensive renovations to The Mount, which is in disrepair. The Company is being assisted in the endeavor by Smith College students." Susan Besaw Walsh, "Theater Company Leases The Mount," *BE*, June 2, 1978, n.p.

4. Teresa M. Hanafin, "Shakespeare Will Buy The Mount," *BE*, September 2, 1978, n.p. The mortgage amount was not determined.

5. Ibid.

6. Avice Meehan, "Tentative Contract is Signed for Purchase of The Mount," *BE*, November 3, 1978, n.p.

7. Ibid. The negotiations concerned whether Altshuler would guarantee payment for the property by Shakespeare & Company with the $500,000 mortgage held by the Foxhollow School trustees (a second mortgage for $250,000 was held by the Chemical Bank of New York; the Lenox Savings Bank held two additional mortgages for $30,000 and

for $35,000). According to Joel S. Greenberg, attorney for the trustees: "The Trustees of the Foxhollow School look with favor on the purchase and will do whatever possible to make that come about. We are assuming that Shakespeare & Company is a legitimate group with some aesthetic worth... Altshuler is asking to be released from certain terms of his contract."

8.   Epstein, *The Companies She Keeps*, 91.

EDITH WHARTON RESTORATION,
OWNER, 1980-PRESENT

1.   Lila Berle to Thomas Hayes, October 3, 1985, EWR. The Endangered Properties Program had been established several years prior to 1980 to operate with a $2 million revolving fund to buy and sell National Historic Landmark properties whose integrity was jeopardized by development or demolition. "National Trust Buying The Mount," *BE*, April 16, 1980, n.p.

2.   Ibid.

3.   Ibid.

4.   Ibid.

5.   Lila Berle to John Frisbee, April 9, 1980, EWR.

6.   Ibid.

7.   Ibid.

8.   "National Trust Buying Mount," *BE*, April 16, 1980, n.p.

9.   Avice Meehan, "Sale of The Mount Approved," *BE*, May 29, 1980, n.p.

10.   Linda Carmen, "Shakespeare & Company Subsidiary Acquires The Mount in Lenox," *BE*, July 2, 1980, n.p.

11.   Ibid.

12.   Ibid.

13.   Lila Berle to John Frisbee, April 9, 1980, EWR.

14.   EWR board roster, June 6, 1980, EWR.

15.   "Variance Approved for The Mount," *BE*, July 24, 1980, n.p.

16.   Ibid.

17.   ZBA restrictions included: 1) Plunkett Street must be clear of parked cars to allow emergency vehicles access; 2) if either organization were to go bankrupt or sell any part of the 50-acre estate or its buildings, a future purchaser would have to come before the ZBA to obtain a new variance; 3) the number of personnel allowed to live in the estate's buildings was limited to 15 in the mansion, 12 in the stable, 12 in the gatehouse, and six in the adjacent cottage; 4) the size of the audience for the outdoor amphitheater was limited to 400 persons; 5) "activities at The Mount [must] be conducted in a manner so as not to disturb neighbors unnecessarily."

18.   In November 1980, EWR appointed Deborah A. Dunning, former director of the Providence Preservation Society in Rhode Island, to be its first full-time director. Dunning's primary responsibility was to explore adaptive reuse of The Mount. Her other responsibilities included "overseeing restoration and repair of the landmark, coordinating fund-raising, restoring the house and its formal gardens, stimulating public interest in the project, and bringing programs related to the restoration and the theater company into the schools" ("Leader Named for Restoration of The Mount," *BE*, November 25, 1980, n.p.). Dunning was supposed to begin her appointment as director in early January 1981 but ill health forced her to withdraw.

19.   "Former Monument Teacher Named to Post at The Mount," *BE*, January 30, 1981, 9. Brolli, who had a back-

ground in local real-estate and antique sales and experience in "restorations, renovations, moving houses to new sites, and designing additions to complement existing structures," had resigned from teaching at Monument Mountain Regional High School the previous September.

20.   Interview by the author with Dorothy Carpenter (Foxhollow class of '68), September 11, 1994.

21.   Charles Bonenti, "Vanishing Craft Reapplied at The Mount," *BE*, May 7, 1982, 20. GE donated the materials used to make the molds.

22.   AMF — who had initiated the first restoration of The Mount — became ill in 1981. Before she died on December 20, 1981, at age 83, she was pleased that the restoration of the drawing room ceiling was underway. Julie Sell, "Foxhollow School Founder Given Tribute at The Mount," *BE*, October 18, 1983, n.p.

23.   Carpenter was disappointed with the result, which she felt was due to a too-limited budget that did not allow for full and appropriate restoration of the drawing room ceiling.

24.   Harold Holzer, "Edith Wharton's First Real Home - Remembering Life and Work at The Mount," *American Heritage*, September 1982, n.p.

25.   Julie Sell, "The Mount Names First Director; 'Turning Point' in Finances Cited," *BE*, date unknown, c. Spring 1984, n.p. (Hayes's title later became president). Hayes was vice president of development and public relations for the Springfield, Massachusetts, Library and Museums Association, Inc. He had previously served as director of development at the Caramoor Center for Music and the Arts, Inc., in Katonah, New York; had headed public relations for the Peabody Institute of John Hopkins University in Baltimore; and had been a director of media services at the National Trust for Historic Preservation in Washington, D.C.

26.   Ibid.

27.   Ibid.

28.   Ibid.

29.   Months later, Mary Misch, the executive secretary of EWR who had overseen day-to-day operations since Brolli's departure, resigned.

30.   On September 10, 1990, *BE* announced that S&C was "heavily in debt" (Abby Pratt, "Shakepeare & Company Heavily in Debt," *BE*, September 10, 1990, B-1); one week later the paper reported that the company owed $300,000, including approximately $39,000 to EWR (Abby Pratt, "Shakespeare & Company Will Owe $300,000, memos say," *BE*, September 18, 1990, B-1). Hayes said that he had "referred the matter to an attorney." Tensions between the two organizations continued to escalate over monies owed to EWR and the ways and the extent to which S&C was utilizing the house and the grounds.

31.   William F. Semanie, EWR board co-chair, explained in *BE* that the board of directors "all agreed that the task in front of us is something that is going to be very energetic and needs some different kind of talents...to bring us where we have to go during the next five years" (Mary-Jane Tichenor, "Edith Wharton Chief Resigns," *BE*, May 16, 1992, n.p.). Semanie noted that in recent years, EWR's board "has been able to raise barely enough to pay the bills for the programs and salaries for the staff... The board is going to go in a new direction and come up with something that's going to involve some new talents and a whole new approach to the restoration." Hayes remained with EWR through the fall of 1992; his wife, Joy, stayed on as administrative assistant until June 1993.

CHAPTER 9

Outbuildings

1. See RWBL, *EW*, 100. By 1938 the estate had grown to 157 acres (see 1940 Tax Assessment for CVA).

2. BBD, *ALAAMP-TM*, 62.

3. "ML," *BRT*, 2. The gate of The Mount — with its classical style and concave sections — resembles other gates known to have been designed by H&K, for instance, Brookhurst and Eastover (Fahnestock) in Lenox.

4. Reynolds is also listed in Lenox Town Directories of the period.

5. L and L, *LEW*, 242. EW to MF, July 3, 1911.

6. Ibid.

7. See *LEW*, 254. EW to SN, August 26, 1911.

8. The house was rented at one point by AMF to the Bergen family (sometime in the late 1960s). Their daughter, Delphine (now Delphine Phelps), attended the Foxhollow School, class of '73.

9. "The Lenox Cottagers," *BRT*, July 23, 1904, 6. The 1905 information may be found on microfilm at the Berkshire Athenaeum in *The Pittsfield Sun*.

10. RWBL, *EW*, 159.

11. EW, *The House of Mirth* (New York: Charles Scribner's Sons, 1905), 66.

12. AMF, "EW-M," 7.

13. "ML," *BRT*, 1.

14. The Whartons had a Pope-Hartford motor car, purchased in early July 1904. See *BRT* for July 9, 1904 ("The Lenox Automobilists"). The Whartons' Pope-Hartford was also mentioned in several other issues of *BRT* (see Chapter 5).

15. "ML," *BRT*, 2.

16. Howard Nott Palmer, "Stable Planning," *The Architectural Review*, 1902.

17. From information in the 1901 Official Catalogue of the Lenox Horse Show at Highlawn Farm, Friday, October 4, 1901, LnL. The Whartons also had a horse named Countess (*LnLf*, September 20, 1902, 1).

18. GL, "EW," 17.

19. "ML," *BRT*, 2.

20. Much of the information on William Parlett was furnished to the author by Mrs. Virginia (Pratt) Agar, the daughter of Mr. Parlett's daughter Cicely Parlett (later Pratt). Mrs. Agar now lives in Connecticut; her son John now owns his great-grandfather's watch presented by EW. John Agar, Mr. Parlett's great-grandson, was married to Jane Kammerer at The Mount on September 9, 1989.

21. L and L, *LEW*, 152. EW to MF, June 8-11, 1908. Mrs. Agar remembers that her grandfather was interested in birds.

22. See Chapter 5 (also Note 46, Chapter 5).

23. CVA, "SRAAAT," 6.

24. AMF, "EW-M," 3-4.

25. BBD, *ALAAMP-TM*, 64.

26. The farmhouse across the road from the complex was clearly part of the property again by the time of the Van Andas' occupancy. Handwriting (believed to be that of AMF)

on the back of a c. 1942 photograph states: "This is my favorite house of all right down on the lake. It has no electricity in it & is inhabited by the groom and his wife. They have been there for years & I couldn't move them but may have to in the future."

27. GL, "EW," 17.

28. "ML," *BRT*, 2.

29. *The Berkshire Gleaner*, April 5, 1905, Lee, Massachusetts. EWR is indebted to Cornelia Brooke Gilder for material from this local newspaper.

30. See RWBL, *EW*, 136.

31. Ibid., 160.

32. EW, *ABG*, 125.

33. CVA, "SRAAAT," 6.

34. Ibid., 5.

Selected Bibliography

BOOKS

Amory, Cleveland. *Who Killed Society?* New York: Harper and Brothers, 1960.

Bell, Millicent. *Edith Wharton & Henry James: The Story of Their Friendship*. New York: George Braziller, 1965.

Benstock, Shari. *No Gifts From Chance: A Biography of Edith Wharton*. New York: Charles Scribner's Sons, 1994. Copyright (c) 1994 by Shari Benstock. Used by permission of Scribner's, a Division of Simon & Schuster.

Craig, Theresa. *Edith Wharton — A House Full of Rooms: Architecture, Interiors, and Gardens*. New York: The Monacelli Press, 1996.

de Wolfe, Elsie. *After All*. London: William Heinemann, Ltd., 1935.

Dwight, Eleanor. *Edith Wharton: An Extraordinary Life*. New York: Harry N. Abrams, Inc. 1994. All rights reserved.

Edel, Leon, ed. *Henry James — Letters Vol. IV (1895-1916)*. Cambridge, Massachusetts: The Belknap Press of Harvard University Press, 1984. Copyright (c) 1984 by Leon Edel, Editorial. Copyright (c) 1984 by Alexander R. James, James Copyright material. Used by permission of Harvard University Press.

_____. *Henry James—The Master: 1901-1916*. New York: Avon Books, 1972. Copyright (c) 1972 by Leon Edel. Used by permission of HarperCollins, Publishers.

Epstein, Helen. *The Company She Keeps — Tina Packer Builds a Theater*. Cambridge, Massachusetts: Plunkett Lake Press, 1985.

Lewis, R. W. B. *Edith Wharton: A Biography*. New York: Harper & Row, 1975. Used by permission of HarperCollins, Publishers.

Lewis, R. W. B. and Nancy Lewis, eds. *The Letters of Edith Wharton*. New York: Charles Scribner's Sons, 1988. Copyright (c) 1988 by R. W. B. Lewis, Nancy Lewis, and William R. Tyler. Used by permission of Scribner's, a Division of Simon & Schuster.

Lubbock, Percy. *Portrait of Edith Wharton*. London: Jonathan Cape, 1947.

Metcalf, Pauline C., ed. *Ogden Codman and The Decoration of Houses*. Boston: David R. Godine, 1988.

Powers, Lyall H., ed. *Henry James and Edith Wharton Letters: 1900-1915*. New York: Charles Scribner's Sons, 1990. Copyright (c) by Lyall H. Powers. Used by permission of Scribner's, a Division of Simon & Schuster.

Wharton, Edith. *A Backward Glance*. New York: Appleton-Century Company, Inc., 1934. Copyright (c) 1933, 1934 by Charles Scribner's Sons; Copyright (c) 1961, 1962 by William R. Tyler. Used by permission of Scribner's, a Division of Simon & Schuster.

_____. *The Ghost Stories of Edith Wharton*. New York: Charles Scribner's Sons, 1973.

_____. *Italian Villas and Their Gardens*. New York: The Century Press, 1904.

_____. *A Motor-Flight Through France*. New York: Charles Scribner's Sons, 1908.

Wharton, Edith and Ogden Codman, Jr. *The Decoration of Houses*. New York: Charles Scribner's Sons, 1897.

ARTICLES AND ESSAYS

"Albert R. Shattuck Dies at His Villa in Lenox." *The Berkshire Evening Eagle*, November 5, 1925.

"Albert R. Shattuck Dies of Heart Attack." *The New York Times*, November 5, 1925.

"Altshuler Alters Resort Plan." *The Berkshire Eagle*, April 5, 1979.

"Berkshire Institutions Given Sizable Bequests by Mrs. Shattuck's Will." *The Berkshire Evening Eagle*, March 6, 1935.

Besaw, Susan M. "Bible Speaks Pays $600,000 to Buy Foxhollow Site in Lenox." *The Berkshire Eagle*, September 20, 1976.

_____. "Foxhollow is Placing Students, Teachers." *The Berkshire Eagle*, August 31, 1976.

_____. "Foxhollow School Closing Because of Rising Costs." *The Berkshire Eagle*, August 24, 1976.

"Body [A.R. Shattuck] Will Be Taken to New York." *The Berkshire Evening Eagle*, November 6, 1925.

Bonenti, Charles. "Vanishing Craft Reapplied at The Mount." *The Berkshire Eagle*, May 7, 1982.

Brown, Ralph E. "Committee Planning Restoration of Edith Wharton House in Lenox." *The Berkshire Eagle*, March 11, 1975.

Carman, Linda. "100 Visit The Mount." *The Berkshire Eagle*, July 3, 1978.

_____. "Mount Tank Expected in 2 Weeks." *The Berkshire Eagle*, July 18, 1979.

_____. "Resort Selling Wharton Mansion." *The Berkshire Eagle*, October 8, 1977.

_____. "Shakespeare & Co. Subsidiary Acquires The Mount in Lenox." *The Berkshire Eagle*, July 2, 1980.

"Carr Van Anda Dies Suddenly." *The Berkshire Evening Eagle*, January 29, 1945.

"Carr V. Van Anda." Editorial, *The New York Times*, January 30, 1945.

"Carr V. Van Anda, Noted Times Editor, Dies Here, Aged 80." *The New York Times*, January 29, 1945.

Champlin, Richard. "Col. Hoppin's Newport." *Newport History* 59 (Winter 1986): 28-35. Newport Historical Society, Newport, Rhode Island.

Coles, William A. "The Genesis of a Classic." Introduction to Classical America's edition of Edith Wharton's and Ogden Codman's *The Decoration of Houses*. New York: W. W. Norton and Company, 1978. Used by permission of Classical America.

"Col. Hoppin, 74, Architect and Painter, Dead." *New York Herald Tribune*, September 10, 1941.

Conroy, Ralph. "A Time of Transition at Foxhollow: The Second Headmistress Takes Over." *The Berkshire Eagle*, October 27, 1970.

Ferree, Barr. "Talks with Architects: Mr. F. L. V. Hoppin on the House and Garden." *Scientific American Building Monthly* 35 (March 1903): 47, 61.

"Former Monument Teacher Named to Post at The Mount." *The Berkshire Eagle*, January 30, 1981.

"Fox Hollow, for Girls, Aged 13 to 18." *The Berkshire Evening Eagle*. April 3, 1939.

"Fox Hollow School to Move From Rhinebeck to Holmwood." *The Berkshire Evening Eagle*, April 1939.

"Foxhollow Pays $18,000 for the Van Anda Place." *The Berkshire Evening Eagle*, August 21, 1942.

"Foxhollow Puts Mount on Market to Raise Funds." *The Berkshire Eagle*, July 1, 1976.

"Foxhollow School Buys The Mount, Lenox." *Daily Republican*, August 18, 1942.

"Foxhollow School Buys Mount to Use with Present Buildings." *The Berkshire Evening Eagle*, August 17, 1942.

"Foxhollow School Has Spacious Rooms in New Building." *The Berkshire Evening Eagle*, September 12, 1942.

"Foxhollow School Petition Being Heard by Land Court." *The Berkshire Evening Eagle*, May 20, 1943.

"Foxhollow's Miss Farrell to Retire as Principal." *The Berkshire Eagle*, August 8, 1970.

"Francis Hoppin." National Cyclopedia of American Biography, vol. 31. New York: James J. T. White, 1944.

"Funeral of A.R. Shattuck." *The New York Times*, November 7, 1925.

Goldberger, Paul. "Edith Wharton's Home: An Unusual Rescue." *The New York Times*, August 7, 1980.

"Grant Obtained for Work on Edith Wharton's Home." *The Berkshire Eagle*, January 22, 1976.

Hanafin, Teresa. "Shakespeare Will Buy The Mount." *The Berkshire Eagle*, September 2, 1978.

Hawes, Alexander, Jr. "The Mount, Home of Edith Wharton, Eligible to be National Landmark." *The Berkshire Eagle*, February 11, 1972.

"Historic Home Up For Sale." *The Springfield Republican*, November 5, 1978.

Holzer, Harold. "Edith Wharton's First Real Home — Remembering Life and Work at The Mount," *American Heritage*, September 1982.

Hoppin & Koen. "Some Country and City Residences." *The New York Architect* V (July 1911): 149-156.

"Leader Named for Restoration of The Mount." *The Berkshire Eagle*, November 25, 1980.

"Lenox." *The Berkshire Evening Eagle*, May 17, 1912.

"Lenox Arts Center to Lease The Mount." *The Berkshire Eagle*, April 13, 1976.

"Lenox Building Qualifies for $6,300 State Grant." *The Berkshire Eagle*, March 13, 1974.

"Lenox ZBA Hears Petition for Changes at The Mount." *The Berkshire Eagle*, July 9, 1980.

Marshall, Scott. "Employee — E. R. Wharton." *VISTA from The Mount*, Spring/Summer, 1987.

_____. "The 'Original' Mount in Astoria, N.Y." *VISTA from The Mount*, Winter 1988-89.

_____. "Whatever Happened to Teddy Wharton?" *VISTA from The Mount*, Winter 1987-88.

Meehan, Avice. "Foxhollow Trustees OK Aid to Theater Group." *The Berkshire Eagle*, April 8, 1980.

_____. "The Mount, Acreage May Be Sold by April." *The Berkshire Eagle*, January 4, 1980.

_____. "National Trust Steps in to Buy The Mount for Theater Group." *The Berkshire Eagle*, February 25, 1980.

_____. "Sale of The Mount Approved." *The Berkshire Eagle*, May 29, 1980.

_____. "Tentative Contract is Signed for Purchase of The Mount." *The Berkshire Eagle*, November 3, 1978.

Metcalf, Pauline C. "Elegance without Excess: Ogden Codman in New York." *Newsletter — Preservation League of New York State*, Winter 1986, vol. 12, no. 1.

"The Mount in Lenox." *Berkshire Resort Topics*, September 10, 1904.

"Mr. Wharton's New Home." *Lenox Life*, August 17, 1901.

"Mrs. Albert R. Shattuck, Once Imprisoned in New York by Robbers, Dies." *The Berkshire Evening Eagle*, March 1, 1935.

"Mrs. Van Anda Dies in New York." *The Berkshire Evening Eagle*, February 18, 1942.

The National Trust. *Belton House, Lincolnshire*. Herts: The Stellar Press, 1985.

"National Trust Buying Mount." *The Berkshire Eagle*, April 16, 1980.

"New Lenox Resort Plans Season Opening July 15." *The Berkshire Eagle*, July 2, 1977.

"Novelist's Former Home in Need of an Underwriter." *The Albany Times Union*, August 2, 1976.

Owen, Russell. "Van Anda A Savant in Diverse Fields." *The New York Times*, January 30, 1945.

Palmer, Harold Nott. "Stable Planning." *The Architectural Review* (1902).

"Pendennis." "The Thinking Heart: An Impression of Mrs. Edith Wharton at Close Range." *The Book News Monthly* 26 (November 1907): 171-173.

Pratt, Abby. "Shakespeare & Co. Heavily in Debt." *The Berkshire Eagle*, September 10, 1990.

_____. "Shakespeare & Co. Will Owe $300,000, Memos Say." *The Berkshire Eagle*, September 18, 1990.

"Renovation of The Mount Considered." *The Berkshire Eagle*, December 7, 1977.

"Sale of Jewels, Furniture and Objets d'Art of the Late Mrs. Shattuck of Lenox Brings $84,687." *The Berkshire Evening Eagle*, October 22, 1935.

Sell, Julie. "Foxhollow School Founder Given Tribute at The Mount." *The Berkshire Eagle*, October 18, 1983.

_____. "The Mount Names First Director; 'Turning Point' in Finances Cited." *The Albany Times Union,* c. Spring 1984.

"Sewage Disposal Problems Seen in New Use of Mount." *The Berkshire Eagle*, September 6, 1978.

"Shakespeare & Co. Must Get $120,000 by April 11 to Purchase The Mount." *The Berkshire Eagle*, February 26, 1980.

"Shattuck Art Collection Nets $84,687 in Sale," undated and unattributed newspaper clipping in the auction catalogue, c. October 1935.

"Shattuck Buys the Wharton Property." *The Berkshire Evening Eagle*, September 11, 1911.

"Shattuck Heirs Divide $500,000 Trust Fund." *The New York Times*, November 20, 1926.

"Shattuck Robbery. Inside Story Told. Pittsfield Link-up. Chief Took a Hand. Banker in Council. Pinkertons Here." *The Berkshire Evening Eagle*, March 9, 1935.

Siegelbaum, Dee. "National Landmark in Lenox a Sickly, White Elephant." *The Albany Times Union*, August 2, 1976.

Tichenor, Mary-Jane. "Edith Wharton Chief Resigns." *The Berkshire Eagle*, May 16, 1992.

"Three Houses at Aiken, S.C., Hoppin & Koen, Architects." *Architectural Review* IX (September 1902): 114.

"Two New Offers Made for Foxhollow." *The Berkshire Eagle*, October 13, 1976.

"Van Anda Estate Sold." *The New York Times*, August 19 (?), 1942.

"Van Anda Estate to Appeal Value Placed on 'Mount.'" *The Springfield Republican*, March 19, 1942.

"Variance Approved for The Mount." *The Berkshire Eagle*, July 24, 1980.

Walsh, Susan Besaw. "Theater Company Leases The Mount." *The Berkshire Eagle*, June 2, 1978.

_____. "U.S. Grant of $10,130 Set for The Mount." *The Berkshire Eagle*, December 6, 1977.

Wharton, Edith. "A Little Girl's New York." *Harpers* 176 (March 1938): 356-364.

Williamson, S.T. "The End of a Quest — Stranger Than Fiction." *The New York Times*, November 15, 1925, IX.

Wilson, Richard Guy. "Edith and Ogden: Writing, Decoration, and Architecture," in *Ogden Codman and The Decoration of Houses*, Pauline C. Metcalf, ed., Boston: David R. Godine, 1988.

_____. "Picturesque Ambiguities: The Country House Tradition in America." *The Long Island Country House 1870-1930*. Southampton, New York: The Parrish Art Museum, 1988.

UNPUBLISHED SOURCES
(MANUSCRIPTS, PROPOSALS, ETC.)

Baker, Wendy; David Bennett; and Diane Dierkes. *A Landscape Architectural Analysis and Master Plan for The Mount.* Prepared for the Massachusetts Council on the Arts and Humanities, Edith Wharton Restoration, Inc., and Shakespeare & Company. Harvard Graduate School of Design, 1982.

Bennett, David H. "From the Ground Up." Slide lecture.

Curtis, William Derbyshire. "A Daily Reminder of Important Matters." Notations in his diary for the year 1911. Collection of the Lenox Historical Society.

Farrell, Aileen M. "E.W. — Mount." Manuscript from the Foxhollow School Archives.

------. "Edith Wharton at The Mount," typewritten essay and manuscript from the Foxhollow School Archives.

------. "The Mount," text for a brochure for the restoration of The Mount from the Foxhollow School Archives.

"French Furniture of the Eighteenth Century, Queen Anne and Georgian Silver, Chinese Porcelains, Property of the Estate of the late Mary Strong Shattuck, New York and Lenox, Mass.," auction catalogue for public sale October 17, 18, and 19, 1935. New York City: American Art Association/Anderson Galleries, Inc., 30 East 57th Street.

Krausnick, Dennis. Proposal attached to General Operating Support Form 102, March 6, 1980.

Palermo-Schulze, Carole. *Summary for the Restoration of the Formal Gardens at The Mount.* Prepared for Edith Wharton Restoration, 1985.

Peck, Amelia. *Restoration Plan for the Interior of The Mount, Lenox, Massachusetts.* Thesis for the Division of Historic Preservation, Graduate School of Architecture and Planning, Columbia University, 1984.

The Preservation Partnership. *Project Work Documentation for Development Project Application — The Mount.* FY 1981.

Siegel, Stuart. *The Architecture of Hoppin & Koen.* Graduate thesis for the Department of Architectural History, University of Virginia, 1980.

Wharton, Edith. "Life and I." Yale Collection of American Literature, Beinecke Rare Book and Manuscript Library, Yale University.

Williamstown Regional Art Conservation Laboratory, Inc.: Inspection Report for Edith Wharton Restoration, 1985.

ARCHIVES, MUSEUMS, LIBRARIES

Avery Architectural and Fine Arts Library, Columbia University, New York. 1901 Hoppin & Koen floor plans and elevations.

Beinecke Rare Book and Manuscript Library, Yale Collection of American Literature, Yale University, New Haven, Connecticut. Edith Wharton Archives: unpublished memories of Edith Wharton; Edith Wharton correspondence; photographs of houses and gardens.

Berkshire Athenaeum, Pittsfield, Massachusetts. *Berkshire Resort Topics* for 1903,1904; *Lenox Life* for 1899-1902; *Pittsfield Sun* for 1905; and other papers on microfilm; town directories.

Berkshire County Probate Court, Pittsfield, Massachusetts. Wills of Albert R. Shattuck and Teddy Wharton.

Berkshire County Registry of Deeds, Pittsfield, Massachusetts. Deeds for sale of The Mount in 1911-12, 1938, 1942, and 1975-76.

The Berkshire Eagle, Pittsfield, Massachusetts. Clippings archive.

Edith Wharton Restoration Archives, The Mount, Lenox, Massachusetts. "Alterations to residence of E. R. Wharton, Esq., Lenox, Mass." (1907 floor plans); Butler's Pantry Cutout Box sheet; guides' training material; summary of restoration funds received since 1980.

Foxhollow School Archives, The Mount, Lenox, Massachusetts.

Lee Library Association, Lee, Massachusetts. *The Berkshire Gleaner* for 1903 and 1905.

Lenox Historical Society, Lenox, Massachusetts. "A Daily Reminder of Important Matters," diary of William Derbyshire Curtis.

Lenox Library Association, Lenox, Massachusetts. "List of Cottages, July 1909" (printed by Louis Regnier); 1901 Official Catalogue of the Lenox Horse Show at the Highlawn Farm, Friday October 4, 1901; and Van Anda, Carr V., "Statement of Reasons for the Attached Application for Abatement of Taxes on the Property of Louise D. Van Anda," Lenox, Massachusetts, September 26, 1940.

Redwood Library and Athenaeum, Newport, Rhode Island. "Lodge, Stable and Residence, E. R. Wharton, Lenox, Mass." Unpublished account books of the Hoppin & Koen firm.

Society for the Preservation of New England Antiquities — Codman Family Manuscripts Collection, Boston, Massachusetts. Codman letters and floor plans.

PART TWO

Existing Conditions, Problems of Repair, and Recommendations

JOHN G. WAITE ASSOCIATES,
ARCHITECTS, PLLC
ALBANY, NEW YORK

PRESENT-DAY PHOTOGRAPHS
BY JONAS DOVYDENAS

Existing Conditions, Problems of Repair, and Recommendations

This recording of the exterior and interior existing conditions and related problems of repair was carried out in 1986-87. All of the information reflects the situation at that time. More current information has been appended to some of the descriptions to reflect certain significant changes made since that date.

Exterior Problems of Repair

The exterior of The Mount is very deteriorated due to the modest quality of its original construction and decades of neglect, which would have affected even the most permanent building. Virtually all of the exterior components require either substantial conservation or complete rebuilding or replacement. The highest priority is the stabilization and restoration of the exterior building fabric to make the house impervious to weather and structurally sound.

MAIN ROOF

The main roof was repaired in the decade prior to 1987. That work included replacement of some damaged slates and the installation of new copper flashings. Although recently installed, the copper has been scoured and eroded by microscopic particles of slate washing over it. This scouring has prevented the formation of a protective patination normal to the oxidation of copper; the soft, unprotected copper will eventually erode, allowing water to penetrate the most vulnerable roof areas near gutters and downspouts.

Some of the new flashings, as well as the copper flat-seam roof at the upper level, have been soldered together using excessive amounts of solder. These joints will quickly fail, as the solder expands and contracts at a rate different from that of copper, causing the joints between the metal pans to separate.

A number of slates are cracked or broken. Others have slipped out of position because of nail failures.

The original built-in roof gutters have been relined with pans of copper soldered together. The excessive expansion and contraction of the metal sheets will cause the joints to separate. When enough joints fail, the entire gutter will need to be replaced, since it is very difficult to make long-lasting repairs to the broken joints.

The existing ferrous-metal ridge flashings have not been repaired in many years. The steel is badly rusted in places, and there has been an almost complete

FIG. 89 *The Mount today, west elevation.* (JGW)

failure of the protective paint coating. Many of the fastenings have failed, and a number of flashings are loose. The new copper flashings overlap the steel in many areas, resulting in additional damage and electrolytic or galvanic corrosion between the two metals.

The chimney and dormer flashings have broken down in places; they need to be repaired or replaced. In some areas there are no cap flashings. Where this occurs, the details need to be redesigned so that effective, two-part flashings are installed.

Many of the copper leaders are broken and/or no longer connected with the original below-grade drainage system, damaging portions of the walls and terrace by conducting water onto, rather than away from, the building.

DORMERS

The original wood dormers are badly in need of repair. The paint is badly weathered, and much of the wood has decayed; the sills are especially deteriorated. All deteriorated paint needs to be removed and the decayed wood treated with consolidants before repainting.

CHIMNEYS

The stucco coating on the chimneys has failed in many locations. Repairs have been made with Portland cement, a non-compatible material, compounding the problems. In some areas the stucco is rust-stained from the iron chimney caps.

Even recently repaired flashings are in poor condition. The old sheet-steel base flashings are badly deteriorated and have not been painted in many years. The installation of copper cap flashings over the steel base flashings will result in galvanic corrosion, which will eventually destroy these flashings. Some of the chimneys retain their original cast-iron caps; others have been removed, and one has been covered with cement stucco.

Photographic evidence indicates that a chimney was removed from the southeast corner of the mansion in July 1979. This chimney was constructed of wood framing with a stucco finish and was a decorative, non-active chimney. There are several other chimneys on the house that are decorative and non-active. This important architectural feature should be restored to its original appearance.

FLAT ROOF

The recently repaired flat roof over the south wing consists of an asphalt sheet material. The roofing has buckled, and some of the joints have opened. The damaged roofing needs to be removed and replaced by an elastomeric membrane roof. The edge flashings are oversized and do not replicate the appearance of the original.

Early photographs record a now-missing wood parapet wall at the outer edge of the roof. This important decorative architectural feature should be restored to its original appearance.

CUPOLA ROOF

The original flat-seam terne-plate roof on the dome has been replaced by a standing-seam copper roof. The new roof has a different appearance from the

FIG. 90 *The cupola on the roof of the mansion is listing, and structural repairs and wood stabilization are necessary.* (JD)

FIG. 91 *The Mount today, east elevation.* (JGW)

189

FIG. 92 *Deterioration and staining of stucco on the east elevation outside the east guest room, caused by a steel fire escape. Some shutters are missing.* (JD)

FIG. 93 *Wall deterioration and failing gutter system on the east elevation beside the south "blind" French door of the drawing room.* (JD)

FIG. 94 *A section of deteriorated cornice on the west elevation. Also evident is deterioration of the chimney, dormer, window frame, and failed gutter/leader system.* (JD)

FIG. 95 *The original oval window in the pediment on the east elevation needs to be replicated using pieces of the original window.* (JD)

original, and the use of copper sheets adjacent to the iron finial will result in electrolytic corrosion because of the dissimilar metals. The sill base flashings of the cupola are of lead-coated copper.

The sheet-copper roof on the cupola has buckled due to the excessively large-sized pans that were used; the edges of the sheet-metal roofing are lifting at the base of the dome.

The filigree iron dome-like finial that covers the chimney flue should be cleaned of rust and pollutants and then primed and painted.

When this work is done, the weather vane should be checked for stability and repaired.

LIGHTNING ARREST SYSTEM

The existing lightning system has become detached from the building in many locations. The entire system should be checked by a certified lightning-rod installer.

SKYLIGHT

The original steel-and-glass skylight is badly deteriorated. It must be restored by removing the rust and stabilizing the steel framework, replacing the damaged glass, installing new flashings, and reputtying and painting.

WALLS

The exterior walls were originally coated with a lime-and-cement stucco, which gave the building a monolithic appearance. Stone quoins were simulated in this material. The stucco has been damaged by water leaks from the cornice and downspouts, as well as by normal weathering. In many locations, the stucco has disintegrated or spalled, exposing the back-up construction to the elements.

Where repairs have been made, Portland cement has been used, which is considerably harder, less porous, and less plastic than the original lime-and-cement mixture. The Portland cement patches have contributed to the further deterioration of the original stucco.

When the building was used as a school, four steel fire escapes were attached to the exterior walls. When two of these were removed, some of the steel supports were left embedded in the walls. These remnants have continued to rust, badly staining the stucco.

The stucco should be restored by removing all damaged material and raking out all of the cracks. The walls should be patched with a lime-and-cement mix that matches the original stucco in composition, porosity, texture, and color.

Deep-seated rust stains should be removed using chemical cleaning agents and poultices.

The stucco walls rest on a stone foundation of tooled white marble on the west facade and the same material as a water table on the terrace sides. This material needs to be cleaned and the joints repointed. The stone at the junction of the terrace and north and east facades is in a very deteriorated state.

CORNICES

The decorative wood cornices are badly deteriorated because of long-term leaks in the built-in gutters and decades of little or no maintenance. The wood cornices need to be cleaned of loose and deteriorated paint, then treated with epoxy consolidants and fillers. Missing elements should be reproduced in wood, exactly duplicating the original design.

WINDOWS

The windows need extensive consolidation and filling; the sills are in especially poor condition. The sash need to be removed so that they can be repaired or rebuilt. Missing or badly damaged elements, such as parting strips, need to be replaced.

Broken panes need to be replaced with new glass and all of the lights reputtied. Metal weatherstripping should be installed.

The missing sash should be restored to the oval window opening in the east pediment.

Most of the original blinds (shutters) need extensive stabilization or rebuilding; missing blinds need to be replaced with reproduction units.

SERVICE PORCH

The internal structure of this wood porch should be investigated. All surfaces should be cleaned of loose and deteriorated paint. Missing elements should be reproduced in wood and deteriorated elements treated with epoxy consolidants and fillers. The column bases are in particularly poor condition.

TERRACE

The terrace consists of brick and marble paving on a concrete slab partially on-grade and partially over basement areas, where the concrete slab is supported by steel beams. The terrace is seriously deteriorated because of lack of maintenance and water penetration caused by the breakdown of the original downspout/underground drainage system. Many of the bricks have been displaced; in some areas bricks have been reset in Portland-cement mortar, which has caused additional problems.

Water has percolated through the concrete slab causing corrosion of the steel beams over the basement. Temporary supports have been installed to support the deteriorated structure.

The east and south sides of the terrace rest on a fieldstone foundation wall. Portions of the wall need to be repointed or rebuilt because of moisture damage. Sections of the south wall have been rebuilt with Portland-cement mortar, which is both physically incompatible with the original construction mortar and visually inappropriate.

The perimeter of the terrace is defined by a marble and cast-stone balustrade with a stairway to the garden on the east side. The rails and balusters are generally in poor condition. Many of the joints of the stone handrail and base are open and exposed to water penetration.

Freezing and thawing of water have broken open the cast-stone elements, exposing the steel reinforcing rods. As the rods rusted and expanded, further damage occurred.

Extensive work is required to stabilize and repair the terrace. All of the paving must be removed and the slab either consolidated or replaced. The underground drainage system must be made operational.

FIG. 96 *The four columns of the service porch were originally round, as this c. 1946-50 photograph confirms (see Fig. 71). The car has been identified as a 1946 Oldsmobile.* (FHS)

FIG. 97 *The brick paving in front of the drawing room doors has settled.* (JD)

FIG. 98 *A pier on the north end of the terrace, showing stucco finish that has fallen off, exposing the interior brick. Iron railings were installed in the late 1980s to stabilize the balusters.* (JD)

FIG. 99 *The terrace in the early 1980s, showing brick paving and the south section of the Palladian staircase. Note the hole in the center of the pier cap where a decorative obelisk was originally attached. Photograph by Warren Fowler.* (EWR)

FIG. 100   *The niche and lion's-head fountain in the early 1900s, showing the original details. Seated (from left): George Cabot (Bay) Lodge, Elizabeth (Bessie) Lodge, and Teddy Wharton. Photograph probably taken by Edith.* (BL)

FIG. 101   *The niche and lion's-head fountain today (compare to Fig. 44).* (JD)

Deteriorated steel support beams need to be replaced. An elastomeric membrane should be installed over the concrete slab and the brick paving restored.

Many of the balustrade components will have to be replaced with new cast-stone elements. Others can be stabilized using epoxy consolidants. The stone steps from the terrace to the garden need to be reset; individual treads require localized repairs.

Over the years, the niche has been simplified. The decorative elements of this important feature should be restored in stucco to their original configuration. The lion's-head fountain should be made operational.

FIG. 102   *Areas of cracked, loose, and missing brick on a section of the forecourt wall south of the "blind" door.* (JD)

The rusticated wall, which has been modified in detail, should be restored. (There is a fine Wharton-period photograph illustrating these missing details.)

The long-missing cast-stone obelisks and sculptures should be restored to the balustrade piers. These elements are shown in historical photographs.

FORECOURT WALL

Continuous exposure to weather and lack of maintenance have caused the deterioration of this brick wall. There are areas of cracked, loose, and missing brick, particularly at the base of the wall. All loose and flaking paint should be removed. Improper pointing should be removed, and the joints should be repointed using mortar that matches the original in composition. Deteriorated brick should be replaced. The wall should be repainted as determined by the paint analysis.

PAINT INVESTIGATION

The color and type of the original finishes should be determined for wood surfaces such as the cornice, windows, doors, and blinds, as well as for the stucco surfaces and such features as the filigree chimney cap on the cupola and the weather vane.

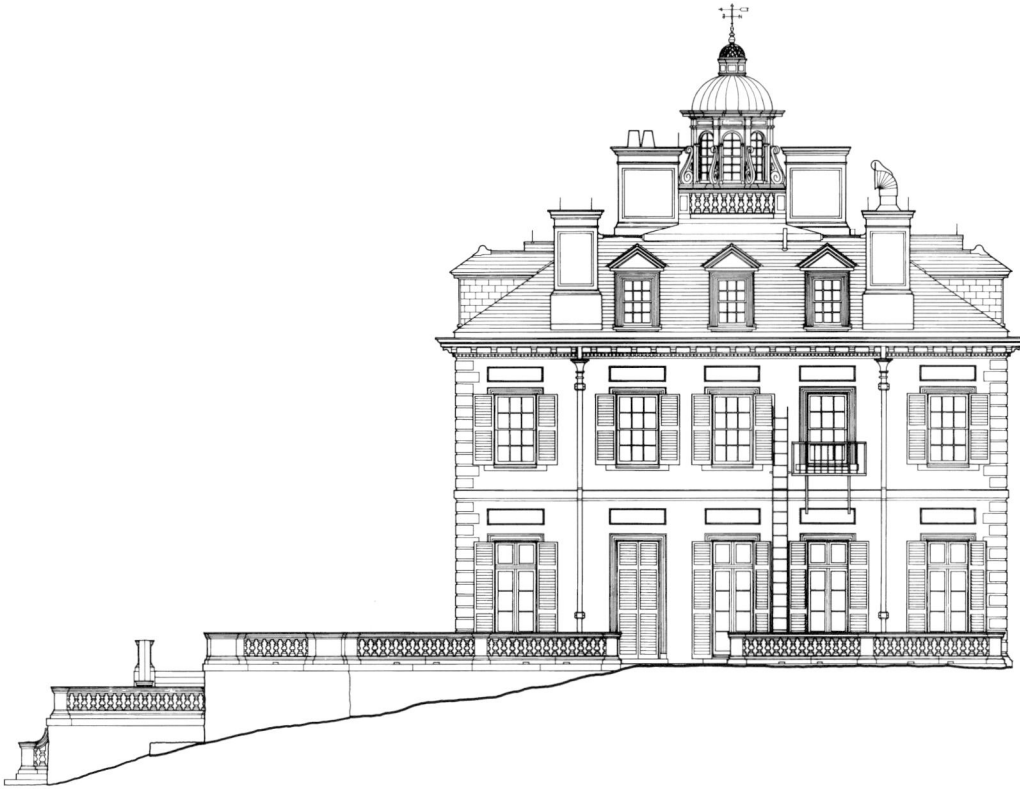

FIG. 103 *The Mount today, north elevation.* (JGW)

Interior Existing Conditions and Problems of Repair

The interiors of The Mount were examined and analyzed to document the existing conditions, determine where repairs are needed, and to provide a better understanding of the changes and modifications since initial construction. The primary focus has been the appearance and conditions that existed during the Whartons' occupancy.

The examination included visual investigation and description, measuring and drawing, and photographic documentation.

Although the building is occupied, many of the rooms are sparsely furnished. This facilitated the visual investigation. In a few rooms in the basement service areas there were so many objects that access was not possible. It is important that subsurface elements of the building exposed during future work be carefully documented to confirm or alter conclusions found in this study.

The results of a preliminary paint analysis of some of the important spaces were compared with the extant information concerning color schemes in 1904. In each instance, the current analysis confirmed those descriptions.

A complete paint analysis is recommended for both the exterior and interior. This information will permit accurate restoration and provide a better understanding of changes made by the various owners. This can be accomplished by comparing paint layers on various surfaces within a space, by the collection and study of relevant documentation, and by the study of early photographs. Only the gallery, library, drawing room, dining room, and Edith's boudoir are recorded in Wharton-period photographs, and it is only the library photographs that provide a sense of the entire room. To date, no Wharton-period photographs of the bedrooms or the service spaces have been found. Such spaces were rarely recorded by the camera.

An excellent illustrated article, "The Mount in Lenox," in the September 1904 issue of *Berkshire Resort Topics*, provides a brief tour of the house, commencing in the forecourt and moving from the entrance hall up into the formal rooms on the main floor. Edith Wharton's boudoir is also mentioned.

The investigation revealed that the Wharton-period interiors are remarkably intact; except for painted finishes and furnishings, the formal rooms retain their original character. Modifications occurred mostly in secondary areas of the house.

It is unfortunate that few original furnishings remain. The handful of objects that do survive include the drapery poles in the library, the large cabinet in a guest bathroom (203), and the wall

193

FIG. 104   *One of the doors to the terrace on the main floor, with original cremone bolts from Sterlin in Paris.* (JD)

FIG. 105   *Settling of the original terrazzo floor and its marble border to the right of the mantel in the dining room.* (JD)

FIG. 106   *The failing gutter/ leader system outside Edith Wharton's library, which has caused deterioration of both the stucco exterior and the brick terrace.* (JD)

mirrors in the bathrooms (212 and 214). Although none of these objects is intrinsically valuable, the fact that they survive makes them important.

Surviving decorative elements include the various lighting devices, primarily wall brackets, and the very fine door and window hardware. The beautifully detailed ormolu hardware, including box locks, knobs, levers, cremone bolts, and the two missing finials from the wrought-iron stair balustrades, was manufactured by Sterlin, located at 39 rue de Richelieu, Paris. These fittings are stamped with the trademark "ST." The supplier was probably located in New York City but remains unknown.

A set of 1901 drawings by Hoppin & Koen survives, including plans of the four floors and the roof, four exterior elevations, and two sections. Unfortunately, they do not record the house exactly as constructed. Some details differ significantly, for example, a loggia across the front of the main floor gallery and the arrangements of Edith's bedroom suite.

The drawings seem to record accurately the usage of rooms and the locations of lighting fixtures, heating devices, and plumbing fixtures. Some materials are also recorded. The room descriptions in this report note differences between the actual plan of the space and the Hoppin & Koen plans. Additional surviving Hoppin & Koen drawings delineate an elaborate scheme for the forecourt and two large pavilions at the corners of the terrace.

In general, similar problems of repair are found in each room throughout the house. Some problems can be blamed on the poor construction and design deficiencies. These problems are most noticeable in the floor settlement occurring in the primary rooms of the main floor, the drawing room, and the dining room, as well as the marble floors of the second-floor bathrooms. This also includes the water damage to the rooms beneath the terrace.

Roof and gutter leaks and general deterioration are caused by the lack of adequate maintenance. Neglected plumbing has also been the cause of extensive damage to interior finishes.

Further problems can be attributed to many years of institutional use. The wear and tear on the doors, hardware, and various surfaces is very apparent.

Modifications made by the various owners can also be looked upon as problems. The insertion of partitions and the removal of original finishes and details have resulted in damage to the house. All of these changes should be reversed so that The Mount, as Edith Wharton knew it, can be better understood and fully appreciated.

GROUND FLOOR

Room G-1 Entrance Hall

This inviting room, with its cool tile floor, low-vaulted plaster ceiling, mirrors, and formerly the sound of running water in the marble fountain, served as an introduction to the house. Remarkably, all original architectural finishes survive in relatively good condition, although the focal point, the original bronze statue of Pan that ornamented the fountain, was removed in the 1970s. It is on loan to the Berkshire Museum in Pittsfield.

Restoration will include minor repairs to the various surfaces, the reinstallation of the statue of Pan, and the restoration of the fountain. If its original appearance can be determined, the lighting should also be restored.

FLOOR: Original 9-inch-by-9-inch quarry tiles laid in a simple grid pattern. The tiles are well preserved and require only regular maintenance.

WALLS: The original wall surfaces are of ornamental plaster on wood lath arranged in various architectural forms including pilasters, recessed panels, relief surfaces, and various moldings. A shallow plaster niche is centered in the east partition. The wall panels include raised surfaces molded to simulate falling water. This detail reinforces the hall's grotto-like character. The wall surfaces are in good condition, with only minor hairline cracks and some loose paint.

CEILING: The original shallow vault is divided into three bays by two broad shallow ribs and is formed of plaster on lath. The surface is plain. There are several areas of cracked plaster and faulty patches. After adequate plaster repairs are made, the surfaces should be painted in their original colors.

CORNICE: Original, continuous molded plaster entablature composed of a plain frieze and unornamented cornice. This feature pushes forward above the door and window openings and above the pilasters and niche. There are minor breaks along the top edge of the cornice and several large vertical cracks. Once these damaged areas are repaired, the entablature should be painted in the original color.

BASEBOARD: The original narrow base is formed of verde antique marble and extends around the room. It is generally in good condition, although two plinth blocks are missing under the door and window surrounds in the southeast corner.

DOORS: There are three original openings; all of the original doors survive in good condition and in situ.

G1-1: Pair of oak entry doors, each leaf with four panels. The original decorative ormolu hardware

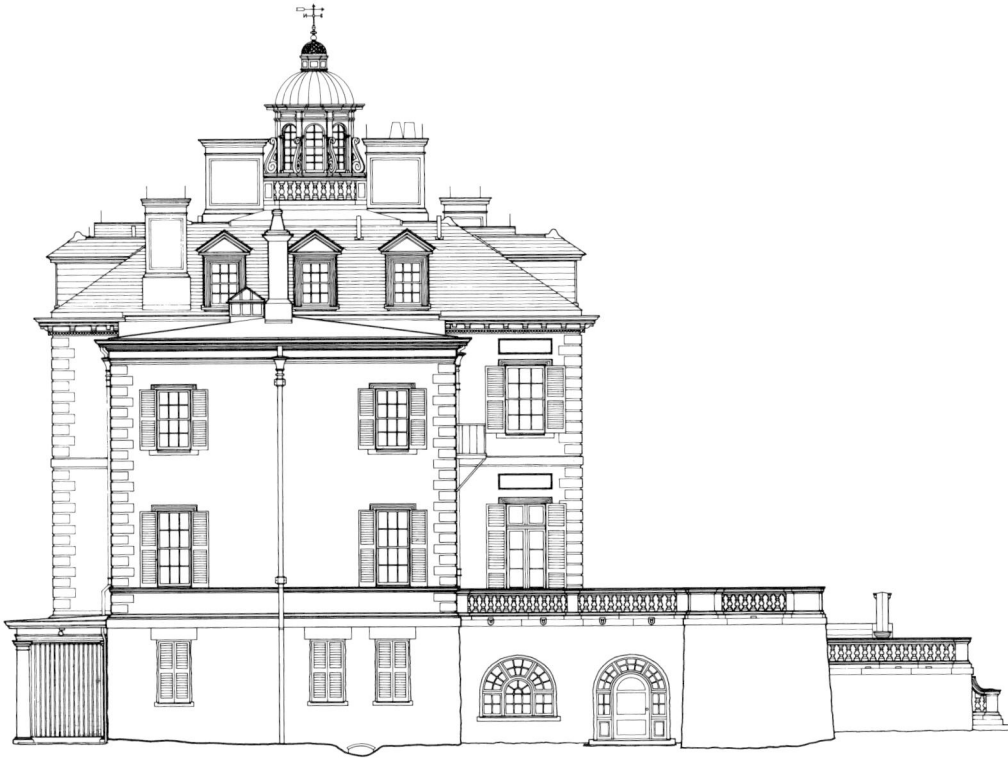

FIG. 107 *The Mount today, south elevation.* (JGW)

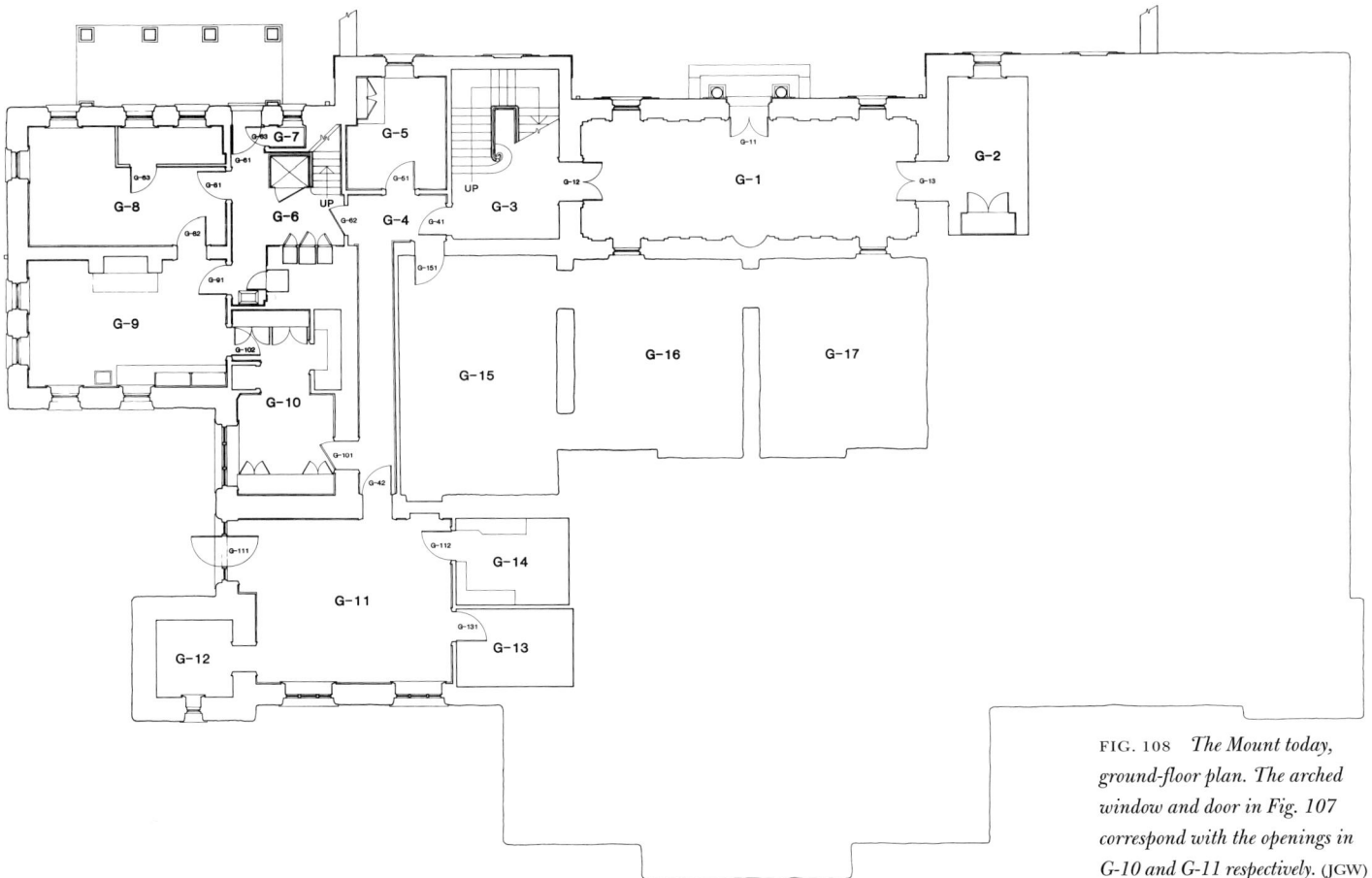

FIG. 108 *The Mount today, ground-floor plan. The arched window and door in Fig. 107 correspond with the openings in G-10 and G-11 respectively.* (JGW)

includes hinges, vertical slide bolts, and locks. The lefthand lock and knob are missing.

The doors should be cleaned and refinished. The hardware should be cleaned and the missing rim lock restored. The later bolt and chain latch should be removed and, if necessary, more appropriate models should be substituted.

G1-2: Pair of painted wood doors, each leaf with three clear glass lights above a raised recessed panel. The bottom of the inner stile of the left leaf is split. The molded wood trim rests on marble blocks; the left one is missing, the other is loose. Original hardware survives, including the ornate ormolu hinges, rim locks, and slide bolts. One hinge-pin cover is missing. The door should be repaired, the hardware should be cleaned, and the missing elements should be restored.

G1-3: Pair of painted wood doors, each leaf with three mirror-glass panels above a raised recessed panel.

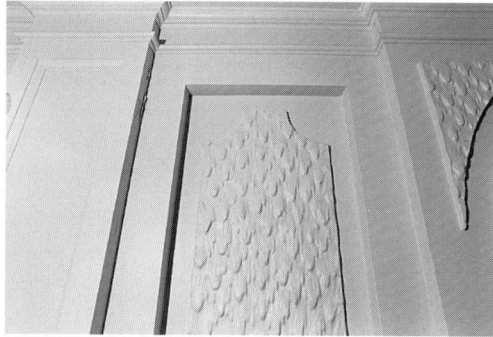

FIG. 109   *The plaster walls of the entrance hall have a pattern that simulates falling water.* (JD)

WINDOWS: There are four original window openings. Two of these are internal and open into basement rooms G16 and 17. The two windows in the west wall open to the forecourt and feature six-over-six double-hung sash secured with thumb latches.

Two identical sash are located in the east wall; both are filled with mirror glass.

HEATING: Original cast-iron radiator situated behind the grille below the southeast internal window. The wood cover is deteriorated, and the marble base is loose. The cabinetry and base should be repaired, and this should remain the location of the heat source when the system is renewed.

LIGHTING: The two silver-plated incandescent wall brackets are not original. A c. 1942 photograph illustrates two marble pedestals supporting bronze and porcelain electrified candelabra. They were placed next to the east wall in the same relative positions as the current fixtures. These pedestal fixtures may be original. There is no evidence for a suspended ceiling fixture, and the ceiling is too low to accommodate one.

EQUIPMENT: The electrical switches are of various periods; the push-button type are the earliest and possibly the originals. A recently installed thermostat is located in the reveal of the northeast interior window.

FIG. 110   *The entrance hall, looking south into the staircase hall, 1985 (compare to Fig. 49).* (EWR)

OTHER FEATURES: The original white marble fountain base and bowl is still situated in the niche. There is evidence of wiring for a light. There is old BX electrical cable in the wall behind the fountain. The statue of Pan has been removed.

PAINT INVESTIGATION: A careful analysis should be made of all painted surfaces to determine the original color scheme and finish.

RESTORATION PROGRAM: The entrance hall and adjoining public areas should be restored to the Wharton period, as they are the first spaces seen by a visitor and introduce the other important rooms.

The tile floor should be cleaned and maintained. All plaster surfaces should be repaired. The cornice has several damaged areas. The two missing marble plinth blocks need to be found or replicated and reinstalled. All the woodwork, including the doors, should be repaired.

Hardware should be cleaned and made operable and the missing lock and knob restored to door G1-1. The existing lighting is not original, and the elaborate pedestal fixtures shown in the 1942 photograph may not date from the Wharton period. If the pedestal fixtures can be found, they should be restored to their positions. The marble fountain should be fully restored and the statue of Pan, or an exact reproduction, placed in its proper position. All original finishes should be restored.

Room G-2 Gift Shop

Now the gift shop, this small room is described as the coat room on the Hoppin & Koen floor plan and as the cloak room on the 1940 Van Anda floor plan included with the Application for Abatement of Tax on Real Estate. If the gift shop is moved to larger quarters, this room should be restored to its original function.

FLOOR: Recently applied wall-to-wall carpet probably covers the original quarry tile. The 1940 Van Anda survey refers to a tile floor. This surface should be uncovered, repaired, and cleaned.

WALLS: Painted canvas applied over furring strips. This surface is applied over vertical wood boards (visible on the east wall). There is a simple, low chair rail and evidence of coat-hook rails on the north and south wall surfaces approximately 5 feet 6 inches above the floor. The canvas surface, which may be original, is damaged with buckling and peeling paint.

The canvas should be carefully analyzed for original appearance.

CEILING: Wood boards, approximately 5 inches wide, running east-west, are covered with a deteriorated

coating of plaster and/or paint. There is evidence of a canvas covering, which would probably match the canvas on the wall surfaces.

The proximity of this room to the unexcavated crawl space to the east may have resulted in a moisture problem on the walls and ceiling.

The canvas should be restored to the ceiling surface, and the correct color replicated.

CORNICE: There is a narrow wood molding, located approximately 1 inch below the wood ceiling surface, which represents the level of the canvas ceiling.

BASEBOARD: Original plain low wood base.

DOORS: Original opening in the south wall.

G1-3: Pair of wood-paneled doors (mirror panels on the hall side) set in a deep reveal. Original hardware includes an ormolu lever handle, locks, and hinges. New brass slide bolts are applied to the east leaf to enable locking from the shop side.

WINDOWS: Original opening in the west wall with six-over-six double-hung sash set in a deep wood reveal and secured with a thumb latch. The wood sill is split.

HEATING: Single cast-iron hot-water radiator marked with the H.B. Smith logo. An awkwardly positioned feed pipe extends out from the east wall above the radiator. There is an original small ornamental grille above the baseboard on the north wall, probably for ventilation.

LIGHTING: The original lighting is unknown. Recently installed ceiling-mounted track lighting

FIG. 111 *The original coat room was converted into a book and gift shop by Edith Wharton Restoration in 1985. In the background is a large wood cabinet that may be original.* (EWR)

now provides illumination. Surface-mounted electrical cable enters the room through the heat-pipe hole in the east wall.

EQUIPMENT: Telephone wire attached to the baseboard along the north and west walls.

OTHER FEATURES: A possibly original large wood cabinet is set against the east wall and features a pair of paneled doors and a full cornice. The doors include original ormolu knobs and a recent slide bolt. The lefthand door leaf needs repair. Recently installed sales-shop counters, cabinets, and wall-mounted glass shelving now furnish this small room.

PAINT INVESTIGATION: A careful paint analysis should be made of all original surfaces to determine and restore the original color scheme. The existing canvas should be analyzed for any special finish.

RESTORATION PROGRAM: This room can again function as the coat room for visitors once the gift shop is moved to more spacious quarters. Appropriate secure storage units may be needed for visitors' valuables while they tour.

The original finish on the walls and ceiling, if canvas, should be restored.

The original tile floor should be cleaned and repaired after the carpet has been removed.

All woodwork should be repaired, including the split wood window sill.

The original lighting should be restored.

All phone wires should be removed.

All painted and finished surfaces should be restored to their original appearance.

Room G-3 Staircase Hall

This dramatic space houses the primary stairway ascending to the *piano nobile* (first floor). The room retains all of its original architectural character, including the elegantly detailed wrought-iron handrail of the stair.

FLOOR: The original oak parquet flooring is laid in a hexagonal pattern. The floor is in good condition and requires only proper maintenance. The floor is currently covered by wall-to-wall carpeting installed in 1991.

WALLS: Original plaster on lath in a bold, rusticated pattern. There are numerous cracks, chips, and areas of loose paint. The plaster is damaged next to the door leading into the service-wing hall.

CEILING: Original plaster on lath forms the ceiling and the underside of the staircase. Areas of cracking and loose paint on all surfaces.

CORNICE: Original plaster cornice. Several vertical cracks and areas of damaged plaster exist next to the stairwell opening.

BASEBOARD: Original verde antique marble base, which should be cleaned.

DOORS: Two original openings and doors, which provide access to the entrance hall and service hall.

WINDOWS: Natural light is provided by the window at the first-floor level.

HEATING: The original cast-iron hot-water radiator is concealed behind the iron grille set in the east wall. This should remain the location for a new heat source.

LIGHTING: What may be the original incandescent fixture consists of an opal glass globe (globe not original) suspended from a brass chain.

There are three recently installed metal-can spotlights mounted on the ceiling at the head of the stair soffit.

Original or early push-button electric switch on the south partition.

OTHER FEATURES: The original wood stairway ascends to the first floor in three runs. The continuous closed stringer supports an elaborately ornamented wrought-iron handrail. This rail spirals at the bottom newel above a broadly curving first tread. Treads and risers are now partially covered with a carpet runner. The stairway is in good condition except for a split bottom tread, loose crown molding on the first run of the baseboard, and the missing urn-like finial formerly ornamenting the top of the newel. This finial probably matched the one now missing from the second-floor stair, which is illustrated in an old Van Anda-period photograph. When repairs are made, these important features should be restored.

PAINT INVESTIGATION: A careful paint analysis should be made of all original surfaces to determine the original color scheme.

RESTORATION PROGRAM: The flooring remains in good condition, requiring only careful cleaning that will not damage the patina.

The plaster walls, cornice, and ceiling, including the underside of the stair carriage, require repair and patching.

The marble baseboard is in good condition but must be cleaned.

The woodwork is in good condition, but there is a loose panel molding on the door into the service hall. All hardware should be cleaned and made operable, and an appropriate knob should be restored to door G4-1.

The original ceiling light needs to be cleaned and rewired.

Less obvious emergency lighting should be installed. The historic ceiling fixture can be wired into an emergency system.

As part of the restoration of the stairway, the missing newel finial should be put back in place.

Room G-4 Service Hall

This hall is part of the service-corridor system that joins the various rooms in the service wing. Originally this space was continuous with corridor G-6.

FLOOR: Original poured concrete. Surface is scored in a grid pattern to duplicate the appearance of the marble floor in room G-10. The west portion is covered in green vinyl tile of recent date but now deteriorated.

WALLS: Original plaster on wood lath with beaded-board wood wainscot. Areas of cracked and loosened water-damaged plaster, particularly on the south wall of the narrow corridor leading to the former laundry room.

A recent gypsum-board partition and a doorway separate the hall from its continuation to the south, now referred to as hall G-6.

The moisture problem must be corrected prior to any repair of the plaster or wainscot.

CEILING: Original plaster on lath with a smooth painted finish. Plaster cracks and loose paint.

CORNICE: The plaster wall and ceiling surfaces meet at a right angle with no cornice molding.

BASEBOARD: Original 10-inch-high molded wood baseboard.

DOORS: There are five original openings leading from this corridor, each retaining the original door. A recent sixth opening and door now separate the corridor from its continuation (G-6).

G4-1: Original three-panel door and ormolu rim lock and hinges. The metal knob and black ceramic knob are not original. The door has a split stile and loose panel molding.

G4-2: Original paneled door with three panels on the laundry room side and five panels on the corridor side. The original butt hinges, knobs, and escutcheon plates are intact. A padlock has been added on the hall side.

Door openings G5-1, G10-1, and G15-1 are original and retain their trim. The deep-paneled reveal of door G15-1 has damaged and missing panels.

WINDOWS: There are no window openings in this hall.

HEATING: The only heat would come from the corridor's proximity to the boiler room.

FIG. 112 *Extensive water damage to the plaster of the south wall of the service hall reveals the wood lath beneath. The original beaded-board wood wainscot is visible at the bottom.* (JD)

LIGHTING: An original incandescent ceiling fixture survives in the east corridor, but the glass shade is missing. Additional lighting is provided by a recent plug-in fixture clipped to a pipe near the ceiling.

PLUMBING: Iron pipes of various periods run below the ceiling surface. The pipes form a grid upon which various materials are stored improperly.

PAINT INVESTIGATION: All surfaces should be investigated to determine the original finishes.

RESTORATION PROGRAM: All of the service spaces should be restored as much as possible to their original appearance. Service spaces are frequently considered unimportant in a restoration, but in reality a full understanding of the house and its occupants cannot be achieved without them.

The vinyl floor tiles should be removed and the original concrete surface restored.

All plaster surfaces need to be restored. There is extensive water damage to the south partition of the long corridor. The wood wainscot in this area must also be repaired. This work should be carried out only after all water penetration problems are resolved.

The door to the former laundry room (G4-2) is extensively damaged and must be restored. The paneled reveal of the door into the boiler room must also be repaired. The gypsum-board partition and doorway should be removed to restore the hall to its original length.

The original lighting fixture should be cleaned and rewired, and the missing shade restored. The recent lighting must be removed. Additional fixtures may be installed if they are sympathetic to the original.

All plumbing and other pipes and wiring should be inspected and repaired. Any unnecessary or unused non-original elements should be removed. The pipe grid near the ceiling should not be used as a storage area.

Original surface finishes should be restored.

Room G-5 *Mechanical Room*

The Hoppin & Koen floor plan labels this as the "Lamp Room," a designation that would not be unusual in a large nineteenth-century household. The Mount has always been electrified, but there was probably some use of oil lamps and, of course, candles for the dining room.

The surfaces in this small room are in a very deteriorated state. The original mechanism that operated the elevator is in the southeast corner. There is a dangerous mix of exposed electrical and telephone wiring and leaking water pipes in this room.

FLOOR: Original smooth-finished poured concrete. The deteriorated portion near the piping should be repaired.

WALLS: Original plaster on wood lath above and below a chair rail. The plaster is very deteriorated, and both plaster and lath are missing in some areas. Remaining plaster should be stabilized, and missing plaster and lath should be restored.

CEILING: Original plaster on wood lath with areas of cracking and fallen plaster above the window.

CORNICE: No cornice in this room.

BASEBOARD: No baseboard in this room.

DOORS: There is an original opening in the east wall.

G5-1: Original three-panel wood door with original hardware. A diagonal metal brace has been installed on the room side.

WINDOWS: Original opening with six-over-six double chain-hung wood sash. The molded wood trim surrounds a deep reveal. Several telephone junction boxes should be removed from their position in this opening.

HEATING: An original iron-pipe radiator is attached to the ceiling above the window.

LIGHTING: A ceramic fixture wired to BX electrical cable is mounted on the ceiling.

PLUMBING: An array of pipes is located just below the ceiling. A cast-iron drain pipe is partially embedded in the west wall and extends down into the concrete floor.

EQUIPMENT: Remnants of the original elevator mechanism. Extensive telephone wiring is located on the south wall. Recently installed electrical service boxes are attached to the closet enclosure.

OTHER FEATURES: A bi-level cupboard is situated in the southwest corner. Access to the lower brick portion is through a pair of paneled wood doors secured by a padlock. The smaller upper cupboard is enclosed by beaded-board doors.

PAINT INVESTIGATION: All surfaces should be investigated to determine the original finishes.

RESTORATION PROGRAM: This room was always minimally finished. There apparently was never a baseboard.

All surfaces should be restored to their original appearance.

The water leaks should be repaired prior to any restoration work.

The deteriorated portion of the concrete floor needs repair, and all damaged plaster surfaces should be restored. In some areas the wood lath is missing.

The wood door should be repaired so that the temporary brace can be removed.

All non-original non-functioning mechanical equipment should be removed.

If the current electrical panels and telephone equipment are to remain in this space, they should be installed in a less intrusive manner.

The original elevator mechanism should be preserved in place.

All surfaces should have their original finishes restored.

Room G-6 *Stair/Elevator Hall*

This hall was formerly a continuation of the corridor (G-4) beyond the recent north partition. Several important original features survive here, including the service stairway and elevator and the large built-in ice box.

FLOOR: The original poured concrete floor is covered in recent green vinyl tile, which is now deteriorated.

WALLS: Original plaster on wood lath with a high beaded-board wood wainscot. There are areas of cracked and loose plaster and faulty repairs.

CEILING: The original plaster ceiling has been replaced or covered with gypsum board. Water penetration has caused the gypsum to deteriorate, resulting in open joints and exposed nails.

CORNICE: No cornice in this room.

BASEBOARD: Original 10-inch-high molded wood baseboard.

DOORS: There are four original door openings. The fifth opening, a recent addition, separates the hall from its north extension.

G6-1: This is the original service entrance door, which is arranged with three panels. Above the openings there is a three-light transom. The original hinges survive, but the door knobs are missing. The door now operates with recently installed hand grips, a closer, and a dead bolt.

G6-2: Original three-panel door and hardware. The padlock is a recent addition.

G6-3: Recent solid flush door with contemporary hardware. This door and opening should be removed.

WINDOWS: Natural light enters this hall from the first-floor window located on the service stair. This opening retains the original six-over-six double-hung sash.

HEATING: No heating provided.

LIGHTING: A single original incandescent wall bracket is attached to the corner of the ice box. The shade is missing. The incandescent ceiling fixture with a glass "school house" shade is a later addition.

PLUMBING: An original iron utility sink with a stone back splash and original faucet is still in use next to the east partition.

EQUIPMENT: Original built-in ice box with six paneled-wood doors secured with brass latches and hinges. Additional pairs of doors are located on the side of the unit. A refrigerator was designated on the Hoppin & Koen floor plan.

OTHER FEATURES: Original wood service stairway, composed of seven risers to the first landing, seven to the second, and three risers to the first floor, arranged around an open well, which houses the elevator. The treads are very worn. The wood handrail attached to the wainscot is a later addition.

Original service elevator, manufactured by the Otis Elevator Company (600-pound capacity) and enclosed in a wire-mesh cage. The steel cab features a window (broken wire glass) and a rosette in the ceiling for an incandescent light fixture.

PAINT INVESTIGATION: All surfaces should be investigated to determine the original finishes.

RESTORATION PROGRAM: The vinyl floor tiles should be removed and the original concrete surface restored. All plaster surfaces need to be repaired. The gypsum-board ceiling should be replaced with plaster.

Damaged areas of the wood wainscot should be repaired.

The original exterior door should be repaired and the proper hardware installed.

The original light fixture should be cleaned and rewired and an appropriate shade installed. The later ceiling fixture could be retained and should be rewired.

All damaged portions of the original elevator should be repaired and made operational only if this does not destroy the original character of the artifact.

The original finishes should be restored.

FIG. 113 *The original built-in ice box on the east wall of the service hall opposite the service elevator.* (JD)

Room G-7 Toilet Room

This very small toilet room is located under the second run of the service stairs and is now used as a closet. Original surviving finishes include the white marble floor, plaster walls and ceiling, and the beaded-board wainscot. The original toilet has been removed. The window retains the original six-over-six double-hung sash.

PAINT INVESTIGATION: All surfaces should be analyzed to determine the original finishes.

RESTORATION PROGRAM: All surviving original surfaces should be repaired and restored to their original appearance.

Room G-8 Servants' Dining Room

Formerly the servants' dining room, this space has most recently functioned as a combination ticket office and dressing room for Shakespeare & Company. Though in poor condition, most of the original finishes survive.

FLOOR: Green vinyl tile of recent origin, which is loose and deteriorated from water penetration, laid over original wood flooring.

WALLS: Original plaster on wood lath with a high beaded-board wood wainscot. Evidence of some loose and cracked plaster.

CEILING: The original plaster-on-wood lath ceiling is very deteriorated with some areas of fallen plaster. It is now covered by a recent suspended metal frame-and-panel ceiling. The original ceiling should be restored.

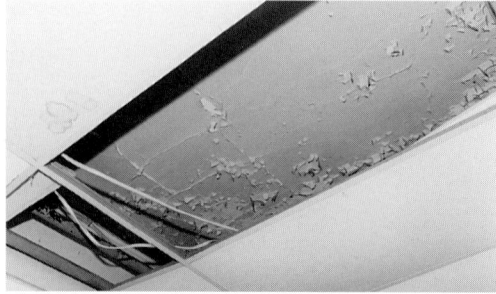

CORNICE: Original narrow wood picture molding just below the plaster ceiling.

BASEBOARD: Original 10-inch-high molded wood baseboard.

DOORS: There are two original door openings.

G8-1: Original three-panel wood door with all hardware intact. The lock rail, on the room side, is in a very deteriorated condition.

G8-2: Original three-panel wood door with all hardware intact. Metal brace repair at top.

WINDOWS: There are four original openings, which retain their six-over-six double-hung sash. Two of the openings are now enclosed by the recently constructed ticket booth.

HEATING: Original large cast-iron radiator placed below the south window.

LIGHTING: The original ceiling fixture has been replaced with a fluorescent fixture mounted in the suspended ceiling. The Hoppin & Koen floor plan indicates a single centrally placed ceiling fixture.

PLUMBING: Recent copper pipes for the first-floor bathroom are located above the suspended ceiling.

OTHER FEATURES: Recent plywood enclosure in the northwest corner, which housed the ticket booth.

PAINT INVESTIGATION: All surfaces should be analyzed to determine the original finishes.

RESTORATION PROGRAM: Regardless of future use, all surfaces should be restored to their original appearance. The tile flooring should be removed so that the original wood flooring can be repaired and restored.

All plaster surfaces need to be repaired. This includes the deteriorated plaster ceiling now covered by the suspended ceiling, which must be removed.

Both doors need to be repaired, and all hardware should be cleaned and made operable.

If the bathroom on the floor above is to remain in use, then the recently installed exposed pipes should be concealed.

An appropriate incandescent ceiling fixture should replace the fluorescent fixture.

Original finishes should be restored.

Room G-9 Dressing Room (Original Kitchen)

This large well-lit room is the original kitchen used by the Whartons and the Shattucks. The kitchen was moved to the first floor for the Van Andas by 1940. This room currently serves as a dressing room for Shakespeare & Company. The Hoppin & Koen floor plan illustrates the kitchen as it remains today, including the locations of the sink, counter, and cupboards.

FLOOR: Original narrow tongue-and-groove wood flooring, which runs north-south. Very worn with traces of a green paint.

WALLS: Original plaster on wood lath and high beaded-board wainscot. Areas of cracked, deteriorated, and missing plaster.

CEILING: Original plaster on wood lath. Water has damaged the plaster and paint in the northeast corner.

CORNICE: No cornice.

BASEBOARD: Original 10-inch-high molded-wood baseboard.

DOORS: There are three original door openings.

G9-1: Original three-panel wood door with all hardware intact except for missing knobs. Top rail and stile reinforced with a T-bracket.

WINDOWS: Four original window openings retain the original six-over-six double chain-hung sash secured with thumb latches.

HEATING: Original cast-iron radiator placed below the south windows.

LIGHTING: Evidence of an original incandescent ceiling fixture and two later ceiling fixtures. These have been replaced by three suspended fluorescent fixtures.

PLUMBING: Exposed pipes near the ceiling in the northeast corner. Pipes of various periods suspended below the ceiling.

EQUIPMENT: The original kitchen sink is missing, replaced by an old small soapstone utility sink removed from another location.

Recently installed ventilation fan placed above the stove recess.

Two early, possibly original, electric bells attached to the north wall.

OTHER FEATURES: The projecting chimney mass centered on the west wall was the location of the original cooking stove. Recess and chimney breast faced with glazed white brick. Opening spanned with a massive gray stone lintel. There is a gray stone hearth set into the floor. The lower portion of the recess is now filled with a painted wood insert.

FIG. 115 *The original kitchen after conversion by the Foxhollow School into a chemistry lab, c. 1944. This view of the southwest corner shows a portion of the original cooking stove and the glazed white brick on the chimney mass. Photograph by Joseph W. Overlock (see also Fig. 79).* (FHS)

The original painted wood cabinets and cupboards survive along the east wall. The cupboard doors are missing. The original countertop terminates in a very deteriorated wood drain board, which extended to the missing sink. An original marble backsplash is in place on the wall.

PAINT INVESTIGATION: All surfaces should be analyzed to determine the original finishes.

RESTORATION PROGRAM: The original kitchen is the most significant of the service spaces and should therefore be restored very carefully. This would include the installation of an appropriate stove and sink, if the appearance of the missing originals can be determined.

The sink was probably the same or similar to the original extant sink upstairs in the former butler's pantry (108).

The wood flooring should be restored to its original finish.

All plaster surfaces should be repaired after all possibility of water penetration has been eliminated.

Door G9-1 needs repair, and the missing knobs should be restored.

The wood wainscot needs general repair. The white paint should be removed and the original varnished finish restored.

The missing doors to the upper cupboards need to be fabricated and installed.

Recently installed equipment should be removed, including the fan located above the stove recess. Original equipment, such as the electric bells on the north wall, should be conserved.

An appropriate incandescent fixture should replace the recent fluorescent fixture on the ceiling.

All surfaces should have their original finishes restored, including the varnished finish of the doors, trim, and wainscot.

Room G-10 Storeroom (Original Service Room and Scullery)

The former scullery and service room is located both within the confines of the house and under the terrace. This unusual location has resulted in severe deterioration and dangerous conditions. This room has several interesting features and merits restoration. The Hoppin & Koen floor plan shows a countertop instead of the closet in the northwest corner.

FLOOR: Original white marble tiles (14 inches by 14 inches) laid in a grid pattern. Cracked tiles indicate some settlement.

There is an original wood floor in the closet.

WALLS: Original plaster on wood lath and 54-inch-high beaded-board wood wainscot. Very deteriorated from water penetration.

203

Small vents near the ceiling (some retain original ornamental iron grilles) to allow ventilation between stone wall and plaster.

CEILING: Original plaster on wood lath. Plaster failure and deteriorated paint due to severe water penetration.

CORNICE: No cornice.

BASEBOARD: Original molded wood baseboard.

DOORS: There are three original door openings.

G10-1: Original three-panel wood door with hardware intact except for missing knob on the hall side.

G10-2: Original closet door with hardware removed.

G10-3: Original three-panel wood door with hardware intact.

WINDOWS: Single original large arched opening with six glazed sash in a radiating pattern. Remnants of frame for hinged inside screening. Deteriorated from water.

HEATING: Single original cast-iron radiator, rusted.

LIGHTING: One original incandescent ceiling fixture with opal glass shade suspended from a metal chain.

Later metal ceiling fixture, shade missing.

PLUMBING: Exposed pipes near ceiling, deteriorated and leaking.

Cast-iron leader pipe in the north wall. Wall deteriorated due to leaking pipe.

Underside of first-floor kitchen sink is visible in the deteriorated ceiling of the closet.

EQUIPMENT: Recently installed electrical box mounted on the wall. Dangerous wiring.

OTHER FEATURES: Original built-in wood cupboards, sink set in marble counter top, and marble backsplash.

The original dumbwaiter shaft projects from the south wall, now covered with gypsum board.

The original closet features wood flooring, plaster walls, and built-in shelves.

PAINT INVESTIGATION: All surfaces should be analyzed to determine the original finishes.

RESTORATION PROGRAM: Like the kitchen, this interesting space should be restored. Two important features are the marble counter with sink and the dumbwaiter shaft. These features are shown on the Hoppin & Koen floor plan.

Prior to any restoration work, serious water penetration from the terrace and from the damaged cast-iron leader in the north masonry wall must be corrected.

The plaster surfaces are very deteriorated and must be repaired.

The marble flooring shows slight settlement, possibly due to the long history of water penetration.

Woodwork repairs include work on the water-damaged window and frame and the fabrication of the missing closet door.

The dumbwaiter shaft needs to be repaired and reconstructed at first-floor level. It has not been determined if the cab is still in place in the shaft.

The original ceiling light fixture needs to be cleaned and rewired.

All original finishes should be restored.

Room G-11 Storage Room (Original Laundry)

The original laundry was formerly a very fine room featuring an elegant marble floor and large arched windows. Unfortunately, this interesting room has deteriorated severely due to water penetrating from the terrace above. The Hoppin & Koen floor plan includes four wash trays (tubs) in front of the windows in the east wall and a stove in the northwest corner. A stove was not actually placed in that position because it would have blocked the door into a storage room.

FLOOR: White marble and black slate tile floor arranged in a geometric pattern surrounded by a simple black slate border. The floor is very soiled, and several tiles are damaged, loose, or missing.

WALLS: Original plaster on metal lath and 54-inch-high wood beaded-board wainscot. All surfaces severely damaged from water penetration.

Small vents near ceiling (some retain original ornamental iron grilles) to provide ventilation of the wall cavity.

CEILING: Exposed brick jack-vaults with iron supports. The original flat plaster ceiling deteriorated and was removed.

FIG. 116 *Damaged and missing white marble and black slate tiles in the original floor of the laundry room.* (JD)

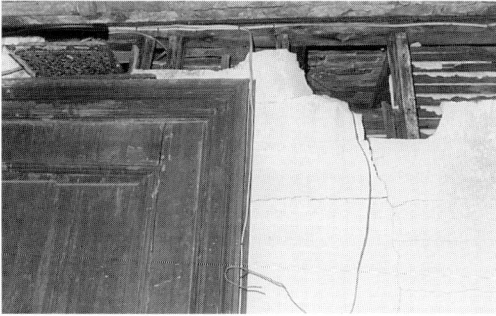

CORNICE: No evidence of a cornice.

BASEBOARD: Original 10-inch-high molded wood baseboard.

DOORS: Five original door openings.

G4-2: This opening retains its original three-panel door set in a deep-paneled reveal. Very deteriorated from water penetration.

G11-1: Original three-panel wood door with hardware. Keyhole escutcheon missing, recent padlock.

G11-2: Original door removed. Inner wood grille door to wine cellar.

G11-3: Exterior doorway centered in the arched window opening. Three-panel door with plywood panels. Inside screen door.

G12-1: Original three-panel door set in a deep-paneled reveal.

WINDOWS: Three original arched openings with glazed sash in a radiating pattern around a central casement sash. The opening in the south wall surrounds the exterior doorway.

HEATING: Not determined due to crowded condition of the room.

LIGHTING: Original incandescent wall bracket on the west wall. Two recent spotlights and a fluorescent ceiling fixture.

PLUMBING: Iron pipes below the ceiling surface. No accessible evidence for the original laundry fittings.

EQUIPMENT: Recently installed surface-mounted electrical cable and miscellaneous wiring.

OTHER FEATURES: Original or early wood shelf supported by iron brackets on the north wall. It should be preserved in place.

Recent storage racks.

PAINT INVESTIGATION: All surfaces should be analyzed to determine the original finishes.

RESTORATION PROGRAM: This interesting room warrants careful restoration. The large windows and the marble floor made this a very fine laundry room.

The most serious problem is the water penetration from the terrace above.

All plaster surfaces are severely damaged and must be repaired. The original flat plaster ceiling needs to be completely reconstructed. The iron-and-brick vault structure should be inspected for structural stability.

The flooring needs considerable repair; tiles are missing.

The wood wainscot is water damaged, and the finish is deteriorated.

Of the original doors, G4-2 must be completely rebuilt, and door G11-2 is missing and must be fabricated.

The exterior door and window opening in the south wall have been damaged by water (the damaged stone wall has been temporarily stabilized) and must be restored.

The original incandescent wall light must be cleaned and rewired.

Any additional lighting should be in keeping with the character of the room.

All exposed cable and wiring should be removed from the room. Any new wiring should be concealed.

The long-term restoration would include the reinstallation of original laundry fittings such as the tubs, three of which are located in the adjacent storage room (wine cellar).

All surfaces should have their original finishes restored.

FIG. 117 *Severely damaged plaster walls of the original laundry room and exposed brick jack-vaults located directly under the terrace are exposed in the upper half of the image. In the upper left corner an original ornamental iron grille above a door is falling away from its frame.* (JD)

FIG. 118 *The arch over the entrance (Door G11-3) to the laundry room has been supported until the terrace is restored.* (JD)

Room G-12 *Servants' Toilet/Storeroom*

The Hoppin & Koen floor plan designates this small square space as a storeroom, but a penciled correction notes it as a servants' toilet. The marble tile flooring continues into this space, and a small window in the east wall provides some natural light. The room was inaccessible at the time of the room investigations, but it is clear that the space suffers from considerable water damage like the laundry room. The original toilet has been removed.

PAINT INVESTIGATION: All surfaces should be analyzed to determine the original finishes.

RESTORATION PROGRAM: Of primary concern is the elimination of water penetration from the terrace.

All surfaces should be repaired and restored to their original condition.

Room G-13 *Closet/Storeroom*

The Hoppin & Koen floor plan designates this room and its neighbor (G-14) as a single large room called the trunk room, but it was constructed as two rooms. The 1940 Van Anda floor plan refers to this room as the wine closet. It probably functioned as such for the Whartons also.

This room has suffered severely from terrace-water penetration. Much of the plaster has fallen from the walls and ceiling.

PAINT INVESTIGATION: All surfaces should be analyzed to determine the original finishes.

RESTORATION PROGRAM: After the water penetration has been corrected, all surfaces should be restored to their original condition and finishes. The missing outer door (G11-2) should be found or fabricated and reinstalled.

Room G-14 *Closet/Storeroom*

The Hoppin & Koen floor plan designates this room and its neighbor (G-13) as a single large room called the trunk room. Actually, the storage space was constructed as two rooms. The 1940 Van Anda floor plan refers to this room as the basket closet. It now functions as a storeroom.

This room has suffered severely from terrace-water penetration. Much of the plaster has fallen from the walls and ceiling.

PAINT INVESTIGATION: All surfaces should be analyzed to determine the original finishes.

RESTORATION PROGRAM: After the water penetration problem has been corrected, all surfaces should be restored to their original condition and finishes.

Room G-15 *Boiler Room*

This room has maintained its original function. The Hoppin & Koen floor plan refers to this space as the furnace and coal room. The original furnace would have consumed a vast amount of coal, but the location of the storage bunker and the way the coal was delivered to it have not been determined. The 1940 Van Anda plan indicates that space G-16 was the fuel room.

Only minimal finishes are found in this large space directly beneath the dining room.

FLOOR: Poured concrete, cracked and deteriorated around the boiler. This floor may be original.

Raised concrete platform for the boiler.

Metal plates covering a trench west of the boiler.

WALLS: The north, east, and west walls are laid in irregular stone with brick at openings. Surfaces covered in whitewash.

The south wall is of rough plaster on wood lath with a small area of horizontal tongue-and-groove beaded board, which covers a former doorway into the hall.

CEILING: Original rough plaster on wood lath attached to the first-floor framing (which supports the terrazzo floor of the dining room).

The structure was exposed when recent supports were installed to reinforce the first floor. The supports are composed of beams (three 2-inch-by-11-inch members bolted together) supported on a series of hollow pipe columns. Three old, possibly original, 4-inch-diameter iron columns are still extant in adjacent positions.

CORNICE: No cornice.

BASEBOARD: No baseboard.

DOORS: There are three original functioning openings. An original opening in the east stone wall is now filled with concrete block. A former opening in the south partition is covered with horizontal boards.

G15-1: Recently installed flush metal fire door placed in the original wood frame opening with plain trim.

The two masonry openings in the north wall were never finished with doors or trim.

WINDOWS: There are no window openings although there is evidence for internal openings in the east wall, which formerly opened into room G-14.

HEATING: Heat supplied directly from the boiler.

LIGHTING: Single suspended (braided wire) incandescent fixture, which is old and possibly original.

PLUMBING: Large steel tank on pipe supports next to the boiler (possibly covered in asbestos).

Recently installed steel water tank labeled Extrol. Numerous water and heating pipes extending across the ceiling.

EQUIPMENT: Old oil tank located next to the east wall.

Oil-fired hot-water boiler labeled "The H.B. Smith Co. Inc."

RESTORATION PROGRAM: The immediate goal should be the removal of the heating apparatus and mechanical equipment from this room and room G-17 to an underground mechanical vault located outside the house.

The dining room floor structure should be investigated to insure its stability.

Room G-16 Storage Room (Former Fuel-Storage Area)

This roughly finished room was apparently used for coal storage. It now functions as a general storage room. The Hoppin & Koen floor plan shows this area as unexcavated, but penciled notations indicate the two openings in the south wall for access to this room.

The 1940 Van Anda plan labels this space "Fuel."

FLOOR: Poured concrete, probably original.

WALLS: Laid up in irregular stone with brick at openings. Surfaces covered in whitewash.

CEILING: The wood joists are covered in lath and rough-finished plaster.

Recently, four hollow-pipe columns and a built-up wood beam were installed to help support the ceiling joists, which in turn support the terrazzo floor of the drawing room.

CORNICE: No cornice.

BASEBOARD: No baseboard.

DOORS: Three original masonry openings, never including doors or trim.

WINDOWS: An opening in the west wall contains one of the mirror glass "windows" that ornament the east wall of the entrance hall.

HEATING: Some heat may be supplied by the radiator located in the west wall "window" niche.

LIGHTING: Single utilitarian wall-mounted porcelain fixture on the west wall.

PLUMBING: A 6-inch-diameter cast-iron soil pipe runs along the west wall and above the door on the south wall. It enters the ground in the southwest corner.

EQUIPMENT: An early fuse box (active) is attached to the north wall.

OTHER FEATURES: An old, possibly original, stud-and-horizontal-board enclosure is located in the northeast corner, finished in whitewash. Recently constructed plywood addition with access door.

RESTORATION PROGRAM: All original or early devices and equipment, such as wiring and fuse boxes, should be preserved in place in a non-functioning state.

The floor structure of the drawing room above should be investigated for stability.

Room G-17 Furnace Room

In 1939 the Van Andas installed a new hot-air furnace and air-conditioning plant in this room; the original system installed by the Whartons was housed here. The Hoppin & Koen plan labels this space as unexcavated but also shows a penciled-in circle, which may represent a furnace. This would have been the hot-air furnace that heated the main portion of the house. The room has always functioned as a utility space, with very few architectural finishes.

FLOOR: Poured concrete, probably original.

WALLS: Laid up in irregular stone with brick at openings. Surfaces covered in whitewash.

CEILINGS: Original first-floor wood framing with "defening," a type of early sound insulation, between the wood joints.

Later application of a fire-retardant asbestos board. Some of this has been removed above the furnace. Recently, four hollow-pipe columns and a wood built-up beam were installed to help support the ceiling joists and terrazzo floor of the drawing room.

CORNICE: No cornice.

BASEBOARD: No baseboard.

DOORS: One original opening into room G-16; it never included a door or trim.

There is a small opening in the north wall, which provides access to the crawlspace beneath the library.

WINDOWS: An opening in the west wall, spanned with a wood lintel, contains one of the mirror-glass "windows" that ornament the east wall of the entrance hall. The backside of the sash is covered in horizontal beaded board.

HEATING: Heat supplied directly from the furnace.

LIGHTING: Single utilitarian wall-mounted porcelain fixture with spotlight.

PLUMBING: A 6-inch-diameter cast-iron soil pipe runs along the west wall.

EQUIPMENT: A recently installed Magic Chef oil-fired forced-hot-air furnace replaced an earlier model. Various overhead sheet metal ducts contemporary with the furnace.

A mix of pipes and telephone cables covers the ceiling.

RESTORATION PROGRAM: The furnace should be removed to an isolated location such as an underground bunker outside of the house.

The floor structure and foundation of the drawing room should be investigated for stability.

First Floor (Main Floor)

Room 101 Staircase Hall

This elegant stairway is the primary access from the ground-floor entrance hall to the important rooms on the first floor. The hall retains its original architectural character with the exception of the chandelier, which is of a later date. A Wharton-period photograph of the gallery (102) looking south shows part of this hall, including the edge of a chandelier, which appears to be the same as the two fixtures used in the gallery at that time. All three of these fixtures have been replaced.

FLOOR: Original gray-and-white terrazzo with a white marble border.

WALLS: Original plaster on lath with applied moldings forming panels. There is a wood-paneled area above the arched door openings. Two large antique oil paintings on canvas are framed by wood moldings and topped by rectangular plaster panels with classically detailed ornament. These works of art need conservation. Evidence of plaster cracking with significant damage in the northeast and southeast corners and above the door into the dining room.

CEILING: Original smooth plaster on lath. Large gypsum board patch damaged by water in the southwest sector.

CORNICE: Original plaster cornice (run in place) with cracks and small areas of damage. Severely water damaged above the painting on the south wall.

BASEBOARD: Original low flat marble base extends around the floor. A wooden base extends around the stairwell.

DOORS: Three original openings. The arched opening in the north wall never included doors.

The molded wood trim of each opening terminates on small marble plinth blocks. The west plinth block is cracked and broken.

FIG. 119 *The Mount today, first-floor plan.* (JGW)

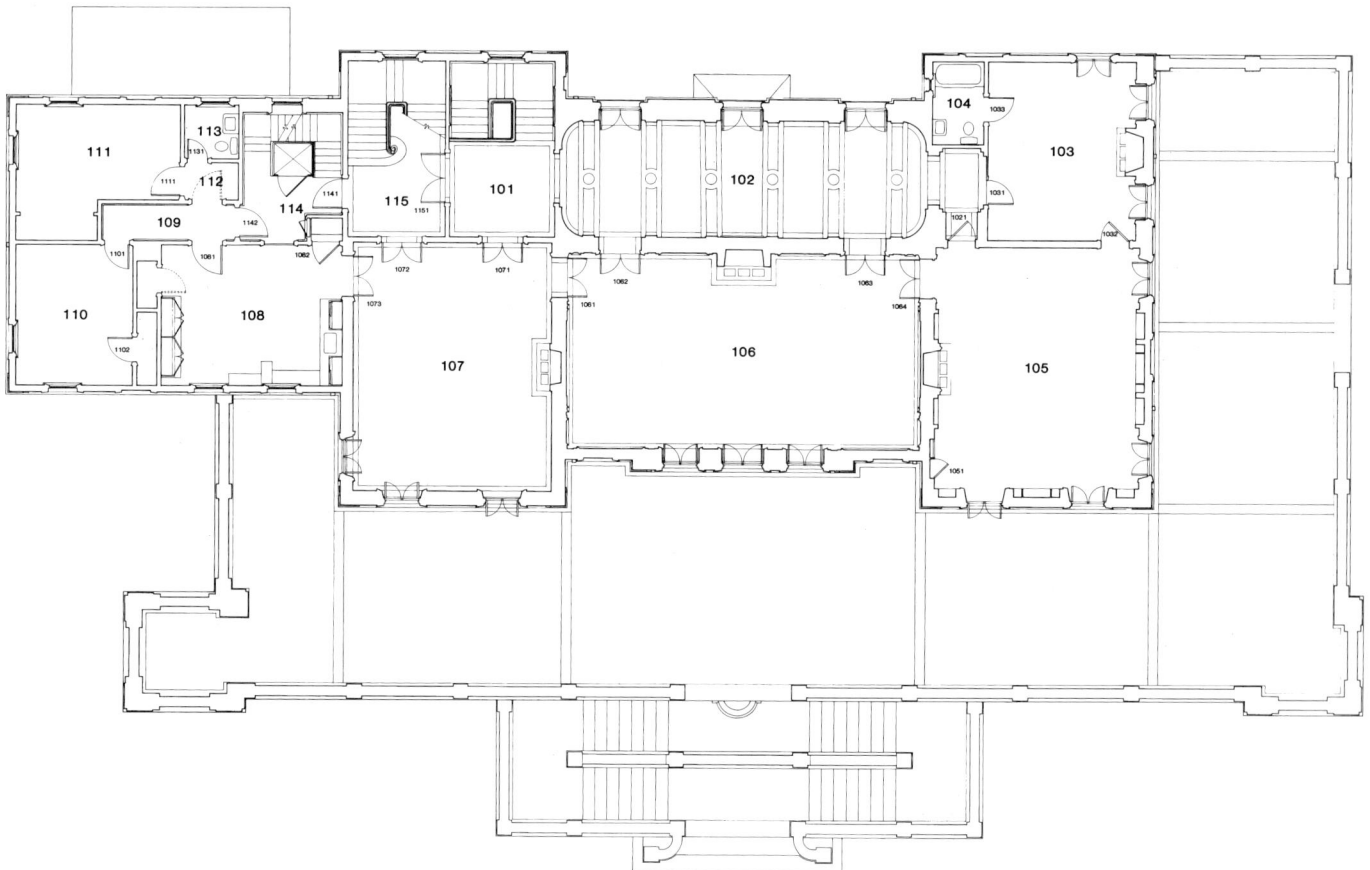

1151: Original pair of paneled and glazed wood doors with semicircular wood-and-glass transom above. Original ormolu hardware.

1071: Original pair of wood doors, each leaf with three panels. Original ormolu hardware.

WINDOWS: Original opening in the west wall. The sash consists of a pair of inward-opening wood casements topped by a fixed transom with two lights. Full wood architrave and paneled apron.

Original ormolu cremone bolt. The ormolu hinges have been painted white.

HEATING: No heating at this level.

LIGHTING: The original chain-suspended incandescent crystal chandelier is partially visible in a Wharton-period photograph of the gallery (102). The current five-arm glass incandescent fixture matches those now in the gallery and is illustrated in a photograph taken in the Van Anda period.

OTHER FEATURES: The original elegant wood staircase ascends from the ground floor and terminates in this hall. The ornate wrought-iron handrail terminates at the south wall and rests on a low wood base.

PAINT INVESTIGATION: A preliminary paint investigation confirmed the results of the 1985 study. The walls were initially painted a light blue-green; the applied moldings and the lower stair rustication were covered in a pale warm gray. A further investigation should include all surfaces.

RESTORATION PROGRAM: Because the staircase hall is architecturally intact with all of its original details, the restoration involves only routine mainte-

nance and repairs and the recreation of the original paint scheme. An attempt should be made to locate or recreate the original chandelier.

The terrazzo floor and marble base should be cleaned. The broken marble plinth block should be repaired. Prior to repair of any damaged plaster, the second-floor bathroom plumbing above the hall should be in good condition. Ideally, the plumbing should be disconnected at the basement level so that there will be no future danger of water damage to the plaster or the oil paintings.

All plaster surfaces should be repaired, including the gypsum board patch in the ceiling.

All hardware should be cleaned and made operable.

The two large oil paintings are significant aspects of the hall's decor. They should be removed, conserved by a qualified technician, and reinstalled.

All painted finishes should be restored.

Room 102 Gallery

The gallery, one of the most impressive rooms in the house, introduces the surrounding public rooms, including the den, the library, and the drawing room. This vaulted space is recorded in a Wharton-period photograph that looks south into the stair-

FIG. 120 *Detail of the painting on the north wall of the staircase hall.* (EWR)

FIG. 121 *Looking up from the staircase hall towards the gallery, with wrought-iron railing in the foreground, 1989. Photograph by Victoria Beller Smith.* (EWR)

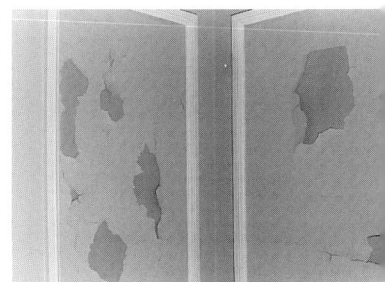

FIG. 122 *Deterioration in the southwest corner of the staircase hall adjacent to the two paintings.* (JD)

FIG. 123   *The gallery during the Whartons' occupancy, looking south towards the staircase hall, date unknown.* (BL)

FIG. 124   *The gallery today.* (JD)

case hall. The gallery was lined with numerous art objects and furnishings. Two diminutive "crystal" chandeliers were suspended from the vault.

The Hoppin & Koen floor plan shows the gallery as a much narrower space with an outdoor loggia extending along the west side.

FLOOR: Original white marble and terrazzo floor arranged in a pattern of bands and rondels. The floor has settled toward the center, resulting in cracking and separation from the marble base along the east wall.

WALLS: Original plaster on lath divided into five bays by projecting plaster columns. The north and south walls form an apsidal configuration with semidomes joining the vaulted ceiling.

The center bay of the east wall retains the original round-topped mirror secured in a molded wood frame with wood panel below. This mirror is visible in the Wharton-period photograph.

CEILING: Original plaster on lath vaulting in a complex arrangement of paneled ribs and cross vaults and terminating in semidomes.

CORNICE: Original projecting plaster cornice. The corona and cymatium, extending into the door and window recesses, are crafted in wood.

BASEBOARD: Original variegated marble base with a plaster crown molding. The marble has come loose below the center window and below the wall mirror (related to floor settlement).

DOORS: Four original openings. The north and south arched openings provide access into the staircase hall and the library and den. These openings were not designed for doors.

1062-1063: Arched openings each with plain deep reveal and semicircular paneled lunette with a central rondel motif. Original pairs of paneled doors. A marble plinth block is missing from the left base of the architrave of the south arched opening.

WINDOWS: Three original arched openings with deep unpaneled reveals. The openings are filled with pairs of inward-opening casement sash (each sash with ten lights) and a glazed nine-light semicircular lunette. There is a wood-and-plaster paneled apron below. The original ormolu hinges and cremone bolts remain.

HEATING: Single original cast-iron grille set in the east wall for hot-air system.

LIGHTING: Two glass and silvered-metal, five-arm incandescent chandeliers suspended from chains. These fixtures are shown in a Foxhollow-period photograph. They replaced the fixtures illustrated in the Wharton-period photograph.

EQUIPMENT: Recently installed thermostat next to the mirror panel. What may be an original service call-button is located on the pilaster to the south of drawing room door 1063.

PAINT INVESTIGATION: A preliminary investigation revealed that the walls were initially painted in the same light blue-green and pale warm gray used in the staircase hall. Further analysis should include all surfaces.

RESTORATION PROGRAM: In general the gallery is in very good condition. The most apparent problem is the deflection of the terrazzo floor surface and the resultant loosening of some of the marble base.

Damaged plaster should be repaired, particularly below the windows and along the cornice. The marble baseboards should be reset where loose or missing.

All hardware should be cleaned, and the Wharton-period chandeliers should be restored to the room (either the originals, reproductions, or old fixtures that are similar in appearance).

The Wharton-period paint scheme should be restored.

Room 102A Vestibule

This small transition area provides access to the den and the library.

FLOOR: Original white marble and terrazzo.

WALLS: Original plaster on lath.

CEILING: Original plaster on lath.

CORNICE: Original projecting plaster cornice.

BASEBOARD: Original variegated marble base with a plaster crown molding.

DOORS: Two original openings.

1031: The opening into the den features a pair of paneled wood doors (the west leaf is false and not visible on the inner side). The semicircular lunette is ornamented with a sculpted marble rondel depicting an infant with a crucifix. Original ormolu hardware and recent lock.

102A1: Three-panel wood door with original ormolu hardware. The middle hinge is missing its upper ormolu cap. The brass door stop set into the floor may be original.

PAINT INVESTIGATION: The original paint scheme duplicates that in the gallery.

RESTORATION PROGRAM: All surfaces should be cleaned, repaired, and painted as needed. Care should be taken when cleaning the marble relief above the entrance to the den.

Room 103 Den

The Hoppin & Koen floor plan refers to this room as the den, with a doorway connecting this room to the library penciled in.

All of the architectural details are intact.

FLOOR: Original oak parquet floor.

WALLS: Full paneled walls composed of wood stiles and rails surrounding a lath-and-plaster field. Applied plaster ornament. Below the chair rail there is a paneled dado.

Minor plaster cracks and loose paint on various surfaces.

There are two original oil-on-canvas paintings, in need of conservation, mounted above the doors in the south wall.

CEILING: Original plaster on lath unornamented ceiling and cove. Minor cracks and evidence of old repairs.

CORNICE: Original plaster cornice ornamented with acanthus leaves, marred by ceiling cracks, especially above the northeast window.

BASEBOARD: Original low wood base with an ovalo molded crown.

DOORS: There are three original openings.

1031, 1032: Original three-panel wood doors identical in detailing and hardware. The original hardware consists of ormolu and enamel-finished rim locks and knobs and three ormolu butt hinges.

FIG. 125 *Damaged variegated marble baseboard in the gallery beside the south doors into the drawing room.* (JD)

FIG. 126 *Marble rondel above door 1031 in the gallery's vestibule depicts an infant with a crucifix.* (JD)

FIG. 127 *The den today, north wall and northeast corner.* (JD)

FIG. 128 *Original jib door, east wall of Teddy Wharton's den, opening into Edith's library, designed by Ogden Codman, Jr.* (JD)

Both doors are missing two pairs of ormolu hinge-cover finials. Door 1031 has an added "Keil" surface-mounted lock. Door 1032 has a simple slide bolt on the bathroom side.

1033: Original jib door with applied moldings to match the surrounding paneling. The original ormolu and enamel rim lock survives on the library side, but the three hinges have been replaced. The north jamb is deteriorated.

WINDOWS: Three original window openings. The west opening retains the original inward-opening wood casement sash (each leaf with three lights) and an upper two-light fixed sash. Original ormolu cremone bolt and hinges. The north openings feature inward-opening French doors (each leaf has four lights) and upper two-light fixed sash. The west sash has an ormolu cremone bolt and three pairs of hinges; the east sash is designed so that the "doors" are operable from the exterior. There is a pair of ormolu-and-enamel rim locks. The original exterior knob and inside lever are missing.

HEATING: A typical iron grille covers the hot-air heat duct in the southeast corner.

LIGHTING: There were never any attached fixtures in this room. There are two original electrical floor outlets with brass cover plates (the caps are missing).

PLUMBING: An access panel for the bathtub plumbing, dating from the tub installation, is located in the dado in the southwest corner.

EQUIPMENT: A small round metal plate set into the floor below the west window may be an early or original outlet for a telephone.

Recent telephone jack attached to the dado on the west wall.

Original servant call-button set in the trim of door 1031.

OTHER FEATURES: Original projecting chimney breast and fireplace mantel centered on the north wall. The overmantel includes a large mirror (the glass with mirror disease) surrounded by ornamental plaster motifs including a medallion with a cameo-like profile. The original projecting red marble mantel includes an inlaid marble hearth (cracked), an ornamental cast-iron firebox lining (back plate cracked), and a tile firebox hearth (several damaged tiles).

PAINT INVESTIGATION: The 1985 paint investigation and the reference in the 1904 issue of *Berkshire Resort Topics* agree that the walls were covered in a cream paint with white moldings. This should be confirmed.

RESTORATION PROGRAM: This room requires only routine maintenance and repairs to restore the space to its original condition. There are no known Wharton-period photographs that illustrate the furnishings.

The plaster should be repaired and the floor refinished.

The cracked tiles and iron fireback can be left as they are because the fireplace should not be used. If the adjoining room (104) is restored (and the tub removed), then the plumbing access panel can be removed and the dado restored.

The north jamb of the jib door (1033) needs to be repaired, and more appropriate hinges should be installed.

All surfaces should have their original finishes restored.

Room 104 Bathroom (Former Lavatory)

Only a toilet and lavatory were originally located here. The bathtub was installed during the Foxhollow period. The Hoppin & Koen plan calls this room the toilet.

FLOOR: Original white marble tile. Some areas of staining.

WALLS: Plaster on lath with deteriorated conditions and poor repairs. The tile surrounding the tub is a later addition. Some tiles are cracked, and two replacements do not match.

CEILING: Original plaster on lath with coved surface at perimeter.

CORNICE: Original narrow plaster molding below the plaster cove.

BASEBOARD: Original white marble base with molded crown, loose behind the toilet and next to the tub.

DOORS: The molded wood door trim rests on marble plinth blocks, which are loose.

WINDOWS: The original narrow opening retains the two-over-two sash with a fixed top light secured by a thumb latch.

HEATING: Original cast-iron hot-water radiator.

LIGHTING: Two wall-mounted incandescent porcelain fixtures, possibly original, flank the medicine cabinet.

PLUMBING: All of the fixtures are replacements or additions. Ceramic tank toilet marked "Standard." Ceramic lavatory marked "Case" on chromed metal legs. The enameled iron tub is an addition to the space.

EQUIPMENT: The metal and beveled glass mirror cabinet set in the south wall may be an original feature. Various additions include the towel bar, paper-towel dispenser, and paper-cup dispenser.

PAINT INVESTIGATION: Original finishes should be determined.

RESTORATION PROGRAM: The plaster should be repaired, and the marble flooring and base should be cleaned and repaired. If evidence is found concerning the original plumbing fixtures, they can be restored; the tub should be removed.

The original paint scheme should be restored.

Room 105 Library

Where other important rooms have been repainted several times by successive owners, the oak paneling in the library appears exactly as it did in several Wharton-period photographs.

FIG. 129 *Detail of the ornamental plaster medallion of a Roman emperor's head, designed by Ogden Codman, Jr. (compare to Fig. 52).* (JD)

One significant change was the modification of the French doors in the southeast opening to provide safe egress during the occupancy of the Foxhollow School (the same modification was made in the dining room).

The second change is mystifying. Wharton-period photographs show the plaster entablature with a "white" finish. That surface is now finished in oak graining, imitating the paneling below. A preliminary paint investigation revealed the following sequence of paint layers on the original white plaster:

cream (a primer), orange/tan, red/brown, and a glaze. These last three layers create the oak graining. Significantly, there are no layers of dirt between the white plaster and cream layer or between the cream layer and the graining, indicating that the applications occurred within a fairly short time and that the graining may date from late in the Whartons' occupancy. As it now exists, the entablature correctly relates to the walls and not the ceiling. More sampling will be necessary to make a final judgment.

The original wood drapery poles and rings at the head of each of the four window openings remain. Although the support brackets appear to be recent, they are of a type available in the Whartons' time. Some of the poles are cut, indicating previous use, probably at Land's End in Newport, Rhode Island.

The significant settlement of the structure at the south and east ends and the location of a functioning bathroom on the second floor above the north end of the library will affect the room's restoration.

The masonry terrace, which extends along the length of the garden facade, is a significant but troublesome feature. Improper drainage coupled with poor maintenance has allowed water to penetrate into the foundation of the house. Settlement in the library, drawing room, and dining room may be caused by a rotted wood plate, deteriorated floor joists, or settlement of the foundation. Further probing is necessary in the basement and crawl space as well as some excavation where the terrace joins the building. Replacement of deteriorated wood and additional support of the floor structure may be necessary.

The condition of the marble floor and base indicates a long history of water-related problems in the bathroom (208) above the library. The plumbing should be disconnected at basement level to ensure the long-term preservation of the library and its contents.

If the bathroom is to be functional, the piping under the marble floor and in the wall below must be analyzed, repaired, and maintained prior to any restoration work in the library.

FLOOR: The original oak parquet floor is scratched and worn. The surface slopes inward from the east wall. A small section of parquet is missing from the northwest corner of the hearth.

CORNICE: Plaster entablature composed of a plain frieze and a projecting cornice, now painted to imitate the oak paneling. The Wharton-period photographs show this plaster work unpainted. There is water damage from the bathroom above.

BASEBOARD: Low plain oak base integral with the paneling.

DOORS: Three original door openings. A fourth door opens into a small narrow closet.

1051: Original pair of oak three-panel doors. The right leaf is fixed. The hardware matches the original hardware on the other doors, but there is evidence of a previous lock treatment.

WALLS: Original oak paneling to the bottom of the entablature. The north, south, and east walls incorporate built-in recesses with adjustable shelves. Applied carved ornamentation appears above the door openings and the shelves. The large plaster-surfaced panel centered on the west wall originally featured a tapestry, illustrated in Wharton-period photographs.

The paneling has dropped and become loose due to the floor deflection.

CEILING: Original plaster on lath with a simple cove rising from the cornice. Fine cracks and some loose paint.

1061: Pair of paneled oak doors opening into the drawing room. Original ormolu-and-red-enamel rim lock.

102A1: Oak three-panel door opening into the vestibule. Original hardware. One of the ormolu hinge finials is missing.

1033: Oak three-panel door. The outside face incorporates the details of the den wall treatment. The hinges have been replaced.

WINDOWS: Four original window openings that retain their original sash. The southeast window

FIG. 132 *The library today, northeast corner. The original, gilt wood drapery poles with pineapple finials and drapery rings survive from the Whartons' occupancy.* (JD)

was modified during the Foxhollow period so that the sash opens outward; it has panic hardware. The top and bottom keepers of the removed cremone bolt survive.

The openings include pairs of French doors (each leaf with four lights) and fixed two-light transoms. The original hardware includes a pair of ormolu-and-red-enamel rim locks with lever handles and ormolu-and-red-enamel cremone bolts.

HEATING: A bronze-finished grille for the hot-air system is incorporated into the bottom of the bookcase west of the fireplace.

LIGHTING: The Wharton-period photographs illustrate several table lamps but no permanent lighting fixtures.

Two post-Wharton-period, ormolu electric wall brackets flank the tapestry panel.

The brass-covered floor outlets are original. Only one retains an original brass cap.

FIG. 133 *Drawing room, southeast corner, during the Whartons' occupancy.* (BL)

EQUIPMENT: Original servant call-button next to the drawing room door.

Recent thermostat in the northwest corner.

OTHER FEATURES: The original fireplace is centered on the south wall. The bolection-molded architrave is of a mottled green marble. This stone work has come loose from the wall. The hearth is of red and green marble, and the firebox includes an original ornate cast-iron fireback; the iron side-plates are replacements. The tile hearth surface is very deteriorated.

The original gilt wood drapery poles with pineapple finials and drapery rings have been modified and may have been used in an earlier Wharton house.

PAINT INSPECTION: The plaster entablature is covered in a layer of white paint (perhaps a primer) and the current oak graining. The absence of dirt between any of these applications (especially in a room heated by hot air) makes it likely that the graining was applied early and may date to the Wharton era.

RESTORATION PROGRAM: The plumbing in the bathroom on the bedroom floor above the library should be disconnected to protect against further water damage.

The cause of the floor deflection should be determined and the problem alleviated. It may not be possible to make the floor level.

The floor should be carefully cleaned to restore its original appearance.

All plaster surfaces should be repaired and their original finishes restored.

The modified French doors should be restored to open inward and the missing hardware replicated. All hardware should be cleaned and made operable. The red enamel finish should be restored. Remove the ormolu wall brackets, and repair the oak paneling where damaged. The brackets should be preserved in the collection.

The green marble mantel must be resecured to the chimney face. The fireplace should be only ornamental; therefore the deteriorated tile need not be replaced.

Room 106 Drawing Room

The drawing room is the largest room and may be the most architecturally elaborate room at The Mount. All of the original detailing survives, although some elements, such as the boldly ornamented plaster ceiling, were severely damaged by water and have been poorly repaired. The one surviving Wharton-period photograph illustrates only a portion of the southeast corner. Photographs taken during the Foxhollow period show the room furnished with an assemblage of French-style furniture of unknown origin. The Hoppin & Koen floor plan shows five window openings in the east wall, but only the center three were actually constructed as real openings. The two outermost openings are blind windows on the exterior.

FLOOR: Large expanse of gray-and-white terrazzo with white marble border. There are pink terrazzo panels in the window reveals. Deflection of the wood floor structure beneath the terrazzo has caused extensive east-west cracks and the deformation of the surface in the northeast corner. Some of the border marble has also cracked.

WALLS: The surfaces are arranged with panels, doors, and window openings. Wood stiles and rails surround flat, plastered surfaces. Applied plaster floral-and-ribbon ornaments on the east and west walls.

The large central panels on the north and south walls originally included tapestries (the south one is illustrated in the Wharton-period photograph). Foxhollow-period photographs illustrate smaller tapestries inserted in modified panels.

What may be two original picture pins survive high on the east wall. All walls show cracked plaster. The damaged plaster at the north end of the east wall may be the result of the floor deflection and/or water penetration from the terrace.

CEILING: Original ornate plaster on lath ceiling, extensively repaired. Ornamented with applied cast-plaster rosettes and garland bands. Water penetration from above caused severe deterioration. Nine original rosettes survive in place. The early-1980s restored cast-plaster ornament is of poor quality.

CORNICE: Original full plaster entablature with an unornamented frieze. There is a poor repair in the southeast corner. Two modillions are broken above the fireplace (caused by the attachment of theatrical spotlights on these delicate plaster ornaments).

FIG. 134 *The drawing room today, southeast corner.* (JD)

BASEBOARD: Low wood base with an applied crown molding. The floor settlement has opened a space beneath the baseboard in the northeast corner.

DOORS: There are four original door openings in the room. All of the openings retain their original matching pairs of three-panel doors. The molded wood architraves support a carved pulvinated frieze and a broken pediment. The original hardware

FIG. 135 *Original drawing-room ceiling rosette.* (JD)

FIG. 136 *Cast-plaster rosette, installed in the early 1980s.* (JD)

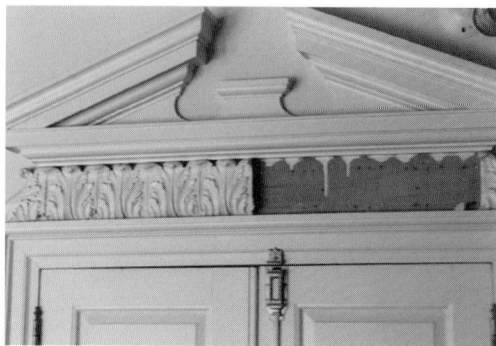

FIG. 137   *Plaster acanthus leaf ornament over the north drawing room doors was damaged by repeated door slamming in 1994.* (EWR)

includes pairs of ormolu-and-enamel rim locks with knobs, slide bolts, and three pairs of hinges. The top ormolu hinge cover is missing from one of the cast-iron hinges on library door 1061.

WINDOWS: Three original window openings in the east wall. The inward-opening French casement sash (each leaf with four lights) are topped by fixed two-light transoms.

The deep wood reveals are paneled. The original hardware includes ormolu-and-enamel cremone bolts and iron hinges with ormolu covers. Each pair of sash have three pairs of hinges. The curtain rods are recent.

HEATING: A single metal grate for the hot-air system is set into the dado next to door 1063.

LIGHTING: There have never been any permanent fixtures in this room.

There is an original electrical floor outlet with a brass cover plate in front of the center window. Later outlets are in the baseboard.

FIG. 138   *Original fireplace and cast-iron firebox liner illustrating the sacrifice of Isaac by Abraham.* (JD)

EQUIPMENT: There is an original servant call-button mounted on the right side of the center window and an original or early telephone jack(?) mounted on the floor in front.

Recent thermostat located next to the dining-room door.

OTHER FEATURES: Original fireplace and mantel centered on the west wall. Massive projecting pink-and-red/brown variegated marble mantel with an inlaid marble hearth and an elaborately ornamented cast-iron firebox liner. The firebox hearth is covered with ceramic tiles, several of which are cracked and deteriorated.

The overmantel features a framed panel with a rounded pediment supported on consoles, all in plaster.

PAINT INVESTIGATION: A preliminary paint analysis revealed a blue/gray ground finish and white moldings. This agrees with the description published in a 1904 issue of *Berkshire Resort Topics* which stated: "The room is painted in a bluish-gray tint, with white moldings and ceiling..." The 1985 study found that the walls were initially painted in shades of cream and off-white. Further analysis should be made.

RESTORATION PROGRAM: Proper repair of the elaborate plaster ceiling is paramount. The original ceiling and ornament should be retained, the improperly restored portions should be removed and accurate ornaments applied.

After external forces are investigated as a cause for the settlement along the east wall of the terrace (the column supports in the basement rooms below may have solved the problem), the plaster wall surfaces can be repaired. The cornice should be repaired and left free of lighting or other devices.

The walls should be painted in their original blue/gray-and-white scheme and original, large tapestries should be restored to the north and south panels.

The fireplace should not be used, and therefore the damaged tiles need not be replaced.

Room 107 Dining Room

This large and elaborately detailed room has many ornate plaster decorations. The two original oil paintings are an integral part of the decor; they require cleaning and conservation. This room retains some original Wharton-period furnishings, such as the four Rococo-style bronze wall sconces from Land's End. Originally gas, they were electrified when installed at The Mount.

One rather poor Wharton-period photograph shows one of the wall brackets, elegant French-style

FIG. 139 *The dining room, looking towards the northwest corner, during the Whartons' occupancy.* (BL)

FIG. 140 *The dining room today, looking towards the northwest corner.* (JD)

FIG. 141 *Applied wall garland of flowers, fruit, and fish, designed by Ogden Codman, Jr.* (JD)

caned dining chairs, and a rather conventional Victorian table hiding beneath the table cloth.

FLOOR: Original gray-and-white terrazzo with a white marble border. The floor has deflected, and three extensive north-south cracks have developed. The marble border has settled in front of the windows. The floor was recently shored up from the basement boiler room.

WALLS: Original lath-and-plaster wall surfaces with applied wood moldings forming panels above a chair rail. The pilaster-like projections on the north and south walls are of wood and originally were ornamented with applied garlands. Two large oil paintings in elaborately carved frames are incorporated into the panel arrangements of the south and north walls.

CEILING: Unornamented plaster on lath. The lack of cracks indicates that this surface was recently repaired and painted.

CORNICE: Plaster entablature with a plain frieze and egg-and-dart molding. Vertical cracks in several locations and in poor condition along the north and south walls.

BASEBOARD: Low wood baseboard with an applied crown molding. The base has separated from the floor along the wall west of the fireplace due to the floor deflection.

FIG. 142 *Over-door panel with molded plaster relief of an urn overflowing with leaves and flowers, designed by Codman.* (JD)

DOORS: There are four original door openings. All doors consist of identical paired three-panel doors; three open into the dining room and door 1064 opens into the drawing room. The trim includes a molded architrave incorporating an elaborate over-door panel with molded plaster relief.

The hardware on doors 1071, 1072, and 1073 consists of the original ormolu locks, hinges, and slide bolts. Door 1073 is missing the upper keeper of the slide bolt.

WINDOWS: Three original window openings. The French casement sash (each leaf with four lights) are topped by fixed two-light transoms. The sash open inward except where modified to open outward in the northeast opening. The original hardware consists of ormolu cremone bolts and iron hinges with ormolu cover finials (three pair of hinges for each opening). The south window in the east wall is missing one hinge finial.

The northeast door was modified during the Foxhollow period, and panic hardware was added to each leaf. Portions of the original hardware survive, including the keepers for the cremone bolts and six of the ormolu caps on the hinges.

HEATING: A single metal grate, for the hot-air system, is mounted in the dado west of the fireplace.

LIGHTING: Four ormolu brass Rococo-style electrified wall brackets (originally gas fixtures) installed during the Wharton period and formerly used at Land's End. The original cloth-covered wiring, in a precarious condition, is still in use.

EQUIPMENT: Recently installed thermostat located next to the staircase hall (101) door.

OTHER FEATURES: Original fireplace and mantel centered on the north wall. The bolection-molded surround is composed of red-and-white mottled marble. Small breaks in the horizontal members have been glued. The badly deteriorated hearth is formed of the same marble with black stone inserts. Ornamental cast iron lines the firebox, which has a tile floor.

Above the surround there is a horizontal panel with applied-plaster ornaments. The overmantel features a large oil-on-canvas painting (the mate to the painting on the south wall), secured in an ornate, carved wood frame.

PAINT INVESTIGATION: A preliminary paint analysis uncovered cream-colored walls with the decorative molding and ornaments picked out in white. This subtle combination may be the "white, paneled with stucco" referred to in an article in the 1904 issue of *Berkshire Resort Topics*. Further analysis should be made.

RESTORATION PROGRAM: When the floor structure has been stabilized, the plaster walls and cornice can be repaired. The ornaments missing from the pilasters flanking the door should be restored. All surfaces should be painted in their original colors. All three window openings should be weather-stripped and made operational. The leaves of the northeast opening should be repaired to open inward, and all missing hardware should be restored.

The oil paintings should be removed for cleaning and conservation and then reinstalled.

The four light fixtures should be cleaned and rewired.

Because the fireplace should not be used, the deteriorated tile need not be replaced.

Room 108 Kitchen (Former Butler's Pantry and Brush Room)

The area included in the present kitchen, created by the Foxhollow School, was formerly partitioned into two rooms: the butler's pantry to the north and the brush room to the south. There was a dumbwaiter in the southeast corner of the former butler's pantry; the shaftway can still be seen in the former scullery (G-10) on the ground floor. These room designations were found on the Hoppin & Koen floor plan. The brush room is referred to as a pantry on the 1940 plan included with the Abatement of Tax on Real Estate.

FLOOR: The original floor is visible in the south closet and consists of 3 1/2-inch-wide tongue-and-groove boards, which run north-south. The floor is now covered by vinyl tile, which is very worn in some areas and depressed into the wood floor. Leaking pipes have caused the floor boards beneath the sink cabinets to deteriorate.

WALLS: Some original plaster on lath with repairs made during remodeling. The east wall retains a high beaded-board wainscot, now painted white, but originally with a varnished oak finish.

CEILING: Some original plaster on lath with recent gypsum board repairs. Extensive water damage, racks, and loose plaster.

CORNICE: No evidence of a cornice.

BASEBOARD: Original wood base with applied crown molding.

DOORS: There are currently five original door openings in this room.

1073: Original pair of paneled wood doors opening into the dining room. The small, ornate oval knobs are original. Four hinge locations on the architrave indicate that there was a second pair of doors that opened into the butler's pantry. The Hoppin & Koen plan shows a swinging door in this position.

1081-1082: Original three-panel wood doors and molded wood architraves. The original hardware includes iron butt hinges, mortise locks, and wood knobs. Door 1081 was the original access into the south room. Door 1082 opens to a small closet. There is an original pair of paneled closet doors above this opening. This closet is penciled in on the Hoppin & Koen first-floor plan.

1083: This original opening formerly provided access to the butler's pantry from the hall (114). A recent flush solid-core door with masonite panel above now fills the opening.

1084: Original opening to closet. The molded wood trim survives with hinge locations on the east jamb. The door was removed prior to 1986 but has been restored.

WINDOWS: Two original window openings with six-over-six double-hung wood sash. The molded wood trim matches that around the doors. These windows were originally in separate rooms.

HEATING: Single plain cast-iron radiator with exposed piping to third floor of the service wing.

LIGHTING: Two recently installed incandescent ceiling fixtures, one with missing shade.

PLUMBING: Original ceramic sink, badly worn and cracked, set in wood cabinet with marble top and high marble back splash. The sink retains original knobs, spigots, and pipes below. Later copper pipe repairs.

EQUIPMENT: Recent gas range, refrigerator, and telephone.

OTHER FEATURES: Original built-in oak cabinetry (now painted white). Above the sink and set against beaded-board backing is a two-tiered arrangement of pairs of glazed sliding doors topped by six single, small-paneled hinged doors.

Similar oak cabinetry is located against the south partition. This unit was located against the now-removed south wall of the butler's pantry. Recently the wood counter top was covered in plastic laminate.

The closet in the south partition retains original shelves and cabinets with the original varnished wood finish.

FIG. 143 *One of four original ormolu brass Rococo-style electrified wall brackets, brought from Land's End to The Mount.* (JD)

221

The original dumbwaiter (from room G-10 below) was located between the windows in the east wall. It opened to the butler's pantry.

PAINT INVESTIGATION: All surfaces should be investigated to determine the original colors and finishes, particularly after the two rooms were joined.

RESTORATION PROGRAM: This space could be restored as two separate pantries. The cabinetry should be reinstalled to the reconstructed south wall of the butler's pantry, and the dumbwaiter should be reconstructed.

Numerous items require repair, including cracked and water-damaged plaster walls and ceiling and the original wood floor covered in vinyl tile. All of the woodwork and cabinets should have the varnished oak finish restored. The missing and replaced doors should be restored.

Simple period ceiling light fixtures should replace the recent fixtures.

Note: This analysis records the present kitchen as it was in 1988. In the spring of 1995, extensive restoration work was done, including the restoration of the original varnished oak finish; restoration of the original paint colors to the walls and ceiling; patching of ceiling and wall plaster; removal of the vinyl tile floor and installation of a pine-plank floor; removal of the recent flush solid-core door from and the installation of an oak door in opening 1083; restoration of an original servants' bell on the west wall of the butler's pantry; and re-enameling of the butler's pantry sink. An island for modern conveniences (sink, stove, and dishwasher) was installed in the center of the room, allowing the restoration of the surrounding historic fabric and the recreation of the feeling of the barrier that originally divided the butler's pantry from the brush room during the Wharton period.

Room 109 Service Hall

This narrow hall was originally a continuation of the stair hall (114). The partition separating these spaces was constructed later. This space survives largely intact, including the original finish on the woodwork and original equipment such as the electric wall bracket and the servants' call-box.

FLOOR: Original 3 1/2-inch-wide tongue-and-groove pine boards, which run north-south. The finish is deteriorated.

WALLS: Original plaster on lath with some cracking and areas of loose material on the west partition.

NORTH: Recent gypsum-board partition with doorway to separate hall from the stair hall.

EAST: Area with improper gypsum-board repair.

SOUTH: Original door opening removed and partition constructed in gypsum board with reproduction baseboard. The Hoppin & Koen floor plan

indicates a doorway in the south partition opening into the cook's room, which was probably removed by the Foxhollow School.

CEILING: Original plaster on lath.

CORNICE: No evidence of a cornice.

BASEBOARD: Original wood base with crown molding and original varnished finish. Reproduction base at south partition probably installed by the Foxhollow School.

DOORS: There are three surviving original openings. Openings 1081 and 1101 retain the original panel doors.

Opening 1121 is missing the door. This doorway originally provided access into the butler's room, according to the Hoppin & Koen plan.

The recent opening (1142) has a flush hollow core door and simple ranch trim.

The former door opening into Room 111 was probably removed by the Foxhollow School.

WINDOWS: There are no windows in this hall. When this space included the stair hall, natural light was provided by the window lighting the stairway.

HEATING: Originally heating was provided by the radiator in the stair hall.

LIGHTING: The original brass incandescent wall bracket attached to the west partition is now loose. This fixture is indicated on the Hoppin & Koen floor plan.

EQUIPMENT: Attached to the east partition there is what appears to be an original wood-and-glass cabinet housing a servants' call-box. It was manufactured by the Berkshire Electric Company in Pittsfield, Massachusetts. An indicator-box is illustrated on the Hoppin & Koen plan in a position just south of door 1083.

The recent Honeywell thermostat replaces an earlier one. Old green wall paint is visible in this position.

PAINT INVESTIGATION: A careful paint analysis should be made of all surfaces to determine the original decorative scheme.

RESTORATION PROGRAM: As part of the long-term restoration program, the doorway formerly in the south partition should be recreated. If the recently installed doorway separating this hall from the stair hall is to be retained, a more appropriate door and proper detailing should be used. Further investigation may reveal whether the baize door shown on the Hoppin & Koen floor plan was actually installed. All surfaces should be repaired and plaster should replace all gypsum board surfaces. The original electric wall bracket should be rewired.

Room 110 Original Housekeeper's Room

The Hoppin & Koen floor plan indicates this large space as the housekeeper's room, although the butler's pantry cutout box lists it as the cook's room. The room was converted into the kitchen during the Van Anda residency and is illustrated as such in early Foxhollow School photographs.

The doorway in the west partition, which opened into the former cook's room (now Room 111), has been removed, and a new oak floor has been installed over the original floor. These changes were accomplished by the Foxhollow School when the room was converted to a dormitory.

FLOOR: Narrow tongue-and-groove oak floor installed over the original wider boards. The stained and varnished surface is very worn.

WALLS: Original plaster on lath exhibiting numerous cracks and loose paint.

CEILING: Original plaster on lath with a small gypsum board repair in the northeast corner. Numerous cracks, loose plaster, and poor repairs. Evidence of water damage.

CORNICE: Original narrow wood picture molding.

BASEBOARD: Original 10-inch-high molded wood baseboard with its original unpainted varnished finish.

DOORS: There are two original door openings. A third opening (in the west partition) was removed late in the occupancy of the Foxhollow School.

1011-1012: Original three-panel wood doors with all hardware intact including the wood knobs. More recent hardware (bolts, etc.) has been installed.

WINDOWS: Two original window openings retain the original six-over-six double chain-hung sash secured with thumb latches.

HEATING: One plain cast-iron radiator and exposed pipes near ceiling for third floor (of service wing) radiator.

LIGHTING: Old incandescent ceiling fixture (perhaps installed when this room functioned as the kitchen for the Van Andas). Original push-button light switch next to hall door.

PLUMBING: Any plumbing that was included in the Van Andas' kitchen has been removed.

EQUIPMENT: Recent surface-mounted armored cable and electrical outlets.

Wall-mounted box for speaker connections and numerous wires (all property of Shakespeare & Company).

OTHER FEATURES: Original closet as illustrated on the Hoppin & Koen floor plan.

PAINT INVESTIGATION: A careful analysis should be made because an earlier study (by William Hickman) indicates an interesting original wall color.

RESTORATION PROGRAM: The long-term goal may be to recreate the original plan of the servants' wing, including the doorway in the west partition.

The immediate problems include the repair and stabilization of all plaster surfaces and the removal of inappropriate wiring. The floor needs to be cleaned and varnished. The original color scheme should be restored.

Room 111 Original Cook's Room and Butler's Room

This large room was apparently converted to a dormitory late in the occupancy of the Foxhollow School. Two closets were removed and a partition was built to create the small hall and toilet room (112 and 113). A door opening was removed from the east partition.

The Hoppin & Koen floor plan cites the south end of this room as the cook's room, while the north end, separated by a closet partition and including the present hall and toilet room, was to function as the butler's room. Like the adjoining Housekeeper's Room, these spaces were probably office/sitting rooms rather than living quarters. The butler's pantry cutout box suggests that the cook's room was actually used as the chef's room.

During the Van Anda ownership, the former room in the southwest corner was used as the staff dining room, while the butler continued to use the original north room as a sitting room.

The modifications made during the last years of the Foxhollow School left little trace of the rooms' original character.

FLOOR: Narrow tongue-and-groove oak flooring installed over original wider boards, probably by the Foxhollow School. The stained and varnished surface is very worn, and the boards have buckled from extensive water damage.

WALLS: Original plaster on lath, which is cracked and irregular. There is a deteriorated surface with loose paint on the west wall. The former door openings in the east and north partitions (present closet rooms) are filled with gypsum board. The north partition was constructed to enclose a toilet room and small hall.

CEILING: The original deteriorated lath-and-plaster ceiling survives above a recently installed metal-frame-and-panel suspended ceiling. This surface is soiled and water stained.

CORNICE: No cornice in this room.

BASEBOARD: Original 10-inch-high molded wood baseboard. The base on the north partition was installed late in the Foxhollow School period.

DOORS: One opening (1111) created when the original two rooms were combined. The three-panel door, trim, and hardware, including the wood knobs, are original materials reused in this position.

Two other original openings have been closed in with gypsum board.

WINDOWS: Two original window openings, which retain the original six-over-six double chain-hung sash secured with thumb latches.

HEATING: One plain cast-iron radiator and exposed iron pipes to the third floor of the service wing above.

LIGHTING: One recent ceiling fixture inserted in the suspended ceiling.

PLUMBING: Recent copper pipes for bathrooms above.

EQUIPMENT: Recent surface-mounted electrical outlets, one attached to the south window sill.

OTHER FEATURES: Closet recess with framed opening. A pair of sliding doors has been removed. This closet was created when the room was converted to a dormitory by the Foxhollow School.

PAINT INVESTIGATION: An analysis should be made of all surfaces to determine the original decorative scheme.

RESTORATION PROGRAM: The long-term goal should be the recreation of the original Wharton-period floor plan, including the reconstruction of the closet partition between the two former rooms and the reopening of the former two doorways. The bathroom (113) created late in the Foxhollow School period would be removed.

All plaster surfaces should be restored and the suspended ceiling removed. The possibility of removing the water-damaged floor and restoring the original floor beneath should be investigated.

The original paint schemes should be restored to the two reconstructed rooms.

Room 112   Vestibule

This vestibule is a small portion of the original butler's room illustrated on the Hoppin & Koen floor plan. The present configuration was created late in the Foxhollow School period to add dormitory space. The present doorway in the east partition was the original access from the service hall into the butler's room.

FLOOR: Narrow tongue-and-groove oak flooring installed over original wider boards.

WALLS: Original plaster on lath survives on the north and east partitions. The other walls were created when the former butler's room was modified by the Foxhollow School. There are plaster cracks in the north wall and above the hall door.

CEILING: Recent suspended ceiling as found in Room 111, with the original plaster ceiling above.

CORNICE: No cornice in this space.

BASEBOARD: The original wood baseboard survives on the north and east partitions. The remaining base is a replication.

DOORS: The only original opening is in the east partition (1121), but the door has been removed.

Doorway (1111) was created when the original room was modified by the Foxhollow School. The three-panel door, trim, and hardware are original material, reused in this position.

The doorway into the toilet room (1131) includes a hollow-core flush door with a simple ranch-mold architrave, part of the Foxhollow School remodeling.

WINDOWS: There are no windows in this space.

HEATING: No heating.

LIGHTING: No lighting.

PAINT INVESTIGATION: The analysis should determine the original color scheme for the butler's room, as well as the first scheme used as part of the Foxhollow School remodeling.

RESTORATION PROGRAM: The long-term goal should be the recreation of the original floor plan. This would mean the loss of the toilet room. The deteriorated plaster must be repaired and the suspended ceiling removed.

Room 113   Toilet Room

A portion of Room 111, the small vestibule (112), and this toilet room were formerly a single large room noted on the Hoppin & Koen floor plan as the butler's room. The current arrangement was created late in the Foxhollow School's occupancy. Originally, there was no toilet room on this floor of the service wing, indicating that the former butler's room, cook's room, and housekeeper's room functioned as sitting room/offices and not as sleeping areas.

FLOOR: Green 9-inch-by-9-inch vinyl tile installed by the Foxhollow School. The blue tiles beneath the toilet are recent replacements.

WALLS: The north and west walls are of original plaster on lath. There are some plaster cracks behind the radiator. The east partition is of recent origin.

CEILING: Recent suspended ceiling as found in Room 111. The original plaster ceiling survives.

CORNICE: No cornice in this space.

BASEBOARD: Original wood baseboard survives on the west wall. The remaining base copies the original finish.

DOORS: Recent opening with flush hollow-core door and ranch-mold architrave.

WINDOWS: One original window opening that retains the original six-over-six chain-hung sash secured with a thumb latch.

HEATING: One small plain cast-iron radiator below the window.

LIGHTING: Recent incandescent ceiling fixture.

PLUMBING: Ceramic lavatory and tank toilet marked "Crane," installed when the bathroom was created.

PAINT INVESTIGATION: Analysis should determine the original color scheme for the butler's room, as well as the scheme used when the toilet room was first created.

RESTORATION PROGRAM: The long-term goal should be recreation of the original floor plan, resulting in the loss of the toilet room.

Immediate restoration includes the repair of deteriorated plaster wall and ceiling surfaces, the removal of the suspended ceiling, and the repair of the tile floor surface.

Room 114 Stair Hall

The existing plan of the stair hall generally follows the scheme as drawn by Hoppin & Koen with one exception: the plan does not include the kitchen closet, which projects into the northeast corner of the hall. Apparently this was an afterthought, as it is penciled-in lightly on the original drawing. At the location of the recently installed flush door in the south partition, the Hoppin & Koen plan shows a swinging door labeled baize door. It has not been determined whether this fabric-covered door was actually installed. The most significant features in this space are the service elevator and the stairway that wraps around the shaft on three sides.

FLOOR: Original 3 1/2-inch-wide pine tongue-and-groove flooring, which runs north-south. The finish is deteriorated except around the edges.

WALLS: Original plaster on lath. Numerous cracks and some loose plaster on the south partition.

The projecting corner of the kitchen closet is finished with a metal bead, which is exposed where the plaster has fallen off.

Original beaded-board wainscot on all walls and the stairway matches that found in the butler's pantry portion of the present kitchen (108).

The wainscot retains the original varnished finish, but the wood has numerous scratches and dents.

CEILING: Original plaster on lath. Numerous cracks and peeling paint. Loose plaster on the underside of the stair carriage.

CORNICE: No cornice.

BASEBOARD: Original wood base with applied crown molding and varnished finish. Very scratched and dented.

DOORS: There are three door openings in this hall. The openings in the north and east partitions are original. The opening into the south hall is a recent addition but may replace an original feature.

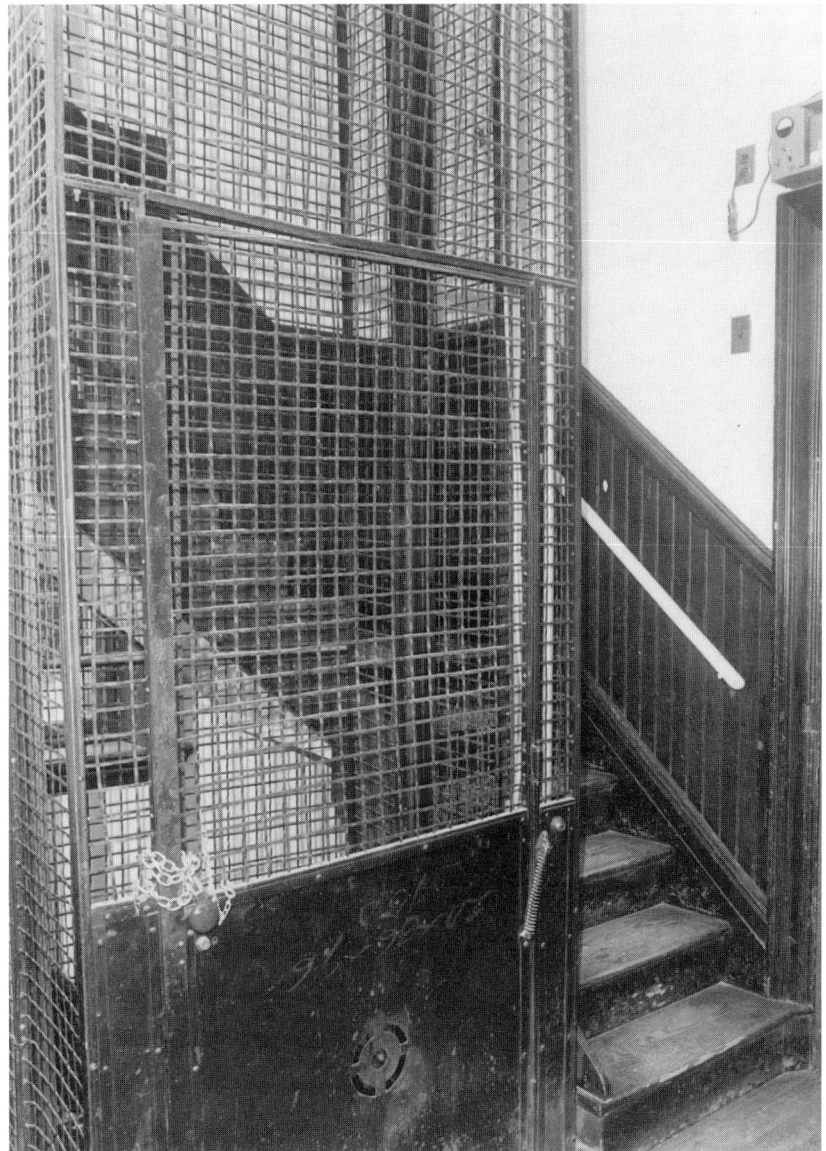

FIG. 144 *The original service stair surrounds the original elevator cage in the service wing.* (JD)

1141: Original opening and molded wood trim. Recent flush solid-core door with conventional hardware and door closer. The door is shorter than the original opening; a transom panel has been inserted above.

1042: Recent flush hollow-core door and simple ranch-mold trim. Conventional hardware and door closer. There may have been a baize door in this location. The wainscot in the stair hall does not extend beyond this doorway into the service hall, which would indicate that there was always a separation at this point.

1083: Original opening into the former butler's pantry. Recent flush solid-core door with masonite panel above. Original three-panel door has been removed.

ELEVATOR: Original steel-plate and wire-screen door with brown ceramic knob.

WINDOW: One original opening in the west wall above the stairway. Molded wood trim and six-over-six double-hung wood sash with metal thumb latch.

HEATING: Single plain cast-iron radiator and two exposed pipes to floor above.

LIGHTING: Two original electric wall brackets, one with bent arm and replaced socket and the other, on the stair landing, retaining only the ornamental wall plate (the arm and socket are missing).

PLUMBING: Protruding bronze pipe and valve, marked "Crane," located in the south partition at 6 feet above the floor.

FIG. 145 *Detail of the now-missing finial in the staircase hall, c. 1942.* (FHS)

FIG. 146 *The newel post at the foot of the staircase today, without the urn.* (JD)

EQUIPMENT: Original built-in wood fuse box with old exposed wiring. An identification sheet labels this object the butler's pantry cutout box. Later metal fuse box.

Recent battery pack for an emergency light located in the adjacent stair hall (115), set above the architrave of door 1141.

Recent alarm bell and on-off switch.

OTHER FEATURES: Original wood service stair with three runs to the floor above. The treads and landings are very worn. Later wood handrail attached to the wood wainscot.

The stairway surrounds the original caged elevator shaft on three sides, as is shown on the Hoppin & Koen floor plan.

PAINT INVESTIGATION: All surfaces should be investigated to determine original colors and finishes.

RESTORATION PROGRAM: The proper doors should be restored to the original openings. Further investigation should be made to determine if there was a baize door in opening 1142.

All deteriorated plaster surfaces should be repaired, and all woodwork should be restored. The floor needs refinishing.

The two original electrical wall brackets should be rewired and restored. The emergency lighting system should be modified to conceal the battery packs.

All finishes should be restored, including the metal elevator shaft enclosure finish.

Room 115 *Staircase Hall to Second Floor*

The staircase hall provides access to the bedroom floor and is separate from the main stairway, which rises from the ground floor to the *piano nobile*. Both stairs are identical in detail and provide an elegant connection to each floor.

The staircase hall differs in minor details from the Hoppin & Koen plan. The bottom riser of the staircase was constructed with a much bolder curve than illustrated, and two pilasters flanking the stairway were not built. The pair of glazed doors opening into the stair hall from the outer stair hall are shown on the original plan as a single swinging door flanked by glazed sidelights.

There are no known Wharton-period photographs of this area, but one can see the oil painting above the door (1141) in the south partition in a Wharton-period photograph of the gallery. The canvas appears as a dark object through the closed glazed door separating the primary stair hall (101) from the second-floor stair hall (115).

A photograph taken late in the Van Anda occupancy shows the now-missing urn-like finial mounted on top of the newel post at the foot of the staircase.

FLOOR: Original gray-and-white terrazzo with a white marble border.

WALLS: Original plaster on lath with applied plaster moldings forming panels. Numerous cracks, chips, and breaks and diagonal cracks on the south stair wall. The damaged area above the base on the north wall may relate to water damage on the opposite side of the partition.

The panel above door 1141 includes wood moldings that frame a painted canvas of a cupid with flowers, possibly by an anonymous eighteenth-century artist.

CEILING: Original smooth plaster on lath on the ceiling and the underside of the staircase. There are several poorly repaired cracks and areas of loose paint.

CORNICE: Original plaster cornice (run in place), cracks at corners, and several areas with vertical cracks.

BASEBOARD: Original low flat mottled marble (breche) base with a molded plaster crown. The marble is loose in several locations especially along the south partition.

DOORS: Three original door openings. The molded wood trim of each opening terminates on small marble (breche) plinth blocks.

1151: Original pair of paneled and glazed wood doors with a semicircular wood-and-glass lunette above. Original hardware, including an ormolu and enameled box lock with a lever handle, ormolu slide bolts, and six ormolu hinges (seven decorative hinge finials are missing). This pair of doors is shown in the closed position in a Wharton-period photograph of the gallery.

1072: Original pair of panel doors (opening into the dining room), with original ormolu knob and escutcheon.

1141: Original opening with recent solid-core flush door. This door is shorter than the original and now has a wood panel above. Recent brass-plated knob and butt hinges.

WINDOWS: Original opening in the west wall. The wood sash is composed of a pair of wood casements topped by a fixed transom with two lights. Full wood architrave and paneled apron. The lower sash appears to open inward but is blocked by the staircase. The original hardware includes an ormolu cremone bolt and three hinges (the fourth was never applied behind the stair carriage).

HEATING: No heating.

LIGHTING: Two ormolu three-branch wall brackets with electrified candles, recently rewired. These fixtures may date from the Wharton period, although the Hoppin & Koen floor plan does not show fixtures in this location.

One recently installed emergency spotlight attached to the architrave of door 1141 with the battery pack located in the service stair hall (1114).

EQUIPMENT: Recent ceiling-mounted smoke detector.

OTHER FEATURES: Original elegant closed-string wood staircase, which ascends to the bedroom floor in three runs (nine risers to landing, three risers to landing and 11 risers to second floor). The bottom tread curves around the newel. The landing floors have shifted away from the baseboard but seem stable.

The ornate wrought-iron handrail spirals around the newel and ascends in a continuous run to the second (bedroom) floor. The handrail pattern matches that of the main stairway.

The newel is capped by a bronze base (secured with three screws and stamped "ST") to which was originally screwed a metal (?) urn-finial visible in the Van Anda-period photograph. The same "ST" (Sterlin) mark is also found on the ormolu door knobs in the house.

PAINT INVESTIGATION: A thorough paint investigation should be made to determine the original decorative scheme.

RESTORATION PROGRAM: The stair hall is architecturally intact with one exception. The original door, leading into the service wing, was recently replaced by an inappropriate smaller flush door (1141). The original door or an exact replica should be restored.

Extensive repairs need to be made, including the stabilization and repair of the plaster walls, ceiling, and cornice after ensuring that the plumbing in the second-floor bathroom (203) is sound. The plumbing should be disconnected at the basement level so there is no danger of water damage. The marble base should be resecured along the north partition.

All hardware should be cleaned and made operable and the missing hinge finials restored. The missing urn newel ornament should be found or a replication produced using the old photograph as a guide.

The oil painting must be removed, conserved, and reinstalled.

Finally, the painted decor should be restored based on the paint analysis.

Second Floor (Bedroom Floor)

Room 201 Second Floor Hall

The second floor hall differs from the Hoppin & Koen plan in minor details. The original plan includes two doorways from the hall (202A and 202B) into what is labeled Mr. Wharton's bedroom (Room 211); there is a single doorway into this bedroom from the hallway, which seems to be more practical.

The early plan illustrates a bathroom and closets in the area actually constructed as a single large bathroom (208). The two doors shown, which would have joined Mrs. Wharton's bedroom and boudoir through the bathroom, were never executed.

The dark and utilitarian nature of this space was exacerbated when the Foxhollow School constructed a partition and doorway, which until recently cut off the main stairway and its window from this hall.

The Hoppin & Koen floor plan designates the larger area, at the head of the stairway, as the staircase hall and the corridor beyond the arched opening in the north partition as the gallery.

FLOOR: Original flooring composed of 2 1/2-inch-wide tongue-and-groove boards, which run north-south. The floor sags between the east and west partitions.

WALLS: The original walls are plaster on lath ornamented with plaster moldings forming panels. All surfaces have cracks, and a large section of molding is missing from the southeast corner.

The north partition includes a broad arched opening that gives access to the gallery.

The stairwell had been enclosed by a gypsumboard partition, constructed by the Foxhollow School (removed in 1990-91), which included a doorway.

CEILING: Original plaster on lath. Numerous areas with plaster cracks, poor patching, and loose paint.

CORNICE: Original plaster cornice (run in place) with numerous vertical cracks and separation in the southeast corner.

BASEBOARD: Original low wood base with crown molding.

DOORS: Three original openings with doors and an original archway.

2011: Original three-panel wood door and molded wood architrave. The original hardware includes a pair of ormolu hinges, ormolu and enamel box lock, and two oval knobs.

2012: A three-panel door that replicates the original second-floor door type. Simple plain board architrave and hardware consisting of a pair of plain butt hinges and mortise lock. The wood knob and

rectangular keyhole escutcheon appear to have been removed from a door in the service wing, installed by the Foxhollow School (removed 1990-91).

2013: Original arched opening with wood trim and flattened arch with plain key block.

2031 AND 2131: Original openings, doors, and hardware.

WINDOWS: This hall originally received natural light from the window in the west wall of the stairwell.

HEATING: No heat.

LIGHTING: Chain-suspended incandescent ceiling fixture with replacement glass shade. This fixture may be original and matches the intact fixture in the ground floor stair hall (G-3). The Hoppin & Koen plan shows two wall fixtures flanking door 2131.

A recent battery-powered emergency light is attached to the east partition near doorway 2131.

EQUIPMENT: Recent battery-operated smoke detector on ceiling. Fire-alarm bell and switch on the east partition.

OTHER FEATURES: Two large knotty-pine two-drawer chests built in against the west partition by the Foxhollow School (removed in 1990-91).

PAINT INVESTIGATION: A thorough paint investigation should be made to determine the original decorative scheme.

RESTORATION PROGRAM: The second-floor hall is architecturally intact. The cause for the floor deflection should be determined and corrected, if possible. All plaster surfaces should be repaired and missing elements restored.

The cracked panel and loose moldings of the door to Room 213 should be repaired. All hardware should be cleaned and made operable. The later glass shade on the light fixture should be replaced by one more appropriate. The original paint scheme should be restored.

Room 202A and 202B Hall (Gallery)

This long, dark hallway is divided into two sections by a plain narrow arched opening, which was constructed to mask the chimney flue from the drawing room fireplace on the floor below.

FLOOR: Original 2 1/2-inch-wide tongue-and-groove pine boards running north-south. The floor deflects at the south end.

WALLS: Original plaster on lath, including a simple wood chair rail. The rail was removed from the area behind a later wood chest built against the east par-

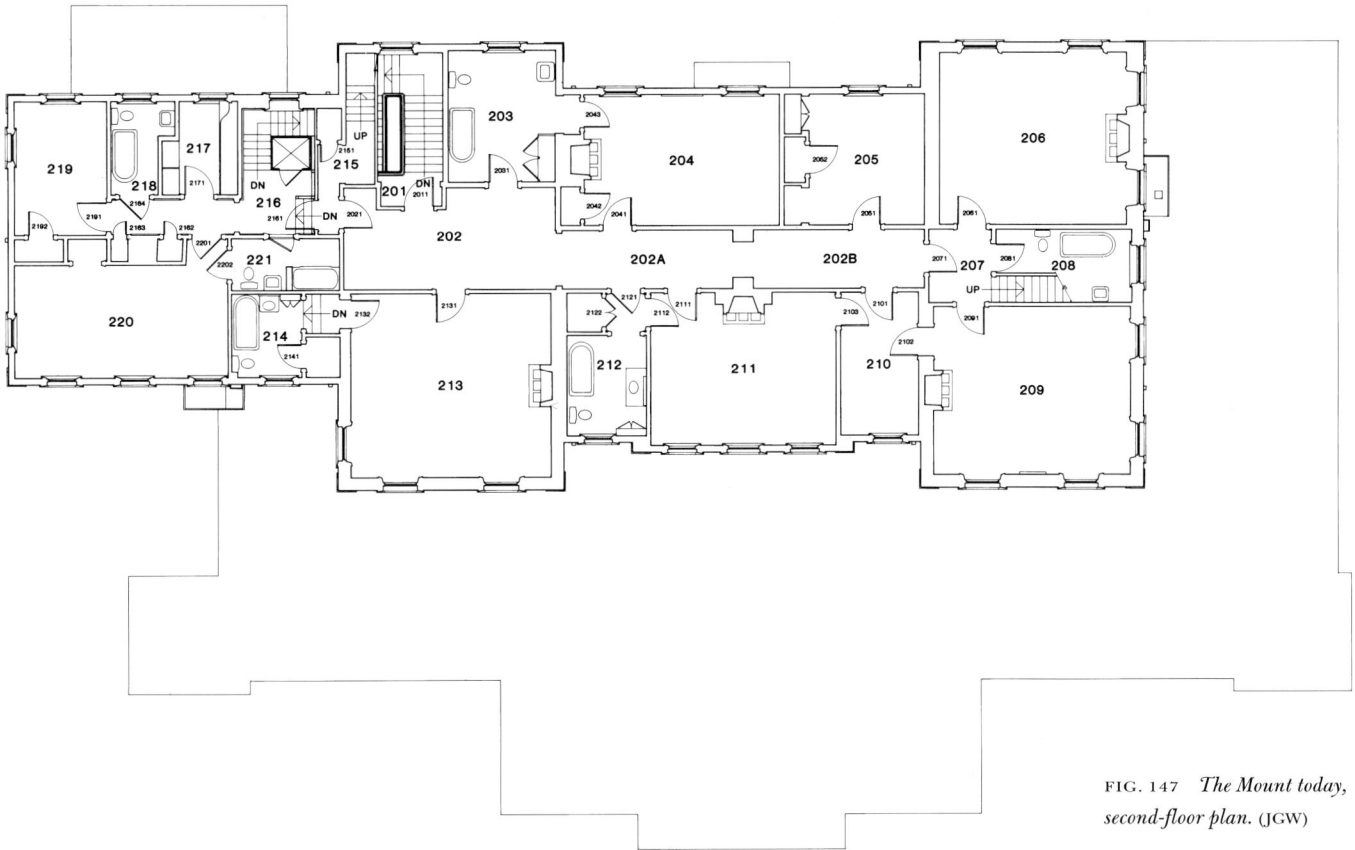

FIG. 147 *The Mount today, second-floor plan.* (JGW)

tition at the north end of the hall (202B); the chest was removed in 1989. The plaster is very deteriorated, particularly the east partition in 202A. This is related to the sagging floor and the east partition in 202B where the plaster has separated from the lath. Numerous diagonal cracks and deformations.

CEILING: Original plaster on lath. Numerous cracks, sagging plaster, and areas of poor patching.

BASEBOARD: Original low wood base with crown molding.

DOORS: Six original openings and doors. The doorways into rooms 204 and 205 appear on the Hoppin & Koen floor plan but not on the Van Anda plan included with the 1940 Abatement of Tax and Real Estate, which illustrates a doorway opening from the staircase hall (202) into the southeast corner of a bedroom (204).

Each of the three-panel wood doors retains the original ormolu brass hardware, including hinges, oval knobs, and box locks.

WINDOWS: There are no window openings.

HEATING: No source for heat.

LIGHTING: There are two incandescent ceiling fixtures, which appear to be original. An ornamental metal ring supports a large frosted-glass globe.

Fixtures are shown in these positions on the Hoppin & Koen plan.

EQUIPMENT: Recent electrical and telephone wiring attached to the baseboard and extending around doorway 2071 at the northeast end of the hall.

Brackets for a fire extinguisher attached to the south face of the archway.

PAINT INVESTIGATION: All painted surfaces should be investigated to determine the original finishes.

RESTORATION PROGRAM: Although the architectural character of this hallway is intact, many of the surfaces are very deteriorated. The floor deflection and the cracked plaster may be a result of the original construction, in which this hall, the adjoining rooms to the east with their partitions, and the central fireplace mass are supported by the structure that spans the drawing room below.

All plaster surfaces need to be repaired and stabilized. A large section of plaster has come loose from the lath support along the east partition.

All doors and hardware should be repaired, and the original light fixtures should be cleaned and rewired.

The chair rail should be restored where the two built-in chests have been removed. The original paint scheme can then be restored.

Room 203 Bathroom

This is the largest bathroom in the house, and it can be entered from the hallway and from guest room 204. The Hoppin & Koen plan illustrates this space as it appears today, except that no lavatory is illustrated in the plan.

FLOOR: Original white marble floor of 12-inch-by-12-inch tiles set in a grid pattern. The marble needs cleaning, and the surface has settled considerably in front of doorway 2043. There are several cracked and irregular tiles around the toilet.

WALLS: Original plaster on lath with simple wood chair rail. Cracks on all surfaces and movements in the wall surface around the hall doorway (2031). The painted surface is peeling behind the bathtub and toilet.

CEILING: Original plaster on lath.

CORNICE: Original deep plaster cove with a molding along the bottom edge.

Horizontal cracking in the cove along the west wall. Separation from the plaster ceiling along the east partition.

BASEBOARD: Original white marble base. A portion behind the cabinet in the northeast corner has been cut and may be removed. Base has separated from the south and west walls, and the marble floor has deflected beneath the base below the lavatory.

DOORS: Two original openings and doors.

2031: Wood three-panel door. The panel molding is loose. The molded wood trim has deflected, causing splitting in the top of the architrave. The marble plinth blocks are loose. The original hardware includes butt hinges with ball finials and oval ormolu brass knobs and box lock. The two glass push-plates and slide bolts are later additions.

2043: The east side of the architrave is split, and the marble plinth blocks are loose. The original ormolu brass knob and plain keyhole escutcheon are intact. The glass push-plate is a later addition.

Original arched opening centered in the north partition. Plastered reveal with white marble base and wood chair rail.

WINDOWS: Original opening with six-over-six, wood double-hung sash. Original wood architrave resting on the marble base. Plastered apron below the wood sill. The sash is secured by an original latch. The plaster is cracked, and the painted surface is peeling.

HEATING: Single cast-iron radiator below the window.

LIGHTING: Original incandescent wall bracket as shown on the Hoppin & Koen plan. The bulb socket has been replaced.

PLUMBING: The original toilet and lavatory have been replaced. The current white ceramic tank toilet is labeled "Standard." The white ceramic lavatory is supported by two chromed metal legs. Original iron and white-enamel bathtub set on massive console supports and what may be the original or early plumbing fittings.

The piping for the original wall-mounted toilet tank is still in place on the south partition.

OTHER FEATURES: A large, c. 1880s painted-wood case piece is fixed in the northeast corner. Stylistically, the cabinet predates the construction of The Mount, but it is not known when it was placed in this position. Wallpaper behind the cabinet indicates that it was not installed at the time of construction. The marble baseboard has been modified to accommodate the cabinet.

PAINT INVESTIGATION: All surfaces should be investigated to determine the original finishes. There appears to be wallpaper behind the cabinet in the northeast corner.

RESTORATION PROGRAM: The primary concern is to determine the cause of the floor deflection along the north wall. The marble floor tiles need to be repaired, and the loose marble baseboards and plinth blocks should be reattached. All plaster surfaces should be repaired.

Both doors need to be repaired, including portions of the trim.

All hardware should be cleaned and made operable and the enamel finish restored to the box locks.

The plumbing should be disconnected at basement level. This will ensure the preservation of the stair hall and its oil paintings below this room.

Wharton-period fixtures should replace the recent toilet and lavatory.

The original decorative scheme should be recreated. This will involve investigation of the wallpaper concealed behind the large cabinet.

Room 204 Guest Room

This large room and the adjoining smaller space to the north are both labeled as guest rooms and shown connected by a doorway on the Hoppin & Koen floor plan. They may have functioned as a guest suite (with larger room 204 as a boudoir and smaller space 205 serving as a bed chamber) or as separate bed chambers, although the smaller would have lacked a connecting bathroom. The use of the rooms probably varied depending on the number of guests at The Mount.

The 1940 Van Anda floor plan shows the two rooms connected. The connecting doorway was probably removed during the Foxhollow years.

FLOOR: Original 2 1/2-inch-wide tongue-and-groove pine boards, which run north-south.

WALLS: Original plaster on wood lath with a simple 3 1/4-inch-wide wood chair rail located at 2 feet 7 inches above the finished floor.

A doorway in the north partition has been filled in. Cut lines in the chair rail and baseboard and cracks in the wall plaster give evidence of the original opening.

Areas of deteriorated and poorly repaired plaster and peeling paint.

A large plate-glass mirror in a simple painted wood frame is attached to the west wall and rests on the chair rail.

CEILING: Original plaster on wood lath.

CORNICE: Original plaster cove enclosed by plaster moldings.

BASEBOARD: Original 5-inch-high wood base with bullnose crown molding. Area of later base in the position of the former doorway in the north partition.

DOORS: Three original openings and doors. A fourth original opening, in the north partition, was removed during the Foxhollow years.

2041, 2042, 2043: Original three-panel wood doors and 5-inch-wide molded wood architraves. The original hardware on each door includes a pair of bronze hinges, ormolu box lock, and oval knobs. The locks feature painted (enameled) panels in poor condition. Later brass slide bolts on the hall door and bathroom door.

WINDOWS: Two original openings with six-over-six, double, chain-hung wood sash. The 5-inch-wide molded wood architrave extends to the floor and encloses a plastered panel below the window sill. The sash are secured by brass thumb latches.

The thin configuration of the exterior wall structure is evident at these windows. The exterior stucco is applied to wood framing, not masonry.

HEATING: Original 7 1/2-inch-by-12-inch iron grille set in the east partition as part of the hot-air heating system.

LIGHTING: Two original double-arm bronze incandescent wall brackets with exposed bulbs. The original shades are missing. Fixtures in these positions are indicated on the Hoppin & Koen plan.

EQUIPMENT: Two original service call-buttons next to the hall doorway.

OTHER FEATURES: The original fireplace is centered on the south partition as indicated on the

Hoppin & Koen plan. The small projecting classically detailed mantel and the hearth are of gray marble. The hearth has three light gray marble insets. The fire box is lined with cast iron and has a recent cast-iron Franklin stove placed in the opening.

The closet is indicated on the Hoppin & Koen floor plan.

The Van Anda floor plan indicates access from the hall (202) through this closet. There is no evidence that this modification was ever made.

PAINT INVESTIGATION: All surfaces should be investigated to determine the original finishes and colors.

RESTORATION PROGRAM: This room retains all of its original character. Restoration will involve the repair and stabilization of the plaster wall and ceiling surfaces and the cornice. All hardware should be cleaned and made operable and the enamel finish restored to the box locks. The missing closet door should be restored (the door was reinstalled after 1986). The original electric wall brackets should be cleaned and rewired.

The large plate-glass mirror attached to the west wall and the nature of the wall finish behind it should be investigated further.

All original finishes should be restored.

Room 205 Guest Room

Of the three guest rooms located on the second floor, this is the smallest. It was probably both part of the suite formed by its original connection to guest room 204 and an independent bedroom. Two arched recesses in the south partition provide architectural interest, but unlike the other bed chambers this room lacks a fireplace. The original doorway connecting to guest room 204 was probably removed by the Foxhollow School.

FLOOR: Original 2 1/2-inch-wide tongue-and-groove pine boards running north-south. A metal electrical chase has recently been attached to the floor along the north and west walls.

WALLS: Original plaster on wood lath with a simple 3-inch-wide wood chair rail located at 2 feet 7 inches above the finished floor. Two plastered arched openings in the south partition incorporate shallow plastered recesses. The southeast recess originally included a doorway to room 204.

CEILING: Original plaster on wood lath.

CORNICE: Original plaster cove enclosed by plaster moldings.

BASEBOARD: Original 5-inch-high wood base with a bullnose crown molding.

DOORS: Two original openings and doors. A third doorway was located in the partition beyond the southeast arched opening. This feature was probably removed during the Foxhollow period.

2051, 2052: Original three-panel wood doors and 5-inch-wide molded wood trim. The original hardware on both doors includes a pair of iron and ormolu hinges with ball finials, ormolu box lock with enameled panel, and small oval ormolu knobs. The inside knob of the closet door (2052) is missing.

WINDOWS: One original opening centered in the west wall with six-over-six double chain-hung sash. The 5-inch-wide molded wood architrave extends to the floor and encloses a plastered panel below the window sill. The sash is secured with a brass thumb latch.

HEATING: Original 7 1/2-inch-by-12-inch iron grille located in the east partition as part of the hot-air heating system.

LIGHTING: Simple original incandescent metal bracket attached to the east partition. Exposed bulb with no shade. A fixture is indicated in this position on the Hoppin & Koen floor plan.

EQUIPMENT: An electrical channel with three double outlets was recently attached to the floor along the north and west walls.

Two original service call-bell push-buttons are located in the trim of the hall door (2051). They are marked "housemaid" and "servants' hall."

OTHER FEATURES: The southwest arched recess incorporates an original low wood cabinet with a pair of six-panel wood doors that open to shelves. The top surface consists of a gray marble slab with a beveled front edge. There is a 1-foot-4-inch-high gray marble backsplash attached to the back and side walls, with plaster above the marble. A wash bowl and pitcher that would have been useful because of the lack of connecting bathroom, may have been placed here, reinforcing the notion that this space was sometimes used as a separate guest room. Inappropriate metal brackets (supporting wood shelves) have been installed on the back wall of this recess.

The closet appears on the Hoppin & Koen floor plan; the vertical mirror attached to the closet door is a recent addition.

PAINT INVESTIGATION: All surfaces should be investigated to determine the original finishes and colors.

RESTORATION PROGRAM: This room retains all of its original character, except for the original doorway formerly located in the partition beyond the southeast arch. This feature should be restored if this guest suite is to represent the conditions extant during Edith Wharton's occupancy.

All plaster surfaces should be repaired and stabilized.

The hardware should be cleaned and repaired, and the enameled finish on the box locks restored.

The original electric wall bracket should be cleaned and rewired.

The electrical track and outlets should be removed from the floor surface.

The telephone junction boxes on the window and the trim should be removed.

The mirror should be removed from the closet door, and the inappropriate wood shelves eliminated from the southwest recess.

Room 206 Boudoir

The boudoir, designed by Ogden Codman, is architecturally intact. All of the ornamental details are preserved, including the eight decorative floral canvases set into the walls. This is the only room on this floor documented by a Wharton-period photograph. It records the northeast corner and shows the fireplace, a window, and three of the wall canvases. The window is draped simply with a printed (toile) fabric. The same fabric appears to be covering a sofa and chair. The painted canvases have the same dark quality in the photograph that they exhibit today. One of the canvases on the south wall is reflected in the mirror over the mantelpiece.

The Hoppin & Koen floor plan includes a door in the east partition to connect the boudoir to the adjoining bathroom. A second door in the bathroom

FIG. 148 *Edith Wharton's boudoir, north wall and northeast corner, during her occupancy.* (BL)

FIG. 149 *The boudoir today, north wall and northeast corner.* (JD)

would have opened directly into Mrs. Wharton's bedroom. These doorways were never constructed, and the current arrangement of the boudoir is what was actually built.

FLOOR: Original oak parquet floor arranged in a pattern of diagonal squares. This surface is framed by a simple strip border. The finish is worn and there are areas of black staining.

WALLS: Original paneled composition of wood stiles and rails framing flat, recessed plaster fields. Each wall features a symmetrical arrangement of panels, doors or windows, and inset oil paintings. There is a low dado with plain, recessed panels on each wall. The central panel of each wall includes a recessed canvas and is ornamented below the cornice with applied foliate swags and a central rondel. The eight painted canvases are secured behind wood moldings.

There is some separation of the wood panel components and cracking of plaster surfaces. The chair rail has shifted in the northeast corner.

CEILING: Original unornamented plaster on lath.

CORNICE: Original molded plaster cornice ornamented with a leaf motif. There are several vertical cracks, which may indicate that the cornice was installed in sections rather than run in place and then ornamented.

BASEBOARD: Original low wood base with an applied crown molding.

FIG. 150 *One of the boudoir's applied foliate swags and a central rondel, designed by Ogden Codman, Jr.* (JD)

DOORS: Single original opening and door. A second doorway, shown on the Hoppin & Koen floor plan, was never constructed. Codman's arrangement of canvases on the east partition precludes the positioning of a door shown on the original plan.

2061: Original three-panel wood door and bolection-molded architrave. The hardware includes a pair of iron and ormolu hinges and an ormolu and enamel box lock with oval knobs. There is a simple escutcheon plate on the hall side.

Later additions include a name plate on the outside and a recent slide bolt on the room side.

WINDOWS: Four original openings with six-over-six double chain-hung sash. Original bolection-molded architrave extending to the floor and paneled apron below the sill. The two windows in the north wall have deep reveals. Each sash is secured by a brass thumb latch.

HEATING: Original painted iron grille located in the dado of the east partition as part of the hot-air heating system.

LIGHTING: The original Hoppin & Koen floor plan indicates four wall brackets, but there is no physical evidence that such fixtures were installed. Probably Codman's design scheme with painted canvases precluded the placement of electric wall brackets here.

The Wharton-period photograph does not include any lighting devices.

EQUIPMENT: Two original staff call-bell push-buttons are located in the wall next to the door architrave. They are finished with mother-of-pearl insets.

Possibly original push-button electrical switch located below the service buttons.

Three electrical floor outlets of later origin but possibly in original locations.

Three telephone jacks; the one mounted on the south partition baseboard may be early.

OTHER FEATURES: The original fireplace is centered on the north wall as indicated on the Hoppin & Koen floor plan. The projecting mantel features a bolection-molded architrave and an applied shelf, both formed from a mottled red-and-white marble. The hearth is of the same marble and includes three black marble inserts. The hearth has settled slightly below the floor plane. The bottom of the firebox is formed of black tiles, of which nine are broken. The firebox is lined with ornate cast-iron panels. The back panel is cracked.

The overmantel includes an original inset horizontal mirror with a deteriorated silvered backing. One of the eight original floral canvases is positioned above the mirror. The complete painting is clearly illustrated in the Wharton-period photograph.

A second, larger mirror is installed in the center, paneled bay of the south partition just above the dado. Reflections from the mirror would be most visible from a sitting position. Edith Wharton's desk was centered between these two mirrors.

PAINT INVESTIGATION: A preliminary paint investigation revealed that the paneled and ornamented walls were originally covered in a pale yellow followed by a pale blue; further analysis is necessary. Approximately ten layers of paint were revealed on these surfaces.

RESTORATION PROGRAM: The boudoir, Edith Wharton's bedroom (209), and the library are the three rooms most intimately connected with Edith Wharton and therefore merit very careful restora-

tion. This elegant room retains all of its original character and is in good condition.

The wood-and-plaster wall surfaces show evidence of minor cracks and separations, and there are several vertical cracks in the plaster cornice. The parquet floor should be cleaned carefully so that the patina is not removed.

The eight oil paintings should be removed, cleaned, conserved, and reinstalled.

All hardware should be cleaned and made operable and the enameled finish restored to the box lock.

The cast-iron fireplace lining needs to be cleaned and polished with stove blacking. The fireplace should not be used.

All original painted finishes should be restored.

Room 207 Passage

The Hoppin & Koen plan includes this passage, although the actual number and arrangements of doors differ from what is shown on the original plan. This small and somewhat dark space functioned as the entrance to and buffer for Edith Wharton's private domain.

FLOOR: Original oak parquet floor arranged in a pattern of diagonal squares. The finish is very worn.

WALLS: Original plaster on wood lath with a simple wood chair rail. Bad cracks and loose plaster in the southeast corner. The cracks continue up into the cornice, and there are plaster cracks above each door.

CEILING: Original plaster on wood lath. Cracks along the edge of the ceiling.

CORNICE: Deep molded plaster cove with molding at the upper and lower edge. Severe horizontal crack in the cove along the east partition and a large crack in the northeast corner.

BASEBOARD: Original low wood base with a molded top.

DOORS: There are four original openings and doors. The bathroom door (2081) was relocated in the partition when the stairway was constructed during the Foxhollow period.

Only the door from the gallery opens into the space (202B).

The Hoppin & Koen floor plan includes a doorway in the south partition into the dressing room separating Edith Wharton's bedroom from her husband's room. This doorway was never constructed.

2071: Original three-panel wood door and molded wood architrave. The upper door panel is loose, as is the outer molding. The original hardware includes a pair of iron-and-ormolu hinges and an ormolu-and-enamel box lock with oval knobs.

The lock keeper is missing, and one hinge finial has been removed.

The other openings (2061, 2081, 2091) retain the original doors, trim, and hardware.

The opening to the stairway was created during the Foxhollow period.

WINDOWS: There is an original transom-like window at the top of the north partition. There are four large square openings, two of which retain glass. The two east openings were closed when the stairway was constructed during the Foxhollow period.

HEATING: There is no heating.

LIGHTING: Old, possibly original, incandescent ceiling fixture. The glass shade is missing. The Hoppin & Koen plan indicates a fixture in this position.

EQUIPMENT: Original push-button light switch next to the hall door.

Old wiring protrudes from the south wall next to the hall door.

PAINT INVESTIGATION: All surfaces should be investigated to determine the original finishes.

RESTORATION PROGRAM: If the stairway is removed from the bathroom, the north partition can be restored. This work would include the opening of the two transom panels above the stair entrance door.

All plaster surfaces need repair, including the cornice and ceiling.

The parquet floor should be cleaned and the finish restored.

The doors need repair. All hardware should be cleaned and made operable. The enamel finish should be restored to the box locks.

The ceiling light fixture should be carefully cleaned and rewired and a proper glass shade installed.

All original painted finishes should be restored after repairs have been made.

Room 208 Bathroom

This room is part of Edith Wharton's private suite, situated between her boudoir and bedroom. The Hoppin & Koen floor plan illustrates a bathroom and closet in the area that currently includes only the bathroom with no direct connection from the bathroom to the boudoir and bedroom.

During the Foxhollow years a stairway was constructed from the attic story down through this space to the passage (207).

FLOOR: Original white marble floor, composed of 12-inch-by-12-inch tiles set in a grid. The marble is soiled, stained, and has minor cracks. The tiles have settled in the northeast corner and beneath the toilet.

WALLS: Original plaster on wood lath with a simple wood chair rail. Numerous cracks and loose paint and an irregular damaged area above the lavatory. The chair rail has pulled away from the east partition.

CEILING: The original plaster ceiling has been removed or covered by a panel system secured by moldings.

The ceiling was disturbed when the stairway was inserted during the Foxhollow period. The surfaces are crazed, and paint is loose.

CORNICE: Originally there was no cornice. A narrow wood molding was installed during the Foxhollow period.

BASEBOARD: Original white marble base with a molded top edge. It is cracked and loose below the lavatory and behind the toilet and bathtub.

DOOR: One original door and opening. The opening was moved a few inches to the west when the stairway was constructed.

2081: Original wood three-panel door. The upper and lower panels and moldings are loose, and the door is in a rough condition. The original architrave was reused when the opening was moved.

The original hardware includes two iron-and-ormolu hinges, a partially enameled ormolu box lock, and oval knobs. The beveled-glass hand plate was probably installed during the Foxhollow period.

WINDOWS: Original opening with six-over-six wood double-hung sash. The molded wood architrave rests on a wood sill at chair-rail level. The bottom of the stop at sill level has separated into a large crack. The metal thumb latch is broken.

A horizontal transom-like opening is located at the top of the south partition. The opening features two large glass panes, one of which is cracked. This original feature allowed natural light to reach the passage (207).

HEATING: Single small cast-iron radiator against the north wall.

LIGHTING: Two original incandescent single-light wall brackets flanking the lavatory. The original shades (glass?) are missing. Above the lavatory between the brackets is an ornamental brass cover plate of unknown origin.

The Hoppin & Koen floor plan indicates a single wall bracket above the bathtub.

PLUMBING: The original toilet and lavatory have been replaced. The white ceramic tank toilet is labeled "Standard."

A pipe protruding from the wall above the toilet may relate to the original wall-mounted tank.

FIG. 151 *Edith Wharton's bedroom today, northeast corner.* (JD)

The white ceramic lavatory is of recent origin.

Original iron-and-white-enamel bathtub set on massive console supports and what may be original or early plumbing fittings.

The plumbing has leaked, causing damage to the library below.

EQUIPMENT: Several towel racks of varying periods, none original.

PAINT INVESTIGATION: All surfaces should be investigated to determine the original finishes.

RESTORATION PROGRAM: It is important that all plumbing be disconnected to eliminate danger of water leaking into the library below.

The cause of the floor deflection should be determined and corrected. The marble floor should be repaired, reset, and cleaned, and the marble baseboard should be secured to the wall. All plaster surfaces should be repaired, including the ceiling.

If the stairway is to be relocated, then the plaster ceiling should be restored and the doorway placed in the original position.

The door needs to be repaired, the hardware should be cleaned and made operable, and the enamel finish should be restored to the box lock. The toilet and lavatory should be replaced with fixtures that duplicate the originals.

Repairs should be made to the damaged window stop, and the cracked glass in the south partition transom should be replaced.

The two wall brackets need to be cleaned and rewired and appropriate shades installed.

The original paint scheme can be restored after all repairs have been made.

Room 209 Edith Wharton's Bedroom

The architectural finish in this important room, even on the small, elegant marble mantel, is very basic in its detail.

The Hoppin & Koen plan includes a doorway in the west partition opening directly into the bathroom, a single window on the north wall, a small window in the south wall, but no doorway into the dressing room (210). The room as actually constructed included a door opening into the dressing room but no doorway to the bathroom.

FLOOR: Original oak parquet floor arranged in a pattern of diagonal squares. This surface is framed by a simple wood border. The finish is worn; many of the individual pieces that became loose were resecured by surface nailing.

WALLS: Original plaster on wood lath with a simple wood chair rail on all walls. The plaster is generally in good condition with some cracks between the north windows.

CEILING: Original plaster on wood lath is in good condition, with only hairline cracks.

CORNICE: Original molded plaster cornice attached to wood lath. There are several vertical cracks and water damage on the north wall.

BASEBOARD: Original low wood base with an applied crown molding.

DOORS: Two original openings and doors.

2101: Wood three-panel door in damaged condition. The upper and lower panels are loose, and the applied panel moldings on the hall side are damaged. The original hardware includes a pair of iron-and-ormolu hinges (one of the ormolu finials is missing) and an ormolu-and-enamel box lock with oval knobs. There is a small metal card holder on the lock rail (hall side), probably from the Foxhollow period. The brass slide bolt is recent.

2102: Wood three-panel door set in a deep-paneled reveal. The recently installed clothes hanger bar indicates that this recess is serving as a closet. The original ornate oval knob is in place. The glass push-plate may date to the Foxhollow period.

WINDOWS: Four original openings with six-over-six double chain-hung wood sash. The molded wood architraves extend to the floor, and there is a paneled apron below each sill. The lower sash are secured by metal thumb latches.

HEATING: Original painted iron grille located next to the mantel on the south wall. This is part of the hot-air heating system.

LIGHTING: The Hoppin & Koen floor plan indicates two fixtures on the east wall and a single fixture on the north wall.

The fixtures in place today reflect the original construction. There are four electric wall brackets. The two single brackets on the west partition may have flanked the bed. A pair of double-light brackets on the east wall may indicate the location for a dressing table. The frosted-glass, tulip-form shades are recent replacements. One shade is missing.

EQUIPMENT: Three original staff call-bell push-buttons are located on the trim of the hall door (2091).

The telephone cable next to the door in the west partition and the thermostat mounted on the south wall are recent additions.

OTHER FEATURES: The original fireplace is centered on the south wall as shown on the Hoppin & Koen plan. The simple but elegant small mantel is a mottled gray marble. The top member of the inner surround is damaged; broken pieces have been resecured with extensive cracks evident. The firebox is lined with unornamented iron plates.

The gray marble hearth has three cracks, and the firebox has several damaged tiles.

The mantel is attached directly to the wall surface with no projecting chimney breast.

A large framed mirror is attached to the wall surface between the windows of the east wall.

PAINT INVESTIGATION: A careful paint investigation should be made of all surfaces. Traces of wallpaper should be sought behind the wall brackets and the large mirror attached to the east wall.

RESTORATION PROGRAM: This bedroom warrants great care in its restoration.

All plaster surfaces should be repaired after all possibilities of external water penetration have been eliminated. Damaged woodwork needs to be repaired, particularly the panels and moldings of door 2091. The clothes rod should be eliminated from opening 2101. The parquet floor should be carefully cleaned so that the patina is not removed.

All hardware should be cleaned and made operable and the enameled finish restored to the box locks. The original electric wall brackets need to be cleaned and rewired, and proper shades should be installed.

The marble mantel should be repaired. The restored fireplace should not be used.

All original surface finishes should be restored.

Room 210 Dressing Room

The only difference beteen this small room and the Hoppin & Koen floor plan is the placement and direction of the door swings. The original floor plan identifies this as the dressing room, a connecting

FIG. 152 *The three original staff call-bell push-buttons in Edith Wharton's bedroom. The top one reads "House Maid," and the bottom "Svts Hall." The center unmarked one probably called her personal maid (compare to Fig. 157).* (JD)

FIG. 153 *The original mantel on the south wall of Edith Wharton's bedroom is made of a French gray-and-black melange marble. The top section of the shelf needs repair.* (JD)

passage between the Whartons' bedrooms and a clothes storage area.

The ceiling was damaged by water, and a large section of that surface has been replaced with gypsum board.

FLOOR: Original narrow tongue-and-groove boards running north-south. The finish is very worn.

WALLS: Original plaster on lath with a simple molded wood chair rail. All walls show evidence of cracking, and the south wall has been damaged by water. The east wall may have been resurfaced in gypsum board.

CEILING: Only the west quarter of the original plaster on lath ceiling survives. The remaining surface is a gypsum-board replacement.

CORNICE: Plaster cove and ceiling molding terminating along the bottom edge in a molded band. Only the west quarter of this cornice survives intact. Part of the cove and bottom molding survives on the north and south partitions; this feature is missing along the east wall.

BASEBOARD: Original simple low wood base with a molded crown.

DOORS: Three original openings and doors. All three doors are identical in detail and open into this space.

2101: Wood three-panel door and molded wood architrave. The top panel has a vertical split. The original hardware includes a pair of iron butt hinges with ball finials and an ormolu-and-enamel box lock and oval knobs. The two glass push-plates probably date from the Foxhollow period. Curiously, the 1940 Van Anda floor plan does not indicate a doorway in this location.

2102: The top panel is partially split. A single glass push-plate was probably added during the Foxhollow period.

2103: The two glass push-plates may date from the Foxhollow period.

WINDOWS: One original opening with six-over-six double chain-hung wood sash. The molded wood architrave extends to the floor, and there is a paneled apron below the sill. The sash and stops are recent replacements and have not been painted.

HEATING: No evidence for heating.

LIGHTING: The wall bracket indicated on the Hoppin & Koen plan was never installed. The existing simple incandescent ceiling fixture appears to be original. The glass globe shade is missing.

EQUIPMENT: A single original staff call-bell push-button is located on the door architrave of opening 2103. An original push-button light switch is located nearby on the wall surface.

OTHER FEATURES: Three recently applied wood strips are attached to the south partition.

A small iron nut and bolt protrudes from the east wall near the baseboard. This is part of the support for the exterior fire escape.

PAINT INVESTIGATION: All surfaces should be analyzed to determine the original color and finishes.

RESTORATION PROGRAM: The missing plaster surfaces of the wall, ceiling, and cornice must be restored. All of the woodwork must be repaired, including the cracked door panels.

The strip flooring should be cleaned so that the patina is not removed.

All hardware is to be cleaned and made operable and the enameled finish restored to the box locks.

The ceiling fixture needs to be cleaned and rewired; the missing glass shade should be replicated.

All original painted finishes should be restored.

Room 211   Teddy Wharton's Bedroom

This comparatively small but bright room has the distinction of being located below the central pediment of the east facade. The Hoppin & Koen floor plan refers to it as Mr. Wharton's bedroom.

The room has been damaged by settlement in the drawing room directly below. Leaks from the bathroom directly above resulted in the collapse of several feet of the plaster cornice in 1985. Although in a deteriorated state, the room is architecturally very much intact. The focal point is the bold black-and-white marble mantel centered on the west wall.

FLOOR: Original narrow tongue-and-groove boards running north-south. The finish is very worn, and the floor surface slopes to the north and south, due to the deflections in the drawing room below.

WALLS: Original plaster on lath with numerous cracked and deteriorated areas, particularly on the north and south partitions.

A simple molded wood chair rail extends around the room. This element is in a higher position on the east wall due to the settlement of the two flanking walls. Part of the north partition was repaired recently with gypsum board.

CEILING: Original plaster on lath in a very deteriorated condition. Extensive water damage and areas where the finish coat has come loose, exposing the undercoat.

CORNICE: Original molded plaster cornice attached to wood lath. There are numerous damaged areas; a large section has collapsed along the south partition, exposing the wood lath. Deteriorated area along the chimney breast.

FIG. 154 *Teddy Wharton's bedroom today, east wall.* (JD)

BASEBOARD: Original low wood base with an applied crown molding.

DOORS: Three original openings and doors. A fourth doorway, shown on the Hoppin & Koen floor plan on the north side of the chimney breast, was never constructed.

2111: Wood three-panel door and molded architrave. The upper and lower panels are loose. The original hardware includes a pair of iron butt hinges with ball finials, an ormolu-and-enamel box lock, and oval knobs. The two glass push-plates probably date from the Foxhollow period. The small slide bolt is a recent addition.

2112: This door is the same as 2111. Settlement of the partition has caused the door to shift within the frame. The two glass push-plates probably date from the Foxhollow period.

2103: This door is the same as 2111.

WINDOWS: Three original openings with six-over-six double, chain-hung sash. The molded wood architrave extends to the floor, and there is a cracked plastered apron below the sill.

The sash are secured by thumb latches.

HEATING: The original ornamental cast-iron grille is situated in the floor in the northeast corner. This is part of the original hot-air system.

LIGHTING: The Hoppin & Koen plan indicates two wall brackets on the south partition and a single bracket on the north. Actually, two electric ormolu brackets flank the central window. These fixtures originally held glass shades.

EQUIPMENT: Two original staff call-bell push-buttons (one labeled house maid) are located on the architrave of the hall door 2111.

Two old or original push-button light switches survive on the west partition.

A small metal plate set into the baseboard of the south wall may be an early or original outlet for a telephone. Nearby is a more recent telephone jack.

OTHER FEATURES: The original fireplace is centered on the west partition and projects from a broad chimney breast. The simple but elegant small mantel is formed from a bold black-and-white marble. The deep firebox has a plain iron plate lining. The projecting hearth is formed of the three red marble insets and a black-and-white marble border. The south corner of the border is damaged. Several of the black tiles in the firebox are cracked.

PAINT INVESTIGATION: All surfaces should be investigated to determine the original finishes.

FIG. 155 *South wall of Teddy Wharton's bedroom, showing the large section of the original plaster cornice that collapsed in 1985, exposing the wood lath.* (JD)

RESTORATION PROGRAM: The attic plumbing should be disconnected to prevent water damage to this room or the drawing room below.

The conditions in this room should also be analyzed as part of the structural inspection of the drawing room and the east wall where it meets the exterior terrace.

This room requires considerable plaster repair. All gypsum board repairs should be replaced with plaster. The missing section of cornice should be replicated.

Damaged woodwork needs to be repaired and the door panels resecured.

The wood floor should be cleaned so that the patina is not removed.

All hardware should be cleaned and made operable, and the enamel finish restored to the box locks. The two original electric wall brackets need to be cleaned and rewired. Glass shades should be placed on these fixtures.

The marble mantel should be cleaned. The iron firebox should be polished with stove blacking, but the fireplace should not be used. The damaged tiles, therefore, need not be replaced.

All original finishes should be restored.

Room 212 Bathroom

The Hoppin & Koen floor plan illustrates this bathroom much as it exists today. Minor differences include the never-installed door separating the small vestibule from the bathroom proper and the existing pair of closet doors, which the plan shows as a single door.

The original marble-topped lavatory and the enamel bathtub survive, as do some original or early furnishings, such as the large mirror and the wall cabinet.

FLOOR: Original white marble floor composed of 12-inch-by-12-inch tiles set in a grid pattern. The marble needs cleaning; the surface has settled in the southwest corner where there are some loose tiles.

The vestibule area has a floor composed of narrow tongue-and-groove boards that match those in the bedroom.

WALLS: Original plaster on lath with a simple wood chair rail on the north and south walls.

The plaster has numerous cracks, areas of loose paint, and gypsum-board repairs on the east wall and the bottom of the west partition.

CEILING: Four large composition-board and gypsum-board panels with joints masked by wood moldings. This surface replaces an original plaster ceiling.

CORNICE: Applied wood molding that abuts a wood strip attached to the ceiling. This cornice and the integral detailing of the ceiling are an early modification.

The vestibule retains the original plaster cove, which is water damaged. The bottom applied molding on the east side is missing.

BASEBOARD: Original white marble base with integral molded top edge. The base is loose along the south and east walls.

DOORS: There are four original openings, three of which have doors.

2121: Original three-panel wood door and molded wood architrave. The bottom panel has a loose molding. All of the original hardware, hinges, lock, and knobs remain in place. Curiously, the 1940 Van Anda floor plan does not indicate this opening.

2122: Original pair of wood three-panel doors. All of the original hardware remains in place. The Hoppin & Koen plan indicates a single door, apparently never built, in this position.

2123: Original opening with molded wood architrave. There is no evidence that a door was positioned in this opening as indicated on the original plan.

2112: Original door and hardware.

WINDOWS: Single original openings with six-over-six double-hung sash. The molded wood architrave extends to the top of the marble base. The original plastered apron has been repaired with gypsum board. The sash is secured by a thumb latch.

HEATING: Single small cast-iron radiator below the window.

FIG. 156 *The original marble-topped lavatory on the north wall of Teddy Wharton's bathroom.* (JD)

LIGHTING: Single original electric wall bracket in the position shown on the Hoppin & Koen floor plan. The bulb socket has been replaced.

PLUMBING: Original marble-topped lavatory with high marble back splash. Oval white ceramic sink bowl. Marble apron supported by a pair of nickel-plated legs.

Original iron-and-white-enamel bathtub set on massive console supports. Recent black steel shower-curtain support.

White ceramic tank toilet, which replaces the original toilet with wall-mounted tank.

EQUIPMENT: Two early and possibly original metal towel bars attached to the north partition and now painted the wall color.

Recent toilet-paper holder attached to the window sill.

OTHER FEATURES: Early, possibly original, large wall-mounted wood cabinet with a pair of paneled doors and glass shelves.

Large vertical plate-glass mirror with a decorative painted wood frame. The top fits into the wood molding of the cornice. The original finish of the frame should be determined. This may be original.

The condition and finish of the wall surfaces behind this mirror and the wall cabinet should be investigated.

PAINT INVESTIGATION: All surfaces should be investigated to determine the original finishes.

RESTORATION PROGRAM: The plumbing should be disconnected at basement level to prevent further water damage to the drawing room below. The cause of the floor deflection should be determined prior to resetting the loose marble tiles and baseboard.

All plaster surfaces should be repaired, and gypsum board patches should be replaced with plaster.

The original condition of the ceiling needs to be determined.

All hardware should be cleaned, restored, and made operable.

If the room is fully restored, the original toilet type should replace the existing one.

All original surface finishes should be restored, including those on the towel bars, the mirror frame, and the wall cabinet.

Room 213 Guest Bedroom

Unlike the other bedrooms (including the west guest suite), this large room features no cornice or chair rail. The only ornamental feature is the marble mantel centered on the north wall. Further physical investigation may reveal that an original cornice was removed, perhaps when the ceiling was repaired.

It has been assumed that the Whartons used this large room as their primary guest room. The two subsequent owners used it as the master bedroom. It is the largest room on the second floor.

The layout of the room generally follows the Hoppin & Koen plan with two exceptions. The original floor plan includes a closet door in the south wall; as actually constructed, the closet space is entered from the adjoining bathroom. The original plan also illustrates a narrow window in the north wall, but this opening was never constructed.

FLOOR: Original narrow tongue-and-grove boards running north-south. The finish is worn.

WALLS: Original plaster on lath. The walls were repaired and painted in July 1986.

CEILING: The ceiling has been repaired recently and is in good condition.

CORNICE: No cornice.

BASEBOARD: Original low wood base with an applied crown.

DOORS: Two original openings and doors.

2131, 2132: Wood three-panel doors and molded architraves.

The inside face of the hall door is covered by a large mirror set in a wood frame. This feature is old and may be original. The hardware consists of a pair of butt hinges and simple ball finials and an ormolu box lock with oval knobs.

The bathroom door retains the original hardware. The box lock is painted blue.

WINDOWS: Three original openings with six-over-six double, chain-hung wood sash. The molded wood architraves extend to the floor, and there is a wood paneled apron below the sill. Original thumb latches secure the sash. Recent glass and aluminum inside storm sash.

HEATING: The original simple cast-iron grille is located in the north wall near the mantel. This is part of the original hot-air system.

LIGHTING: Two original ormolu double-arm electric wall brackets between the east wall windows.

The current silk shades have replaced the original glass shades.

The Hoppin & Koen plan indicates two fixtures in this same position.

EQUIPMENT: Recently installed thermostat in the west partition near the hall door.

OTHER FEATURES: The original fireplace is centered on the north wall. The marble mantel projects directly from the wall with no visible chimney breast. Red-and-white mottled marble similar to the boudoir mantel (209). The hearth is composed of the same red-and-white marble with three black marble insets showing evidence of cracking. The firebox is lined with plain iron panels, and the floor is covered in glazed black tiles; approximately 13 are damaged.

PAINT INVESTIGATION: All surfaces should be carefully investigated to determine the original finishes.

RESTORATION PROGRAM: The room has been repaired recently. Future investigations should seek to determine whether the room originally featured a cornice and chair rail.

The floor needs cleaning and careful refinishing.

The door hardware should be cleaned and made operable, and the enameled finishes should be restored.

An investigation should determine if the large mirror attached to door 2131 is original.

The small cracks in the marble fireplace should be repaired.

All surfaces should have the Wharton-period finishes restored.

Room 214 Guest Bathroom

The Hoppin & Koen plan shows the closet with access from the bedroom, but a second doorway is penciled in on the bathroom side. The bedroom steps are penciled in on the drawing.

No lavatory is included on the original plan.

The details in this room match those found in the other primary bathrooms on the second floor.

FLOOR: Original white and gray 12-inch-by-12-inch marble tiles set in a grid pattern. The surface needs cleaning but is in good condition.

The original three-riser stair is constructed with wood treads and risers.

WALLS: Original plaster on lath with a simple wood chair rail. The surfaces are in good condition. The walls were repainted in July 1986.

CEILING: Plain flat panels in composition board or gypsum board with joints marked by wood moldings. What appears to be a painted canvas covering is loose on the northeast panel.

CORNICE: Applied wood molding that abuts the wood dividing strips on the ceiling.

BASEBOARD: Original white marble base with integral molded top edge. It is loose along the east wall and broken along the wall behind the tub and toilet.

DOORS: Three-panel wood door with a molded wood architrave terminating on marble plinth blocks. One of these blocks has been removed and placed behind the radiator.

The original hardware consists of a pair of plain butt hinges with ball finials, an oval ormolu knob, and a small iron box lock marked "ST."

The door opening at the foot of the short run of stairs never featured a door.

WINDOWS: One original opening with six-over-six wood double-hung sash. The molded wood architrave extends to the base and terminates on marble plinth blocks. These blocks are loose on both sides. The sash is secured by an original thumb latch. Recent aluminum and glass interior storm sash.

HEATING: Single small cast-iron radiator below the window.

LIGHTING: Original electric wall bracket with later silk shade. The bulb socket is a replacement.

PLUMBING: Original white ceramic lavatory (marked "Pat.d Nov. 4, 1902") set on a single turned and tapered pedestal leg. The faucets are replacements. Original iron-and-white-enamel bathtub set on massive console supports. The original pipes survive but the faucets and shower were replaced in 1986. Recent white ceramic tank toilet marked "Standard." Pipe in wall for original wall-mounted toilet tank.

EQUIPMENT: Glass shelf at the foot of the tub supported on old metal brackets. Old glass and metal towel bar, possibly original.

OTHER FEATURES: Early, possibly original, large wall-mounted wood cabinet with a pair of paneled doors and glass shelves.

Large vertical mirror in a plain molded wood frame set on top of the chair rail behind the lavatory. This may be an original furnishing.

PAINT INVESTIGATION: All surfaces should be analyzed to determine the original finishes, including the wall surface behind the mirror and cabinet.

RESTORATION PROGRAM: If this is to remain a functioning bathroom, then all pipes should be inspected and replaced as necessary. The original lavatory and tub should be preserved. The original type of toilet should replace the existing fixture.

The ceiling needs to be probed further to determine the original condition.

The loose marble baseboard and the plinth blocks must be resecured.

The light fixture should be cleaned and rewired.

All original surface finishes should be restored, including those of the mirror and wall cabinet.

Room 216 Servants' Hallway

The Hoppin & Koen floor plan represents the hall as it appears today, with the exception of the partition and door, probably dating from the Foxhollow School period, which separate this hall from the attic stairway.

FLOOR: Original tongue-and-groove pine boards running north-south. The finish is worn.

WALLS: Original plaster on lath with a full beaded-board wainscot and a 3-inch-wide molded wood chair rail. The varnished finish survives on the woodwork.

The plaster walls are continuous around the stairwell surrounding the elevator shaft. The north partition, which compromises the balustrade, is a later addition.

CEILING: Original plaster on lath. Loose and damaged area above the stairway and elevator.

The sides of the original skylight originally opened to provide ventilation. The shaft is sheathed in beaded board. There are attic access windows in the east and west faces of the shaft.

CORNICE: No evidence of a cornice.

BASEBOARD: Original 10-inch-high wood base with molded crown.

DOORS: Seven original openings and doors.

2162, 2163: Original narrow three-panel wood doors and 5 1/2-inch-wide molded wood architrave. The original hardware consists of a pair of bronze butt hinges, mortise lock, and wood knobs. Door 2163 is missing its knobs.

2181: Three-panel wood door and 5 1/2-inch-wide molded architrave. The original hardware is in place, including the wood knobs.

WINDOWS: Natural light is available from the skylight.

HEATING: No heating.

LIGHTING: Original electric wall bracket on the west partition.

EQUIPMENT: Recent telephone and electric wire-mold runs above the doors of the east partition.

OTHER FEATURES: Original wood service stair with three runs down to the first (main) floor. The treads and landings are very worn. Later wood handrail attached to the wood wainscot.

The stairway surrounds the original caged elevator shaft on three sides. The elevator terminates at this floor.

Short three-riser wood stair with balustrade connecting the servants' wing to the main house.

PAINT INVESTIGATION: All surfaces should be analyzed to determine the original colors and finishes.

RESTORATION PROGRAM: All deteriorated plaster surfaces should be repaired and varnished finishes on all woodwork should be restored. The skylight should be restored as part of the re-roofing work.

The missing wood knobs should be restored to closet door 2163.

All surfaces should have the original finishes restored.

Room 217 Linen Closet

This small narrow room functioned as the linen storage area, and both the Hoppin & Koen plan and the 1940 Van Anda plan identify it as such. The room received natural light and ventilation from a large window in the west wall.

FLOOR: Original tongue-and-groove pine boards running east-west. Refinished in the spring of 1988.

WALLS: Original plaster on lath. Original built-in linen storage units against the north and south partitions. The room was painted in the spring of 1988.

CEILING: Original plaster on lath.

CORNICE: No cornice.

BASEBOARD: Original wood base with molded crown.

DOORS: Single original opening and three-panel wood door. The original hardware is extant, including the wood knobs. Recent added lock and turn latch.

WINDOW: Original opening with six-over-six wood double-hung sash. Sash secured by a thumb latch.

HEATING: No heating.

LIGHTING: Original ceiling-mounted incandescent fixture.

A dangerous condition exists where a recent wall-mounted outlet has been wired to the ceiling fixture.

OTHER FEATURES: Original built-in shelves and storage units as shown on the Hoppin & Koen floor plan. Two of the storage drawers are missing.

PAINT INVESTIGATION: All surfaces should be analyzed to determine the original finishes.

RESTORATION PROGRAM: All plaster and wood surfaces should be repaired. The ceiling light fixture should be rewired and the later outlet removed.

If the two missing drawers cannot be found, new units should be fabricated.

Room 218 Bathroom (Housemaid's Closet)

The Hoppin & Koen plan labels this small narrow room as the housemaid's closet. A slop (utility) sink is shown in the northwest corner. The conversion to a bathroom probably occurred after the Wharton period. The 1940 Van Anda plan labels the room W.C. When the bathtub was installed, the door had to be reversed to open into the hall.

FLOOR: Original tongue-and-groove pine floor covered by a single sheet of battleship linoleum. Original white marble slab set into the floor beneath the lavatory (former location of the utility sink).

WALLS: Original plaster on lath. Some patched areas and visible cracks. The sink alcove is lined in 5-foot-high white marble panels. The room was painted in the spring of 1988.

CEILING: Original plaster on lath.

CORNICE: No cornice.

BASEBOARD: Original wood base with molded crown.

DOORS: Single original opening and three-panel wood door.

2181: The original varnished finish survives on the hall side, but the room side has been painted white. The door originally opened into the room, but the swing was changed when the bathtub was installed.

WINDOWS: Original opening with six-over-six wood double-hung sash. The architrave terminates on a projecting molded wood sill.

HEATING: Single small cast-iron radiator below the window.

LIGHTING: Incandescent ceiling fixture with glass shade. Above the lavatory is the fitting for a wall bracket.

PLUMBING: The original utility sink has been removed. The fixtures installed when the room was converted into a bathroom include the enameled cast-iron bathtub raised on four claw feet and the white ceramic tank toilet. Both of these fixtures probably date from the Shattuck occupancy. The white ceramic lavatory supported on chromed metal legs is more recent.

OTHER FEATURES: Narrow wood shelf resting on top of the marble wainscot on the west wall.

Box-like shelf attached to the wall above the toilet (removed after 1986).

PAINT INVESTIGATION: All surfaces should be analyzed to determine the original finishes, as well as the finishes applied when the space was converted to its current use.

RESTORATION PROGRAM: This room could be restored to its Wharton-period appearance or maintained as a bathroom. The linoleum floor is old and could be retained.

Room 219   Maid's Room

The Hoppin & Koen floor plan designates this as the maid's room. Since there was originally no bathroom nearby, the maid must have used the attic bathroom. It is possible that the housemaid's closet (218) was converted into a bathroom during the Wharton period.

The 1940 Van Anda plan designates this space as the servants' sitting room.

FLOOR: Original tongue-and-groove pine floor running north-south. Refinished in the spring of 1988.

WALLS: Original plaster on lath. The north end of the east partition originally opened to a doorway that gave access to the original sewing room (220). The room was painted in the spring of 1988.

CEILING: Original plaster on lath; minor cracks and loose plaster above hall door.

CORNICE: Narrow 2-inch-wide wood molding at the junction of the wall and ceiling.

BASEBOARD: Original wood base with molded crown. The crown molding is loose along the north and south walls.

DOORS: Two original openings and doors. A third doorway at the east end of the room was walled in. This was removed in 1988.

2191: Original three-panel wood door with hardware intact including the wood knobs.

2192: Original three-panel wood door to closet with hardware intact.

WINDOWS: Two original window openings with six-over-six double-hung wood sash secured by thumb latches. Molded wood architraves terminate in projecting wood sills.

HEATING: Single cast-iron radiator positioned beneath the west window.

LIGHTING: Single brass incandescent wall bracket attached to south wall as indicated on the Hoppin & Koen floor plan.

PAINT INVESTIGATION: All surfaces should be analyzed to determine the original finishes.

RESTORATION PROGRAM: The goal should be to restore the space to the Wharton period, regardless of the intended function. All surfaces should have their original finishes restored.

Plaster surfaces should be repaired, especially loose ceiling plaster.

The loose baseboard moldings need to be resecured.

The original electric wall bracket should be cleaned and rewired.

Room 220 Sewing Room

This large bright room has four windows overlooking the walled garden. The Hoppin & Koen plan refers to it as the sewing room. There is a direct connection from this space to the maid's room (219). In 1988, this room and rooms 218, 219, and 221 were refurbished for use as an apartment for an Edith Wharton Restoration employee. In 1990, they became the offices of Edith Wharton Restoration.

FLOOR: Original tongue-and-groove pine floor running north-south. Refinished in the spring of 1988.

WALLS: Original plaster on lath. Several areas of cracked and loose plaster particularly beneath the east windows. The room was painted in the spring of 1988.

CEILING: Original plaster on lath. The center section of the ceiling has a large area of water-damaged plaster.

CORNICE: Narrow 2-inch-wide wood molding at the junction of the wall and ceiling.

BASEBOARD: Original wood base with molded crown.

DOORS: Three original openings, which retain their paneled doors.

2201: Original three-panel door with the original hardware, including the wood knobs.

The inside face of the door is deeply scratched, probably by a pet dog.

2202: Original closet door with three panels and original hardware. An electric push-button switch was mounted in the door frame so that the light came on when the door was opened.

2203: Original three-panel wood door and hardware.

WINDOWS: Four original openings with six-over-six double-hung wood sash. The molded wood architraves terminate on projecting wood sills.

HEATING: Single cast-iron radiator positioned between two windows in the east wall.

LIGHTING: Original brass incandescent ceiling fixture with an opal glass "school house"-type shade. The shade is old but may not be original to the fixture. The Hoppin & Koen plan indicates a light in this position.

EQUIPMENT: Attached to the north wall is an original wood and glass cabinet housing a servants' call-box. It was manufactured by the Berkshire Electric Company in Pittsfield, Massachusetts (under Holtzer's Patent). An indicator-box is illustrated on the Hoppin & Koen plan in the same position. The call-box bells were for Edith Wharton's boudoir, bedroom, and bath.

PAINT INVESTIGATION: All surfaces should be analyzed to determine the original finishes. All painted woodwork in this room and the other rooms in the service wing should have the varnished finishes restored.

RESTORATION PROGRAM: Prior to any restoration work, the roof should be renewed to prevent water penetration.

The floor should be carefully refinished, and all plaster surfaces need to be repaired.

The ceiling light should be cleaned and rewired.

Room 221 Bathroom (Dress Closet)

The Hoppin & Koen plan notes this interior space as the dress closet. Access was from the sewing room, and a glazed sash, high in the west partition, could be opened to provide ventilation.

The room was converted into a bathroom by the Foxhollow School. Most recently the space was remodeled into a kitchen for the employee apartment created in the servants' wing in 1988.

The following notes record the room as it functioned as a bathroom.

FLOOR: Original narrow tongue-and-groove pine boards running north-south (refinished in the spring of 1988).

WALLS: Original plaster on lath. Attached to the north partition is a 4-inch-wide wood rail fitted with large brass hooks spaced at 10 inches on center. Patched areas in the plaster wall indicate the locations of additional rails. The room was painted in the spring of 1988.

CEILING: Original plaster on lath. There is a later ceiling vent in the northeast corner.

CORNICE: No cornice.

BASEBOARD: Original wood base with molded crown.

DOORS: Original opening and three-panel wood door. The door retains the original hardware.

WINDOWS: Single original small opening set high in the west partition. The hinged wood casement sash swings into the room and is glazed with obscured glass.

HEATING: No heat.

FIG. 157 *The original cabinet housing the servants' call-box, which was manufactured by Berkshire Electric Company in Pittsfield. The three slots read (from left): "Mrs. Wharton's Boudoir," "Mrs. Wharton's Bedroom," and "Mrs. Wharton's Bath."* (JD)

LIGHTING: Simple porcelain socket with pull-chain set in the ceiling. Recent incandescent chromed metal-and-glass fixture above the lavatory.

PLUMBING: White enamel tub and lavatory and ceramic tank toilet arranged against the east partition. These fixtures probably date from the Foxhollow period.

PAINT INVESTIGATION: All surfaces should be analyzed to determine the original finishes.

RESTORATION PROGRAM: Since the above analysis was completed this room has been converted to a kitchen. It could be restored as the dress closet or maintained as a kitchen, depending on the ultimate use of this portion of the house.

Attic

The servants' rooms in the attic encompass the floor space above the bedroom floor of the main portion of the house. The construction generally follows the 1901 Hoppin & Koen floor plan. That plan includes some penciled-in modifications.

All of the rooms appear to have been quite comfortable, and all receive ample natural light from the dormer windows, with the exception of room 310 (originally this room included space 309), which has as its window the small oval opening that ornaments the east pediment.

The original plan remained intact until the Foxhollow School created an additional bathroom (309) and a second means of egress (stairway 306).

All of the original architectural detailing survives, although hard usage is apparent on many surfaces.

The most interesting architectural feature is the cupola, which can be reached from the stairway located in the central hallway (302). This elegant structure creates an important visual note to the exterior of the house and provides some natural light to the attic corridor.

In the attic crawlspace, below and just to the north of the cupola, what appears to be the original water system for the house remains intact. The main component of the system is a large open tank lined in lead, measuring approximately 6 feet wide, 15 feet long, and 2 feet deep. The tank is constructed of two-by-fours, which are laid flat and interlocked to form walls. It is supported on large wooden beams and by the chimney mass, with the northwest corner being hung by steel straps from the roof framing.

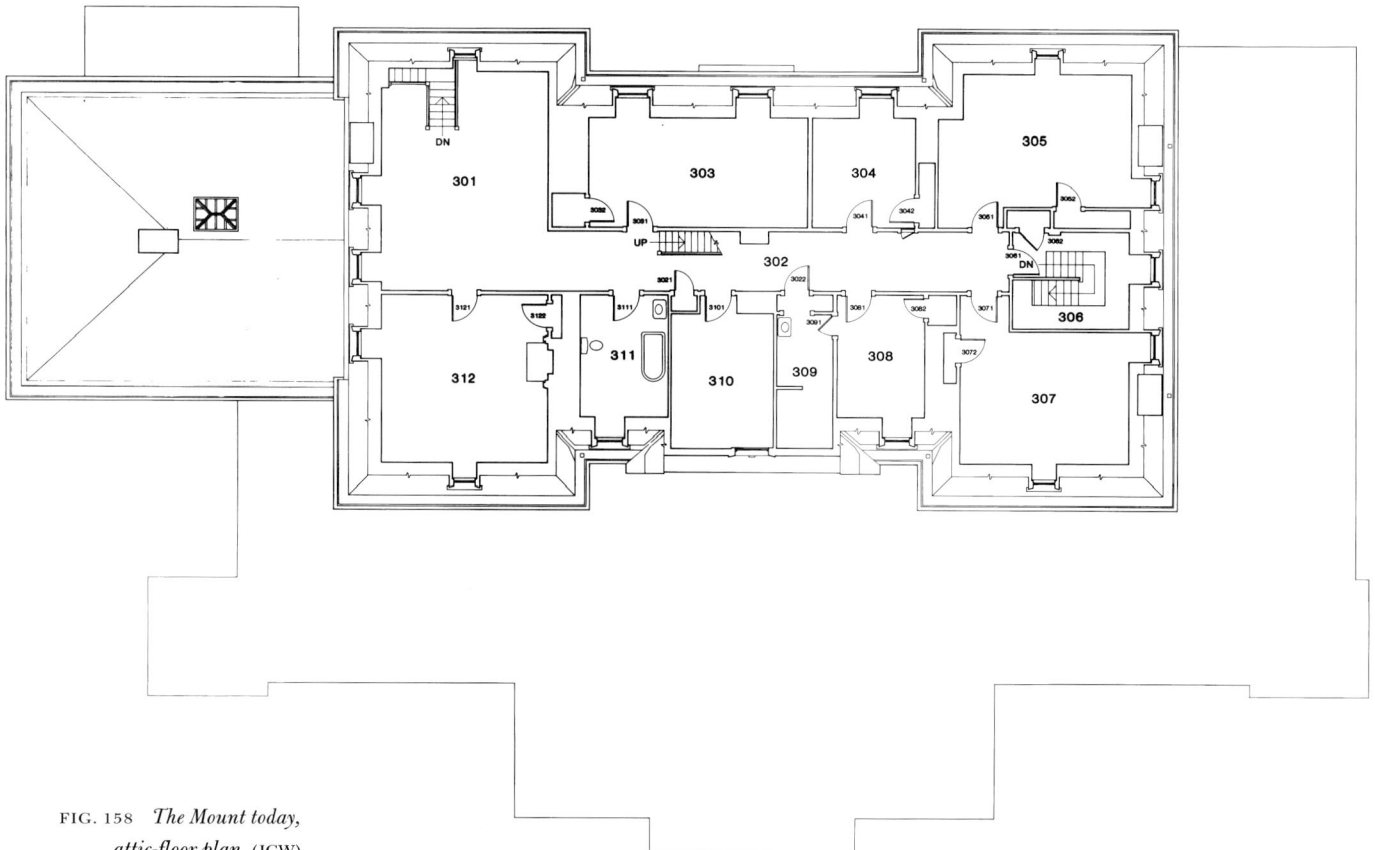

FIG. 158 *The Mount today, attic-floor plan.* (JGW)

Water was either collected from the roof into this tank or pumped up several stories to the tank to be distributed throughout the building for bathing, washing, and cleaning.

The stairway to the cupola and the stair that ascends from the second (bedroom) floor to the attic have the same detailing with regard to balusters, railing, and ball finials. All rooms in the attic have the same architectural detailing, which differs from that found in the service wing. Both the door architraves and the doors themselves are completely different from those in the service wing. In the attic, the architraves are composed of a simply molded surround that joins at the head of the opening in corner blocks ornamented with a circle bulls-eye motif. The doors feature an arrangement of five narrow vertical and horizontal panels. The hardware duplicates that used in the service wing. Narrow three-light transoms are incorporated into the architrave above each door.

In general, attic problems relate to water penetration from the roof and wear on finishes from hard usage.

There are many areas of deteriorated, loose, and cracked plaster and areas with poor plaster repairs.

The narrow-board pine floor has lost much of its finish.

No restoration or repair work should begin until the roof and gutters have been thoroughly restored.

Room 301 Stair Hall

The Hoppin & Koen plan labels this the stair hall, but its size and number of windows make it likely that this was more than just a passage.

The 1940 Van Anda plan indicates that the space was used for trunk storage.

All of the original architectural features appear to have survived.

RESTORATION PROGRAM: The pine floor needs to be refinished, and the plaster walls and ceiling need to be repaired. All faulty earlier patching should be redone. The north stair balustrade needs to be resecured.

Surface-mounted wiring and the inappropriate incandescent ceiling fixture should be removed.

If the paint investigation reveals that the woodwork was originally finished with a varnish, then that surface finish should be restored.

Room 302 Hall

This long central hall provides access to all of the attic rooms. The most interesting feature is the stairway to the cupola and the plaster arch that spans the

FIG. 159 *The long central hall on the attic floor, with the stairway to the cupola.* (JD)

hall beyond the stair and houses the chimney flue, which rises up through the cupola and terminates in the cast-iron crown beneath the weather vane.

RESTORATION PROGRAM: The pine floor needs to be refinished. The various areas of cracked and water-damaged plaster should be repaired. All poorly executed plaster repairs should be redone. Restore the missing section of baseboard on the east wall and the missing section of trim to doorway 3061.

All surface-mounted wiring should be removed.

The old electrical fuse box in the west partition should remain in place.

All surfaces should have their original finishes restored.

FIG. 160 *Water penetration from the roof has caused deterioration of the plaster walls along the stairway to the cupola.* (JD)

247

Room 303 Bedroom (Office)

The Hoppin & Koen plan defines this area as two separate bed chambers, but penciled marks on the drawing indicate that it was to be constructed as the single large space that exists today.

All original features survive, including the electric wall bracket.

RESTORATION PROGRAM: The floor finish needs to be renewed, and the plaster surfaces need repair. The closet has a large gap in the plaster between the ceiling and the wall surface. The original electric wall bracket needs to be cleaned and rewired, and the missing bracket should be restored to the north partition where the back plate remains in place.

All surfaces should have their original finishes restored.

Room 304 Bedroom (Office)

This small room appears as shown on the Hoppin & Koen floor plan. The pine floor has been painted.

RESTORATION PROGRAM: The water-damaged plaster of the dormer ceiling needs to be repaired.

The wood window sill is deteriorated and needs replacement.

All surfaces, including the floor, should have their original finishes restored.

Room 305 Bedroom (Office)

This room retains its original architectural character and follows the Hoppin & Koen floor plan.

RESTORATION PROGRAM: The pine floor needs to be refinished.

The plaster ceiling is badly deteriorated in the southeast corner from water penetration. There is a chimney on the roof above this damaged area.

The original wall bracket should be cleaned of paint and rewired.

All surfaces should have their original finishes restored.

Room 306 Bedroom (Stairway)

This small room was formerly a bedroom; the closet survives from that usage. The stairway was constructed by the Foxhollow School to provide a second means of egress from the attic floor. This resulted in modifications to Edith Wharton's private bathroom directly below. Although the stairway changed the function of the room, it damaged only the floor.

RESTORATION PROGRAM: The stairway should be removed and the pine floor restored.

Apparently the door to the hall (3061) was also replaced; the original door should be restored. Areas of plaster ceiling need to be repaired and poorly done patching replaced. A historic light fixture should be installed and the missing wood closet door knob put back in place.

All surfaces should have their original finishes restored.

Room 307 Bedroom (Office)

This former bedroom retains its original architectural character.

RESTORATION PROGRAM: The floor needs to be refinished, and the baseboard along the west partition should be renailed.

Areas of cracked and water-damaged plaster need to be repaired. A gap between the wall and ceiling plaster is visible in the closet.

The recent light fixture should be replaced with one of the historic wall brackets.

All surfaces should have their original finishes restored.

Room 308 Bedroom (Office)

The Hoppin & Koen plan represents this small room as it appears today except for the narrow door opening in the south partition. This feature may have been constructed when the bathroom was created in Room 309.

RESTORATION PROGRAM: The floor should be refinished.

Cracked and damaged plaster and a large area of loose plaster in the ceiling must be repaired.

The narrow doorway (3091) should be removed when the adjoining room is restored.

Room 309 Storage Room (Former Bathroom)

This narrow, dark room was originally part of room 310. The south partition was constructed by the Foxhollow School so that a bathroom could be created here. Water leaking from this bathroom damaged the drawing room ceiling below in the early 1970s. The plumbing fixtures have been removed. Access to this room was created in the west partition through a former closet that opened from the hall (3022).

RESTORATION PROGRAM: The south partition should be removed and the original room configuration restored. The closet arrangement should be rebuilt.

Room 310 Bedroom (Office)

This unusual room is located behind the central pediment of the east facade. The small oval window ornaments that pediment. The original delicately detailed sash has been removed. The wood floor is now covered by vinyl tile.

RESTORATION PROGRAM: The north partition and vinyl-tile floor should be removed to restore this interesting room to its original condition.

All surfaces should be repaired and restored. The missing oval window sash should be put back in place.

Room 311 Bathroom

This bathroom, included on the Hoppin & Koen plan, was designed for the servants who occupied the attic bedrooms. The plan shows a closet in room 310, which projects into the northwest corner of the bathroom. The closet is crossed out in pencil and apparently was never built. The room features the same white marble floor and baseboard that appears in the second (bedroom) floor bathrooms of the main house.

RESTORATION PROGRAM: The plumbing should be disconnected at basement level to prevent water damage to the important rooms directly below this bathroom.

The cause of the floor settlement should be determined and corrected. The marble floor and base need to be cleaned.

Damaged plaster should be repaired, especially in the ceiling above the lavatory.

The missing marble base and wood chair rail in the northwest corner indicate that there may have been some sort of built-in lavatory cabinet.

All surfaces should have their original finishes restored.

Room 312 Bedroom (Office)

This large room follows the Hoppin & Koen plan and incorporates the penciled-in changes, including the addition of the fireplace and the elimination of one of the two closets. The 1901 plan refers to this as a servant's bedroom, but the 1940 Van Anda plan labels it the servants' sitting room. The fireplace makes this room more important than the other attic rooms. The pine mantel is very simple in detail and appears to date to c. 1820-40. The woodwork, excluding the baseboards, has had the later paint removed to expose the natural wood.

An original wood-and-glass cabinet housing a servants' call-box is attached to the west wall. It was manufactured by the Berkshire Electric Company in Pittsfield, Massachusetts (under Holtzer's patent) and is identical to the one on the north wall of the original sewing room (220). No call-box was indicated on the Hoppin & Koen floor plan for this room; instead an indicator was called for on the north wall of the adjacent stair hall. The existing call-box was connected to the east guest room, west guest room, and the small guest room (their labels remain intact). The labels and names for these rooms are original to the Whartons' occupancy.

RESTORATION PROGRAM: The wood floor should be refinished. Damaged and cracked areas of plaster need to be repaired.

The original electric wall bracket should be cleaned and rewired.

The fireplace should not be used.

All surfaces should have their original finishes restored, including the bare woodwork.

Recommendations

PRESERVATION OBJECTIVES

The Mount is a remarkable, early twentieth-century American country house. It is of major architectural and historical significance and has survived with most of its original building fabric intact. The unique cast of characters involved in the creation of The Mount produced a house of unusual distinction that merits the most careful building conservation. This care is necessary to ensure the long-term preservation of the house without compromising its architectural integrity.

The Mount should be accurately restored to the appearance it had while owned by Edith Wharton. Since so much of the original building fabric survives and because there is a wealth of documentation from literary sources, this objective may be accomplished without conjecture or whimsy. Eventually the entire house, including the service areas and the attic floor, should be restored.

The goal of complete restoration should be independent of any proposed uses for the house beyond that of a house museum. Both the exterior and interior appearance of each surface and space should reflect the intent of Edith Wharton and of the architects and should not be compromised by frequently changing ideas about usage. Any insertions necessary to accommodate a certain function must not damage the historic fabric of the building and should be easily removable.

Fortunately, the majority of the changes made at The Mount by successive owners are reversible,

FIG. 161 *The courtyard entrance today.* (JD)

building might well be consumed by the process of renewal. Current and future maintenance and repair work should be carefully programmed and delineated to preserve the integrity of the building.

Routine maintenance should be an integral part of the program for accomplishing preservation and restoration objectives. A well-defined long-range maintenance program will also help to ensure that maximum results are achieved within the constraints of available funding.

BUILDING USES

There should be no question that the primary reason for the preservation of The Mount is its intimate connection with Edith Wharton. Like her writings, it is one of her creations. Because of this relationship, The Mount should be restored as a period house museum. All of the spaces should be interpreted as they would have appeared and functioned during the occupancy of Edith and Teddy Wharton. It is important that visitors be shown the "upstairs" and "downstairs" of The Mount so that they can gain an accurate understanding of the way the house was used by the Whartons.

It is unlikely that many of the original furnishings will ever be returned to the house. The few extant Wharton-period photographs can assist in refurnishing The Mount, but acquiring similar objects will entail great expense. Therefore, many of the rooms may remain devoid of appropriate furnishings for some time.

It is important that sympathetic alternative uses be explored for some of the spaces. The public rooms could be used for small seminars and conferences. Historically The Mount has been a place where ideas were exchanged. This was true in Edith Wharton's time, as well as during the tenure of the Foxhollow School. Museum offices and support areas could be housed in some of the secondary spaces.

The merits and problems of maintaining staff offices in the servants' wing should be considered, but the spaces should still be restored to the Wharton period.

The gift shop should be moved to a larger space, such as ground floor room G-8. The nearby exterior door could then be used as an exit by visitors.

MECHANICAL/ELECTRICAL SYSTEMS

All of these systems are inefficent and obsolete, or nearly so. In some cases they are dangerous.

The existing heating system includes components dating from the original construction, the 1940s, and more recent renewals. There are two

although considerable work may be needed to accomplish the restoration goal.

Because maintenance has been deferred over the past several decades, a substantial amount of work is needed to make the building simply weather tight and safe. A very significant part of the problem involves the obsolescence of mechanical systems, including heating, plumbing, and wiring. If this work is not carried out in accordance with the best modern standards of building conservation, the

large furnaces in the basement under two of the most significant rooms in the house. This system does not meet modern museum standards of adequate temperature or humidity controls and represents an unnecessary hazard.

The basic original electrical system, with later piecemeal additions, is at best inadequate. The wiring is dangerous in some areas, particularly where it has come into contact with leaks from the terrace and deteriorated plumbing. The existing system should be removed and a new system installed that meets modern standards for museum use. This work would include the rewiring and repair of all surviving historic light fixtures.

It is recommended that the HVAC system and electrical equipment be removed from the mansion and placed in a new building southwest of the house either wholly or partially underground. This will allow for periodic maintenance and renewal without subjecting the house to trauma.

FIRE DETECTION AND INTRUSION DETECTION

The very minimal fire-detection system is not complete or adequately sensitive. A new system should be installed, consisting of low-voltage ionization detectors highly sensitive to combustion. The detectors should be zoned and connected to a central annunciator panel linked directly to the fire department. The detectors should be installed as inconspicuously as possible.

A new intrusion-detection system consisting of magnetic door and window contacts, ultrasonic motion detectors, and photo-electric cells should be installed.

PRIORITIES

Category 1
Emergency Stabilization

Temporary repairs to roofs, terrace, and other areas with water penetration problems.

Category 2
Exterior Restoration

Repair and replacement of roof and rainwater system.

Restoration of the north and west terrace and stairway.

Restoration of exterior stucco.

Restoration of exterior woodwork, windows, and porch.

Category 3
Mechanical/Electrical System

Construction of new isolated systems facility.

Installation of electrical and security systems.

Installation of heating and air-conditioning system.

Category 4
Interior Restoration

Ground floor.

First floor (main floor).

Second floor (bedroom floor).

Service wing.

Attic.

Category 5
Site Restoration

Forecourt.

Landscape immediately adjacent to the house.

John G. Waite Associates, Architects, PLLC

John G. Waite Associates, Architects, provides nationally recognized leadership in the preservation, restoration, and reuse of historic buildings. A partial list of the firm's portfolio includes some of the most significant structures that comprise our national psyche, including Mount Vernon in Virginia; the Jeffersonian Precinct at the University of Virginia in Charlottesville; Blair House (The President's Guest House) in Washington, D.C.; Tweed Courthouse in New York City; and the Lincoln Memorial in Washington, D.C.

Through years of experience in their respective fields, the staff — which includes architects, architectural historians, historic-interiors specialists, and building-materials conservators — has developed the wide range of skills in architectural and decorative conservation necessary to undertake the most meticulous restoration work. The firm has expertise in such diverse areas of historic preservation as the development of historic structure reports, the restoration of significant public buildings, the adaptive use of historic landmark buildings, and the design of new buildings in historical contexts. Individuals in the firm have published widely on architectural history and preservation technology. The firm specializes in preservation technology, particularly the identification and analysis of building-fabric deterioration and remedial treatments required to accomplish long-term preservation.

JOHN G. WAITE

In his thirty-year career, John G. Waite has largely redefined the preservation and restoration of historic architecture in America. His nationally recognized practice has been responsible for the restoration of many of America's most significant buildings.

When Waite began his career America was just becoming aware of its architectural heritage, and historic preservation techniques were in their infancy.

Early on, Waite appreciated the complexity of responsible restoration and advocated a multidisciplinary approach that would include archeologists, historians, technologists, and craftsmen whose specialties would be coordinated by the architect. He built his practice based on this concept. Today his firm's unusual breadth of disciplines is well recognized.

One of Waite's major contributions to restoration methodology was the development and refinement of the historic structure report, which has become the recognized tool for gathering essential information for planning a preservation project. His firm has produced HSRs for more than one hundred buildings, including many of major national significance, such as The Octagon, Mount Vernon, Monticello, and the University of Virginia.

Waite has published more than fifty articles and books. His book, *Metals in America's Historic Buildings*, issued by the U.S. Government Printing Office, is the recognized standard in the field.

Waite is a frequent lecturer on historic preservation to professionals, college students and faculties, and the general public. He serves on many national and local preservation boards. He was a founder of the Society for Industrial Archaeology and currently chairs an agency dealing with preserving historic bridges.

John G. Waite's consistent, meticulous, and intelligent preservation of American architecture has greatly enriched the field of historic preservation.

Key to Illustration Sources

AAFAL   Avery Architectural and Fine Arts Library, Columbia University in the City of New York

AP   AP/Wide World Photos

BA   Berkshire Athenaeum, Local History Room, Pittsfield, Massachusetts

BL   Beinecke Rare Book and Manuscript Library, Yale Collection of American Art,
Yale University, New Haven, Connecticut

CP   Culver Pictures, Inc., New York, New York

EWR   Edith Wharton Restoration Archives, The Mount

FHS   Foxhollow School Archives, Edith Wharton Restoration, The Mount

JD   Jonas Dovydenas

JGW   John G. Waite Associates, Architects, PLLC, Albany, New York

LL   Lilly Library, Indiana University, Bloomington, Indiana

LNL   Lenox Library Association, Lenox, Massachusetts

MMA   Photograph and Slide Library, The Metropolitan Museum of Art, New York, New York

NPG   National Portrait Gallery, Smithsonian Institution, Washington, D.C.

S&C   Shakespeare & Company, Lenox, Massachusetts

SM   Collection of Scott Marshall

SPNEA,   Society for the Preservation of New England Antiquities,
CFMC   Codman Family Manuscripts Collection, Boston, Massachusetts

The text for this report has been set electronically using the digital Monotype Bulmer, redrawn by Ron Carpenter. This version is based on types cut by William Martin and used by the printer William Bulmer, circa 1790.